Praise for
The Complete Single Mother,
Third Edition:

"Comprehensive and compassionate, *The Complete Single Mother* will guide you to make good decisions for your children and yourself. Each updated edition only makes it more relevant and reliable."

—Barbara Meltz, parenting columnist for *The Boston Globe*, author, *Put Yourself in Their Shoes: Understanding How Your Children See the World*

"From conception to the teen years and from de-stressing to dealing with the ex from hell, *The Complete Single Mother* is the definitive guide to life for solo moms. Don't consider single motherhood without it."

—Ariel Gore, editor/publisher of *Hip Mama*

"*The Complete Single Mother* offers comfort, common sense, experience, encouragement and more than a few laughs. The sophisticated and psychologically savvy advice is invaluable no matter what the single mom challenge. This book is absolutely a 'must-get' for all single moms."

—Tammy Jones, founder of *SingleRose.com*, Resource for Single Mothers, and author of *Single Mother Sentiments*

"This is the most helpful, empowering resource single moms have looked to for over a decade. Written in a friendly and supportive way; no question goes unanswered, no topic avoided. The third edition even includes minibios of notable single moms which offers added reassurance and inspiration for women who aspire to create balanced, well informed, confident lives."

—Sheila Ellison, author of *The Courage to Be a Single Mother* and founder of SingleMomsConnect.com

"Single moms will refer to this marvelous book time and again. It offers practical advice on everything including pregnancy, special needs children, money issues, relationships and stepfamilies. And it does so with encouragement, intelligence, and humor. It's the Single Mother's Bible!"

—Ellie Slott Fisher, author of *Mom, There's a Man in the Kitchen and He's Wearing Your Robe: The Single Mother's Guide to Dating Well Without Parenting Poorly*

"As I read this new version of the absolute single mother 'Bible' I couldn't believe how much incredibly important information delivered with heart, hope and laughter is packed in. If you are a single mom, toying with the idea, or know one . . . you must get this book!"

—Patrice Karst, author of *The Single Mother's Survival Guide*

"The book provides a much-needed service to single moms. It is extremely valuable for the authors' reassuring, common sense advice. . . . Since the single mothers I encounter are always full of questions, I recommend this book as a practical guide to raising children of either sex. Engber and Klungness address these mothers' specific, often urgent concerns in a warm and conversational style. . . . Inviting and nonjudgmental in tone, this guide draws readers into its wise counsel on what it takes to be a responsive, empathetic parent. . . . The authors' gift to single parents is the strong message that they are not alone, and they can succeed as other single parents have done and are doing. The expanded third edition speaks with understanding to many circumstances of single parenthood, including those single by chance or by choice. . . . *The Complete Single Mother* is a tremendous gift to women who are raising children alone, and I thank the authors for revising and expanding it to educate and reassure today's single moms."

—Peggy Drexler, Ph.D., author of *Raising Boys Without Men*

"*The Complete Single Mother* is just what it says—complete! There is no other book about single parenting like this one, which has an answer for any question a single parent would ask. Readers are sure to find their particular situations and interests within these pages, which can offer much-needed comfort to single parents who may feel alone and misunderstood. I can confidently recommend this book in my practice to moms and dads who are dealing with specific problems that are not typically written about in the parenting field. I especially appreciate the philosophy that Engber and Klungness promote regarding the importance of always putting kids' needs first."

—Diane Chambers Shearer, author of *Solo Parenting: Raising Strong & Happy Families* and publisher of *The Peaceful Co-Parent* newsletter

The
Complete
Single Mother

Third Edition

The Complete Single Mother
Third Edition

Reassuring Answers to Your Most Challenging Concerns

Andrea Engber
Leah Klungness, Ph.D.

Adams Media
Avon, Massachusetts

Published by Adams Media, an F+W Publications Company
57 Littlefield Street
Avon, MA 02322
www.adamsmedia.com
ISBN 13: 978-1-59337-490-7
ISBN 10: 1-59337-490-9
Printed in the United States of America.

J I H G F E D

Library of Congress Cataloging-in-Publication Data
Engber, Andrea.
The complete single mother : reassuring answers to your most challenging concerns /
by Andrea Engber and Leah Klungness.—3rd ed.
p.   cm.
ISBN 1-59337-490-9
1. Single mothers—United States. 2. Parenting—United States. I. Klungness, Leah.
II. Title.

HQ759.45.E54 2006
306.874'32'0973--dc22
2005021885

This publication is designed to provide accurate and authoritative information with regard to the subject matter covered. It is sold with the understanding that the publisher is not engaged in rendering legal, accounting, or other professional advice. If legal advice or other expert assistance is required, the services of a competent professional person should be sought.
—From a *Declaration of Principles* jointly adopted by a Committee of the American Bar Association and a Committee of Publishers and Associations

Many of the designations used by manufacturers and sellers to distinguish their product are claimed as trademarks. Where those designations appear in this book and Adams Media was aware of a trademark claim, the designations have been printed with initial capital letters.

Interior illustrations by Lynn Jeffrey and Jim Hunt.

This book is available at quantity discounts for bulk purchases.
For information, please call 1-800-289-0963.

To our children, Spencer, Sarah, and Andrew,
who taught us to live joyfully in the present.
And to our sisters, the single mothers who have
inspired us through their strength, hope,
and the community they have brought to
the new American family.

CONTENTS

--------------------------------- PART 1 ---------------------------------

THE MANY FACES OF
SINGLE MOTHERS TODAY

PART 2

BECOMING YOUR OWN BEST PARTNER

PART 3

RAISING GREAT KIDS WITH CONFIDENCE AND COURAGE

——————————— PART 4 ———————————

YOUR CONNECTION TO THE REST OF THE WORLD

ACKNOWLEDGMENTS

Sometimes those to whom we are most grateful cannot be thanked enough. Often those who offered their deepest support and encouragement are no longer around to receive the thanks.

I thank my late mother, Florence, who released me from her hold, but only after seeing to it that her constant refrain, "You can do anything you set out to do," had sunk in. To the spirit of Sherman Engber, the man who raised me, I owe deep gratitude for meeting the challenge by marrying my independent single mother and for loving me out of choice and not because he "had to." As real a daddy—if not more so—as any birth father could hope to be, he taught me that love has less to do with blood than unconditional acceptance. My parents also taught me their roles were genderless, as my father, a tall, strong Bogart type, shopped and cleaned house while my mother, a former model, maintained the car and rewired our apartment.

I owe endless thanks to Sally McMillan, my agent, for preparing me for the rough process of writing such a book. With painstaking guidance, she returned the proposal four times before submitting it. Yet, because of her I have confidence and skills I never knew I possessed.

To Laura Morin, my first editor at Adams, I am deeply grateful for her trust in me, for being there at the eleventh hour, and for laughing at the right times. Kate Epstein and the staff at Adams deserve praise, too, for standing behind this edition 100 percent.

My thanks to *Working Mother* magazine; Universal Press Syndicate; Shòshana Alexander, author of *In Praise of Single Parents*; *American Baby* magazine; Jane Mattes, founder of Single Mothers By Choice; Gary Nielson and Carolyn Beyrau at the *Charlotte Observer* for giving me my first real break as a columnist; Moms Online and Oxygen Media for allowing me to become a "Web Journalist"; Bob, who massaged my tired feet when he would much rather have been doing something else; and my extended family of friends, particularly Cordelia Williams, Maxine Fairchild, and Tere Wood.

Probably my earliest thanks should go to Linda Dillon, who may have influenced me more than she knows. My first best friend did not realize it at the time, but she gave me much comfort when she matter-of-factly retorted, "So you'll raise the baby without him," after I whined about being dumped by my son's father. That's just what I did.

Finally, to my son, Spencer, the most beloved person in my life, for picking pretty flowers for me just when I lost sight of what is really important and for forgiving me for being such a workaholic: it is for him and all the children of the new American family that this book is written. —A.E.

Many people give unselfishly of their time, experience, and wisdom to keep my professional life and my personal world on course. We all need a support system to sustain us. I deeply appreciate my loving children, my loyal friends, and my generous colleagues. Many of these people would be embarrassed to be singled out for recognition. To these supportive and altruistic individuals I make a promise: to continue to devote myself to helping others grow, achieve, and move forward, with hope for a bright future and barely a backward glance at the shadows from a difficult past. —L.K.

INTRODUCTION

I first met my coauthor, Dr. Leah Klungness, in 1993, but we were unknowingly connected to each long before that.

Ten years before we met, Leah watched the moving van pull out of the driveway of her recently sold house in Syracuse, New York. Excitedly, she packed a few last-minute items to take with her to her new home. Her husband, already relocated in Charlotte, North Carolina, was waiting for the van and his family to follow. Leah, a school psychologist, and her two children, Sarah, then three, and Andrew, eight, were saying their good-byes to the house when the phone rang. Leah ran to pick up the phone, expecting her husband to fill her in on the final details of the move. Instead, he informed her that he didn't think they should be married anymore and that she and the kids should move in with her mother. Then he promptly hung up.

She was dazed. "I just couldn't believe it!" she said. "There went most of my life—my bed, my furniture, every towel, plate, and cooking utensil, every toy and book my children had ever had—in that van heading toward our new home while he's telling me on the phone that he's found a new life! How could he just say he didn't think we should be married anymore? And what was wrong with me not to even notice any red flags?"

After stumbling around in shock for what seemed like ages, she gathered up the remains of her life—two flimsy suitcases, her children, $500, and whatever energy she could muster—and dragged herself off to her mother's, trying not to scrape her chin on the ground.

Like many other unprepared women whose husbands abruptly left them, Leah's entrance into single motherhood came with no warnings and no instruction manuals—only unanswered questions, paralysis, and fear.

She had already been accepted to the University of South Carolina's psychology doctoral program, and she embarked on a plan of action to get her Ph.D. while raising her two young children alone. "I was planning to attend school while living in Charlotte anyway. Why change my plans just because I was no longer married?"

The following August, just a few months after her husband had left her and her children, Leah packed up from her mother's house, and she, Sarah, and Andrew moved into their new apartment in Columbia, South Carolina. "One of the driving forces I credit for motivating me to find us an apartment was that I wanted to get out of my mother's house, fast!" she says. "True, we should welcome any options and choices we have when first faced with a disaster such as a husband bailing out. But living at my mother's with my two children was certainly not one of them."

When they arrived in Columbia, Leah knew no one—she had no child care, no family, and no support network. But she made a commitment to herself that "come hell or high water," she would complete her education. "I was determined to do what I always wanted to do—get my Ph.D. and become a psychologist with my own successful practice," she remembers. It was a major undertaking, trying to single-handedly raise two kids with no child support, get enough sleep, find time to cook, clean, earn money, study, and write her dissertation, but she met all the challenges head-on.

After extensive planning and artful prioritizing and compromising—which is much of the meat for this book—Leah's hard work and commitment started to pay off. Even though the family budget was painfully tight and the only one without homework in the evenings was little Sarah, Leah began to feel that she was making some real progress. She earned her Ph.D. in the spring of 1986 and was on her way to becoming a licensed psychologist. Leah and her children eventually moved back to New York, where she opened up a practice on Long Island, counseling families, children, and individuals, most notably single mothers.

Leah's life remains an example of perseverance and commitment. Her former husband has lost all meaningful contact with his children. Leah's son, Andrew, is an attorney on the West Coast, and her daughter, Sarah, is a college graduate completing a degree in nursing.

Just a few months earlier and only a few miles away in Charlotte, North Carolina, I was going through my own dramatic entry into single motherhood. I was suffering from contractions, alone, in the parking lot of a local hospital because I refused to go in before midnight. The hospital's billing cycle started at 12 A.M., and it was only 11:00 PM. There was no way I was going to let them charge me their daily rate of $700 for just sixty minutes! Especially when I had no health insurance.

Needless to say, the grunting and groaning that accompanied the contractions caused quite a commotion because nearby members of the hospital's staff came rushing out to the parking lot, pushing a wheelchair, and politely shoving me in it. They raced me into the emergency entrance, where I had to go through more than the usual red tape of entering a hospital since I was uninsured, unmarried, and unprepared. ("Pack what bag? The baby wasn't due for two weeks, and I was in the middle of a huge project at work!")

My live-in partner had decided on Labor Day 1985, to leave town when I was four months pregnant at age thirty-six. Actually, he told me a day earlier that he was going on a job interview that Monday and would return the middle of the following week. At 4:00 A.M. the next morning, I awoke to the sounds of grinding gears and crunching gravel. I ran to the window and saw Jerry pull out of the driveway in a truck with his motorcycle on board and a trailer pulling his boat behind him. Someone else was driving his car.

I waited one week, two weeks, a month for him to return, but no word. I couldn't ignore the sneaking suspicion that this was no ordinary job interview. During this time, I called at least fifty hospitals to see if they had anyone fitting his description, just to help prolong my denial. Four and one-half months later, on January 3, 1986, when I had my son, Spencer, I got the hint that Jerry was not coming back. It wasn't until April of that year that he briefly showed up to see if I still wanted him. Somehow, I couldn't forgive this guy who had left me on Labor Day and showed up on April Fool's Day.

Even though I was a new MOM (Mother Outside of Marriage), like single mothers through divorce, I went through the usual course of dealing with loss, starting with denial and overstaying my welcome in the depressed and anger stages. I became obsessive. Being dumped was enough, especially if you've never been the dumpee. But to be pregnant with my thirty-sixth birthday only a week away was awful. On top of that, I had lost my partner to a woman who was twenty-five years his junior. My self-esteem was signaling "major meltdown."

Things got even worse. When Spencer was only nine months old, I was fired from my seven-year job as art director of an advertising agency. My boss was uncomfortable having an unmarried mother on staff and found an excuse to terminate me, giving me only one hour to pack up and go. All this occurred only days after I had major home improvements and repairs completed. How was I going to pay for all of it when I was still paying off the costs of Spencer's birth, not to mention day care, food, and shelter costs?

Hitting bottom, it seemed that I had no choice but to accept the situation and stop feeling like a victim and get on with it. My mother's often-used refrain, "sink or swim" couldn't have spoken to me at a better time. I had actually made myself sick from the depression and anger and feelings of bad luck I had internalized. I decided to channel all that negativity into some productivity, thereby freeing up my creative energy. In fact, it actually occurred to me (although in retrospect) that the father of my child was someone with whom I did not want to spend the rest of my life. I also realized that had I not lost my job that I would still be working as an art director and copywriter in a mediocre job and not doing what I really wanted to be doing with my life. In a sense, both my boss and Jerry had done me a huge favor.

I ran a lucrative advertising and design service for a few years before the recession hit. By the time it caught up with me, most of my clients were already gone. But I was smart enough to sock away what I could when things were good, and by now my house was almost paid for.

Christmas 1990 was the turning point when I became aware of the purpose of my life. While sitting in the pediatrician's office (for my son's umpteenth ear infection), I was thumbing through all the magazines boasting the same articles on "How to Avoid Stress" and "Supermom Burnout." You know the ones—they advise you to get your husband to help out more. "That's it," I said, leaping out of my chair. "Well, excuse me, but I forgot to bring the man who's supposed to bring out the trash."

With that, I started Single Mother, a newsletter that prides itself as "a support group in your hands," and founded the National Organization of Single Mothers, Inc. (NOSM) because there wasn't anything out there for women like me. I knew there must be more of us. I started selling subscriptions on the street, on airplanes, in stores, and anywhere I thought I could spy a distressed-looking single mom.

NOSM grew to become a network that was more than committed to helping single parents successfully meet the challenges of daily life. The organization and its publication, Single Mother, became the voice of more than 11 million single mothers. Single Mother has become the country's only national newsletter dealing with single-parenting issues in an upbeat, practical, and positive light. The organization has linked families through a network of empowerment.

One day, Leah was reading the New York Daily News when she saw an article about me and the Single Mother newsletter. (Normally, she wouldn't be caught dead reading anything other than the New York Times, but thankfully her son insisted on getting the New York Daily News for the sports section.) She was so impressed with what she read that she contacted me immediately and said she wanted to be part of this network that helped empower single mothers. Leah offered the perspective of one who experienced divorce and had attained her dream in spite of it. She shared her knowledge and success by contributing to *Single Mother*, even before we met in person in June 1993.

We realized that single mothers needed a book they could pick up anytime and anywhere that would reassure them when sometimes the challenges of single parenting seemed impossible. We also were tired of seeing the confidence of "real" single mothers shot down by the debates over family values on television, radio, and in the news. This lifestyle boasts popular celebrity status in Hollywood and Nashville. (Single motherhood is fairly popular among country singers.) But the unfair stereotyping, poor publicity, and inaccurate analyses of studies that was the usual rhetoric began brewing a backlash against mothers raising their children without a husband at home. Economics played a major role, too. It seemed okay to be a single mom if you were a rich celebrity, such as Jodie Foster, Farrah Fawcett, Cher, Glenn Close, Madonna, Tanya Tucker, or a Spice Girl, but not okay if you were an average American woman.

Because Leah and I not only knew that the stereotyping of single mothering was false but also that single parenting actually could be a healthy and empowering experience in a woman's life, we needed to supply more information and more encouragement to prove that this was true. So we wrote this book.

The Complete Single Mother offers a fresh perspective to raising a family solo through its realistic, upbeat, and positive approach. Packed with valuable information, the book takes women through the first stages of accepting their single-parent lifestyle, whether by choice or chance, to enabling them to unleash their creative potential to be a successful individual, parent, valuable friend, and worker. Here is a book that will answer all the questions you may have about single mothering but were either too busy or too afraid to ask because you felt that no one had the answer anyway.

The Complete Single Mother is for the new generation of mothers (and men, too, who are single parents) who will bring with them a new set of family values that are actually good and necessary for this country's survival. The single parent is bringing back community by seeking extended families, teaching that self-reliance is healthier than codependency, and proving that a family is not defined by who heads it, but rather by its ability to love and share and make its members feel safe. Whether by choice, chance, or other circumstance— adoption, divorce, death—if you are or will be a single mother, *The Complete Single Mother* offers reassuring answers for your most challenging concerns. For relatives, professionals, and others who work with and counsel single moms, this book can serve as an invaluable resource and reference guide, too.

The Complete Single Mother is for everyone who is affected by single mothering today. But, most of all, this book is for the woman who needs encouragement, confidence, and practical advice. It will help her organize her life around the realities and strengths of single parenting and not around others' expectations of who she is or should be.

—A.E.

PART 1

THE MANY FACES OF SINGLE MOTHERS TODAY

1
The Heroic Single Mother

Heroes don't do the easy thing but do the right thing. Heroes are courageous, stand up under fire, and sacrifice for the good of others. Heroes have had to face some form of injustice or inequity and are often lonely. Heroes know how to take care of themselves. Single mother heroes take care of themselves by setting boundaries, establishing priorities, and making creative compromises. You help others everyday by the example of your own successful single parenting.

The burden you bear in parenting without a partner in a society that provides so little support for parents is certainly unjust, although you may have chosen this way of parenting. (You probably didn't have as many choices as you would have liked.) Because of this injustice, it's easy for single mothers to fall into the victim trap, but this is a most unproductive, senseless way to live. We are all victims of something larger than ourselves at one time or another. Whether you're divorced because your husband slept around or whether you knew your baby's father for only a short period, if you want to succeed as a hero, not a victim, you should first recognize that you have made choices, even if you were not conscious of them at the time. Recognize that you have a choice in how you will play the cards you now hold."

In spite of a culture that has failed to meet the needs of single mothers because of weak child support enforcement, inflexible employers, prohibitive child care costs, and schools that are slow to recognize the single mother's schedule, most single mothers are doing a very good job. They are showing that self-reliance is the key to a joyful and productive life.

From this moment on, if you have ever felt like a victim, tell yourself that you will no longer be a victim in your eyes or in anyone else's. If you've been viewed as villainous because you've made choices that didn't agree with others' expectations, let it go. As a woman and a mother, you are powerful.

OUR GODDESS HISTORY

Long before the age of Christianity, even before Judaism, Islam, and classical Greece, much of civilization on Earth revered the "Goddess Mother." The Goddess culture valued and respected women—the human creators, sustainers of life, and nurturers of the earth—in the symbolic role of mother.

Countless stories celebrate the remarkably creative goddess. Most often they were mothers who were not attached to a male partner. The Greek single mother goddess Demeter went into the underworld to search for her daughter Persephone. The myth tells us that it is the recurring loss of her daughter Persephone which creates the seasons. Legend tells us that Demeter spewed forth the seasons as she emerged

LOVE HURTS

Before giving in to the hype of Valentine's Day by drowning yourself in mounds of chocolate you felt compelled to buy, consider this: Aphrodite, the Greek goddess of beauty and love—or Venus, as the Romans called her—was a single mom with many children, most notably Cupid (or Eros to the Greeks). The Venus De Milo may be depicted armless, but legend says she wrapped her arms (and legs) around some powerful gods with which she dallied. In other myths, she is said to have been born pregnant with the little blindfolded matchmaker in diapers who would shoot his love arrows into unsuspecting victims. When her son once complained about being stung by a bee, mom replied, "If the bee sting is painful, what pain, Eros, do you suppose all your victims suffer?" Ouch!

from her winter darkness of mourning her daughter's loss, and their reunion was celebrated as spring.

In some of these early societies and in many aboriginal cultures, there was no fatherhood as we know it. In fact, renowned anthropologist Margaret Mead was among the first to call fatherhood a social invention.

Resurrect the goddesses who lived before you by reclaiming the goddess inside you. Be proud of what you achieve in caring for yourself and your children. Remember you are a hero.

YOU ARE NOT ALONE

The U.S. Census Bureau has acknowledged that one of the most profound changes in family composition to have occurred during the past quarter century was the tremendous increase in the number of single parents. According to the most recent data, more than 28 percent of all births were to single women. The steepest increase was among college-educated women and those with professional or managerial jobs. The Census Bureau also reported that 53 percent of first births were to unmarried women.

There are now more than 12 million single mothers in the United States.

The National Center for Health Statistics notes a shift in the typical age of the unmarried mother. Increasingly, single mothers are older than they used to be. When once births to teenagers were epidemic, the latest figures show births to women under twenty have declined. The birth rate for unmarried women in their early twenties through midthirties has soared.

Analysts give economic and cultural reasons for the rapid increase in the number of single mothers outside of marriage. More women in the workforce today see less of a gap between their earnings and those of men working similar jobs. As a result, women don't feel as pressured to marry as they did decades ago. The women's movement has left many women with a new sense of independence. Many women no longer trust the institution of marriage, while the social taboos that have discouraged unmarried births have waned. Single mothers are found within every ethnic, economic, and religious group.

MEETING THE CHALLENGES HEAD ON

Let's face it. Times are changing. A family is not defined by who heads the household.

Those who most openly criticize the choice of single mothering are often people with their own unresolved family issues. For example, some women may not be able to separate from their own abusive relationships, or perhaps they secretly desire a child of their own. They may envy your freedom or feel threatened by the control you have taken over your own life. Unfortunately, there are those who feel that being in any relationship is better than living single. Not true. Psychologists report that the single-parent household, in many cases, is preferable to a two-parent situation, especially if there is constant arguing, substance abuse, or physical or emotional battering.

If you are a single mother, you're not alone. Even if:

♦ Your child's father left you.

♦ Your mate announced he doesn't want to be a father.

♦ You're pregnant, and he's got the bankbook.

♦ Your fiancé died, leaving you pregnant and sort of widowed.

♦ You left an abusive relationship.

♦ Your ex-husband wants nothing to do with you or your child.

♦ Your ex-partner wants nothing to do with you or your child.

♦ Your child was the result of donor insemination or adoption.

You can achieve whatever it is you want out of life. In fact, many women are convinced they would not have accomplished their desired goals had they not had to learn to rely on their own abilities and wit. Thousands of women have not only survived single motherhood but have also emerged as powerful and dynamic people whose hidden talents and resources would have been dormant if they had not accepted the challenges of single parenting as an opportunity for personal growth.

Don't confuse the challenges of single parenting with hard luck or unfortunate circumstances. No one says this will be easy. It's frustrating to be expected to perform the lion's share of work both in and outside the home.

With some energetic and creative thinking, a bit of planning, and The Complete Single Mother *as a companion, you can not only raise happy, healthy, and productive children but you will also be able to become the person you were meant to be— strong, decisive, independent, courageous, and, above all, a joyful woman.*

2

When You're a Mother Outside of Marriage by Chance

The majority of single mothers who have never been married to their children's fathers are what's called "single mothers by choice," but this does not reflect everyone's reality. Although this category is far better than such demeaning phrases as "knocked up" or "mother of an illegitimate child," many of these women actually became mothers by chance.

In this book, we refer to all Mothers Outside of Marriage as MOMs. The MOM tag includes those who became mothers by accident, those who prepared for motherhood "just in case," those who consciously chose to become pregnant, and adoptive mothers. Many MOMs by chance share the insight that on some level they arranged the circumstances to allow for the possibility of motherhood. Truthfully, most MOMS by chance thought at one time or another of mothering solo. The woman who has made the life decision that she does not ever want children and finds herself pregnant has experienced an accident. It remains her choice, however, whether to perceive this accidental pregnancy as an unexpected tragedy or as a happy surprise.

Whatever label you may find appropriate or useful for your particular situation, the most important thing, of course, is that *all* women with children are simply, in the final analysis, mothers.

IF YOUR MATE DOESN'T SHARE YOUR FEELINGS

You're not alone if you find yourself in a relationship with a man who doesn't want children but never made this clear. Somehow, this doesn't seem to be a problem at first. You may have kept your desire for motherhood well hidden. Your mate may have remarked in

MEET THE NEW MOMS ON THE BLOCK

According to the U.S. Census Bureau 2003 report, fully 22 percent of single moms in the United States have never been married. The other 10 million single women raising children measured by the Census Bureau break down as follows:

+ 12 percent are separated.

+ 35 percent are divorced.

+ 3 percent are widowed.

passing, "I may want kids, but not now, not for a long time." You didn't want to push him, and so you waited for a more opportune moment to discuss marriage and fatherhood. Typically, it is only after you announce your pregnancy that any serious discussion begins.

Many MOMs say they knew deep in their hearts that their former partners were not father material. It often takes a few years to become aware that perhaps you stayed in such a relationship to allow yourself at least the option of motherhood, whether or not the father was willing to participate. At first, it may appear that he is the only reason you are a single mother, but when you examine the matter further, you may find that you weren't really surprised by his decision not to be a father.

"MY BOYFRIEND CAN'T MAKE UP HIS MIND. . . ."

I've been in a relationship for five years with someone who has decided not to be a father. I am considering having a child on my own. I don't want to spend my life waiting for

my boyfriend to maybe change his mind so I can have a child. I know definitely that I want to be a mother and to have a baby fairly soon, but fatherhood is just not in his life plan. I wouldn't want my baby's father to be someone who didn't want to be a father, anyway.

You're right—you can't make your boyfriend want to be a father and willingly assume all the responsibilities of parenthood. If remaining childless or postponing the decision to start a family is not right for you, then your decision to have a child as a single mother is the best one for you and your child. You need to feel confident that single motherhood is right for you. Feeling confident about this important life decision is the first step in successful single mothering.

YOUR PARTNER LEFT YOU

In a sense, the man who announces "I don't want a baby" has left you emotionally, especially if you discussed having children together. No matter what circumstances surround single motherhood, loss is a central theme. Even women who consciously choose single motherhood by donor insemination are dealing with a type of loss—in this case, the loss of a dream family complete with father, two kids, two cars, and a dog and cat.

If your boyfriend ended the relationship with you because he did not want children, ask yourself whether this is truly a tragedy or whether he may in a sense have done you a favor. If you take an honest look inside yourself, you may find that, even if you can't have the "dream family," you still really want to be a mother. It is not always easy to allow ourselves this conscious choice. Therefore, many of us use the end of a relationship as an excuse to be a "victim" of single motherhood.

If your pregnancy was planned but the father disappeared, never to be seen again, or you had the major breakup scene, assess the situation carefully. You will find that most likely there was some indication that becoming a father was not a commitment this man wholeheartedly sought.

Of course, there are no guarantees in life. Perhaps your pregnancy stirred up painful feelings in your partner, and he saw fleeing or breaking up as the only way out. You're likely to experience this abandonment as akin to experiencing a sudden death in the family. In a sense, you feel widowed, but more unsettled and bewildered, because widows at least know that their partners did not want to abandon them, but rather were taken from them against their will. When your partner leaves without explanation, you may wonder if there was anything you could have done to prevent it. Probably not, but there is something that can be prevented now, and that is blaming yourself. It is not your fault.

IF YOUR PARTNER HAS PROBLEMS

When I told my live-in partner of five years that I was pregnant, he simply said, "You decide," and went into the bedroom to watch TV. He's always been emotionally distant and a bit of a couch potato. Lately, he has been sullen and drinking pretty heavily, but only on weekends. Yet, he always appears sober and well groomed,

has never become physically violent, and faithfully shows up for his job, which he claims to hate, every Monday morning. I want this baby but feel unhappy and cheated. How can I decide whether or not to have this baby with him?

This is the most common question MOMs ask themselves after learning that they are pregnant by a partner of many years. First, it would be wise to look at the reasons you were drawn to this relationship. Perhaps sex with this person is more than satisfying. Maybe he's good-looking, has a good job and plenty of money, and drives a nice car. In spite of his weekend drinking, he might still be dependable enough—at least when it's just the two of you. Feeling cheated, however, is not surprising. After all, this person has put up many walls to resist communication and genuine intimacy. This might be his way of protecting himself and avoiding closeness to anyone, even you and your baby. If he is dispassionate and disconnected from others, it seems in character for him to be apathetic about your announcement. The fact that he shows up for a job he says he hates after a weekend binge means that he might have problems even he does not recognize. Binge drinking is a serious red flag, which should not be ignored. Having a baby might be a distraction from

his own issues, and maybe this is why he doesn't have an opinion one way or the other. It also seems that he expects you to take most of the responsibility for this decision, which means he is unlikely to be an active participant in raising your child.

It's important to weigh the benefits of this relationship against the disadvantages. More importantly, keep in mind that communication is essential to any relationship. Without it, you are only going through the motions of being in a partnership and are cheating yourself in the long run. Raising a child with a mate who has poor communication skills may not be wise, since people who tend to be disconnected with others have a way of sending out mixed signals—confusion that no one needs, especially children.

"I GOT PREGNANT FROM A BRIEF AFFAIR. . . ."

I'm a single mother by choice, sort of. At thirty-five, I found myself pregnant after a brief affair with a younger coworker from my office. So far, I'm delighted that I have a healthy daughter, but I also feel a little embarrassed about how I got pregnant in the first place.

Unless your reasons for having a child are based on a need to get back at someone, to shock your family, to rope someone into a commitment, or to ease your loneliness, there is no reason to be embarrassed. The delight and joy you feel about your daughter's arrival is the way it should be. Raising children in today's world is always a challenge, but if you welcome motherhood, how you got pregnant is insignificant. What really

---

> ### ⭐ SINGLE MOM OF NOTE
>
> **Sarah Bernhardt,**
> **First Lady of Theatre**
> Born Rosine Bernard in 1845 in Paris to an unmarried single mother of Dutch-Jewish descent, Sarah was baptized at twelve and brought up in a convent. A year later, she began winning prizes for her noteworthy acting.
>
> Sarah's affair with a Belgian nobleman left her pregnant with her only son, Maurice, when she was eighteen. She continued to pursue her career until her death, appearing on the stage around the world even after her leg was amputated in 1915. Sarah and Maurice, who became a writer, were always close and she died in his arms at the age of 79.

matters is how you mother on a day-to-day basis. If this brief affair fulfilled your needs in the moment, chances are your delighted outlook on motherhood stems from the benefits you consciously sought out from that experience.

IF YOUR BIRTH CONTROL DIDN'T WORK

No birth control method is 100 percent dependable. Don't berate yourself for contraceptive failure. Even if you think it was because of a hidden wish to conceive that you were careless in the use of birth control, a combination of factors might make this a blessing in disguise. If you've decided to go ahead and have your child, it is important not to blame the birth control but rather to welcome the happy surprise.

When contraception failed and the thought of becoming a mother is something that you can't see in the cards, you may have considered terminating the pregnancy. Yet, countless women report that once they became pregnant that all their earlier refrains of "I can't imagine myself ever wanting kids" disappeared. Still, pregnancy is only one step toward motherhood—it's a lifetime occupation that will change any woman. It is up to you to decide whether that change is right for you.

SPECIAL CONCERN: RAPE

From the college student attending a campus party, to the account executive taking a client to dinner, to the woman introduced to a handsome new neighbor by a mutual friend, every woman is at risk of being raped—and the risk of being raped by an acquaintance is far greater than that of being raped by a stranger. No matter how well you knew this person or how intimate you had become before intercourse, if you said no to him and he continued, this is rape.

If you decide to continue a pregnancy resulting from rape, you should seek counseling from an expert in the field of victim recovery. Consultation with a family law attorney prior to the baby's birth to make sure that your parental rights and the welfare of your child are protected would also be wise. Unless the rapist is convicted of his crime, he could legally pursue parental rights.

IF YOU ARE IN AN ABUSIVE RELATIONSHIP

Relationships can be abusive even if no physical injury occurs. It is emotionally healthy and empowering to end a relationship if you feel you can't be yourself.

Remarks like "but he didn't hit you" or "at least he didn't cheat" are not reasons to stay with someone who belittles you or makes you feel worthless or inadequate.

If you are in a physically abusive relationship, get out now. If you got out of one, be proud of your bravery and honesty. Our society too often credits those who stay in relationships "till death do us part," rather than those who have the courage to get out. You need to be your own best advocate. As many single mothers whose significant others were abusive say, "It was one of the hardest things I have ever done, but I left to save myself and my child."

If you got out of a harmful relationship, try to help those remaining in abusive situations by offering a helping hand to other women in need. Consider volunteering at a battered women's shelter or helping out in other ways in your community.

If you think you are in an abusive relationship but are confused right now, investigate the mental health clinics and women's resource centers in your community, which are often listed in the front of your phone book. You need to talk with someone who can help you sort through your confusion and make safe choices.

WHEN ABORTION IS NOT AN OPTION

You may not believe in abortion. Perhaps you are basically pro-choice, but for any number of reasons, you are not willing to abort this pregnancy. Women who have had previous abortions often feel, by the time they reach a certain stage in life, that "this pregnancy is meant to be."

If lack of money or other barriers imperil your choice to have an abortion if you want one, there may be sources of help you have not considered. Your local chapter of Planned Parenthood may be able to help.

HANDLING YOUR FEELINGS ABOUT MOTHERHOOD OUTSIDE OF MARRIAGE

Before you can rid yourself of the guilt and other burdensome feelings you don't deserve and before you "blame"

anyone else, you need to take an honest look at the circumstances surrounding your becoming a mother. Many women realize that their mates' reactions were not entirely a surprise. Our society still stigmatizes single mothers—you may feel you will receive more sympathy and support if you become one by chance instead of by choice. But if your relationship with the father of your child is not working, give yourself permission to walk away. You can be a great mother.

There Must Be Fifty Ways . . .

There are many other ways that women have discovered motherhood outside of marriage. Do any of these sound familiar to you?

- Sandra, twenty-nine, was in a relationship with a man whose behavior when drinking she detested but tolerated. When she discovered she was pregnant, she urged him to stop drinking, even though deep down she knew she didn't want to marry him, even if he remained sober. She wanted a baby but was afraid to have one on her own.

- Nancy, forty-one, lives on and off with a man who constantly belittles her. Her eleven-year-old son (from a previous marriage) also talks back and is disrespectful to her. Just when she's ready to let her partner know that it's over, his friends and family remind her, "He doesn't beat you or cheat on you. He's good with the kids. What's wrong?" She has resigned herself to waiting to see if things will improve.

- Lisa thought her womanizing boyfriend would commit to a permanent relationship when he found out they were going to have a baby. He split saying the baby wasn't his, and she later learned that he had four other children he also denied fathering. Although she was initially in shock, after thinking about it, she realized there had been red flags all along.

- Janine's partner of four years dropped her off at the hospital shortly before she was to give birth. He drove off and never returned. He left the United States.

- Lili is nine weeks pregnant and is grappling with the decision whether or not to have an abortion. Her boyfriend shows no interest in the pregnancy; yet she feels dependent on him.

Maybe one of these dilemmas sound strikingly familiar to you, or maybe your story is totally unique. Whatever your situation, there will be strong feelings that need to be worked through and serious life decisions to be made.

Getting Rid of Guilt, Shame, and Blame

Sometimes we think after a breakup: "It wasn't so bad. What am I doing now that's better? Why couldn't I have been happy the way it was?" We wonder if we secretly pushed the other person out of our lives. At other times, if we were abandoned or weren't deeply involved, we believe it was our fault because if we had been more lovable we would be with somebody right now. Even if we removed ourselves from intolerable circumstances or left for reasons others plainly understood, we can feel guilty for having made any choice at all.

You're Not a Victim

Being a victim often seems to be the easiest choice to make. Truthfully, few of us are really victims. We have choices.

Facing your feelings is essential, just as it would be if your feelings were associated with any other major life-changing event. The events surrounding single motherhood—divorce, death, giving birth, buying or selling a home, moving, getting or losing a job—already rank high on the list of life's most stressful events. This makes single motherhood particularly challenging.

Take a Thoughtful Look at Yourself

Be honest about your feelings so that you can separate the destructive emotions—the guilt, shame, and blame—from those feelings that are affirming and sustaining. Taking an honest look at your feelings and emotions requires personal courage and sustained effort. The goal is to become more accepting of yourself and to get rid of the victim mentality to which so many single mothers succumb.

Name It, Face It, and Erase It

Guilt must be given a name. Whatever you feel guilty about—dig it up, isolate it, and expose it to the light of day. To name it, you have to be as specific as possible. We are not talking about blanket statements about inadequacy or failing but about identifying as clearly as possible exactly what you feel guilty about. Guilt must be faced. It must be spoken of out loud and looked in the eye. Guilt makes us feel ashamed, or it makes us blame others for our circumstances.

Because there is so much baggage each of us will discover along our way, we must identify the personal life dramas that have caused us to feel vulnerable in the past before we can reconcile our feelings about our guilt. Your feelings can't hurt you. In fact, by listening to them you can learn from them and uncover the joy of single mothering. What can hurt is allowing your feelings to fester, causing you to act out of confusion and make poor decisions. The reward for facing your feelings about your entry into single motherhood is peaceful acceptance of the choices you have made. This acceptance is the first important step to living joyfully and fully in the present.

DECIDING ON THE FATHER'S ROLE

If you are a MOM who has conceived with someone you know (and most have), there are potential legal and emotional issues that can complicate your life. These issues can also involve your child, and you need to be aware that in most states that the biological father's rights are the same whether or not you are married.

When a single mother finds that she and the child's father are not going to have a life together, she needs to define the father's role. It's best to find out what the father's intentions are and get a legal agreement in writing. In that way, if the father claims he wants nothing to do with you or the child but comes back later with threats about his rights as a father, you will have some legal recourse. More likely, if he doesn't want to be involved, you will be left in charge. However, we've all heard stories about the father from the past who declared that he wanted custody of his child, usually after becoming jealous of your new relationship or finding that life away from you and your child hasn't worked out for him the way he had hoped.

Some dos and don'ts for dealing with the father of your child:

♦ **Do** be aware that your attitude toward the father affects your child. Your child will always be a link between you and this person. If you have unresolved issues about the father, seek counseling or bolster your support system before your child is born.

♦ **Do** seek legal counsel if you can't agree on what the father's role will be. Remember, even if this person is the last man on earth you'd like to see raise your child, he and all fathers have rights in every state, whether married or not. Learn about the laws in your state and protect your rights and those of your child.

♦ **Don't** try to rope someone into marriage, thinking that your accidental pregnancy will produce a change of

heart in him. You may actually alien-
ate him more and make him lose his
trust in you.

◆ **Don't** refuse to give your child's father
access to your child just because he
didn't want to get married. If he genuinely wants to be part of your child's
life, don't "punish" him by refusing to
let him in your life. Your child is more
likely to be hurt than your ex.

◆ **Do** communicate with each other.
Agree to provide each other with
current contact information and to
advise the other if you move. This
is especially important if he wants to
remain somewhat connected.

On the other hand, if you are friendly
with the father, you might be fortunate
enough to have a good partnership.
Your child would benefit from the two
of you coparenting, as many divorced

couples are now doing. After all, you
can't have too many adults helping you
raise your child—whether biologically
connected or not.

Regardless of how the father's role is
defined, it is wise to seek legal counsel
during your negotiations regarding visitation and possible child support. Don't
neglect this because you think your
child's father's interests will remain the
same. Paternity can always be established at a later date, if he decides to
do so (see Chapter 8 for information
about establishing paternity). Even if
the father acknowledges paternity, his
level of involvement may fluctuate. For
instance, he may suddenly demand joint
custody, or may try to prevent you from
taking a job that would require you to
move to another state, or might even
challenge your authority to make medical, religious, or educational decisions
for your child.

3

When You're a Mother Outside of Marriage by Choice

If you choose to have a baby outside of marriage, don't feel isolated. Overall, the number of Mothers Outside of Marriage (MOMs) has been multiplying. The growth rate has increased more than 60 percent in the last fifteen years; the highest rates of single moms by choice were among professional women in their thirties.

Statistics show, too, that, contrary to stereotypes about unmarried moms, these "new MOMs on the block" are educated women who have decided that having a child is their number one life priority. A loving and nurturing mother and father might be their preferred choice of family, but these women are realistic about accepting the fact that the "dream family"—the house, dog, white picket fence, and Mr. Right—might not materialize. The new single mother has what it takes to raise a child;

she just needs a little reassurance now and then. She is strong and independent enough not to feel overwhelmed by this responsibility, yet gentle and compassionate enough to give unselfishly to her child.

We refer to all Mothers Outside of Marriage as MOMs, even though circumstances are certainly different for single moms by choice and single moms by chance. In fact, the line between the two groups can be quite blurry.

Many MOMs grapple with their options, which typically include remaining in a dead-end relationship, choosing to conceive, opting for an abortion, or deciding against motherhood. Most MOMs by choice don't necessarily choose single motherhood at a precise time—attending a staff meeting at ten, scheduling a hair appointment after lunch, and at three going

SINGLE MOM OF NOTE

Janese Swanson,
Software Inventor

Raised by a single mom, Janese was often busy fixing toasters and other appliances because her mom couldn't afford to have them repaired. The holder of a Ph.D. and five other postgraduate degrees, in the 1980s Janese created *Where in the World Is Carmen Sandiego?*, the popular computer game. In 1995, Janese Swanson founded Girl Tech, which develops products and services that encouraged girls to use new technology.

Swanson credits her mom for much of her success, but her inspiration soared after giving birth to her own daughter in 1992. When once asked what her vision of joy and happiness was, she said, "I get a lot of joy out of seeing my daughter happy."

to the sperm bank to be impregnated. A single mother by choice usually has spent more time deliberately planning her upcoming motherhood by doing things like putting a certain amount of money away each month, moving to a district boasting good schools, and checking into the family leave programs at work.

Regardless of whether prospective MOMs chose donor insemination, conception with a known donor, or to raise their child on their own after realizing that they did not want to remain in a relationship with the child's father, all women who find themselves MOMs by choice—or sort-of-by-choice—have unique challenges and concerns as well as common feelings and experiences.

ARE YOU READY FOR SINGLE MOTHERHOOD?

Single motherhood may not be for everyone. Here are some issues to consider on the journey to deciding:

◆ Have you decided how you will explain your choice to be a single mother to your son or daughter? You should be able to present your child with a positive view of your family situation.

◆ Have you budgeted for all aspects of childbearing and child care, including donor insemination if you are going that route? You should also make necessary legal provisions for your child should something happen to you.

◆ Have you thought about what you will tell family and friends, and are you prepared for any negative remarks? Knowing how to handle people's offhand comments is important, but be sure you are not simply trying to shock or hurt someone or to prove that you can do something on your own.

◆ Have you resolved any issues about men and relationships, and are you sure that you are not angry at men or trying in some way to get even with a particular man? It's important to place a high value on male and female relationships to give your child a realistic perspective of the world. No matter what the sex of your child, it is most important not to have negative feelings toward men. Also, you need to leave yourself open to the possibility that one day you might become involved in a committed relationship with a man.

- Are you having a baby because you are lonely and need something to fill the void? Hopefully, your life is already rich and satisfying, and you have the ability to mother yourself when needed.

- Have you learned what physical and emotional changes you will go through, before, during, and after childbirth? You should arrange to have a friend, family member, or doula be your labor coach and help you out the first few weeks after birth. Keep in mind that you won't always have a partner to share feelings with you or comfort you during the hormonal shifts and mood swings that go along with pregnancy.

- Do you have a strong support system? Just because you have lunch daily with your female coworkers doesn't mean they will be there for you in the middle of the night. Don't mistake work friends for real friends, and don't overlook those friends you normally would shy away from because professionally you have little in common. You need to create an extended family.

- Do expect your feelings to fluctuate even if you are absolutely certain that it is best to have this child without a father. Because the traditional American dream of husband, home, and family is so emphasized in our culture, you will be going through a normal grieving period over the loss of this dream. Your outlook and the amount of emotional support you receive from others will determine how long you spend grieving for the loss of this fantasy.

No one can resolve all of these questions before their baby is born—and no parent has everything figured out ahead of time! But you may find it helpful to contemplate these issues.

"MY FAMILY IS UNSUPPORTIVE. . . ."

My family says I'm selfish to even consider having a child without a husband. They say I will deprive my baby of a father, but I want to be a mother.

A positive and affirming perspective on your own life is critically important to successful single motherhood. If you are troubled and hurt by your family's reaction to your possible plans for motherhood, consider carefully how your decision to become a single mother will influence your relationship within your family. Many families are initially unsupportive of single motherhood but embrace the notion with love and enthusiasm when the baby does arrive. Many families, however, never get to that point of acceptance, which leaves the single mother with yet another significant loss. Remember that the child of a single woman who chose motherhood will be able to proclaim, "My mom really wanted me!" Isn't that healthier than the comments we hear from parents complaining that their children were "mistakes" or from a friend who attributes his life problems to his parents' revelation that his arrival was a burden?

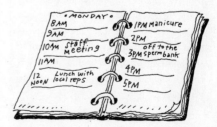

"MR. RIGHT (OR MR. ADEQUATE) HASN'T SHOWN UP. . . ."

Many women are tired of waiting for Mr. Right, or even Mr. Adequate, to show up at their door. He may well appear after the age when you are safely able to bear children. In view of the high divorce rate, many women are choosing to start families outside of marriage since they have no guarantees that a marriage will endure. Some women become pregnant through donor insemination, and others become pregnant by someone they have cared for and been involved with for a long time.

After carefully reviewing your options, you may join the millions of other single mothers who are now starting families. A family is simply a place where one feels loved, safe, and protected. Family has nothing to do with the presence of a man.

TICK TOCK: OVARY ANXIETY

Around the age of thirty, many women start becoming anxious about their biological clocks and their ability to conceive. Sometimes, potential MOMs feel it's now or never. Yet, advances in reproductive medicine have increased older women's options. In addition, many women report that because they waited until they had "lived a little" before having a child, they have more wisdom and patience for child-rearing.

MEET THE MOMs

All significant life decisions bring inevitable challenges—single motherhood is no exception.

- Susan, forty, wanted a baby, but everyone around her was unsupportive. She got pregnant through a longtime friend after deciding against donor insemination. Her family routinely asks her how she could be so selfish as to deprive her child of a father.

- Claire is thirty-eight and getting very anxious about having a child. She's

THE DINNER-DONOR PARTY

One single woman wanting to conceive held a dinner party for her former boyfriends. There she announced her intentions of having a child fathered by one of them if A, they were willing, B, they were worthy, and C, she didn't go the sperm bank route. Two volunteered, while the third said he would think about it. After sizing up her prospects, she made her choice among the league of extraordinary gentlemen who all remarkably stuck around as friends and mentors and role models for her wonderful daughter, now two.

dating someone regularly but doesn't think he would be a good husband or father. Yet, she recently flushed her birth control pills down the toilet.

♦ Bonnie is thirty-two and wants a baby. She does not want to put her life on hold while waiting for a perfect partner. She's doing lots of homework—meeting other MOMs by choice, talking with her doctor, and investigating donor insemination.

♦ Katie has health issues that suggest she may have difficulty conceiving and is under the care of a fertility specialist. Her mother thinks she's crazy to spend so much money on fertility treatments and reminds her how she should have spent more time looking for a husband and less time

pursuing her career. Katie has financial security, a strong network of caring friends, and the desire to have a baby. Yet, sometimes, her mother's words sting and cause her to rethink her desire to be a single mother.

♦ Barbara has a five-year-old daughter through anonymous donor insemination. She is considering joining a sibling registry network to learn about other children conceived with the same donor. She says having her baby was the best decision she ever made.

For more information on single motherhood by choice visit Single Mothers by Choice at *www.mattes.home.pipeline.com.*

HOLD YOUR HEAD HIGH

I sometimes sense that my friends are uncomfortable around me since I became an unmarried mother. Sometimes they're impressed; other times they seem fearful. Why is this?

For reasons of their own, your friends may be threatened by your courage and by your unconventional choices. There's not very much you can do about this— nor should you have to. But it may be that over time you will find that your friends become more accustomed to the choices you have made.

4
Choosing Motherhood Through Donor Insemination (DI)

You may be considering single motherhood or may already have chosen it for a number of reasons: a desire to reproduce the best part of yourself; a strong mothering instinct; the ability to get what you want out of life; and the awareness that your biological clock is ticking away. These reasons for wanting a baby would be the same whether you have a partner or not. In fact, the term "single mother by choice" can be misleading because it implies that the choice was to be single, not to be a mother. Most single mothers by choice prefer to emphasize the "mother" part of the phrase; because although it may not have been their choice to be single, it certainly was their choice to become a mother. Many single mothers by choice eventually "partner," but generally they do not seek a relationship to find a father figure for their children. Single mothers by choice commonly spend a good deal of time planning their entry into motherhood, regardless of their former life style.

IF YOU'VE BEEN IN A RELATIONSHIP

You're divorced—maybe once, or maybe for the second or third time. You have finally decided that Mr. Right may not come along while you are still in your childbearing years, and you feel it is unfair to deprive yourself of a child that you so very much want. Although single mothers by choice are often referred to as never-married, most have been either previously married or in a serious relationship and have decided that having a baby is a greater priority than investing time and energy to seek a new marriage or relationship partner.

Maybe you're like the majority of single women who prefer the "husband, two kids, two cars" approach to family life but find themselves in dead-end relationships. Like divorced women, rather than wait around for the right guy to show up, they have decided that no relationship is better than a bad one and that having a baby solo with one caring parent is better than having two unhappy ones. Moreover, when a woman in a relationship expresses her desire to have a baby, this is usually when her partner's real definition of "relationship" surfaces.

If you currently are involved with a lover who seems ideal for now, once baby and family are mentioned, he may let you know that this is not for him. Rather than denying or ignoring his feelings, it would be better to thank him for his honesty. It is often only after women announce their pregnancies that their partners make it clear they do not want to be fathers, either by saying so or simply by disappearing. Many women in these circumstances want to be mothers and choose to continue their pregnancies. Many of these women would have preferred a different reaction from the father. If the father had warned them early on about his lack of interest in fatherhood, these prospective mothers might have been better prepared. It is far simpler to make informed choices if you know your current partner is not interested in fatherhood.

TO EXIT OR STAY?

I'm involved with a man who wants to spend his life with me but does not want to have children. I want kids, period. Should I leave or stay?

If you are involved in a relationship with someone who does not want children

but you seriously want to be a mother, you have some hard choices to make. It is difficult enough to exit a relationship. Trying to decide whether or not to become a single mother at the same time makes your choice much more agonizing. If you're sure you want to raise a child but this person wants no part of it, then do not involve him. Deception is a sorry beginning to motherhood. If you decide to become pregnant, you need to accept sole responsibility for your decision.

IF YOU'RE READY FOR MOTHERHOOD BUT NOT WIFEHOOD

A number of women are ready for motherhood, but the thought of marriage is not appealing. The institution of marriage is no longer the only road to social advantage and financial security. Many women have attained status successfully without marriage. Having a baby completes a well-planned life. Most single mothers by choice say that if they marry, it will be because they want to and not because they need to. Only a few decades ago, you needed to be married to own a home, have financial security, receive respect from the community, have sex, become a mother, and provide a name for yourself and your child. Whereas at one time the romantic ideal of marriage was for women to get their needs met by someone offering everything they could not possess on their own, now more and more women can choose to remain single because marriage is no longer a financial and social necessity.

Although much has changed today, some women still feel they have failed if they can't find a suitable partner. It's important to keep in mind that getting married is one thing, but staying married is another. If you are choosing single motherhood because you think you would only end up getting divorced anyway, you may be right, but this should not be the sole basis for your decision. Conversely, it is not a wise idea to marry a person strictly because you want to conceive.

"MY BIOLOGICAL CLOCK IS READY TO EXPLODE...."

You're in your midthirties, have achieved a number of your desired goals, and now your ovaries are screaming "We want a baby!" You try to distract yourself with other things, but you still feel so consumed by the desire to have a child that you don't know what to do.

If you feel as though your time is running out, you're not alone. Many women agree that the real push toward motherhood comes from the internal clock setting a time limit.

Your clock should serve only as a gauge to assist you in making your decision; it should not be the only reason to choose motherhood. Don't think you have to have a child before it's too late when you really may not want one. Motherhood simply isn't for everyone, whether married or single.

If you are in your early thirties, in reasonably good health, and fertile, there is no reason to rush into motherhood. In fact, according to some women, you may actually be glad you waited to experience motherhood because at this stage in life you are more mature and patient and can put the whole experience into a more meaningful and realistic perspective.

THINKING IT OUT

Like so many women, you're ready for motherhood, and Mr. Ready for Fatherhood is nowhere in sight. Do you resign yourself to the fact that you may never get married and therefore may never have children? Do you gather as much information as possible about single motherhood and see whether it is an option for you?

Like any life-changing decision,

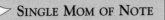

SINGLE MOM OF NOTE

Hollywood

It's not news to anyone that Hollywood hosts a huge share of single moms. Very private single mom stars, such as Jodie Foster and Glenn Close, won't discuss the "father" with reporters, and actor and author Camryn Manheim once was quoted in *People* magazine as saying "There is no father." Tabloids speculate about other unmarried celebrity mothers, but many readers still don't know details about some of their favorite stars. Whether or not known-donor or doctor-assisted donor insemination was the path to parenthood for many celebrities, it's nice to know that if their privacy can be honored, so can yours.

How Old Is Too Old?

People have debated over the right age to have children for years. If you're told you're too young and wait awhile, you may hear that you're now too old. But in today's world, women over fifty are having children, like Aleta St. James, the single mom who became pregnant at fifty-six with the help of her reproductive endocrinologist. St. James, a youthful-looking professional life coach decided it was time to have children when she was fifty-two but endured three miscarriages. After spending two more years working with her doctor, St. James gave birth to twins on November 9, 2004. Although the number of births to women over fifty in the United States amounts to about 250 per year, older women are having babies in other countries, too. In 1994, a woman in Italy gave birth at fifty-three, and a 65-year-old Indian woman gave birth to her son in 2003.

St. James inspires women to go for what they want, but keep in mind, her successful emotional healing practice helped her get there. Financing her fertility treatments totaled around $25,000!

choosing single motherhood has advantages and disadvantages. If you have been thinking about this a lot lately, that's good. Thinking it out enables you to seek out good information. In fact, some women's groups offer talks and workshops for single women thinking of becoming mothers.

Considering single motherhood by choice should include identifying where you are currently in your life and visualizing where you see yourself heading. When a child is an indelible part of the picture you see, with or without a man in the home, you are ready to look at single motherhood as an option.

DEALING WITH DISCOURAGEMENT

I'm thirty-seven years old and want a child terribly. I just ended a five-year relationship with a man who clearly is not good father material. I'd like a child and have researched donor insemination, but my family is making me feel that I am selfish to deprive my child of a father. My parents have been married forty-three years and think I'm nuts to consider this.

You sound too smart to do anything nutty. Your decision should be based upon what you think and not on what others may consider crazy or selfish. First, you've given careful thought to your desire to be a mother and have made the courageous decision not to involve a man who you perceive as less than capable of being a father. You have sorted through some painful emotions. The first step toward being a good mother is wanting a child and then wanting what is best for him or her. Second, you're smart to research carefully all medical and legal aspects of donor insemination because it means that you are giving this important life decision all the focus and attention it merits. Your child will one day benefit from the meticulous care and thought you have given to this decision. The happiest children are the ones who believe unconditionally that their parents consider them a priceless gift.

Tell your folks that rather than depriving your child of a father that you are giving him or her a mother who made it clear that "I wanted you very much."

Do be aware of what's needed to work through the guilt and conflict your parents' reaction may be causing. Remember, they are of a different generation. Reproductive technology in any form is not part of their experience. Embrace the good feeling that you are not adding to the world's problems by having children for the wrong reasons but have chosen single motherhood for the right reasons.

I am strongly considering becoming a single mom by DI. I still hope one day to meet Mr. Right, but now is the right time for me to become a mother. My girlfriends tell me that having a child by DI will be a complete "deal breaker" if I ever meet a man I feel could be part of my future. Is single motherhood necessarily forever?

Many single mothers find satisfying and lasting relationships later on and enjoy the opportunity to parent their children with a loving partner. Will your single mother status limit your chances of finding love? That depends upon the kind of man you are looking to meet. Will you have less time to look for a partner? Yes. Instead of spending time online checking dating sites or sitting in bars looking to connect, you will have the responsibilities of raising a child. You will love and be loved every day. Will men quickly lose interest once they find out you are a single mom? Maybe. You will instantly turn off men who are insecure, immature, self-centered, and not interested in being more than a tall version of a little boy. You will interest men who find a capable, resourceful, and energetic woman fascinating. Will being

a single mother ever be an advantage in the relationship game? Yes. Men interested in fatherhood and possibly more children may see your single motherhood as a welcome bonus. The lack of a former partner whose involvement must always be factored into any couples decision can be a distinct advantage.

WHAT EXACTLY IS DI?

I'm considering donor insemination because I want a baby before I am forty. However, I just can't seem to get past this image I have of me running to the doctor's office with a turkey baster filled with sperm. Can you update me on exactly what DI is? Is it the same as artificial insemination or in vitro fertilization?

The DI procedure is a more accepted way of referring to what was once called artificial insemination. There really is nothing artificial about it, since real human sperm is used. In vitro fertilization (IVF) is a procedure in which the sperm is actually placed in the egg in the laboratory, resulting in the formation of an embryo. Then the embryo is implanted in the uterus of the mother-to-be. This method, much more expensive than DI, is usually used for women with fertility problems.

A popular form of DI actually does rely on a more refined, quite slim version of the turkey baster. Intracervical insemination (ICI) is the most widely used method, the easiest, and the least expensive. ICI requires depositing sperm on the cervix using a slender straw-type device with a plunger on top that pushes the semen through. A plastic coated sponge or cap may be placed into the vagina to keep the sperm near the cervix. This sponge or cap is removed after six hours or so. Although this method appeals to many women because they can perform the procedure privately by self-insemination, most sperm banks recommend having a doctor perform the procedure.

In intrauterine insemination (IUI), sperm is deposited directly into the uterus via a flexible catheter-type device. This method, which must be performed by a physician, allows the sperm to bypass the cervix so that an increased number can reach the uterine cavity and subsequently the fallopian tubes, where fertilization takes place. When IUI is used, it is necessary to separate the sperm from the seminal plasma. This removes prostaglandins and other substances that could cause adverse reactions or severe uterine contractions. To separate the sperm, the sperm will be "washed" in a laboratory prior to the procedure. Sperm washing removes chemicals and bacteria that can cause infections or adverse reactions. The washing procedure may also increase the ability of sperm to fertilize the egg.

No matter which type of DI you and your physician choose, try to relax and focus on the process.

REASONS FOR DONOR INSEMINATION

You may find yourself having to answer questions such as, "Why are you doing this when you can adopt?" or "There are so many children who need a home, why go through the expense and ordeal of donor insemination?" These questions may not come from others but from yourself, as part of the process of deciding to become a single mother by choice.

Many women choose DI because they are uncomfortable with the idea of engaging in sexual behavior for the sole purpose of becoming pregnant. Additionally, women at the height of their desire for motherhood may not know anyone with whom they would have intercourse. Still other women may have a certain person in mind to father their child, but that person may be reluctant to have sexual relations, although he might not object to supplying sperm. Although physician-assisted DI is far more expensive than sexual intercourse, many women who choose this method feel it is safer, less worrisome, and more efficient than conceiving through sexual intercourse. The control over choosing the type of male they would like to have father their child, the reduced risk of HIV transmission, and the freedom from worry about hidden family secrets that a sex partner may harbor, such as inherited mental or physical disabilities, can make DI seem more appealing.

But don't take single motherhood by choice too lightly, whether you plan to conceive through intercourse with someone you know or through donor insemination using the resources of a sperm bank. If you are currently trying to become pregnant, it is imperative that you've carefully weighed all the benefits of single motherhood against the disadvantages. If the advantages clearly outweigh the disadvantages, then single motherhood most likely is right for you. Although there is no perfect situation or time or place to become a mother, you need to be sure that you have explored all your options and are making the best decision for yourself and your child.

Why Not Adopt Instead?

When asked why they chose donor insemination instead of adoption, many women responded that they wanted to experience pregnancy and childbirth, an experience they felt was one of life's most miraculous. Additionally, these women believed they would adopt a second child one day. Even women with fertility problems who are also considering adoption still would like to have the opportunity to reproduce what they feel is the best part of themselves.

Don't feel guilty because you would rather conceive than adopt. This is a matter of personal choice. Perhaps, too, you are hesitant to confront some of the concerns surrounding adoption, but you are willing to confront the challenges associated with conceiving outside of marriage.

ISSUES: THINGS TO THINK ABOUT AFTER YOU DECIDE ON DI

Women who become single mothers by choice through sexual intercourse usually do so with a friend or sexual partner because to them it is more accessible, less expensive, less "clinical," and more natural than going through the donor insemination procedure. Other women choose to self-inseminate with fresh sperm from a friend or other willing donor. Experts believe that self-insemination still takes place, but is far less commonly practiced due to realistic fears about HIV transmission.

I am seriously considering DI with the sperm of a friend who has agreed to be the donor. He is a wonderful man with many of the qualities I would look for in an ideal father. I already know him pretty well, and he is willing to furnish his medical records. What else should I ask?

Before conceiving with a known donor, the first thing to do is consult with an attorney specializing in family law, whether you have met this person only once or twice or you have been close friends for years.

A known donor could one day renege on his promise to stay uninvolved after conception. For this reason, it is crucial to draw up legal contracts in the early stages of planning your pregnancy. There have been cases where men have sued for custody after having a change of heart about being a father or because they are in a new relationship where their wife or partner is unable to conceive. As farfetched as this may seem, you need to be cautious in your decision to become inseminated with sperm from a known donor.

Ask yourself the following questions:

◆ Are you certain that this will never escalate into any type of relationship, romantic or not?

◆ Are you being straight with each other about what is expected from each of you, or are you kidding yourselves? Does either of you think the other will soften up or change his or her mind about the arrangement once conception takes place?

◆ If it is someone who has eagerly offered to be a donor, have you asked why he wants to do this? What would you do if he backed out when the time came, even though he has agreed for now?

- How do you know this person won't change his mind one day and want to become involved in your life? Have you thought out what would happen if he sues for visitation rights or even for custody? Establishing paternity is as simple as sticking out your finger for a blood test. The courts struggle constantly with issues dealing with the underlying question of what constitutes a parental relationship. The bottom line: a known donor will have legal rights, if he chooses to exercise these rights.

- How can you assuage the man's fears that you will one day sue him for child support? Just because you now say you won't, what would happen if you lost your job, your finances took a downturn, or you or your child became sick?

- Can you be sure that he is furnishing all his medical information and has answered every question honestly? Sperm banks employ cutting-edge technology to detect infectious diseases and other potential health risks; the level of testing means that fewer than 3 percent of prospective sperm donors are accepted into the leading sperm banks. Does this man pass every possible health requirement in addition to having tested negative at least twice—with a six-month interval between tests—for HIV? Have you looked thoroughly into his medical history regarding certain physical and mental disorders, including depression, personality disorder, alcoholism, drug abuse, or severe mood swings?

- Have you decided upon intercourse with this person, or do you want to be inseminated with his sperm without the physical entanglement? Intercourse has its advantages: less expensive, enjoyable, and easier to achieve success. But donor insemination is much less emotionally charged. Rarely does DI bring with it intense and unexpected feelings that can complicate your original plans, as can intercourse. Think this out carefully for yourself.

- Have you discussed with this person what you will tell your child? Make absolutely sure that you are both willing to give your child the same factual information and the same emotional message. You are planning to tell your child that you wanted him or her more than anything else in the world. What does he plan to say?

CONSIDER GOING TO THE "BANK"

When artificial insemination, now known as donor insemination, was first used, donors were always anonymous. Keeping "the secret" was considered very important. It was believed that men would never donate sperm, if there was a possibility that their biological offspring might one day search for them. Couples supposedly wanted to protect the husband's sensitivities about his infertility.

As techniques for freezing and thawing sperm were perfected, sperm banks were created. Doctors controlled much of the sperm bank business in the 1950s and 1960s. There was great reluctance to use reproductive technology to help single women become mothers. Specialized sperm banks were created in the 1970s to address the needs of single and lesbian women. Today, about 30,000 women every year from varying family backgrounds are estimated to conceive using DI. There are now approximately 100 sperm banks in the United States. Many sperm banks will also recommend physicians who have experience with DI.

What Can You Find Out about the Donor?

As recently as fifteen years ago, sperm banks furnished little more than a sentence or two beyond information about age and race to guide women in choosing a prospective sperm donor. Prospective donors now fill out lengthy medical and family history questionnaires and must pass rigorous standards for semen analysis, infectious disease testing, and genetic testing and evaluation. Good recovery of sperm after it is frozen is also evaluated. Compare the levels of testing done at each sperm bank. Most women consider the level of testing performed on the donor to be the single most important criteria when deciding which sperm bank to use. All specimens should be quarantined to allow adequate testing for HIV and other infectious agents.

Most sperm banks offer catalogs and online profiles. Donor shopping through a sperm bank catalog or online can ensure that you find someone who is "your type." Good health, intelligence, and physical appeal are just some of the traits you can seek when choosing a donor. You may want someone whose looks are similar to your own or to those of the men in your family, or you may want someone with the same ethnic background. Whether your donor is an athlete, social worker, or college professor is a choice that is totally up to you. You can also choose the sex of your

child by deciding on the "sex preselection" option. Customer service may be important to you, and you may consider a sperm bank with someone available to answer your questions. If you think you may want to conceive more than one child with the same donor, this is the time to make sure the sperm bank you chose can help you make that happen.

Grateful as I am for the possible opportunity to use DI, I am curious why any man would go through all the time and trouble to provide all this personal medical and family information? Should I wonder what motivates these men?

There is no reason to think beyond dollars and cents. Selling sperm is a way for young graduate students, typically saddled with much student loan debt, to earn some cash. Many law students, doctoral students, as well as medical students, are attracted to this opportunity. Some sperm banks specifically advertise the availability of these intelligent and well-educated donors and charge a

"MOM ALWAYS WANTED ME TO MARRY A DOCTOR (OR LAWYER)!"

You did the next best thing, conceiving a child blessed with medical or legal advice genes! Now, when you find yourself explaining to people—and there will always be folks who just don't get the definition of personal—how any man could donate sperm and how a woman would buy and use it, tell them you're no expert, but one day, given her genes, your daughter may become their urologist.

premium price for these sperm and pay the donors a premium as well. Moreover, these young men often do not have an active social life while immersed in competitive studies, which means they do not ejaculate as frequently as sexually active men, a necessary factor in ensuring a higher sperm count. Other men, not necessarily students, are also attracted to the financial opportunity as well as the chance to be part of something greater than themselves. The sperm banks have gotten fairly sophisticated in their screening procedures. Only a small percentage of the donors who apply are actually accepted into most sperm bank programs. Weirdos and others with dubious intent are quickly eliminated as prospective donors.

When You Might Want to Know More

Many women considering DI are concerned about the effect of what some call "genetic bewilderment." Many women are giving thoughtful consideration to what their DI child may want to know in the future about their grandparents, ethnic heritage, and, of course, medical history. Donor children have joined the crusade of many adopted children to gain the right to learn about their biological parents. For these reasons, it is likely that sperm donors will lose much of their anonymity in favor of donor children's rights. Similar to the ideals of the open adoption movement, the so-called open release movement is changing the way sperm banks operate.

When I began considering becoming a single mother through DI, I thought one of the advantages of using a sperm bank would be no messy entanglement with the donor. Many of the sperm banks I am investigating heavily advertise "identity release." What are the advantages of using DI only to have the identity of the donor available to your child? Is there a downside to identity release?

The amount of information you want available to your child about the sperm donor is an important decision you will need to make. It is important that you are prepared to be very honest with your child about the circumstances surrounding his or her birth, as well as comfortable with the decision you make about access to information about the donor. Every sperm bank specifies its policies about release of the donor identity. It is not well understood exactly what will satisfy the curiosity of DI children in the future. It is also difficult to know what additional medical information your child may need in the future from the donor. Many sperm banks provide a picture of the donor now and when he was a baby, responding to the typical desire of most DI children to know exactly what their biological father looks like. Some DI children will obviously want to know more. Some banks offer a video "bio" detailing hobbies and interests and include "a message to you or your future children." Some banks will release the name of the donor at the child's request after the age of eighteen years or older. Certain banks may provide the name of the donor shortly after the baby's birth.

Advocates of identity release believe that the availability of this information prevents children from fantasizing that their father was an escaped serial killer or a member of an obscure royal family. Some banks maintain a sibling registry, which allows children conceived from the same donor to connect. While it is not certain that this option will create some sort of extended family, you may be comforted to know your child will have the opportunity to explore this possibility. There is also the possibility that the donor may change his mind about meeting your child if and when your child decides to locate him. He may have married, and his wife may not be too keen on a relationship between her husband and your child. Some people view sperm donors more like tissue or organ donors rather than biological parents. Even if your child had fairly realistic expectations about the sperm donor, there is always room for disappointment in complicated human relationships.

THINKING CAREFULLY ABOUT ALL THE COSTS

The cost of donor insemination is not limited to money. The time and emotional commitment are significant, just as motherhood will require. If you need additional medical care for infertility, the emotional costs of the inevitable highs and lows will be tremendous. Patience and a positive attitude are particularly important, along with monitoring your ovulation cycles to ensure ideal conditions for conception. Overall, about 70 percent of women with no fertility problems conceive within six cycles. However, sometimes it takes longer to become pregnant, just as it might for anyone conceiving in a more traditional manner. It's helpful to read and post to a message board where DI single mothers offer suggestions, resources, and comfort. Only you can determine how much you want to give to this and when it's time to give up and try another route, such as adoption. Regardless of what happens,

always know that you did your best, and try not to feel like a failure because you were unable to conceive. Remember, you can be a wonderful mother without having to "grow" the baby yourself.

The financial cost for DI varies based on the part of the country in which you are having this procedure done.

DI can cost from $500 to $1,000 for the first cycle and about $300 to $700 for each cycle thereafter. The chance of becoming pregnant from any one cycle of DI treatment is about 15 to 20 percent. Couples without fertility problems have about a 20 percent chance, and DI can be almost as efficient as nature. These numbers include the basic costs of sperm bank registration ($150), health tests (0 to $600), frozen sperm ($135–$265 per vial), ovulation predictor kits ($45–$65), intrauterine insemination ($150–$275 and does not include the sperm sample or associated lab fees), intracervical insemination ($100 and up and does not include the sperm sample), and shipping ($100–$200).

The costs of various enhancements add to the overall cost of DI. Sperm donors who are willing to be identified are paid more, and these costs will be passed on to you, if you want an identity release donor. If you want special donor/recipient matching, a donor audio interview, a donor baby photo, or a more complete donor medical profile, these charges will also be extra. If you want "doctorate" sperm, meaning that the donor is a lawyer, doctor, or Ph.D. or is in the process of earning these advanced degrees, the cost of the sperm vials increases sharply. Expedited shipping will cost more, of course. Weekend appointments add several hundred dollars to the cost. Counseling of various kinds, genetic, intake, or donor selection, are also additional costs. Sex preselection can add as much as $4,000 to the overall cost of DI.

HOW ABOUT FRESH SPERM?

The American Society for Reproductive Medicine (ASRM) recommends that all sperm be frozen for at least six months prior to insemination. The donor is screened at the time of the donation for HIV. The donor is then tested again six months later so that infections undiagnosed at the first screening can be found on the second test. This makes the risk of HIV infection quite small. In fact, most physicians will not allow the use of fresh sperm even if obtained by the patient. Most sperm banks will not ship to your home, but only to a doctor or hospital. There are states in which it is illegal for anyone except a physician to perform DI, including California.

Choosing Your Physician

Fertility specialists by their training and experience are likely to see a woman who wants to get pregnant as having a medical problem. If you have definite fertility issues, this orientation is a blessing. Infertility treatment can be an all-consuming process, with counting and timing your cycles, taking a variety of drugs, and dealing with the emotional drain of unsuccessful attempts to conceive. Unless you have insurance coverage for infertility, however, the high tech procedures, IVF, GIFT, ZIFT, and so on, may be financially impractical as well as highly stressful. For healthy women with no fertility problems, using a fertility specialist may subject you to unnecessary

and intrusive procedures as well as mandatory psychological testing and counseling. DI is one of the few medical "treatments" in which the woman treated is usually perfectly healthy.

Your Physician Should Have a Commitment to DI as a Specialty

Given the emotional and financial costs of DI, it is important that your physician participates in continuing education and stays abreast of medical developments in this field. Be sure to choose a physician who has experience and is comfortable working with single mothers. You also want to be sure to choose a doctor with maximum availability and dependable coverage.

Be Sure Also to Assess the Office Staff

An insensitive staff can raise your stress levels and make the whole DI process more complicated. These people are the "front line" who will coordinate your efforts. Are they aware of the importance of time constraints? You will be charting your ovulation cycle meticulously, and you want to make sure you are inseminated at the perfect time. You would hate to miss an entire month because your best time to try was at 9:00 A.M. on a Sunday. Are they experienced in the thawing and preparing of your frozen sperm sample? Will you be able to call and speak with a nurse regarding a dubious ovulation predictor test result? You want to feel just as confident about the office staff as you do with the physician doing the actual procedure. If you feel uncomfortable with the doctor or her staff, keep looking.

How Long Can You Wait?

Usually when a woman reaches anywhere between thirty-five and forty years of age, her ability to conceive decreases markedly. In women over the age of forty, there is a dramatic decline in fertility. How long is too long to wait? Unfortunately, there are no tests doctors can perform to tell you exactly how

many years of uncompromised fertility you may have left. Women who delay childbearing often have more education, good jobs, and more financial resources. They're socially advantaged but biologically disadvantaged. Balancing work with the desire for motherhood is increasingly challenging, especially since American workers put in longer and longer hours.

WHAT TO TELL PEOPLE

Tell them as much or as little as you want. Your reproductive organs are your own business. People should not assume that you are anxious to give them graphic details about DI or about what it was like to have intercourse with a donor. How and why you chose your donor is private information shared

---

THE DO'S AND DON'TS OF CHOOSING DONOR INSEMINATION

Here is some advice for anyone considering donor insemination.

♦ **Do** get your emotional house in order. Be clear about your reasons for wanting to conceive a child.

♦ **Don't** buy into any guilt others may try to inflict upon you. Their lack of knowledge and understanding should not influence the informed choices you are making.

♦ **Do** have a solid support system in place. Single motherhood is a challenging lifestyle. You need friends who can offer comfort and support. Even single

mothers by choice can at times become overwhelmed.

♦ **Don't** limit your research on donor insemination to just technical facts. Moms who have been there can offer suggestions, emotional advice, and share their experiences. Join a message board, forum, or online support group.

♦ **Do** maintain a sense of humor. If you're asked by well-meaning relatives about what donors are like or why you would choose DI, you can say, "Mom always wanted me to marry a doctor so I thought this was the closest best thing!"

appropriately only with close family and friends. Remember that what you tell others now will certainly be communicated to your child at some later date. If you are mature and responsible enough to become a single mother, you will easily be able to tell the difference between genuine concern and interest and judgmental prying and snooping.

Share the information with which you are comfortable, and try to close all conversations with something like, "Having a child was a real priority for me!" Others will feel the degree of comfort you exude.

IF YOU'RE IN A LESBIAN RELATIONSHIP

Women who plan to raise a family with another woman are good candidates for donor insemination. Most lesbian mothers already have a strong support system in place, usually within the gay and lesbian community. Additionally, if you or your partner are choosing motherhood, your child will benefit from having positive input from two parental role models, as would a child from any loving, two-parent home.

Because women planning to raise children with another woman are as "partnered" as any other couple, this book does not focus on their situation because it deals primarily with those raising children without another supporting parent in the home.

5

Choosing Motherhood Through Adoption

If experiencing pregnancy and delivery or being your child's biological parent is not an essential priority, adoption offers the opportunity not only to love and nurture a child but also to make a significant contribution to our world. Many adopted children would otherwise have faced grim lives in underdeveloped or war-ravaged countries where basic necessities are in short supply and educational opportunities are nonexistent. Other adoptions, especially in cases where the biological parents have died unexpectedly, begin with a tragedy within the immediate or extended family rather than in a country thousands of miles from home.

Some single mothers who've chosen adoption may feel they don't want to add another human being to this already crowded planet, or they may be quite content to skip the infant stage altogether. Still others may have health problems, or may work in occupations that would make carrying a child risky, or harbor concerns about passing along a genetic predisposition to disease or mental illness to another generation. Whatever reasons contributed to your decision, an adopted child, no matter what her history or background, will come to know in a special way how dearly she was wanted and how treasured a part of your family she is. Remember, too, that adoption isn't always a mother's first choice. Most of us have grappled with choices and realized that perfection just wasn't one of them. If you are an adoptive single parent, it's important to get past the events that led up to this decision so that you can enjoy and raise a healthy, happy family. If you're thinking of adoption, you have many options and resources available; so do your homework first.

WHY ADOPTION MAY BE RIGHT FOR YOU

You may know single mothers who have to deal with uncooperative ex-partners or are embroiled in major custody battles, and you never want to find yourself in those situations. Maybe you'd like to have a baby, but because of personal or religious beliefs, bearing a child without a husband is simply not right for you. You're focused and content with making the decision to adopt because you really want to be a parent and raise a family. Others may give you their opinions and advice, but the final decision is to do what is best for you, not for them.

FERTILITY FRUSTRATIONS

Single women who decide on adoption may make this decision because it is physically difficult for them to get pregnant or carry a pregnancy to term. Fertility problems can cause emotional stress, sadness, feelings of loss, and frustration. The tremendous costs of fertility treatments on top of the expense of donor insemination can certainly add to the disappointment of being unable to bear children. You may feel it is unfair to put forth so much effort and receive nothing. It's normal to feel this way, but if adoption is a consideration, there is much hope in knowing that you will realize motherhood eventually. Just don't rush into making a decision while you are still grieving the loss of your imagined pregnancy. Give yourself as much time as you need to accept this loss before you move ahead with possible adoption plans.

There is nothing wrong with choosing adoption as a second choice because you are unable to conceive. The majority of parents who have faced the disappointment of being unable to conceive, whether single women or married couples, have chosen adoption because it gives them the opportunity to fulfill their dreams of being a parent. Infertility stands in the way of becoming a parent to a child that you biologically produce. Adoption removes that obstacle. But adoption won't change the fact that infertility is a fact of life for you.

IF YOU WERE ADOPTED

If you were adopted, you have firsthand experience in what it was like to be raised by parents other than your birth parents. Regardless of your experiences growing up, there most likely were lessons learned that you could apply when raising your own child. Whether from a single-parent household, adoptive family, stepparent family, or traditional two-parent family, most of us say we want to do a better job than our parents did with us. If you were adopted, you have another special connection that can bond you to your adopted child.

HOW TO GET STARTED

Here are some steps to take when considering adoption:

◆ Contact adoptive parent groups such as the National Council for Single Adoptive Parents (www.ncsap.org). The Council publishes *The Handbook for Single Adoptive Parents*, which is the most comprehensive how-to book for single parents who want to adopt.

- Contact your state chapter of the American Bar Association or the American Academy of Adoption Attorneys for referrals to attorneys who are adoption specialists. Remember, laws regarding adoption can vary from state to state. As you consider the type of adoption right for you, make sure you are clear on the laws governing open adoption in your state.

- Word of mouth can bring much success. Let people know that you are interested in adopting.

- Subscribe to *Adoptive Families* magazine (*www.adoptivefamilies.com*). They publish an annual adoption guide that keeps you updated on changing adoption laws and offer a free, eight-page downloadable adoption planner with checklists, timelines, and resources to guide you through the adoption process.

- Seek adoptive parents support forums and organizations on the Internet. The best information comes from those who have been there. Adoptive parents organizations can provide you with lists of agencies but typically do not make recommendations about particular agencies; you should investigate fully any agency you consider. Talk to agency clients. Call your local Better Business Bureau and state adoption unit to see if written complaints have been lodged against the agency.

TYPES OF ADOPTION

You probably weren't prepared for all the different types of adoption that are

---

REALITY BEATS REALITY TV

A birth parent may help make a child, but the day-to-day caregiver upon whom the child relies is the "real" parent. When someone asks you who the "real" father of your child is, remind him or her that love is stronger and deeper than biological connections—that's reality. And this reality triumphed over a short-lived reality television show, *Who's Your Daddy?* Adoptive parents and professionals protested this setup that challenged an adoptive daughter to identify her "real" estranged father from a group of imposters for a lot of cash. A ratings dud, *Who's Your Daddy* quickly met reality and five of the filmed episodes never even aired.

---

available. Most likely, your first concerns were the kind of child you would like to adopt, the costs involved in adopting, and imagining what life would be like as a new mother.

Raising a child is a lifetime commitment, whether you bring your baby home from the hospital or home from an interim care facility. It is important to think ahead about the type of adoption that is most appropriate for you because certain issues will affect your family for a lifetime. Would open adoption, in which your child has access to his or her birth family, be best, or would he or she be best served leaving information about the birth family behind in a war-ravaged country? How will you help your Asian child cope with obvious differences, if you live in a community where all the children come from the local region? Although there are numerous methods of adopting a child, following are descriptions of the three basic types of adoptions, whether domestic or international.

Confidential or Closed Adoption

In this type of adoption, there is no information that could identify the birth parent, making contact almost impossible. The birth parents remain anonymous and are usually matched to the prospective adoptive parents through an agent or adoption specialist. Often, the adoptive mother and birth parents agree that there will be no contact, with the exception that when the child is eighteen that he or she may seek out the identities of the birth parents.

Partially Open or Semiopen Adoption

For many, this is the preferred choice because you can meet the birth parents face to face with the agreement that they will not be involved in your life. You are assured of no disruptions in your home; yet the fear of the unknown has been eliminated because you will have been furnished with social and medical information on the parents and the child. Additionally, when the adopted child grows up and wishes to meet the birth parents, they can be available.

Open Adoption

This is the best bet according to many family experts. This form of adoption involves offering complete information that identifies both sets of parents. Not only do the adoptive parents and the birth parents receive complete information about each other, but there also can exist an agreement allowing ongoing contact, which serves to benefit the child. For many, this contact may provide the opportunity for an extended family, a welcome advantage to all families raising children today.

International Adoption

If you are connected to another part of the world because of family history, your work, or an affinity toward a certain region, you may be an excellent candidate for international adoption. The greater availability of babies makes foreign adoption more attractive. Whatever your reasons for adopting a child from a distant land, you need to gather as much information as possible.

To get started, visit the U.S. Department of State Web site (*www.travel.state.gov/family/adoption html.*) where you can find extensive information about international adoption and the U.S. legal requirements to bring a child adopted internationally back to the United States. Also contact the Joint Council on International Children's Services at *www.jcics.org.*

THE DO'S AND DON'TS OF ADOPTION

- **Do** give yourself time to grieve the loss of your fertility if your decision to adopt is based on your inability to conceive.

- **Do** think carefully about all the different types of adoption and which one might be the best way for you to realize your dream of having a child. There is no single best method of adoption. Much depends on your individual circumstances and what particular qualities you might like your child to have.

- **Don't** expect the "perfect child" because no such child ever existed. Get rid of stereotyped notions, like thinking that children of certain ethnic groups are always successful and obedient students while others should be athletic, musical, or otherwise talented.

- **Don't** delay telling your child that she is adopted. Your child should be made aware that she is adopted from the very first day you bring her home or as soon as she is capable of comprehending the idea.

- **Do** expect your adopted child to have many questions and concerns that will have to be addressed repeatedly as he gets older and particularly during his years in elementary school.

- **Do** make sure that friends and family are prepared with the information you want them to have to help you make your child comfortable with his adopted status.

WHAT ABOUT THE BONDING PROCESS?

I have a biological daughter and have arranged to adopt an infant from Russia. I wonder what the bonding process will be like.

Many mothers who have adopted infants after or while parenting a biological child report that bonding with adopted children when they are very young feels similar to bonding with biological children. Remember, bonding is a process, not an instant rush. Because international adoption often takes time, some moms have been unable to take their children home before two months of age. Although they may have missed having them as newborns, they report that everything else felt the same.

IS INTERNATIONAL ADOPTION SIMPLER THAN DOMESTIC ADOPTION?

Like domestic adoption, international adoption can be accomplished through the help of an agency, attorney, or adoption specialist, depending on the laws in the country from which your baby hails. Don't choose international adoption simply because you have heard that it is not as complex as domestic adoption. This couldn't be further from the truth. Although certain things are simpler in that there may be less rigid criteria for the adoptive parents than in domestic adoption, there are some pitfalls to international adoption that you must consider. For example, because many international children have been abandoned, their personal, medical, and social documents are often unavailable.

You also need to consider how you will handle any obviously different physical characteristics the child may have, any prejudice that may be encountered through others' lack of acceptance of certain ethnic groups, and other issues of parenting an international child such as religious views, social values, and your child's feelings of cultural deprivation.

Like any aspect of adoption or of raising a family for that matter, almost any obstacle can be overcome with love, commitment, and information. It helps to join an adoptive parent support group, particularly one that has members who have adopted children from foreign countries. Also, keep abreast of any changes in foreign governments that will affect the number and availability of children for international adoption.

TIPS FOR ADOPTING A CHILD FROM ANOTHER COUNTRY

◆ Some parents who have adopted children from outside the United States recommend hiring an attorney who deals only in adoptions from the country you choose. For example, if you are planning to adopt a baby from an orphanage in China, an experienced attorney can give you a realistic breakdown of costs, tell you the probable timetable to be

expected, and advise you on exactly what you need to bring for the baby when you travel to the host country.

◆ The majority of international adoptions are handled by private adoption agencies. Public agencies rarely participate in international adoption. If you adopt privately, make sure the agency is aware of U.S. immigration laws. Employ an agency that has extensive experience in international adoptions. Most countries overseas that allow international adoption welcome single-parent applicants.

◆ International adoptions average $20,000 or more, depending on whether you need to travel and reside in the country to complete legal formalities. If the initial figure offered by the attorney is about as much as you can afford, you might want to reconsider or wait until you have more money. Foreign adoption always costs more than anticipated because there are almost always unexpected expenses. Another tip: in addition to the agreed-upon amount of money to begin the process, some agencies or orphanages may request that you provide pictures of your close relatives so that they can match you up with a child who most resembles your family.

◆ Orphanages in foreign countries will usually be able to provide you with some medical and other pertinent information about the child and the birth mother but very little, if anything, about the father. Officials fear that if they press the birth mother too much about the father's identity, they may, out of fear, fail to obtain proper prenatal care and might give birth to a child who will end up on the streets rather than in a loving adoptive parent's home.

♦ The orphanage will send you pictures of your prospective adopted child. You don't have to accept the first child offered to you, although you may feel uncomfortable about refusing a child. Try to remember that no one said you have to save the world. It would not be fair to you or the child for you to adopt a child that you're not sure you can raise; so be certain that you choose a child you really believe would work out best.

Once you have chosen a child, the original birth certificate of the child is destroyed, and a new one is issued with your name.

♦ The amount of paperwork is unbelievable and can be overwhelming for you. An experienced attorney or international adoption expert knows how to wade through it. For example, when you arrive in Colombia for an independent adoption, the attorney will give you a sealed package of papers to present to the officials at the orphanage. Do not even think of breaking the seal. Follow your attorney's instructions to the letter.

♦ Make sure to select a pediatrician ahead of time before you leave the United States to pick up your baby. In case you have immediate questions or there is some emergency or crisis, you can call your own doctor. Be sure to advise your pediatrician of your plan so he or she can be prepared in case you call.

TRANSRACIAL AND TRANSCULTURAL ADOPTION

If you choose to adopt transracially or transculturally, it would be a good idea to join a support group where members share your concern for a positive upbringing for your children and a positive relationship with their racial/cultural background. Keep in mind that children of color have certain concerns that range from skin care and hair grooming to needing a connectedness to others who share their heritage. Racial prejudice remains a sad fact. You need to be prepared to face these prejudices and know how you will handle the situations that you will inevitably encounter. Additionally, you do need to be aware that if you are considering adopting a Native American child that the Indian Child Welfare Act still has strict rules about adopting children of Native American ancestry. Do your homework.

ADOPTING CHILDREN WITH SPECIAL NEEDS

The largest group of children waiting to be adopted is children with special needs. Often called "waiting children," half are children of color, a majority have been physically, sexually, or emotionally abused, a huge number have serious disabilities, and many are older—eight years old and up.

Before you adopt a waiting child, you need to examine your motivations for doing so. Keep in mind, too, that part of the problems these children face is having a history of disappointment and loss due to multiple placements. Don't be scared away because this kind of adoption can bring a special joy and satisfaction to your life, but you must be capable of giving this child all that he or she needs. Insist upon receiving every bit of information on this child, which even means talking with previous foster parents. Explore the availability of ongoing financial and social services support for yourself and your family. Investigate subsidies and assistance you can receive, school services, medical services and coverage, and parent- and community-based support groups. Do your homework and investigate all your options carefully.

LEGAL ASPECTS OF PRIVATE ADOPTION

If you are adopting a child from the same state as your own, jurisdiction—or the authority with the power to interpret the law—is a minor issue. If you choose interstate adoption, you need to be informed about the jurisdictional requirements because every state has its own laws. Suppose you know a potential birth mother in a nearby state whose child you would like to adopt. Your agent or attorney will have to be sure that procedures comply not only with state regulations but also with the Interstate Compact on the Placement of Children.

PLANNING FOR THE COSTS

Adoption costs vary widely, depending on the state and all the bureaucracy and red tape that may be involved. Adoption experts can give you a ballpark figure; so make sure you ask about costs up front.

Keep abreast of changes in federal tax law. Single mothers wishing to adopt can get help from the Internal Revenue Service. Depending upon your income, you may be entitled to a tax credit—a dollar-for-dollar reduction in your taxes—for expenses related to the adoption such as paperwork costs, attorney fees, court costs, and traveling. (Tax credits are even better than deductions, which merely lower your taxable income.) If you think you might be eligible, maintain meticulous records. For more information, contact the IRS and request IRS Publication 968.

Some adoptive parents are also receiving financial help from their employers. A growing number of companies are offering to reimburse some portion of their employee's adoption expenses. The Adoption Friendly Workplace Program currently lists hundreds of companies offering these benefits. Visit their Web site at *www.adoptionfriendlyworkplace.org/employers.asp* for more information. Some employers also offer paid leave or unpaid leave time, above and beyond the twelve weeks allowed under the Family and Medical Leave Act. Check with your own employer regarding benefits to which you may be entitled.

Adopting through public agencies usually incurs minimal or no costs other than attorney fees for finalizing the adoption. Minimal costs are also incurred with foster adoption because this usually involves little or no fees. In this situation, the child is placed in temporary care. Foster adoption, however, is considered a legal-risk placement because the child may be returned to the birth parent's home or eventually be placed with relatives. Adopting a child from a remarriage or from a family member or other known person can be relatively inexpensive. The most expensive adoptions are international or overseas adoptions or where you have a pregnant birth mother whose medical bills you are also paying.

Never proceed with any kind of adoption without professional or legal help, even if it is your sister's child you are adopting!

ADOPTING MORE THAN ONE

Some women just want to double their pleasure. Maybe you came from a very large family and thrived on that, or you feel strongly that siblings should remain together. You may choose to adopt infant twins. Although adopting two or more children will not necessarily double the joys or troubles, the issues that you need to deal with will be multiplied. For example, just as in biological families, sibling rivalry will exist, and those tough parenting stages will be intensified by having to deal with more than one. Your desire and capacity to love and nurture another child should determine whether or not you adopt another child.

EXPECTING THE PERFECT CHILD

I am thinking of adopting an Asian child because they are so smart—as practically perfect as you can get. They excel in school, particularly in the math areas, and I have always adored these children, who look like little porcelain dolls. Plus, money is not an object, and I've lived overseas and can speak a number of languages.

Stop right there. If you expect a perfect child, whether you give birth or adopt, you are setting yourself and the child up for disappointment. Moreover, you need to examine your motives for adopting a particular type of child because you may have unresolved issues surrounding your own abilities. Your affinity for other cultures is your strongest reason to adopt but should not be the major deciding factor. Although speaking your child's language is a boon because you can keep some of his or her culture alive, you still need to look at why you expect your child to fit into a custom-tailored niche. Also, it is unfair to stereotype a child and slot his or her attributes into categories, whether positive or negative. Children need unconditional love and to be accepted for who they are and not what they can do. Think this out a little longer and let the desire for an Asian child be the icing on the cake and not the substance on which your decision to adopt is based.

MOTHERING A DECEASED RELATIVE'S CHILD

If you are thinking of adopting the child of a deceased friend or relative, you need to consider whether you are willing to change your lifestyle and make the commitment necessary to mother this child. Motherhood is a daunting and life-altering challenge for the unprepared woman. What was your relationship with the child prior to her loss? Adopting a child you barely know or have never met can be quite an undertaking, particularly for someone who never gave single motherhood much serious consideration. It may be, however, that you are already a second mother to this child because of your close relationship. In that case, your decision and adjustment will be easier. If you had already agreed to be the child's legal guardian in case of the death of the parent, then you will be more emotionally prepared to face the challenges ahead.

SINGLE MOM OF NOTE

Elizabeth Blackwell,
America's First Woman Doctor
Elizabeth Blackwell graduated at the head of her medical school class in the early 1840s and, unable to find anyone who would hire a female doctor, started her own practice. In 1857, she opened a hospital run by an all-female staff.

An entry from her journal in the year before the hospital's opening shed light on what kept her motivated: *"I feel full of hope and strength for the future. Kitty plays beside me with her doll. She has just given me a candy basket purchased with a penny she earned . . ."*

Kitty was the orphan that Blackwell adopted and raised as her own daughter.

MOTHERHOOD: THE SECOND TIME AROUND

Becoming a single mother through adoption is typically a decision that follows much careful consideration and planning. Adoption is sometimes not a free choice as much as a responsibility accepted in the wake of the last scene in a painful family drama or following an unexpected and sudden tragedy. More than 1.5 million children today are being raised by grandparents without the presence of either parent. Usually, these grandparents are women who have become the custodial parents to their grandchildren because the child's parents are unable or unwilling to assume the responsibility of parenthood. Alcohol and/or substance abuse, mental illness, abandonment, child abuse or neglect, chronic unemployment, incarceration, or death may all be reasons why a grandmother becomes a mother—the second time around.

Assuming this incredible responsibility at a time when many of your peers need only worry about what beach to visit or what time in the day to play golf can be, at least at first, utterly overwhelming. Despite the obvious financial strains and genuine demands on your emotional and physical stamina, most (much older) single mothers report that providing care to their grandchildren, who are, of course, now their children, results in unexpected satisfactions and rewards. The chance to raise a child differently, perhaps correcting perceived mistakes or missteps, is a joy. Nurturing family relationships and continuing family history are sustaining. Children are a strong impetus to continue as a vital and active participant in your community, keeping you active and giving life a renewed purpose.

Your lifetime of experience is your best ally. Knowing that responsibilities cannot be fulfilled without authority, seek legal advice. You will want the power to make the important decisions regarding your child's health and well-being. Any financial arrangements with the birth parents need to be part of any legal agreement reached. Let go of what the neighbors or anyone else thinks. It does not matter, and in any event, at this stage in your life, you don't have the time to care. Expect your neighborhood school to be cooperative and unfazed by your family situation.

You will receive offers of help. Sort through these offers with care. Be selective. Decide what is genuine and what will be of value. Think about the choices, which will add to the comfort, security, stability, and emotional well-being of your newly reconfigured family. Graciously reach out and be thankful for what is truly meant and of lasting value.

Remember to take time for yourself. If you become so immersed in your new family responsibilities that you sacrifice who you are, you will become angry and resentful. All of us benefit from the opportunity to play. Join your children in the recreational activities that you also can enjoy, but don't forget your own needs for fun and relaxation.

Grandmothers assuming the custodial care of a grandchild may find they need financial assistance. Supplemental Social Security, Medicaid, food stamps, reduced school lunch programs, and Head Start or other early childhood programs are all possible sources of help. Contact your local health department or Social Security office for the latest information.

PREPARING YOURSELF AND OTHERS

There are adjustments that must be made before you can begin parenting. Most importantly, you need to prepare yourself and close friends and family members for the fact that your child has come into your life in a different way than most families experience. Because your child's background is different from your own, particularly if you have adopted transculturally or transracially, you should be aware that your child's heritage will be evident in day-to-day activities and will continue to evolve as he or she grows up. The differences should be neither ignored nor played up, but rather celebrated as an opportunity to learn and to grow.

Siblings, grandparents, and the adoptive mom herself must accept the new family member as one who will continue the family name even though there is no genetic connection. Moreover, everyone needs to overcome any overly unrealistic expectations of the child. Although adoption brings with it unique challenges, the child should be treated with the same kind of love and commitment any child deserves.

IF SOMETHING GOES WRONG

No matter how carefully you plan, sometimes unexpected events occur, and you are left with the cruel disappointment of not being able to take home a child you dearly wanted. In some tragic cases, adoptive parents have been forced to surrender a child to the biological parents or to an agency. All these life events are devastating. Do not listen to those who try to offer comfort by saying that you never really knew this child or that the child was not really yours. You suffered a loss as great as that of any biological mother. Allow yourself to grieve and mourn this great loss.

If your efforts to adopt came after unsuccessful treatment for infertility, this new blow can seem especially cruel and undeserved. Take the time to assess your situation and make plans to go forward with your life however you see fit. You are facing intensely personal decisions, and only you can decide what is right for you. Many mothers in your circumstances have taken advantage of counseling or have located a sympathetic support group. Consider these options if you are feeling unable to move ahead or are overwhelmed by your feelings of sadness and loss. Take care of yourself as the first step toward knowing what is the right path for you.

YOUR ADOPTED CHILD

Most likely, life with your adopted child will be normal, as long as your image of normal isn't that of a 1950s TV situation comedy. The time when most trouble occurs is when children reach elementary and middle school, primarily because they spend more time with peers. They may be distressed at the differences they notice between their family and other families. Questions that may bother an adopted school-age child may be: "Was I rejected because I was not smart or pretty enough?" "Were my real parents cruel or careless people who wanted nothing to do with raising a child?" "Was the adoption the tragic result of an accident, misunderstanding, or even a crime?" These questions can stir up feelings of abandonment, grief, loneliness, and guilt. Be there to

listen and offer comfort when you can. Be happy to know that although the teenage years for many parents bring a host of problems, things may actually improve for the adoptive parent because of the groundwork for family communication that already has been established.

TELLING YOUR CHILD ABOUT ADOPTION

The earlier a child is told that he or she is adopted, the better. You should refer to your child's adopted status as soon as the child comes into your life with remarks like "I'm so glad I adopted you!" If you don't do this, the child will view the adoption as some kind of shameful secret and question why his life is shrouded in shame and secrecy.

Some mothers try to wait until the child is of school age, but this is the most difficult time to tell a child. Pre-schoolers are unfazed by the knowledge that they are adopted. Between the ages of six and thirteen, however, children's feelings may change. Even adopted children who have always known are more likely to be troubled by this fact than when they were younger. Adopted children of this age are more likely to show signs of emotional difficulties as a group than biological children. Such signs include depression, withdrawal, aggression, and hyperactivity. By the time biological and adopted children reach late adolescence, however, these group differences are far less evident.

Even though the middle school years are the toughest, you can help your child by discussing the adoption early and as often as is appropriate. Always refer to the adoption in positive terms. For example, assure your child (whether you actually know so or not) that his biological parents loved him and that their decision was based on a desire to do what was best for him. Describe your first meeting with your child in specific and loving detail—emphasize the pleasure that each of you felt and expressed at this first meeting. Make sure also to emphasize how the decision to adopt came from your heart and was based on how you felt about your child as a person. Point out your child's special qualities and how much you love those qualities.

Never deny or minimize the fact that being adopted is different from being a biological child. Adopted children may worry about their birth parents showing up and removing them from the mother they love. Invite your child to discuss these feelings of difference or fear openly, without concern that there is anything wrong with these feelings. Remember that your child is the first and foremost authority on how he or she feels about being adopted. Don't expect your child to resolve all of his or her feelings about being adopted. This process will unfold gradually and continue until adulthood.

Enlist the Aid of Others

Family and friends need to know how they can deal with your child's adoption in a healthy and constructive way. Be sure everyone knows that your child is aware of his or her adoption. Also, let them know how you would like them to respond if your child expresses concerns about being adopted. Do encourage special relationships. A close adult friend who is not a blood relative of yours can be an especially helpful confidant and role model for your adopted child. Like the child, this person is not biologically linked to you but is an integral part of your chosen family. This gives your child a stronger sense of connection to the world around him.

WHEN YOUR CHILD STILL DOESN'T KNOW

I am the mother of a seven-year-old adopted daughter. I have never told her that she is adopted because I thought it would be better to wait until she was older. I can see now that waiting to tell her was not the best choice. Is it too late? How should I handle the situation?

If you have not told your child that she is adopted, then it is time to do so now as positively as you can. It is always recommended that you tell your child early on. For you, the right time is now—better now than later and, certainly, better late than never. Keep the conversation positive. Make sure that your child doesn't get the impression that you are alerting her to bad news. You want your child to understand that this is information that she was entitled to know earlier. Do not tell your child that you delayed because of her inability to understand or accept the news. Make a special, private occasion out of the announcement. Make sure that you allow your child the opportunity to absorb this information and ask the many questions she will pose. This conversation will not be a onetime deal. As your child matures, new questions and concerns will inevitably crop up. Think ahead to anticipate the thoughts and feelings your child will need to discuss with you.

Your heart was in the right place; so forgive yourself. You're working hard to remedy a common mistake, and now it's time to move on.

CHALLENGES TO EXPECT DURING YOUR CHILD'S SCHOOL-AGE YEARS

During the school-age years, trouble-some feelings and behaviors may plague you and your child. For example, you may suddenly hear things from an angry child like "You're not my real mother!" Other problems may include:

♦ Your child may suggest or allege that you kidnapped him.

♦ He or she may have problems getting along with siblings, especially if these are your biological children.

♦ Your child may develop fantasies about being reunited with his or her biological parents.

♦ There may be a reluctance or refusal to cooperate in family activities.

♦ He or she may demonstrate unusual shyness around relatives.

♦ Your child may have intense or inappropriate reactions to TV shows, movies, stories, or pictures featuring parent-child relationships.

How to Meet These Challenges

Feeling like a failure plagues most parents at some time whether they are single or married, have biological or adopted children. Your single mother status plays a relatively small part. It is normal for adopted children to experience some of the toughest times during their school years, but the teen years are tough for any child!

Try the following suggestions:

♦ Being receptive to what you hear without being defensive. Don't say "That's a lie" or "You're wrong," but rather "I'm sorry you believe or feel such untrue things."

♦ Communicating with your child often softens some of the heartache. Make it clear that you understand that he or she is going through a tough time. Emphasize that you are always willing to listen, but mutually respectful communication is expected from all members of the family.

♦ Do seek professional help if there are frequent and intense episodes of sibling rivalry and a consistent pattern of disruption at family gatherings. Trust your instincts if you are anxious about your adopted child's emotional health and seek counseling.

6

Becoming a Single Mother Through Divorce

You've seen them on *Oprah* and in your favorite magazines: stories about women who have overcome the challenges of divorce and found great personal and professional success. Of course, when you're in the throes of an agonizing separation or in the midst of a contentious divorce, it's hard to believe you can ever be happy again, but most likely you will. In fact, according to sociologist Pepper Schwartz, statistics show that most divorced people are happier than people who stay in unfulfilling marriages.

Loss can't be avoided. Everyone experiences loss, whether it is a loved one's death, a child leaving home, the loss of a job, or a divorce. Nobody marches down the aisle expecting to become another divorce statistic. Whether or not you dreamed of the white picket fence, the luxury SUV, and 2.4 children, you are probably wondering whatever happened to your cherished hopes and fantasies.

PARENTING THROUGH DIVORCE

You can minimize the trauma to your children when you divorce by thoughtful parenting. It will help to keep these things in mind:

◆ **Do** remember that children are not miniature adults. Just because your ten-year-old has the vocabulary and mannerisms of a young adult, don't assume that he or she is more emotionally capable than any other ten-year-old. Your child is trying to act bravely in the face of adversity. What your child is really feeling is frightened, and although the divorce may be the best thing for you, your child doesn't see it this way. Be sensitive to how your child views things.

◆ **Don't** stop parenting because you're going through major changes. Your child needs you to be a parent. He or she needs emotional support, consistent routines, and the assurance of love and care.

• **Don't** make your child your confidant, spy, or in-house therapist. This rule applies regardless of the age of your child. Teenage children are no better equipped and sometimes less well equipped to handle divorce than preschool children.

• **Do** keep divorce the business of adults. The ongoing negotiations and legal battles are adult things. Children take what they hear literally. When they hear the phrase "no money," they take that to mean "not a single penny." Lacking experience and maturity, they put two and two together from overheard conversations or inappropriate information offered by adults and almost never come up with four.

• **Do** share information that is relevant to them, however. If there are going to be major lifestyle changes like moving to a different house or a different part of the country, share these plans with your child when they are definite. Telling your child that you might have to do this or might have to move there burdens your child unnecessarily. Much of what you are worrying about now will probably not happen.

• **Do** watch what you say about their father. No matter what he has done and particularly if he spent a significant amount of time with them before the divorce, keep in mind that he is still their father. Everything you say to your children about their father will be dealt with as part of themselves. Telling your children—even if it is the truth—that their father is a lazy, no-good bum may give you the momentary pleasure of knowing that they're siding with you, but what does broadcasting his shortcomings do for them? Positive comments work better, such as saying, "You draw very well. I'll bet you get some of that talent from your father."

• **Don't** publicize your personal life, at least for the sake of the children. You may be ready to announce your availability, especially if you've been in an emotionally dead marriage for years. Maybe your husband left you for someone else, and you are desperate to show the world that you are attractive and desirable. You may have married very young and missed out on a lot, or maybe you just miss sex. You have every right to make happen for you what you feel you need and want. But there is a big difference between what you need and want and what your children need and want. No matter what the circumstances were of your separation and divorce, your children are not yet emotionally ready to support your need for a life of your own. Give them time and keep your lives private.

• **Do** try to live in the present. Today is as important to your children as yesterday or tomorrow. Although it's difficult to focus on your children when so many things in your life are up in the air, try to set aside a small part of each day when you handle "divorce stuff" such as keeping appointments with attorneys or real estate appraisers. Create happy memories now. Small things count the most. Freeze snow today for a snowball fight on the Fourth of July. Count happy memories instead of reading them the usual bedtime story. Bake purple cookies in weird shapes. Let them eat dessert first tonight.

IF THIS WAS YOUR FIRST MARRIAGE

For what it's worth, there most likely are some wonderful memories. There have been times you will never share with anyone else. You built a life together—friends, family, and neighborhood. You may go on to have other weddings or other children, but this was your first wedding and your first child. Because you have not kept your vows to cherish and protect one another, grow old together, and share in your children's growing up, you feel that your dreams for the future are now lost. When you grieve for your loss, also remember that it's okay to delight in the memories.

NOT AGAIN!

This may have been a second (or third) marriage filled with the promise that old mistakes would not be repeated. You did not expect perfection. You knew better this time that a marriage was hard work.

Like many, you probably thought that a second marriage should be the start of a new and different life. Particularly if you had children from the previous relationship, there most likely was great hope that this relationship would bring together a new, blended family. But things have fallen apart, and again it's necessary to grieve for the many hopes, plans, and dreams that are not to be. Equally important, however, is to

cherish the times that were warm and wonderful, too.

WHAT YOU MAY BE FEELING

After a divorce, you may experience a range of feelings about your situation.

Feeling Stuck

There are so many ways to feel stuck. For some, being stuck means being forever labeled and defined as "divorced." For others, it can mean holding on to the painful feelings and unproductive behavior. Psychologists often comment about how one can feel stuck regardless of economic or social status. Some of the most stuck women are in new marriages or relationships—or trying to be—with not a clue as to why they are unhappy.

In essence, being stuck means holding on to ways of thinking and feeling that no longer allow you or your children to move ahead. Rarely does it mean living a life in solitude. However, to avoid living in a self-imposed prison, you have to become "unstuck" because being stuck is not unlike being paralyzed or immobile. To move on, you have to let go.

Feeling Worthless

Even though it is important to remember that no feelings are wrong or unacceptable, don't fall prey to this one—the number one favorite of TV's popular soap operas. Emotions such as sadness, grief, guilt, fear, or anger can all be parts of the growing process, but your basic essence—who you are—should never be attacked by anyone, especially yourself. Feeling worthless is useless, and you need to stop right now! Your confidence needs to be enhanced and protected.

Make a list of the three things you like best about yourself. If you whip up the best tomato sauce in town, have a knack for growing flowers that are the envy of the neighborhood, or have terrific musical skills, write it down. Each morning review your list and add something to it by the end of the week. For example, if your boss praised your reorganization ideas, make sure to add her remarks to your list. If you find getting started or adding accomplishments difficult, ask a trusted friend for help. As you review your growing list of admirable qualities, tell yourself, "My efforts do make a difference. I am accomplishing many important and worthwhile things." There may come a morning when you no longer require the daily reminder and wonder why you even have the list. But it's a good habit to indulge because when you value yourself, you wind up making good choices for yourself and for those you love.

Here are some suggestions to protect your feelings in this vulnerable time:

- **Do** build your confidence. Value and protect it.

- **Do** choose life options that make you independent. Choose to control your own life.

- **Don't** make any long-term commitments right away.

- **Don't** expect a brand-new normal life overnight.

- **Don't** allow yourself to feel like a failure just because your marriage didn't last forever. Partnership contracts can be dissolved when two people can no longer function effectively while connected, not unlike a business relationship. Try to look at this from a logical perspective, not just an emotional one.

- **Don't** underestimate all you have to offer. You have talents, resources, and information to share. Reach out to others with positive energy, and positive energy will be returned to you.

- **Don't** confuse attorneys with friends, lovers, or therapists. Attorneys are paid guides through the legal jungle.

- **Do** tell yourself every day that you will succeed. Learn to say, "Yes, I can do it!" More importantly, believe it.

Feeling Good!

Other women seem obviously devastated by the breakup of their marriages. Their pain is obvious. Frankly, I feel relieved. In fact, I'm thinking of having a divorce party with my girlfriends! What's wrong with me?

It's normal to feel a sense of relief when you exit a marriage that went bad slowly over time. During this long, bad period, you were allowed to work through many of the initial emotions that newly separated or divorced women experience.

Think back through the course of your marriage, and you will remember times of suffering through denial, rage, sadness, and fear. Good for you that these negative feelings are over and that your relief and renewed energy are letting you move ahead!

A divorce party can be a very creative idea, provided it is not a man-bashing festival, but rather a time for women to come together to renew their inherent power. If it helps, a little male bashing can't hurt, but remember, this a time for you to go forward and not to stay stuck in negative feelings. Do what makes you feel good. One recently divorced woman found that having a "funeral" for her husband was a great cathartic. She sent her kids to their grandmother's, invited all her girlfriends over, wore her sexiest black dress, and laughed, cried, ate, and grieved as many do at typical funerals. Even though this ritual allowed her to say good-bye to the dearly departed, she was careful not to involve her children in her method of grieving. Still, after years of misery, her life at last was taking a positive turn.

SHEDDING THE VICTIM ATTITUDE

America seems increasingly comfortable accepting the "victim mentality," which states, "I am not responsible for my actions." Just tune in to any talk show, and you'll undoubtedly find the guest victim blaming his upbringing for the fact that he has lied and cheated on every woman unlucky enough to have crossed his path.

Those who are self-proclaimed victims follow a predictable pattern. When responsibility for personal behavior is jettisoned, there is always a price to be paid. You might notice that many "victims" never seem that happy or successful. They don't seem to have much energy left to point their lives in positive directions. So much energy is spent dwelling in the past.

This is not to say that you haven't been dumped on or suffered some terrible injustice. It's inaccurate to lump all victims into the talk show mold when many women truly are victims of incest or domestic abuse. However, too many divorced women don't realize that they did have choices. The first choice you should make is deciding whether or not you are a victim. Chances are, if you investigate a little further, you may find that you are simply allowing yourself to feel victimized.

DARING DISTRACTIONS

You're going to hurt; don't fight it. But in between feeling and functioning, there's room for some daring distractions to help ease the process of healing. Treat yourself to those sheets your ex absolutely detested, eat food he loved that only you could prepare, or blare country music if he thought it was whiny. Better yet, forget him and have a divorce party. Invite your girlfriends over to watch *Under the Tuscan Sun, Jerry Maguire,* or *Erin Brockovich.* If your friends aren't available, log onto *http://sassypink peppers.com* where you will find fun, friendship, and Abba with this "moving on" support group.

WHEN YOU CAN'T JUSTIFY DIVORCE

My marriage has lacked passion for years. We have separate careers, interests, and friends. My husband does share some of the parenting of our two children but with a lack of enthusiasm and commitment. I have thought for a long time that I would be happier alone. I am having trouble sorting all this out and making a decision. Don't suggest marriage counseling. We've been there!

A large proportion of married women have contemplated ending their marriage at some point. However, only you can decide if the benefits of the marriage outweigh the limitations.

Think about how and why you and your husband created such separate lives. Away from the children, try talking honestly with one another. It is likely he also feels discontent. If counseling has not helped you resolve marital issues, you still need to explore and understand them for yourself, no matter what you decide to do.

Are you better off with him or without him? Make a list of the reasons you might want to stay married and the reasons you might want to divorce. Consider how you might feel sharing your children in a custody arrangement. How would you feel, for example, knowing that you will not always have holidays with your children? Are you ready to give up the good and familiar things you and your husband have created in favor of a future filled with uncertainty and challenge—as well as possibility and promise? Some women unconsciously postpone this decision despite much unhappiness or even abuse,

waiting for another man to come along to rescue them. If this is how you feel, you need to take some time and sort out your feelings about yourself. Why do you think you need a man to survive? For some women whose marriages have lost that essential spark, making the decision to separate is laden with guilt. After all, they think, "What do I have to complain about? He doesn't gamble, drink, or beat me." But don't you think you might deserve more?

If you are afraid to divorce because you don't know how to survive emotionally without a man, get out a sheet of paper and a pen and list all the reasons why you think you are nothing without a man. Then, list all the things you have done in your life of which you are proud. See how many of your accomplishments were not the direct result of your husband's input—things like being able to entertain lavishly on a shoestring budget or helping your company land that new account. Conversely, don't be surprised if a number of your husband's achievements were largely due to you. There is a reason for the saying "Behind every great man is a great woman!"

DOES EVERYTHING REALLY BELONG TO HIM?

My husband and I were married young. I worked at dead-end jobs to help support him while he finished college and graduate school. We have two children, ages four and seven. I quit work because he wanted me to be home full time to care for the children and to manage things at home. He feels that providing the income means he never has to help out at home unless it is his choice. I don't love him anymore,

*and he knows it. He tells me that
if I file for divorce that the children
and I will live in poverty because
the money he makes belongs only
to him.*

Your husband's attitude about his salary reflects what has been eloquently discussed by law professor Joan Williams in her book, *Unbending Gender: Why Family and Work Conflict and What to Do About It.* A significant number of mothers with custody do experience a significant decline in their standard of living after divorce. Many state laws and judicial rulings favor the financial interests of men who have been able to pursue careers without the interruptions of child care or home responsibilities. This is why many divorced men are able to marry younger women and start a second family. Many families' primary asset is the money the husband is able to earn because his career is his sole priority. Courts are reluctant to force a financially independent spouse to reduce his standard of living to pay the living expenses of a financially dependent spouse. This is why only about 8 percent of women are awarded alimony and three quarters of those awards are temporary. This is also why there are income caps on child support awards. These unfortunate facts do not doom you to a life with a man you no longer love. These facts, however, highlight the need for careful planning, competent legal representation, and a realistic understanding of the potential financial pitfalls of divorce.

PREPARING FOR DIVORCE

Be careful about making major financial and career decisions, especially if you're not certain that you are getting divorced. Certainly don't make any joint decisions. For example, this is probably not the time to refinance your home to provide your husband with capital to start his own business. Use your period of indecision as a window of opportunity—a time to plan but not to act. Many divorcing women with children consider keeping the family house in the settlement absolutely imperative for the stability of the children. Houses entail hefty expenses, however, which can leave you house poor. Give careful consideration to options you may need to consider, if you decide to divorce. This is also the right time to take a careful look at your own career. Are you moving in a direction that would allow you to be self-supporting? Does your present job offer the benefits you might need? Consider furthering your education or getting the training you may need a priority so you have better career opportunities and, possibly, more job flexibility.

If you decide to go ahead with the divorce, you should discreetly document your finances and protect your assets before you begin legal proceedings. Work the numbers carefully. Prepare a careful postdivorce budget and make sure you have enough liquid assets to draw upon. These liquid assets are what many matrimonial lawyers refer to as the "war chest." This is especially important if you fear that your husband will be particularly vindictive or angry. If you ultimately decide to stay together, knowing more about your shared finances will strengthen your marriage. Gathering this information will help you better plan and be in a stronger legal position if you do decide to divorce. Don't forget to follow these guidelines:

♦ Remove your name from any joint credit card accounts, and notify credit card companies in writing that you will no longer be responsible for charges made on them. Send the letters return receipt requested and then file all these documents in case you receive bills for your ex-husband's charges at a later time.

♦ You may also want to withdraw half of the money in your bank accounts or ask the bank to freeze the account. Notify your banker in writing, again with a return receipt requested, that you do not want any transactions to occur without both parties being notified.

♦ Close any equity lines of credit you and your husband may have. If you do not do this, you may end up losing your house.

♦ Make a list of everything in your home. Better yet, take photographs or make a videotape of your possessions. If you don't own a camcorder, you can rent one. Keep notes as to value and purchase date. Check your insurance files for these.

♦ Establish a separate mailing address by opening a post office box in your name. You do not have to live in a town to have a post office box there.

♦ Open a checking account in your own name. Apply for credit cards in your own name if you do not already have them.

♦ Do not cosign any loan with your husband. If you do and he later defaults, you will be obligated to pay back the loan in full.

♦ Consider what will happen to your health insurance if you divorce. Find out what your rights are in case of divorce.

Also be sure to make copies of the following necessary documents:

♦ Personal and business income tax returns for the past several years. If you used a tax preparer, this person is required by law to keep copies for three years. Otherwise, log on to *www.IRS.gov* and download Form 4506 (Request for Copy of Tax Form). Complete this form and mail it to the correct IRS office for your state. There is a small fee for each tax year requested. This will give you a photostatic copy of your actual return. This may be preferred for use in Court. (Check with your legal advisor.) Processing time is about sixty days. You can also obtain Form 4506-T, which will give you same-day disclosure of the line-for-line information provided on your return. There is no charge for this information. You must be prepared to verify your identity. If you don't have Internet access, call the IRS (800-829-3676) and request the forms that you need. These forms need not be signed by your spouse, assuming the two of you filed a joint return.

♦ Financial statements from banks and loan applications. Often things overlooked when filing taxes are remembered when trying to prove credit worthiness.

♦ Prenuptial agreements or any other agreements that show how income or assets are to be split.

- Business and home accounting records, including bank statements, ledgers, budget books, and check registers.

- Notes payable to you or by you and outstanding credit card bills.

- Your husband's pay stub, pension agreement, and profit sharing plan or other retirement program.

- Deeds or contracts.

- Personal or business insurance papers.

- Statements from brokerage firms, mutual funds, partnerships, or other investments. This includes appraisals of any collectibles such as antiques, jewelry, or sports collections.

CONSIDER A "DIVORCE SPECIALIST"

As part of the burgeoning divorce industry, some women are consulting with divorce planners or divorce specialists. These individuals are actually called "certified divorce planners" or "certified divorce specialists." These are competing certifications. Check the individual's credentials carefully to make sure that his or her training and expertise address your particular needs. Most divorce planners or specialists are hired by women who have limited understanding of family finances and who really do not know what they should be asking for in the financial settlement. Divorce planners or specialists typically charge about $100 per hour and work with a client for about ten hours. While there are differing points of view about the value of divorce planners or specialists, there is agreement that these services make the most sense when couples have specific financial issues to resolve, such as how to divide up a stock portfolio. Women married at least ten years who might expect alimony as part of the settlement and also with estate assets of at least $250,000 are most likely to benefit from using these services.

HOW TO SELECT AN ATTORNEY

Those who find themselves dissatisfied with their attorney's services or fees probably don't realize that they did have a choice. Although shopping for a doctor or a lawyer should be done with the same patience and thoroughness you would give to purchasing furniture or a car, there is a marked difference: Most people don't know what they want when hunting for a lawyer. Why? Most likely it is because professionals such as doctors and lawyers are usually sought when a person is in a crisis situation, when the potential client is not thinking clearly yet is acting quickly. Moreover, attorneys and physicians often are placed on pedestals, making people feel that the professional is doing them a favor, rather than being in their employ. If you can see this, you shouldn't have too much trouble with the idea that picking an attorney is like shopping for a car. Both need to serve you well and be reliable, affordable, and comfortable.

Most people make do by simply asking a friend or looking up an attorney in the Yellow Pages. Here are some things an informed consumer keeps in mind when attorney shopping:

◆ Call a lawyer referral service. Most communities list phone numbers in their local directories of sources that can refer you to someone who specializes in family law. If you can't locate one in your area, contact your local bar association. Most county bar associations will give out names of lawyers in the area. However, bar associations often fail to provide meaningful screening, which means that those who participate may not be the most experienced or competent.

◆ Another good source of referrals is a community center or public service agency. Your county's battered women's shelter, crisis centers, legal aid societies, women's resource centers or women's commissions, and children's legal services can be of help. Independent paralegals get regular feedback on lawyers' work and can make informed recommendations. If you know of someone who was recently divorced and was pleased with the services of her lawyer, call that lawyer first. If that lawyer cannot take your case, ask for recommendations. Group legal plans, available through some unions and consumer action groups, offer comprehensive legal assistance free or at low cost. Do your homework. Solicit recommendations from a variety of sources and compare the information you receive.

◆ Examine the attorney's areas of specialization or expertise. A common mistake made when asking friends for advice is that they often recommend an attorney whose specialty is in an unrelated field. For example, your brother may have found an attorney who is excellent for his business needs, but this adviser might know little or nothing about divorce or custody law. Avoid giant firms that primarily represent businesses. Such firms know little about matrimonial law and less about keeping costs reasonable.

◆ Keep in mind that just because you see an attorney on a consultation basis does not mean that you need to hire him or her. Most lawyers charge an initial consultation fee, but you should consider this a small price to pay for an opportunity to find the best fit for you and the best bargain. Use this initial appointment to assess whether or not this is the best attorney to represent you in your particular situation.

◆ Tell the attorney the exact nature of your legal problem as concisely as possible. Practice beforehand so you don't get caught up in an emotional discussion, which could wind up being costly. Remember, attorneys aren't psychologists. Don't waste your money venting your feelings. Do that through a support group, your clergyman or counselor, and special friends. Stick to the facts when interviewing a lawyer.

♦ Absolute honesty is essential. Remember, the attorney is bound by a code of professional ethics, and all conversations with the attorney are protected by the attorney/client privilege. But even though you can trust this person professionally, you need to feel trust in him or her as an individual. Get a feeling of whether or not you can communicate comfortably with this person. If you perceive this person as cold or arrogant or if he or she is of a decidedly different personality type from you, the two of you may not work together well. It is better to keep looking.

♦ Determine how much expertise the attorney has in family law. Ask how long he or she has been practicing and how many cases like yours he or she has handled. A competent attorney will welcome your questions. The attorney should be eager to discuss his or her experience and knowledge in handling cases such as yours.

♦ See how realistic the attorney is about settling your case to your advantage. Avoid the attorney who promises you an unrealistically large sum of money. An experienced lawyer should be able to give you a reasonable assessment, but no guarantees. The judge has the final say. Stay away from the expensive, flamboyant media celebrity lawyer. This kind of lawyer would probably pass your case on to a recent law school graduate in his office. Lawyers who make decisions without consulting you, who do not return your phone calls within a reasonable time period, and who generally will not tell you how your case is being handled are all to be avoided.

♦ Ask what your options are. For example, should you go to court, or would it be better to settle differently, perhaps through divorce mediation? If the attorney insists that there is only one way to proceed but does not make it clear to you why there is only one possible course of action, consider leaving. Trust your instincts. Any lawyer who offers to take you to dinner or bed or anyplace else should be avoided like the plague. Their conduct is unethical.

♦ Finally, at the end of the consultation, ask about fees. While most attorneys can't promise an exact figure due to the potential complexity of the case, such as additional court costs or reasonableness of the other party, they should be able to give you a ballpark figure. Most attorneys will

SINGLE MOM OF NOTE

Margaret Sanger

Many people know who Margaret Sanger is—she's the woman who brought birth control to the United States—but few realize that she was a single mother. She and her husband separated in 1914, when their oldest was twelve and their youngest was four. William Sanger continued to live in Paris while Margaret and the children returned to the United States. She was single for eight years until her marriage in 1922.

Margaret Sanger opened the first birth control clinic in the United States and founded the organization that would one day be Planned Parenthood. Her work made it possible for today's women to have birth control options.

require a retainer against which billable hours will be charged. Keep in mind that just because an attorney quotes a high fee that this doesn't mean that he or she is best.

A lawyer is your representative in perhaps the most important issues of your life—custody of your child, child support, your physical protection when domestic violence is an issue, and a fair settlement. As a legal consumer, you have the right to shop around!

CONSIDER MEDIATION

Mediation occurs when, instead of each party hiring a separate attorney, both the husband and the wife agree to a single mediator. It is the mediator's job to reach an agreement regarding all aspects of the divorce, including custody and visitation. The agreement does not have to be fair or equal or right. It just has to be an agreement.

Mediation is not a good choice when your soon to be former husband wields all the power and you cannot negotiate with him on an equal footing. If you are intimidated or in any way fearful of your former husband, mediation is not for you. Mediation is also a particularly poor choice for women who have not worked outside the home or who do not have an accurate accounting of family financial assets. Women who give up too much during mediation for the sake of a quick settlement may have real regrets later when they come to realize exactly what they have given up.

Mediation can be a viable option for couples who need to preserve their working relationships after divorce—like the parents of young children. The com-

promise that is essential for successful mediation is good practice for the years of shared parenting ahead. Communication skills are enhanced. Mediation deals with hard facts only, sidestepping murky emotional issues. Sometimes this approach helps divorcing couples defuse emotional issues and lessen the pain. Couples who have achieved a balance of power and knowledge and are accustomed to consensus building in the workplace can be ideal candidates for mediation. Not only are costs substantially lower, but also there is less animosity and emotional turmoil. Adherence to the agreement is typically greater.

Examine your own situation with care before making any decision about how best to handle the legal matters associated with your divorce.

ANNULMENTS AND *GETS*

Aside from legal considerations, you may have religious issues to deal with concerning your divorce. Your own spiritual advisor is your best source of counsel in personal matters of faith and religious practice.

If you were married, for example, in the Roman Catholic Church, you must receive an annulment (the declaration of a marriage as null and void, as if it never existed) from the Church before it will recognize your civil (legal) divorce. A long and complicated procedure, an annulment is not guaranteed upon request; there must be extenuating circumstances, such as that one party was coerced into marriage. Without an annulment, you are still considered married in the eyes of the Church and consequently cannot remarry in the Church. This is because marriage in Catholicism is considered a sacrament rather than a contractual agreement, as it is in Judaism.

Reform Jews, who are now the largest Jewish movement in North America, believe that civil divorce is sufficient for remarriage. Conservative and Orthodox rabbis will not remarry either a man or a woman until a religious divorce or a *get* has been obtained. A *get* is always issued by a man to his wife, never the other way around. Conservative Judaism has largely addressed the problem of a husband who will not grant a *get* by inserting into the marriage contract a clause empowering a rabbi to force the issuance of a *get*. Orthodox rabbis are increasingly encouraging couples to sign a prenuptial agreement in which the husband agrees to issue a *get* in the case of civil divorce.

In 1992, the State of New York passed an amendment to an existing Domestic Relations Law statute that details a variety of factors that courts are to consider in setting spousal maintenance (alimony) and property division ("equitable distribution") in the event of a divorce. As presently amended, the statute now provides that one of the factors the court shall consider both in determining maintenance and in allocating marital property is the "maintenance (by one spouse) of a barrier to remarriage" (of the other spouse). While neutrally worded, "barrier to remarriage" clearly addresses the withholding of a *get*. Previously, failing to deliver a *get* was essentially a blackmail tactic. The statute gives secular courts leverage to assist women who would otherwise be at the mercy of recalcitrant husbands.

WHEN HE THREATENS TO TAKE THE KIDS

Many husbands will demand custody as a tactic. These men and their attorneys know that losing custody of your child is your worst fear. By making this demand, they hope you will lessen your legitimate demands or accept less than equitable child support.

This is the kind of situation you are paying your attorney to handle. This is a bluff designed to frighten you. If these men wanted custody, they would have demanded it from the very beginning. Your worst nightmare is losing the children. Their worst nightmare is getting the children. Try to put this tactic into perspective and think before you let your maternal instincts dominate your good sense and judgment. However, if you find yourself embroiled in a custody battle, read Chapter 21.

SEX WITH YOUR SOON-TO-BE EX

I am in the middle of a divorce but have had sex twice with my husband. This is confusing things terribly even though we both know it's over. What should I do?

One of the reasons some couples going through even bitter divorces continue to have sex is because it's convenient and certainly safer from a health perspective than sex with a new partner. Many just aren't ready to find another partner. Maybe they are in denial emotionally about the divorce. Their heads are seeing attorneys and signing papers, but their hearts are somewhere else.

A woman may still love her husband and hope that sex will bring him back to her. Some people use sex as a weapon or bargaining tool—for instance, in the case of a man demanding sex in exchange for regular child support payments. This demand, in effect, puts the mother in a position not unlike that of a prostitute. If your ex-husband makes this demand, discuss the situation with your attorney right away.

Having sex with someone you are separating from extorts a great price. The emotional closeness sex brings can be confusing and can hinder your ability to detach from this person—a necessary step to surviving a divorce. See what needs you are trying to fulfill, and try to meet those needs without having sex with your ex. For example, if you need to be reassured that you are still attractive and desirable, try looking in the mirror and telling yourself just that. Remember that sleeping with your ex, or any new love interest for that matter, is not a reliable gauge of your worth as a woman. Learn to love your body, your face, and your talents.

WHAT TO TELL EVERYONE

This is definitely a situation where the less said, the better. The divorce may be taking up 110 percent of your time and energy, but to most other people, the subject is boring. Obviously, some people thrive on other people's pain and love hearing the details. Unless you relish having your life dissected and analyzed by strangers, do not feed the gossip grapevine. Many women find a simple statement like "We reached a point where we no longer could be mutually supportive" or "I'd rather not bore you with these particular personal details" to be the best replies to probing questions. Share your feelings only with those you trust and only if and when you feel like it. Eventually you will need to discuss some aspects of your divorce with pertinent family members—the children's paternal and maternal grandparents, aunts, uncles, close friends, and other relatives—but for now your priority should be to get your emotional house in order.

Your Parents

Your parents may be thrilled, or they may be devastated. They may think that your divorce is a giant blot on the family name. They may tell you that they told you so. It is hard to predict. Ask for their love and support. They may ask what they can do to help. Accept the help, but keep your requests reasonable. Your parents are probably not looking for a major change in their lifestyle or child care responsibilities. Perhaps your mother can pick up your daughter one day a week from school, or your father can fix a few things that need fixing. If they offer money and you need money, accept their offer but keep it a loan, with specified provisions for paying them back. You are not leaving a marriage to become your parents' child once again. Independence is a precious thing.

Your parents will not be better for knowing all the grim details. Your ex-husband will still be part of the children's lives, as will your parents. Telling them things that will make it difficult for them to look him in the eye or to act cordially does no one any good.

His Parents

Having to deal with his family now only on a limited basis might turn out to be one of the unintended perks of your divorce. You may be close to his parents, however, and want to keep up this relationship. Accept that things will be different. It is your former husband's responsibility to tell his parents of your divorce. You have no control over what else he chooses to tell them.

Do not expect your husband's parents to punish him if he neglects his children or fails to live up to his financial obligations. Do not punish them by withholding their grandchildren from them. Your children need their love and support. At the same time, you do not have to put up with any kind of nonsense. If his parents are mean and vindictive, stay away.

Your Boss, Coworkers, and Other Interested Parties

Your boss may like and respect you as a person, but he is not interested in the details of your marital breakup. He is concerned about whether you will be able to do your job as well as you have in the past. He does not want to hear you on the phone endlessly discussing the divorce with your girlfriends or speaking with your attorney. Your attorney works for you. Have him or her call you at home when you can talk without the office gossips on red alert. If you are feeling upset at work, go to the restroom and cry privately. Your coworkers will be sympathetic, but only to a point. Everyone has problems. The woman you may want to confide in and share your daily troubles with may have just found out that she has cancer or that her son is on drugs.

Do not allow your boss to find out about your divorce from someone else. Bosses typically like to be the first to know and hate to be surprised. Tell your boss in a matter-of-fact way and assure him or her that you will continue to produce as you have before. Practice your speech until you can do it in an unemotional way and, definitely, without crying.

Some women report that the best part of working is getting away from the financial and emotional problems that accompany every divorce and concentrating on getting a job done. More than ever, the income is important, and you need to concentrate. Use work as a place to set aside your personal troubles and focus on what you need to do to build your new life.

WHAT TO TELL NO ONE

Accept the fact that most people have a very hard time keeping secrets. That is why attorneys and therapists are called professionals—they do keep secrets. It is absolutely guaranteed that whatever you tell one person, other people will hear about. You may not care. You may feel fine about having the whole town know that your ex-husband liked wearing pink nightgowns to bed. You may want to punish him by having people know that he was unfaithful or cheap or abusive.

But the bottom line is that this is not in the best interests of your children. Depending on how juicy the gossip is, they may be ridiculed by their classmates or may no longer be invited to other people's homes. People have short attention spans. After they are finished with the gossip you spread about him, these same people will turn on you. They will chitchat about why you put up with it or how you are rather cheap yourself. In short, your efforts to muddy his reputation may succeed, but some mud will stick to you and your children. Find healthier ways to rid yourself of the anger you feel—by keeping a journal, talking with a trusted friend, or occasionally just punching a pillow.

RECOVERING FROM DIVORCE AND GROWING BEYOND IT

Most women exiting a relationship feel that their pain is like nothing anyone else could possibly have experienced and that they are the only person in such agony. Death seems appealing— except "What to do with the kids?" It's important to remember that other women have experienced the same feelings. No matter what your individual circumstances, there were feelings of love, commitment, attachment, and belonging. Great energy was focused on creating a life together. To expect to walk away emotionally unscathed is simply not realistic. To punish yourself by expecting instant healing or to deny the experience of loss will guarantee emotional numbness, which is as near to death as you can get while you are still breathing. Still, a few weeks of living in a semicoma after the realization that you are divorced or divorcing is fairly common. It actually seems to serve as a resting period so that you have the strength to complete the grieving process. Then you can begin the divorce recovery process.

Removing the Failure Label

When a woman's sense of personal identity is closely tied to a fantasy picture of marriage, the inevitable collapse of that fantasy can come as a crushing blow. Sadly, too many women define divorce as the ultimate personal failure. The fact that there were two people in the marriage seems forgotten. Yet, accepting responsibility for others' behaviors or for making things go right is something women have been doing for a long time. Even the woman who came into the marriage with a record of success in school or in the workplace can be vulnerable to a crippling sense of failure when her marriage ends in divorce.

Beginning in early childhood, we are expected to "play nicely" as little girls. Girls are brought up not to do things that make other people uncomfortable. As we were growing up, we might have overheard our mothers, grandmothers, or other female family members or friends talking about a particular woman who "just couldn't hold on to her man." Most of us were never quite sure then what that meant, but we knew it was almost the worst thing you could say about any woman. We began as adolescents to define ourselves according to the success or failure of our relationships—unlike boys, who were taught how to succeed in the workplace. Even though the women's movement has brought astounding changes in the last twenty years, many women still allow a "failed marriage" to describe the outcome of their relationship rather than the "dissolution of a partnership."

Regaining Control

Negative, self-destructive feelings can leave you in a frazzle, causing you to feel out of control. Letting go of feelings of failure and helplessness can uncover the strength that you might not even have known that you possessed. This doesn't mean that your life will turn around overnight. Nor does it insulate you from experiencing some bumpy times ahead. But it does mean that control over your own life comes only with the understanding that it is not what happens to you that counts. It is how you decide to deal with what happens that ultimately matters. You may have had no control over events leading up to this moment. Define events as tragic, and your life may indeed be a tragedy. Define yourself as a helpless victim, and you will be just that. But you can take control now. Tell yourself, "I can move ahead. I will move ahead. I am never going to permit myself to be in circumstances like this again." You will have learned from what has happened. You will become smarter, stronger, and better.

Knowing When to Give Up

When one spouse is willing to face an adjudication of contempt, jail, and total destruction, there is very little the other spouse can do to get justice. When one spouse is prepared to do anything to hurt the other and to prevent a fair distribution of assets, sometimes the best thing to do is to give up. Lawyers seldom recommend giving up. It is their training and inclination to figure out how to fight back and get you what is due you. You must weigh the financial and emotional cost of continuing to fight back no matter what.

You shouldn't consider yourself a quitter should you choose to walk away from a spouse who has both the desire and the means to punish and abuse you through unending legal battles. Although in a divorce the first thing you are concerned with is protecting your financial rights, ultimately you have to ask two questions: Am I getting every penny I deserve? Is it worth living my life like this? Go with the answer to the second question.

Thriving after Divorce

Most of us know at least one woman who has survived the difficult and painful adjustment of divorce. She seems to have made the best of whatever her individual circumstances may have been. This woman has turned the divorce into an opportunity for personal growth. New successes, opportunities, personal happiness, and a genuine sense of fulfillment have come her way. She's doing great, and so are her children. This is a family that more than survives—they thrive.

Even if you've been divorced for years, you may still be living in a world that hasn't caught up with the realities of the day-to-day needs and challenges of the divorced woman's life. You need to identify your resources and put them to the best possible use.

Ask yourself how you can go about getting these needs met. What are your resources, and how can these resources be put to the best possible use? Make a list. Ask friends to help you brainstorm. You may find that you have more going for you than you first realized. For example, you may have gardening or cooking talents that you could barter for the tutoring skills of a friend or neighbor. Remember that resources are not just money or possessions. Strong faith is a resource. Belief in yourself is the best resource of all.

HOW TO CUSTOMIZE A LIFE PLAN

Successful people all share two secrets. First they had a vision. Then they executed a plan.

Artists create with a vision of the image or emotion to be portrayed. Painters often rely on a preliminary drawing from which to complete their masterpiece. Writers develop an outline rather than keystroke randomly. Builders follow blueprints.

Like any good sailor, you need to chart a course so you don't just drift. But first you must see where you are going.

Women are typically less prepared than men to create their own vision different from the life that's depicted in fairy tales. Because in real life princes rarely rescue helpless women and because there is no fairy godmother to turn a pumpkin into dependable transportation to take you to a well-paying job with benefits, you need to decide how to make these things happen. Although careful planning and hard work won't guarantee that your life will be heaven, it's the most authentic, productive, and satisfying way to deal with what life offers.

Here are three steps for visualizing where you see yourself in the real world.

1. *Make three wishes and write them down.* Remember to give these some thought because even though you will be utilizing creativity, you don't want to suspend reality. For example, if you dropped out of college after one semester because you never wanted to hear the word "science" again, becoming a world-famous neurosurgeon may not be a realistic wish. However, seeing yourself in the world of medicine may have little to do with longing for the prestige and respect given a doctor or scientist, but rather may be related to an interest in healing or prevention. Consider that you have grown and changed. You may have lacked the discipline in your college years to do the hard work it takes to tackle difficult science courses. Becoming a licensed massage therapist, volunteering at a hospice, or writing magazine articles promoting healthy lifestyles might be realistic. Consider the potential earning power of your dream job. Think beyond just doctor or nurse and research all the possibilities in the health care field. This is just one example. Use your dreams to fuel your efforts to create new opportunities and a brighter future for you and your children!

Likewise, if you are thirty-eight, have two left feet, and never took a dance class in your life, becoming a prima ballerina doesn't look too promising. Yet, if you visualize people, applause, and emotion, the stage may be very important in your vision. Try taking a music class, going to more concerts or ballets, or writing that play that's been in your head for years. Prepare to be surprised by what you find out about yourself.

2. *Review your wish list.* You may wish for a better education or more knowledge of music and the arts. You may wish for companionship or romance. You may wish for greater happiness for your children. You may wish for more peace and serenity in your life. You may wish for more positive relationships with

MY WISH LIST:
1. Learn to play the piano
2. Have more energy!
3. Develop financial security.

your extended family. You may wish for better health, more stamina, or more energy. Wishes that fall under a definite heading like financial security or improved health should give you a clear idea of where your visionary energies should be directed.

3. *Now create a miracle.* Look at your three wishes. Pretend a miracle has happened and your wishes came true. How would things be different? What would have changed? For example, if you wished for more companionship, would you see yourself sitting among a group of adults chatting and laughing on weekends when "Dad" takes the kids, instead of feeling lonesome in your apartment? Would you call some friends and invite them over for a potluck supper and an evening of good conversation? What is available at your local library, college or university, church or synagogue, or other organization? How about organizing a book club, support group, or film society, depending on your interests?

Don't worry; this process doesn't have to be overwhelming. Just take one positive step every day toward fulfilling your wish, and you will be accomplishing a lot.

WEDDING RINGS AND OTHER LEFTOVERS

My marriage has been over for five years. My former husband is happily involved in his new life. I think I'm adjusting okay except that I am still wearing my wedding rings. I can't seem to take them off.

Don't beat yourself up. Rings are powerful symbols of marriage in our society. Receiving your engagement ring brought you a moment of great joy. When the wedding ring was slipped on your finger at your wedding ceremony, it was symbolic of your life together. For you, taking the rings off will be the absolute final end of your marriage. You probably feel unready to date, and so these symbols of marriage don't seem out of place. Maybe a small part of you has not completely accepted the divorce.

When you are emotionally ready, you will take them off. One day you will look at your hand and ask yourself why you are still wearing your rings. You will take them off and not think much about it. Remember to put them in a safe place, but not a place where you have to look at them every day. Your hand will feel strange and light for a few days. Soon, you will forget that you ever wore them.

My husband and I can't seem to decide what to do with our accumulated stuff. He says his new apartment is too small. I find much of it depressing, reminding me of less than great times. I find it interesting that even though we are long divorced, we can't seem to let go of this junk.

"Letting go" is the key phrase here. Whatever this junk is, it has come to represent the last vestige of your life as a couple. Neither of you want to completely let go, or you would have disposed of this depressing stuff long ago.

When you are ready, try this. Say out loud that it is hard to let go of this stuff because it represents the last of your life together as a couple. Grieve and let go. Have a garage sale or rummage sale. Take the money and buy something that

represents a beginning, not an end. Use
the money to begin a stamp or coin collection for your children. Use it to try
something new, like white-water rafting
or canoeing. Give it to a charity whose
work is life affirming and constructive. Make an occasion out of whatever
beginning you choose.

7

Widowed Single Moms

Loss of a spouse ranks high on the list of life's most devastating events. There is simply no aspect of your life that is unaffected. The feelings of grief and loss are indescribable, and you wonder if you will ever again feel joy. In fact, at times, your own desire to continue living may not be all that strong. Much of what you are experiencing may not seem real, only a bad dream from which you will awaken.

But, as everybody most likely keeps telling you, you have your children, and they need you. Your children give you a reason to continue your life with both purpose and happiness. It's hard to believe right now, but there will be joy again in your lives. There will be days ahead not clouded by grief but filled with laughter and fun. By seeking out the joy and happiness in everyday events, you will see the light at the end of the tunnel. If you have hope, the light will grow brighter and stronger.

WHAT YOU MAY BE FEELING

Anger

My husband Tony, a firefighter, was killed while searching for possible victims after a fire in a nearby neighborhood. He was hailed as a hero. After the services were over, I watched his fellow firefighters and their wives return to their homes, sad for the moment but with their own lives unchanged.

I'm so angry that Tony left me alone with two babies to raise. I also can't help feeling anger and blame toward the fire department, toward his parents, who had encouraged his love of the job, and toward the residents of the neighborhood where the fire broke out. What's wrong with me?

Feeling angry is a natural part of grieving. There is nothing wrong with feeling angry. But remember that anger needs to be expressed appropriately without harm to others. Accusing

Tony's parents because they had encouraged his passion for firefighting will not accomplish anything other than prolonging your rage. You could visit Tony's grave and tell him how angry you are at him for leaving. After all, if you didn't love him, you wouldn't feel this way. Allow yourself to feel angry at Tony from time to time, keeping in mind that you are trying to work through this. As the anger dissipates, you might want to tell a few close friends that you felt as if Tony had abandoned you. People will understand.

Inflicting pain on those who share your loss will not make your pain go away. When you realize there is no one to blame, your anger will no longer dominate your life.

My husband, Philip, died of cancer at the age of thirty-eight. There's no one to blame since Philip had lived a healthy life. He received the best of medical care from caring and compassionate physicians. Philip was able to die at home with dignity surrounded by the things and the people he loved. So why do I blame myself and let this anger consume me?

You might be angry at yourself for feeling angry. You may blame yourself for not yet being able to count the blessings of the many good years you and Philip shared or the dignity of his death. Moreover, like many widows, you may be punishing yourself for surviving Philip.

Your feelings are to be expected. Acknowledging the right to be angry at experiencing such a loss is the first step toward a new life. Maybe you are angry that Philip won't be here to help you raise your children or to see the oldest

teen leave for college. Tell him that you are upset he can't be here to help with the endless packing and transporting of belongings that are also college bound.

Continue to chat with Philip now and again. Many widows report taking great comfort from frank discussions about how they are feeling as if their husbands were still physically present. If you are feeling caught up in anger, try talking it out in this way.

Loneliness

Many widows lose not only a husband but also a best friend when their husband dies. This loss of companionship and intimacy is a difficult and painful adjustment. Remember, however, that some people are not capable of having the kind of deep, committed relationship you shared with your husband. You do have that capacity. You will have other relationships in your life that will fill the emptiness you feel now. Perhaps you will choose not to remarry, but your life will fill with rich and fulfilling relationships.

Try to seek out opportunities for companionship and conversation, even if it is just a brief chat with another mother at a Little League game. People may feel awkward and may not know what to say to you, and so often you have to begin the conversation. What you say does not have to be brilliant or witty. You are simply looking for some social contact; so don't set your expectations too high. Small steps will lead to major progress at this difficult time. Give yourself the time to heal. You will always miss your husband, but that sharp edge of loneliness does go away.

Paralysis

Many widows report feeling nearly unable to move for a period of time after their husband's death. Managing daily routines is exhausting. Simple decisions, like what vegetable to give the children for dinner, seem overwhelming. Feelings of low energy, indecision, confusion, and, of course, sadness are quite normal.

Simply put, the death of your husband was a major trauma. You need time to heal and let your emotional energies regroup. If you fight these feelings and force yourself to do more than you are able to do, you will feel worse and be able to accomplish less.

If you find yourself feeling exhausted, indecisive, or confused, lower your expectations for yourself for the time being. Do only what is essential. Whatever energy you can muster up right now should be invested in meeting your emotional and physical needs and those of your children. Let the dust gather, and let others be the stars at work for now. Healing is hard work and should be your main task now.

Worry

There is much to be realistically worried about when your husband dies. Your children are a tremendous source of concern, no matter what their ages. You have worries about finances and matters relating to the proper settling of your husband's estate. You may be worried about employment. You may have to get a job to make ends meet, or you might need to upgrade your job skills. You may be worried about where you are going to live. You may need to move and be concerned about the wheres and the hows.

With all that is on your plate, it would be strange if you were not worried. But endless worry can sap the joy out of life and exhaust you. You need to take control of your worries. Write them down. Rank them according to what is worrying you the most. Then, divide them into two categories: those you can do something about and those that are so far in the future there is nothing you can do about them anyway. Start crossing off the ones you can do nothing about. Prioritize the remainder. For example, which worries would be helped by talking them out with a friend or in a widows' support group? Which concerns don't seem that serious when examined in the light of day? Wondering who will escort you to your son's graduation ten years from now is a bit premature. Maybe your health club membership expired with the death of your spouse. Can you find other ways to benefit from healthy activities and exercise? It is helpful, too, to set aside a certain amount of time each day—say, twenty minutes—devoted exclusively to fretting. Then, when you catch yourself worrying too frequently, you can say to yourself, "This is the wrong time for me to worry!"

Fear

Faced with unexpected challenges, many widows are afraid. They are afraid of being alone, of making the wrong decision, and of facing life and the responsibilities of parenthood. These fears are normal and natural and to be expected. It is important to acknowledge that fear is what you are feeling. Fear that is hidden or unexpressed will be devastating to you. Fear is such a strong emotion that if left unexpressed it will take on many hideous disguises. Fear can literally make you sick. It can look like anger and make you lash out at the very people most important to you. Fear can make you unable to move, like a deer at night with the headlights of an oncoming car bearing down on him.

Make friends with the power of fear. Say out loud, "I feel afraid." Sometimes simply acknowledging that you are afraid is enough for the moment. Fear can be a powerful motivator, or it can stop you dead in your tracks. Unlike other powerful emotions like loneliness, you are the only one who can know what you fear and make a plan for conquering the fear. For example, a very real fear you might have is the fear of the responsibility of raising your children alone. Don't let this fear turn you into a screaming mother from hell when you can allow it to mobilize you into the energetic, resourceful person you are capable of becoming.

Remember, we all have fears. It does not make you weak to be afraid. Often fear means that you are realistic about what you are facing. The real danger is letting our fears ruin our lives by preventing us from finding out where our strengths lie or, worse, making us nonproductive and too dependent on others. Try to live by the adage, "Feel the fear, and do it anyway!"

Unresolved Feelings

Talking it out or in some way expressing your feelings to your late husband is an important part of healing, especially if negative feelings are dominating your life. Perhaps you feel guilty about something you did and want his forgiveness. Perhaps you just want to say you are sorry about a decision or event for which you feel responsible. These feelings must be expressed and put in their proper place for you to move ahead.

Try writing your husband a letter and leaving it at his grave. If this is too public, then burn the letter and scatter the ashes. Maybe it is difficult for you to put your feelings on paper. Make a tape recording and play it at a place where you feel most comfortable. It is not important how you confront these feelings but rather that you do confront them. The only rule is that the feelings get expressed. Give yourself permission to create and enact any ceremony or ritual that will give you the forgiveness or peace you need.

WARDING OFF THE GRIEF POLICE

Among the more unpleasant immediate experiences widows face are the encounters with the "grief police." You know them—the well-meaning friends or people you hardly know who feel free to tell you the "rules" for grieving. These rules take the form of statements like, "He's been dead for six months. Why are you still wearing your wedding rings?" or "A year is long enough to grieve. Get on with your own life." Do not let anyone tell you that there are set timetables for grieving, implying that you are in some way behind schedule. Avoid others' distorted sense of priorities.

Most self-help books and tapes about managing loss are written by members of the grief police. These materials are based on the idea that grief can be managed. Grief, by its very nature, is unmanageable. There is no timetable or step-by-step guide to manage the experience of loss. One widow describes grief like being behind the wheel of a car going sixty miles an hour with no control over the brakes or steering. You just hold on tight.

Keep in mind that although you may never really get over a feeling of loss that you will get through this. When you do, the reminders of this loss in the future will be transformed from painful to poignant. Memories become more bittersweet until one day—as deep as the depths of your sadness and despair are—will come the ability to think of your spouse with warmth and fulfillment.

Remember, too, that there is no hierarchy of grief. Losing a husband of fifty years is not worse than losing a husband of five months or a son of thirty years. Others will be sharing your feelings of grief and loss—his mother, his father, your children. Respect others' unique way of mourning, but at the same time don't let them inflict their rules on you.

Finally, never forget that everyone experiences loss in some form or another. Of course, all grievers believe their pain at a given moment is unlike anyone else's—no one could ever understand the depth or strength of their feelings. But that is because loss is such a personal experience. Like

everything else that occurs in life, you'll get through this, but only if you give yourself permission.

WARDING OFF INAPPROPRIATE QUESTIONS AND COMMENTS

Regardless of the circumstances of your husband's death, you will be astounded at the inappropriate comments and questions. Although tragedy often brings out the best in people, it can also trigger their worst side. Remember to keep in mind the following suggestions:

- Contribute nothing to the gossip mill. People often assume that they have a "right to know." A few people in your life will ask out of genuine concern, but many people are simply curious or looking for gossip to spread. Choose your confidants with care.

- Respect your own privacy. Expect to be asked about the size of your husband's estate, how you are coping without sex, exactly how you plan to handle your money, and on and on. The best way to handle these "none of your business" questions is to say simply that it is a personal matter.

- Keep your sense of humor and use it, when at all possible. Try to keep a slightly amused, slightly surprised tone to your voice when confronted with nosy questions. Try laughing out loud if the question is particularly outrageous.

- When in doubt, say nothing.

FACING YOUR HUSBAND'S BELONGINGS

The most painful and heartbreaking task any widow faces is the disposal of her husband's belongings. Don't let others rush you into this task. Do things as you feel ready. Keep what you want to keep. Your children will want to have pictures and mementos of their father so that he can be remembered. Friends and other relatives might cherish something that belonged to your husband.

If you come across items of unknown value or your husband had a collection of some type, find out the value before giving it away or donating it to charity. Remember again that there is no timetable and that you are free to deal with this task at a pace comfortable to you.

PROTECTING YOUR CHILDREN FROM YOUR PRIVATE PAIN

Activities like writing your deceased husband a letter telling him how angry you are that he died are private matters reflecting adult needs and concerns. You may choose to discuss your feelings with close friends, a trusted clergyman, or a counselor. With few exceptions, however, the activities that accompany these feelings should not be shared with your children, no matter what their age. Your children are dealing with their own issues about their father and cannot shoulder your pain as well.

As you are dealing with your own feelings, you certainly want to help your children confront and express theirs. You might encourage older children to express their feelings in writing or on tape. Younger children can draw or paint. Make sure your children know that they can discuss their feelings with you. If you cannot handle this—and many widows cannot—find a trusted adult in whom they can confide. Counseling can be very beneficial for families when a parent has died.

FINDING SUPPORT AND COUNSELING

Nearly all communities offer counseling and fund support groups for recent widows and their children. These may be available through your local hospital, mental health clinic, church or synagogue, or community center. It is a good idea to seek out these resources for yourself and for your children. Most often widows and their children report receiving great comfort from the opportunity to talk with others who are experiencing the same loss and many of the same kinds of feelings. A support system that enables you and your children to emerge intact from the emotional minefield of the grieving process is very important to your recovery.

If your children do not want to go, gently insist that they try it once or twice. Many children who have overcome the initial reluctance continue willingly. If your child does not want to continue, do not force him. Your child may not be ready for this group experience or for the intensity of individual counseling. Later on, therapy or attending a support group might be just right. Remember, grief is not a timed event, and each of your children will grieve differently. Respect those differences and be ready to accommodate individual needs for private counseling or group therapy.

KNOWING WHEN TO RELEASE THE GHOST

Confronting feelings of anger or guilt and expressing them in some manner to your late husband may be healthy and appropriate. Expressing regret and asking your late husband for forgiveness or understanding can also be part of the normal, healthy grieving process. However, finding yourself conversing with your late husband about what to make for dinner or what movie to see is not healthy.

You will think about your late husband often. When you think of him, remember the love. You must let go of him to move on with your own life. Making his favorite dinner or seeing a movie he would have liked will not fill the void. No kind of meaningful life can be built with a ghost. Release the ghost of your husband. This is key to your survival.

THE YOUNG WIDOW

You may not have realized that widows come in all shapes, sizes, and ages. If you have been widowed while still relatively young and with children living at home, you most likely will receive more support and attention during the time immediately following your husband's death than do older widows. Your husband will have left many friends and survivors, and his parents might still be alive. Although you will want to reach out and accept the help available to you, it is important not to let this support dictate your feelings or shape significantly the plans you will make for the future. Older widows have had a style or pattern of living that they followed. But because of your age, you'll find others urging you to settle into a new life or expecting you to cope as they do. Their

---

SINGLE MOM OF NOTE

**Martha Coston,
Inventor of Signal Flares**
Widowed at the age of twenty-one, Martha Coston (born 1826) was left with four children. She met the challenge of providing for her children by inventing a system of maritime signal flares.

She sold signals to shippers, maritime insurance firms, yacht clubs, and navies across the globe but was undercompensated because she was a woman.

Coston sold her patent to the U.S. Navy in 1856; her flares helped to win battles and save the lives of countless shipwreck victims during the Civil War.

---

needs do not mean you have to stage a show or pretend on their behalf. Let them know that it is precisely because of your age that you don't want to do anything hasty with your life or make too many decisions yet.

Above all else, be kind to yourself. The death of your husband was an enormous loss. Do not make it worse by burdening yourself with having to put on a brave front or feeling you have to create your new life overnight. Let the numb feelings protect you for awhile. Let go of the numbness as you are ready. Your grieving will need to follow its individual course.

My husband recently died in a car accident, leaving me widowed at thirty years of age. I just can't relate to elderly women mourning the death of spouses who didn't have much time left anyway. They don't appear to be in such a state of shock—a number of them tell me they actually feel relieved where I feel practically numb. Why?

Shock and numbness are often the first feelings young widows face. Often their husbands' deaths are the result of accidents, death in the line of duty, or illnesses only rarely found in men so young. The numb feelings are a natural protection; because with little or no time to prepare, there is simply too much to face all at once.

Particularly for young widows who lose their husbands unexpectedly, the feeling of being abandoned is overwhelming. You feel as though your husband has deserted you on purpose. No matter what the circumstances of his death, part of you feels that he had a choice whether to die or not and made a decision to abandon you. Women in their sixties and seventies also report feeling abandoned. But they sense it in a different way, particularly because they weren't left with minor children.

One woman was widowed at twenty-six when her husband died in an airline crash. She described being angry that she was left to face the "frontier" of raising their infant son alone. She knew her husband had nothing to do with the crash and certainly had no wish to die at thirty years of age, but she couldn't help blaming him for leaving her, as irrational and crazy as she thought this was.

NOT QUITE A WIDOW—LEGALLY

I'm in my early thirties and recently widowed, sort of. What I mean is that my fiancé died suddenly from leukemia while I was five months pregnant. I believe he had a little money put away for us, but contact with his family has stopped since my fiancé's death. I feel like I have no one to turn to since my family lives so far away.

Ask yourself if there is anything you can do to maintain relations with your fiancé's family—at least for mutual emotional support. Maybe they are aware of your fiancé's intentions and would like to offer you some assistance. Plus, they might want a relationship, however undefined or remote, with their grandchild, which can be very beneficial for both you and your child. It is not clear why the lines of communication shut down, but maybe you could reopen them. You might also want to check with an attorney to see what legal rights you may have in a situation like this, especially if you know for certain that your fiancé had something to contribute financially to the future of your family. Chances are that he may have set up an account that is in your name, as well as his. Either way, investigate now.

MISSING HIS BODY AND TOUCH

This is the most personal aspect of your loss and probably the most difficult to discuss. Touch is a basic human need. Particularly if your husband's death was sudden or unexpected, loss of his touch makes you feel adrift and incomplete. You will miss his kisses, holding his hand, and his mere physical presence. If your life together as a couple was especially rich and satisfying, you will long for the intimacy and pleasure you brought to one another. These needs will not be easily satisfied.

Some widows try to replace their husbands almost instantly, choosing almost literally the nearest warm body around. This will be a temptation because the pain you feel is so great and the loss so terrible. Looking for a substitute man in haste will almost surely compound your feelings of loss. There will be no shortage of men who will look to take advantage of your situation, particularly for the young widow. Some truly unscrupulous types will seek you out, especially if they think you are a wealthy widow. Their plan is to seduce you and steal your money. This is not to say that every man who might ask you out is a potential felon, but you need to be careful. You have been out of the social scene for a long while. You need to tread carefully and learn the rules and devise your own before you find yourself in a situation you in no way envisioned.

Many widows find that methods of self-satisfaction are the best substitute until they are ready to explore the social scene. Meeting your own needs can also take the form of small luxuries like manicures, pedicures, or massage. These may seem like small comforts in the face of what you have lost, but they may be the best and safest substitute for you now.

GETTING THE HELP YOU NEED

Many people will offer help, urging you to call upon them if you need assistance. Your instincts will tell you who is sincere and who is not. This is not the time to see how absolutely strong and self-reliant you can be. In short, accept the help.

Remember, other people cannot read your mind. You have to ask for what you need. Sometimes the simplest kinds of help are the most needed. If you have been too overwhelmed to cook, ask for a home-cooked meal. Feeling ready for a little entertainment? Ask someone to go to the movies or to the mall with you. Perhaps your children need a ride somewhere that you are having a hard time coordinating.

Asking for and accepting help, particularly during this difficult time, is not a sign of weakness and surely does not predict that you will be unable to forge a new life for yourself and your children. Asking for and accepting help is the first logical step in forging this new life. You have a lot on your plate now. Things will get better. Much of what you are coping with and having to handle, once done, will not have to be a concern again.

RENEW THAT LIBRARY CARD NOW!

However you seek solace, add reading in addition to your list of favorite comfort foods, writing to friends, or soaking in a steamy bath. Sue Miller's *Lost in the Forest* finds a family in turmoil after suffering a loss, but there is hope as you follow their lives while they piece things back together; *Men Don't Leave*, a poignant tale that was also made into a critically acclaimed film; or *The Fourth Hand* by John Irving, in which a new widow uses her passion for the Green Bay Packers to stay emotionally afloat, are stories which can help you feel like an understanding friend is nearby.

SUICIDAL THOUGHTS

It is normal to think about your own death when your husband dies. The desire for reunion, coupled with the feelings of sadness, makes most widows think at least briefly about ending their own lives. The needs of their children and their own healthy desire to live quickly take over. If you have had such thoughts, know that other women have had similar thoughts. Do not punish yourself by thinking that you are insane or a bad person or a terrible mother for letting such a thought even enter your mind.

If you find yourself thinking often about killing yourself and have thought about a plan or possible method, you need to tell someone you trust. You are in serious pain and need help to sort through what you are feeling. No one will think less of you. The loss of your husband is so overwhelming that you are finding it hard to think about continuing to live. Help and understanding are available to you. Ask.

WHEN WIDOW SPELLS R-E-L-I-E-F!

For some women, the death of their husbands brings only relief. Your husband may have physically or emotionally abused you. He may have had a serious drug or alcohol problem. He may have been continually unfaithful to you, causing you humiliation.

Cruel and abusive husbands are seldom mourned as are kind and decent men. If you worked hard at keeping his abusive or addictive behaviors a secret, you may be shocked to hear the comments of others, even at the funeral. Chances are that others were well aware of the kind of man he was and will not expect you to be all that grief-stricken. Your greatest loss at his death might be your pride. Your cherished fantasy that no one else knew may be destroyed.

If you feel only relief, then you have probably experienced much pain and grief during your husband's lifetime. You may have grieved for a loving marriage that never happened. If widowhood comes as a relief, then do nothing more than accept the blessing. You have endured enough. If you have feelings toward your husband that you could not express to him during his lifetime, do it now. Write him a long letter and, if you choose, burn the letter symbolically to express the end of your suffering and unwanted attachment. Enjoy the second chance life has given you. Free yourself from guilt. You have survived life circumstances that would have destroyed a woman of less strength.

The Merry Widow

My husband Jeffrey was a well-respected attorney. He was also a cruel man who ridiculed and demeaned me. As much as the members of our community deeply mourn, frankly I'm not grieving because I know Jeffrey was nothing like the public image he presented. In fact, I've forgiven him, as he begged me to, and am ready to live a little.

Cruel and abusive men often end their lives asking for forgiveness and understanding. You've experienced exhausting emotional pain during the time preceding your husband's death, and so it's likely that you are "thanking" him for leaving, rather than forgiving him his abuses. However, these two feelings can go hand-in-hand, and either way is acceptable. But sometimes one can forgive a little too quickly, as in the case of a woman who was told her husband had only one week left to live. She immediately forgave him for his years of senseless emotional abuse. Feeling as though she had put her feelings in order by being unselfish enough to forgive, this woman went home and disposed of many of her husband's personal belongings, including socks and underwear. But to everyone's surprise, her husband staged a brief yet remarkable remission and was able to go home. Imagine her having to rush out and purchase new underwear and other personals for the husband she had already removed from both her home and her life!

My husband and I were both interviewing divorce attorneys and sleeping in separate bedrooms when he was killed by a hit-and-run driver. I stopped loving him a long time ago. We fought constantly. I often said that, if he died, I was going to cremate him and sprinkle his ashes in the kitty litter. He always told me that if I ever tried to divorce him that he would make every day of my life a living hell. He is buried properly in the family plot, but my feelings are so jumbled that it is hard for me to get through a day. Has any other widow ever felt this way?

Hard as it may be for others to understand, when a husband you no longer love suddenly dies, there is grief and emotional pain just as real as when the husband is cherished. Many women in your circumstances have felt extraordinarily guilty. Husbands and wives often

say things in the heat of the moment that they later wish had never been said. Later on, each may seek to undo the harm their words inflicted. The sudden death of your husband robbed you of that opportunity. While you may have stopped loving your husband, you did not have the opportunity to take back the hurtful things you said, but may not have really meant. The circumstances of your husband's burial suggest that much was said that was meant only to hurt.

While you are no longer married, you need to take time to understand your role in a marriage that you were taking active steps to end. The painful divorce process offers the chance to clear up our own confusion about what went wrong in the marriage. You lost that opportunity. These complicated feelings might be best explored with counseling. Perhaps you made certain choices during the marriage which you now regret. If so, this would also help explain the confusion. You were extremely angry at your husband before he died. You are still angry with him, but now the opportunity to talk things out or settle things between you is gone forever. Given these strong feelings of anger and loss, be kind and patient with yourself. You need time to understand your feelings and to make sense of what you have experienced.

SECRETS AND SURPRISES: THREE SCENARIOS

My husband, Alexander, was a high school science teacher well respected for the personal interest and concern he took in his students. I knew exactly what kind of interest. Alexander was a pedophile. Protected by lax supervision on the part of school officials, my husband had his share of "interesting friends," as he liked to call his latest underage love interest. His sudden death by heart attack was an answer to my prayers, since I always feared exposure and a lengthy prosecution.

When I arrived at the funeral home shortly before calling hours were to begin, I found a strange woman kneeling at the casket sobbing. This strange woman was no stranger to my late husband. I found out she was George's girlfriend of several years! I'm totally speechless.

After going through all the financial records and legal papers that I had never seen until my husband's death, I was shocked to learn that my husband had been stealing from me for years. My retirement savings that I turned over to him for investment purposes had dwindled down to nothing. He even cashed in the life insurance.

There have been countless versions of these stories—the woman who discovered a stash of pornography when she cleaned out her husband's office or the wife who found out that her late husband had not lost money in the stock market but rather had a serious gambling problem. Men you would never imagine as having an affair have been found to have kept mistresses in nice apartments or condos. Regardless of how you discovered your ex's misdeeds or even if you already were aware of his "goings on," this proof can exert some very basic changes in the way you feel about your late husband, someone you thought you knew so well.

Depending on his wicked deed, you may feel any or all of these emotions: shock, devastation, betrayal, humiliation. Remember that you are the victim. Do not berate yourself for not knowing about this part of your husband's life. He invested a great deal of time and energy in keeping this part of his life a secret from you.

Even though you may have been relieved by your husband's death because you knew he had some scary habits, you'll still need to purge some feelings. Keeping a diary or a journal might be especially helpful to you. As you get a better grasp on your emotions, you'll find more appropriate ways to express these feelings.

WHAT TO DO IF YOUR SPOUSE DIES SUDDENLY

Begin by contacting the Social Security Administration anytime at *www.ssa.gov* or at their toll-free number, 1-800-772-1213, on any business day between the hours of 7:00 A.M. and 7:00 P.M. Some businesses advertise that they can provide name changes, social security cards, or earnings statements for a fee. Do not use such services. You can get all these services free from the Social Security Administration.

If you have no credit in your own name, this should be among your first priorities. To build a credit record, you may want to apply for a charge card at a local store or small loan at a lending institution. Ask if the creditor reports transactions to a credit bureau. If they do and if you pay back your debts regularly, you will build a good credit history. You could also consider applying for a secured credit card. In this case, you deposit a certain amount of cash with the credit card issuer in return for a credit line of the same size. If you default on your credit card payments, the bank can seize enough money from your deposit to cover your debt. You can obtain a list of secured credit card issuers from the BankCard Holders of America (BHA) by sending a check or money order for $4.00 to "Secured Credit Card List" BHA Customer Service, 524 Branch Drive, Salem, VA 24153. Avoid calling any "900" phone numbers. You pay for calls with a "900" prefix, and you may never receive a credit card.

Contact your husband's employer in writing regarding his employee benefits and inform them of your husband's death. Include the date of death, your husband's Social Security number, and a copy of the death certificate. Request information about the benefits you should expect to receive, such as 401(k), profit sharing, and life insurance or retirement benefits, and the steps you must take to begin to receive payments.

Under federal law, as a provision of the Comprehensive Omnibus Budget Reconciliation Act (COBRA), you are eligible to continue health insurance coverage under your spouse's health insurance plan for three years at the same price the employer would have paid, plus a small administration fee. You will have to pay premiums, which you might not have had to pay when your spouse was alive. However, you will receive group insurance rates, which will be far lower than you could qualify for as an individual. Furthermore, your dependent children must continue to be covered under your late husband's health insurance policy, and the premiums must be paid under the same terms. Coverage under COBRA is not automatic. You must notify your late husband's employer within sixty days or you lose your right to coverage.

If enrollment under the provisions of COBRA is not available to you, consider enrolling in a Health Maintenance Organization (HMO) or Preferred Provider Organization (PPO). Doing without health insurance coverage is a terrible financial gamble. Avoid this gamble if at all possible.

Determine Your Financial Needs

Your financial needs and goals will depend on many different factors. Much will depend on your age, the age of your children, your employment history and assets, and personal needs and desires. You will make costly mistakes if you do not have a plan. Your plan will depend on what your goals are and what assets are available to you. Following are four tips for protecting your worth:

◆ Hire a lawyer and an accountant you trust. Do not be afraid to ask people you like and respect for their recommendations. These hiring decisions are critical and unfortunately must be made at a time when you feel least able to cope. Invest the time and energy in interviewing people until you find the right fit. Ask about their experience in cases such as yours. Do not be shy about asking about fees and other costs.

◆ Beware of scams. You may be receiving a large lump sum of money from life insurance. Con artists are careful readers of the obituaries; expect to be on the receiving end of a lot of sales pitches and possible con games.

If something sounds too good to be true, it is! Anytime someone is trying to rush you into anything should be a clear signal to you to pull back and reconsider.

- Don't buy, sell, or invest in anything right away. You are coping with enough without having to deal with major decisions such as selling your home to buy a smaller house or condo, investing in hot stocks, or lending money.

- Keep your financial worth private. Many widows have regretted telling their children exactly how much money they had. Older children rarely have any idea how much money is needed to carry on with daily living and feel that the money their mother now has is sufficient to finance any particular whim. Younger children need to be reassured that their needs will be met.

- Additionally, widows who have discussed their assets with relatives or friends were immediately besieged with requests for loans or urged to invest in a "hot stock" or bet a sure thing at the track. Your best advice? Be somewhat vague about your money with friends, children, and relatives.

Review All Your Insurance Needs

In addition to your health insurance coverage, you also need to review your car, life, homeowners, and disability coverage. Homeowners and car insurance may have been under your husband's name and may need to be changed. You should have life insurance coverage for

yourself as part of your overall financial plan.

Revise Your Will

Among your first tasks will be to revise your will and to appoint a guardian for your children in case of your death. After you have settled these matters, tell your children of the plans you have made. Reassure them, particularly if they are young and their father's death was sudden and unexpected, that it is very unlikely that you will die also. This will be a difficult conversation with your children. Set aside a time so that it can occur without interruption and with ample time for all family members to say how they feel. Reactions such as crying are to be expected. However, your ability to answer your children's unexpressed fear about what would happen if you died will be an enormous comfort and an immeasurable aid in their healing.

What to Do about the Death Certificate

Death certificates are issued by the municipality or county in which your husband died. Where your husband died and where you live may be entirely separate locations. You will need a copy of your husband's death certificate to complete much of the business of settling the estate.

These copies need to be what are called "original copies," meaning that they are photostatic copies with the official seal of the issuing government office on them. Ask for ten copies so that you are not caught short.

Keep these copies in a safe place that is readily accessible to you but not where you have to look at them every five minutes. You do not need the constant reminder.

HELPING YOUR CHILDREN FACE THE LOSS OF THEIR FATHER

There will be little of greater concern to you than helping your children deal with the devastating loss of their father. No matter what the age of your children, their feelings and concerns will require much patient understanding and the healing power of time. Here are some thoughts to help you and your children face this painful loss together:

♦ *Let your children teach you about their experience of grief.* No one's love for anyone else is exactly like someone else's. Your child loved his father in a unique and special way. Nobody knows how your child is feeling because nobody else is your child. Help your child find ways to express how he feels and then really listen.

♦ *Explain that death is natural.* Death is not a punishment, nor is it a horrible

experience only for some. Know that not every child will understand death in the same way. Never tell a child that people die because they are bad or that death is like sleeping. You can imagine what young children would do with that information.

♦ *Don't force your kids to understand death.* It is a mysterious stage in the life cycle, and although death is now a secret to us, we all eventually experience it. Some families rely on long-standing cultural traditions about how grief and death should be handled. In other families, death is a forbidden topic. It's best to be available to answer the sensitive questions that your child will pose. But it is important, too, to be able to say simply, "I just don't know."

♦ *Don't expect sudden understanding about God when you explain your religious views about death.* Teaching abstract spiritual and religious concepts is no easy task. As children mature, they are able to understand more and more. While we can teach only what we believe, be careful not to expect too much of yourself. It is a misuse of religious faith to tell a child that a loved one "is in a better place, so it is wrong to feel sad." At the same time, you need not feel guilty or inadequate if you are unable to give specific explanations of God and heaven or whatever your specific beliefs are. Openness to mystery is valuable not only in teaching about death, but also in teaching anything about life.

♦ *Let time help.* Healing is a process, not an event. Children need to face the pain before they can heal, and this takes a long time. Telling children to be strong and get over it is cruel. You may want your children to give the appearance that all is well again so that you can hide from your own pain. But unexpressed grief results in unproductive and harmful behaviors, such as fighting with friends, failing at schoolwork, and demonstrating unsafe and poor behavior. Your children need time.

◆ *Tell the truth.* Children can almost always cope with what they know. Handling what they do not know is the problem. Children will fill in the empty spaces of what they are told with their imaginations. What children imagine is usually far worse than the truth. When children discover that they have been lied to, they feel humiliated and unloved. Lying gives children the message that it is okay to be dishonest at the very times when families should be pulling together.

◆ *Don't wait for one big "tell-all."* Encourage your children to ask questions as they need to ask them. Often children will repeat the same question over and over again. You will be unable to answer some questions. This does not matter. What does matter is that you treat your children's questions with respect and courtesy and try to answer them as honestly as possible.

◆ *Assure your children that they are not responsible.* Children often believe that their thoughts can cause something to happen. For example, a younger child may think that because she constantly left her skates out for her father to trip over that she caused

her father's heart attack. An older child might feel responsible because he secretly wished his father would die for not letting him play video games until his homework was done. Children need to be reassured that nothing they did or thought caused their father to die.

◆ *Expect some physical distress.* Children's bodies will react to the experience of grief. Your child may complain of fatigue, stomach aches, sore throats, or trouble sleeping. You may be told that he is visiting the school nurse with greater frequency. Do not tell your child it is all in his head. He really does feel sick. These physical symptoms are the result of the stress this loss has placed upon your child. He needs support, understanding, and a little extra love and attention. If your child's physical problems persist, it is a good idea to talk the situation over with your pediatrician or family physician.

◆ *Babies need extra comfort, too.* Infants and toddlers are not too young to understand. If infants can give and receive love, then they can certainly grieve. Grieving in children of this age often takes the form of sleep disturbance, regressive behavior like thumb-sucking or bed-wetting,

and strong emotional outbursts. It is important to support and nurture grieving young children, or their capacity to develop trust in the world around them will be greatly diminished. Hugging, holding, and playing with young children are the best ways to offer comfort and support.

- *Dispel the myth that loss means messed-up kids in later life.* The loss of a parent does not automatically lead to maladjustment in adult life. Although many people will take the attitude that your child will be forever emotionally crippled by his father's death, this is simply not true. What will determine your child's adjustment is how your child is helped to mourn this loss. If your child is allowed to express his feelings, ask the questions he needs to ask, and receive the guidance and love he needs, his chances for a meaningful and happy life are good. If your child is not allowed to grieve or is forced to keep to some grief timetable or told that crying or other expressions of feelings are signs of weakness, then no doubt there will be lasting emotional scars.

- *Maintain consistency at home.* Try to keep the household routines as stable as possible. Despite all that you must cope with, it is important that you maintain regular mealtimes and bedtimes. Try to keep the demands on yourself as simple as possible. Gourmet meals are not needed, but your children will be reassured by the order and routine you maintain in their lives.

- *Be patient.* Do not work toward the goal of having your child "get over

it." Children do not "get over" the loss of a father. They learn to live with it, reconcile themselves to it, and make peace with it. Your children will come to the realization that their world is different without their father. As they become more reconciled to his loss, they will look ahead with hope and begin to make plans for the future. They will not forget their father even as their lives go on without him. This process will require patience.

SURVIVING HOLIDAYS AND BIRTHDAYS

That first round of birthdays and holidays after your husband's death is very hard. It is impossible not to remember the special birthday cake your husband baked or the special surprise he arranged last Christmas. There is no reason to forget. Treasure the memory. At the same time, it is important to create new memories. This does not mean that you should completely change all your holiday routines and rituals. Nobody has the emotional energy for that. What you do want to do is to introduce one slightly different twist to the old routines—even something simple like an evening of cookie baking or making a few new ornaments for the tree.

Dad's birthday may bring much remembrance. The first few Father's Days might be even rougher than his birthday. It is best to anticipate these days and make some kind of plan about how to spend the day. One husband and father is well remembered on his birthday by a secret good deed done by each of his children and their mother. Around the dinner table, plans are made and reports of the good deed are shared. Their father's generous spirit is carried on. Instead of sorrowful tears, Dad's birthday is a time of sharing and doing good for others.

YOUR CHANGING SOCIAL LIFE

Immediately after your husband dies, you may find yourself receiving many invitations. After a short while, many of these invitations may stop. The sorry news is that you are probably not as welcome in your previous circle of married friends now that you are a widow. Some people really do consider an "extra woman" a social liability. In short, you will quickly discover who your true friends are. Your true friends will continue to include you in their plans. Those who are not your true friends will loudly proclaim their desire to get together when they happen to run into you at the supermarket, but somehow it will never happen. It is important that you reciprocate the invitations you do receive, even in a limited way. Nobody is expecting you to throw a grand party, but a simple coffee and dessert for a few friends will lift your spirits.

Probably before you have really thought about dating, someone will ask you out or one of your friends or coworkers will want to fix you up with someone. This will be a journey back into the awkwardness you thought you had left behind at fourteen. It feels funny to be having dinner or going to the movies with a stranger. Like that first plunge into the cold ocean, the first date will be the hardest. Take the risk. We are talking about an evening here, not a lifetime commitment.

Remember, however, that your children's feelings and sensitivities need to be kept uppermost in your mind. Your children might be ready to have you date—so ready, in fact, that they ask your date if he would like to be their new daddy. Or they may be so unready to have you date that they embarrass both you and themselves by their rotten behavior when he comes to pick you up. Both these behaviors are clear signals that your children are not ready to participate in your social life even as simple bystanders.

DATING AND SEX

It is best to keep your dating life, particularly in its early casual stages, separate from your children. This means meeting him at the restaurant or having him pick you up at work. If you are dating a "grown-up," he will surely understand your need to protect your children. If he gives you a hard time, this is your first clue that he is probably not worth your time.

Having sex may be the furthest thing from your mind as you take your first timid steps into the dating world. This does not mean that sex is the furthest thing from your date's mind. Be sure you are not sending mixed signals. For example, agreeing to return to his house or apartment after dinner may indicate to him that you are physically interested. If you are not, you need to let him know.

Your first sexual encounter will bring forth many confusing emotions. There is no reason to feel guilty that you want sexual gratification. After all, your husband may be dead, but you are not. Only you know when you are going to be ready, and no one can tell you what is right for you. The best advice is to think carefully before you have sex with someone new. Be clear in your mind about why you are choosing this person and why this feels like the right thing to do now. You need to take responsibility for birth control and practice safe sex.

When you've taken responsibility for your sexual needs, you can allow yourself to enjoy the rest.

DO'S AND DON'TS FOR WIDOWED MOTHERS

* **Do** remember that there is a life to be had without your husband. Building that new life does not diminish the love you shared.

* **Do** not be harsh with yourself if you feel only relief at your husband's death. If this is what you feel, you most likely have good reasons. Put the pain behind you and work toward a healthier, more satisfying life.

* **Do** not project too far into the future. Many things you are worried about today will never happen. Many things will happen over which you will have no control. Focus on today.

* **Do** make fun. Your children and you need the simple pleasures of family life. Cuddle up together on the couch and watch a movie. Make cookies. Take a walk to enjoy the sunshine.

* **Don't** sentence yourself to death by putting up too many walls. Yes, you are vulnerable to future pain, but that also means you are alive.

* **Do** treasure your memories of your husband and allow your children to do the same.

* **Do** make new happy memories together as a family. You cannot keep your home as

a shrine to your late husband or celebrate every holiday in his memory.

* **Don't** try to find an instant replacement or substitute for your husband. A new man will not cure the pain or fill the void of your husband's death. He might be a distraction for you now, but you still need to work through the process of mourning.

* **Don't** let the world take advantage of you. Beware of scams and get-rich-quick schemes. Know that there are men out there who prey on lonely widows. They will try to win your heart to get your money.

* **Do** be open to new opportunities and adventures. The single life is filled with pleasures and excitement if you can open yourself up to the endless possibilities.

* **Do** reassure your child that no angry thought or deed can cause someone to die. People die because they were sick, or injured, or because they got old, but never because of an angry thought or heated words.

* **Do** let your children grieve. Avoid trying to distract them from their feelings. Grieving is a necessary part of life, since all living beings from time to time will experience loss.

YOUR FIRST FAMILY VENTURE WITHOUT DAD

This will be my first summer traveling alone with my two children. My husband used to arrange our vacations, plan the travel routes, and decide where we would all stay. He died two years ago, and I just haven't had the motivation to venture out. I need some encouragement about getting out there and taking over his job.

Don't feel incompetent because your husband arranged your family trips as professionally as a travel agent. You may do a different job. Yet chances are, if you really consider what you and your kids would like to do and not what you think your husband would have wanted, you'll be on the right road in no time. Remember, men and women have different outlooks when it comes to traveling. We've all met the guys who refuse to ask for directions and only rely on outdated maps and moms who want to check their route by asking every gas station attendant for shortcuts.

Think of this as a new venture for you and your kids. Don't try to revisit all the same destinations you did when your husband was alive unless these are places that you truly want to see. For example, were beach trips something your husband loved but, honestly, you could have done without the globs of sun block and the sand sticking around for weeks in the car? Try something different that you and your children might enjoy such as checking out a dude ranch or spending a week in the mountains. If you're not that adventurous, then stick to something familiar, but remember, it doesn't have to be a play-by-play recreation of what your earlier vacations were like. You're bound for disappointment if you have unrealistic expectations.

If you're traveling by car, you have a great opportunity to talk about Dad. Ask the kids if they think Dad would enjoy this trip. Say something like, "Your dad would laugh if he could see us trying to bait our own hooks" or "I'll bet Dad wouldn't enjoy the mountains as much as we do because he liked the hot weather." It's okay to reminisce about previous travels, but don't let the talk turn into negative comparisons. Remember, you're not trying to "please" Dad. Rather you want to bring him along in your thoughts.

PART 2

BECOMING YOUR OWN BEST PARTNER

8

Pregnant? Handling the News

As much as the experience of pregnancy and childbirth bonds us as women and make us part of the wondrous act of bringing new life into the world, not every woman has the same reaction once the news has sunk in a bit. For some younger women, the news is devastating. The emotional maturity as well as the financial and family support needed to handle this event responsibly may just not be there. For many of these women, motherhood is unthinkable at this time in their lives, and so they may choose to terminate the pregnancy. Teenagers may offer their child up for adoption or consider having their parents or other relatives raise their child. For women who are indecisive and debate whether parenthood now is possible, the choice of whether or not to continue the pregnancy can be agonizing. Still, others may follow "I'm what" with "it's about time," particularly if they have been deliberately trying to get pregnant.

Whatever your initial reaction to the news, it's plausible to be "surprised" no matter how sure you thought you were. What is important, however, is that you don't let other people's values dictate what is right or wrong for you, but rather let your heart and your conscience decide what is best. This decision can be more stressful for those who are fairly sure they want a child with or without Mr. Right, but are getting less than supportive messages from family and friends. Find people who are willing to listen to your feelings.

No matter what you see in home pregnancy tests ads, remember that many women react to the news with mixed feelings, whether married or single. You're not alone. Even if this is a planned pregnancy, you may have mixed feelings now that you've successfully conceived.

YOUR TEST IS POSITIVE, BUT HE'S NOT

You've been a little nauseous lately, a little tired and irritable, or maybe your breasts feel slightly tender. Perhaps you just feel a wee bit different than you normally do when you are expecting your period. Even though you are not particularly late, you get a strong feeling (a feeling that you're desperately trying to ignore, of course) that something is happening to your body. Something just makes you say no to that glass of wine with dinner. You tell yourself that if you don't get your period in a few days that you will give yourself a pregnancy test, but you reassure yourself that you are probably not pregnant. But then, if you are, it's not such a bad idea. You would like a child one day, right? It's just that your partner or whomever you've been spending time with may not welcome the news the same way you had hoped. Maybe your partner isn't good news anyway.

You hold your breath as you wait for the little line or dot to show up in the applicator of your home pregnancy test. There it is, and even if you had entertained fleeting thoughts that you could be ever so slightly pregnant, you're now totally dumbfounded. Even though you know the chances of a false positive are extremely small, you run out and buy four more kits. Maybe you even go to a doctor to confirm the results. Like most MOMs—Mothers Outside of Marriage—you didn't actively plan this baby. Your feelings may be influenced by how much involvement the father wants.

If You're Considering Abortion

If you've just learned that you're pregnant and you have no commitment from the father, you may be asking yourself whether or not to abort. You're not the only person who has asked

herself this question, but you are the only person who can answer it.

My pregnancy was really an accident. I used birth control pills up until six months before I became pregnant and relied on spermicides after that. I'm worried that because I became pregnant while using spermicides that it may affect my baby. I want to have this baby but am concerned about spermicides or even the pill damaging the embryo.

More than one-half million women become pregnant each year while using spermicides, and many continue to use them even a few weeks into their unknown pregnancy. No one knows for sure, but it appears that if so many women conceive this way without risk to the baby that it is safe to conclude that there is not much to worry about. If you're really concerned, there are tests that can detect abnormalities early. Discuss your concerns immediately with your doctor. By the way, you don't need to worry about the oral contraceptive usage because you stopped taking birth control pills way in advance of the recommended time to stop.

Bouncing Between Joy and Heartache

Although you may have been initially terrified at the news of your pregnancy, like most single mothers, you decided to keep and raise your baby. Although their pregnancies were neither planned nor purely accidental, MOMs usually report wanting a child. These women's emotions bounce between joy and heartache, however, because they had to endure abandonment, rejection, and other mostly unexpected reactions by the father.

If you have conceived through donor insemination, you may still have mixed feelings about becoming a mother. Congratulations are in order here. Even when physiological changes are causing you to feel strange or uncertain about your decision, remember all women go through confusing feelings during the early stages of pregnancy. Don't underestimate those hormone fluctuations!

IF YOU THOUGHT YOUR PARTNER NEEDED A "SHOVE"

My boyfriend of six years and I can't seem to make the commitment. I thought that when he learned I was pregnant that this would be the push we both needed. But he's acting strange, and I'm not sure if he's even going to stay around.

While it is true that strong relationships often need a little nudge to push them toward making the big "C," don't expect your partner to make a commitment to parenthood if his commitment to you was always lacking. The best way to deal with no reaction, a confused response, or a totally negative or angry reaction from the father is to start focusing more on your life, not his.

"MY PARTNER CAN'T DECIDE HOW HE FEELS ABOUT MY PREGNANCY. . . ."

My live-in partner of two years is undecided about my pregnancy. He says he loves me but doesn't know what to do. I feel like my life is on hold while waiting for him to make up his mind. I had an abortion last year and don't want another one.

It's difficult enough to decide whether and when to become a mother, let alone be uncertain about whether your partner wants to be a father. Again, the level of devotion this person has demonstrated to you during your relationship should be an indicator of how much you should let his reactions affect your decision. For example, wonderful as he is, if this man has a history of unfulfilled promises, then you may be relying too much on his input. Conversely, if this is a man who gives serious thought to every aspect of his life, then be sensitive to the fact that news like this may unbalance him. Surprise pregnancies can often frighten men because they feel that they have lost control over a significant aspect of their life. With time, however, he can get used to the news, and you can both sit down and work out a plan. Still, there is a risk that he may not respond to the news of your pregnancy the way you had hoped. It is for this reason that women are encouraged to look toward motherhood with a can-do attitude, regardless of whether a man is in the picture.

Do keep in mind, however, that some men are delighted with the news of impending fatherhood, although they may not initially show it. This man knows his life will be irrevocably and forever changed. That insight alone will give any mature guy pause for thought. Don't necessarily expect his reaction to resemble yours.

As much as you think you know a person, when you tell the father of your baby-to-be the news of your pregnancy, be prepared for anything. Some women who expect their boyfriends to be elated by the news are blown away to hear statements like "You must be nuts to think that I would marry you" or "How could you do this to me? I'll never give you a dime" or "Get an abortion, or get out!"

It's natural for you to feel ashamed or embarrassed that you could have gotten so close to someone and know so very little about him. After all, they say that the way a couple handles a crisis is what determines whether the relationship will strengthen or deteriorate. Even for engaged women, when a surprise pregnancy is announced to the fiancé, the reaction can be so judgmental and disapproving that these women often wonder why they didn't see any red flags before. It's also very common for a man with whom you've had a brief sexual encounter, or even a long-term sexual relationship, to respond angrily with accusations that you were setting him up. You may hear comments like "It's not my baby," which can make you feel that much more humiliated.

What you need now is emotional support, not verbal assaults. Try to get support from friends and family. Investigate online or "live" support groups. You are not alone in feeling confused and dismayed. Don't set yourself up for more pressure or stress by continuing nowhere conversations with the baby's father. You can, however, be open to the possibility that he may grow to accept the news. It's not uncommon to hear men admit that at first they were unenthusiastic when learning about their girlfriend's pregnancy but later embraced fatherhood without reservation. It's also pretty common that after a man decides to accept the responsibility of fatherhood that the mother-to-be decides she would be better off without him.

If your partner insists you have an abortion, do not succumb to pressure or react hastily—ultimately this is your decision. You will want to discuss your options with your doctor, particularly if you are in midlife or have compromised fertility or other medical issues. Now is the time to evaluate whether this relationship or your desire to have a child is more important to you. No women should have an abortion because a man tells her to.

HAVE YOU RUINED HIS LIFE?

My partner has accused me of trying to ruin his life by becoming pregnant. I feel so upset about this because it isn't true.

Don't let your partner's accusations set you up for a guilt attack. You are not ruining anyone's life, and you are not responsible for his feelings. Your baby's father may be trying to assuage his own guilt about not accepting his responsibility in this pregnancy. This is not to say that he has to burst into a chorus of "Thank Heaven for Little Girls." He need not tell you he's overjoyed when it isn't true. A man, who despite his uncertainty about whether fatherhood is right for him, should be willing to talk rationally. Discussing your feelings calmly and openly is a sure indication of responsibility and maturity—certainly necessary traits for any prospective parent.

Should You Stay with the Baby's Father?

No matter how rocky your relationship, you may simply be staying with the baby's father because, although he was horrified at the news, he didn't rush out and catch the first flight out of town. Counseling can help you decide whether to work it out or move on. Many women still buy into the two-parent ideal and feel they are being unfair to their children by choosing single motherhood. At the same time, however, you know you deserve better than to stay in a relationship that requires constant struggle and possibly a disproportionate amount of compromise. Ending the relationship does not mean that there will be no involvement with the child's father. It just means that what once was the traditional form of parenting most likely won't happen.

If Your Partner Leaves

If your partner can't or doesn't want to deal with the responsibility of fatherhood, he may tell you that:

- He feels tricked.

- He wants you to choose between having an abortion and losing him.

- He thinks you should do what you want.

- He feels he is not ready to be a father.

- He has been through this before and may have another child somewhere.

Unfortunately, these reactions are also the toughest to accept. Try not to become unglued by these comments. Believe it or not, in most cases, the father may have reasons for being unable to stay in this changing relationship that have absolutely nothing to do with you or your child. Don't berate yourself because, as hard as it is to accept this, it's really not a personal attack on you.

RIDING THE EMOTIONAL ROLLER COASTER

Even though you know that you are pregnant, you may periodically forget. Like many single women who claimed they wanted a child someday, you didn't expect it to be like this. Hearing the news from your doctor doesn't necessarily mean that you have accepted the reality of being pregnant.

In a diary she kept during pregnancy, one mother reported how it felt when she first realized she was pregnant. No, it wasn't after the blue line appeared on the pregnancy test or right after her doctor told her she didn't have food poisoning. It was one morning, months later, when she woke up and realized she was very, very pregnant. Wherever she went, it seemed that her blossoming belly arrived there first. It entered the elevator before she did, complained loudly at any uncomfortable moves, and was the first to snuggle down at night. "That's when I knew I had company that was going to stay for a while."

Of course, you already "know" that you're pregnant. After all, you've been told by more than one person, you've been shopping for maternity clothes, it's been all your mother thinks about, and you probably have satisfied some strange food cravings or eaten things you would never have let sit on your plate before. But one day the part of your brain that dictates how you respond or react to things figures out that you're pregnant, too, and all of a sudden you realize that you really are going to have a baby. In the months before, you had been going through the motions of being pregnant because only your rational self knew that you were. The good news about the rest of you catching up with this information is that now you can be comfortable with your pregnancy and start enjoying it.

You don't learn to accept your pregnancy by taking an intensive training course. Acceptance of this momentous life event is a gradual process requiring what you know in your head and what you have come to believe in your heart to join together. Every mother experiences this acceptance in a gradual way, no matter what her circumstances. You can help this process to take shape by talking about your pregnancy with close friends or family, or if you don't

have much local support, join an online forum for single pregnant moms on the Internet. Check out the message boards at *www.singlemothers.org*, *www.singlerose .com*, or *www.singleparentsnetwork.com*.

Enjoy Your Pregnancy!

There is an old saying that you can spot a pregnant woman even if you only see her from the shoulders up. She has a glow and a look of happiness. Well, the glow part might be true, but the look of happiness can vary from woman to woman.

Even women who have desperately tried to become pregnant don't always walk around with a beatific smile on their faces, especially if their pregnancy brings with it nausea, physical discomfort, and swelling. Let's face it: along with the dreamy thoughts of a sweet-smelling, cuddly baby to look forward to are sobering moments filled with such petty annoyances as constant urinating, miscalculating door openings, and those little hemorrhoids you thought only other people got.

But at those times when you do experience that lovely fullness, the deep and soothing satisfaction that was never achieved through eating or even through sex will now seem to transcend all problems of life on Earth. If you allow yourself to bask in the feeling, you, too, can be one of those women who rattle on interminably about how her pregnancy is joy and bliss and, okay, some irritability, too. Most women report that their pregnancy months allowed them to get away with varying degrees of assertiveness they never before would have dared. For example, now you can demand a seat on the bus and still be looked upon as a "lady." You can avoid waiting at restaurants, airports, crowded theaters, and even on line at grocery stores, if you practice some subtle yet feminine grunting. Everyone loves a pregnant woman!

Grieving

If you're pining over your child's absent father or just grieving that you are single, allow yourself your feelings. You may find it helpful to look on the positive side by focusing on:

♦ Increasing your confidence, self-reliance, and peace. This time alone can be one of growth. A healthier set of emotions can emerge just as your child is growing strong and healthy inside you.

♦ Empowering yourself. Take this time to read up on your legal rights. Visit a law library and educate yourself. (Who knows, maybe some of this will filter through to your baby, the future lawyer!)

♦ Reminding yourself that you are part of a fast-growing group of women. Remember, over half of all first births are to single women. Don't let yourself forget that you aren't alone.

♦ Learning what can be changed, what must be accepted, and how you can grow wiser by recognizing one from the other. You may want to keep the lines of communication open with the father, but if your expectations exceed what he is able to give, be careful. Don't focus on his life—work on yours.

♦ Taking a positive action or two. Channel your anger or grief into constructive areas like working out in an expectant moms' class, prepar-

ing your child's room, reading about childbirth, or taking daily walks.

♦ Knowing that there are just no guarantees in life. But the ability to rely on yourself is as close as you can get.

♦ Accepting your pregnancy. Visualize yourself and your child together. Do not think only about snuggling with an infant whose helplessness and total dependency might be overwhelming to you now. Think about having conversations with your child, teaching your child the skills you have mastered, and sharing in activities you enjoy. Imagine you and your child playing together at the beach.

TELLING OTHERS YOU'RE PREGNANT

Tell the people capable of sharing your joy first. This might mean telling the talkative elderly woman who rides the elevator with you every morning, the chatty mailroom clerk, or the man behind the deli counter, even before telling your mother or sister. Why? The joyful responses from friendly acquaintances will fortify you against the disapproving reactions you may experience from others. Don't feel that only unmarried mothers receive negative reactions. Comments ranging from "How can you bring another human being into this sick world?" to "Aren't you concerned about overpopulation?" are routine for married women, too. Of course, if your family will be overjoyed, tell them first.

I'm worried about telling my boss about my pregnancy. What do I need to know?

Know your rights and options before telling your employer. Choose an appropriate time, and share your plans with him or her in a calm and logical fashion. Your boss may not be overjoyed initially, but don't take this to heart. It may mean that he is concerned about your absence from the workforce, as he would be with any productive employee.

If your boss cuts your hours, demotes you, or terminates you and you believe it is because you are unmarried and pregnant or simply because you are pregnant, you have rights. The Equal Employment Opportunity Commission states that discrimination on the basis of pregnancy, childbirth, or related medical conditions constitutes unlawful sex discrimination. Women affected by pregnancy or related conditions must be treated in the same manner as other applicants or employees with similar abilities or limitations. This means that your boss cannot treat a married

---

COMEBACKS TO REMEMBER—JUST IN CASE

Some people make inappropriate remarks or ask rude questions of unmarried expectant mothers without realizing it. Here are some snappy comebacks to offhand comments about your situation:

• *"I just heard you were pregnant. I didn't even know you were married!"* "I'm not married. I hope I'm still pregnant!"

• *"Oh, you poor thing, carrying this baby all by yourself. How do you do it?"* "I think all women carry babies by themselves, don't they?"

• *"Are you sure you know who the baby's father is?"* "No less sure than you are!"

• *"How are you going to have a baby all by yourself?"* "Oh I'm not. I'm having it in a hospital with a doctor, my labor coach, and pain medication . . . just in case!"

• *"You need to find the father of that child right now!"* "Well, if you really need him, here's his address." "How? Check the lost and found?" "But it took forever to get rid of him!"

• *"You need to find a father for that child right now!"* "Okay, but I didn't know I lost one." "Great. Got any tips (and a hot dress I could borrow)?"

• *"Don't you think it's cruel to bring a baby into the world without a father?"* "Actually, I think it's far worse to be brought into the world with the kind of men some children must endure as fathers."

• *"Isn't it selfish depriving your child of a father?"* "In this case I think I'm being generous!" "No, he's getting a mother who really wants him!"

• *"What a cute baby! I'll bet she's daddy's little girl."* "Thanks! But she's her own little girl."

• *"You're not married! How'd you manage to get pregnant?"* A good stare should suffice if an adult asks you this. If a child does, it's best to refer her to her mother.

pregnant employee differently from the way he treats you. Contact your local Equal Employment Opportunity Commission office for more information on hiring, pregnancy and maternity leave, child care, health insurance, fringe benefits, and filing charges of discrimination.

Dealing with Questions about the Father

As you begin to "show," people will start asking you many questions. Strangers on the street will come up to you and pat you on the belly. Nothing in the world attracts more attention than a pregnant woman, except maybe a new baby.

You might be walking down the street one day, and an old acquaintance runs into you and says, "Congratulations! I didn't even know you were married!" Many women find that the second trimester of pregnancy is the easiest; so probably you will be relaxed enough to respond appropriately. You can either ignore the comment and smile graciously, or if you're feeling whimsical at the moment, you might remark, "Well, I had no idea that I was married either!" Depending on the attitude of the person commenting on your marital status, it would be best not to be sarcastic or defensive, but rather to be straightforward and confident. Let people know that their goodwill is helpful and appreciated.

FAMILY PRESSURES AND OTHER REALITIES

My mother and sister keep urging me to marry the father of my child, which is totally out of the question. For that matter, they would have me marry any man with a pulse, just to give my child a "name."

Sometimes parents and siblings are so unable to accept that you will be having a baby on your own that they don't realize they are putting pressure on you. Resist their pushy yet well-meaning efforts by explaining that the baby's father and you are not able to have the kind of relationship a sound marriage requires. Share with your family your plans for taking care of this child on your own. Disclose only what feels comfortable. For example, if the father is to be involved in some way, you may wish to explain what exactly his involvement will entail.

Your decision to have a baby on your own is a new experience for some families, and it is difficult for some families to accept the idea. In fact, you will need to be calm and rational because your news may be met with irrational behavior on their part. Don't try to change them; just seek their tolerance, if not their acceptance and support. Let them know that you wish they would respect your decision, but if they don't, you can bet that threatening them with an ultimatum such as, "If you don't accept my decision, then you'll never see the baby" or "I won't be part of this family anymore" won't work either.

Requesting Assistance from Your Family

It's a good idea, early in your pregnancy, to determine the amount of help, if any, you can expect from your family. The important thing is not to make assumptions about what family members are willing to do. For example, just because your sister is great with her three little ones and really seems to enjoy staying home with them does not mean automatically that she will be happy to watch your baby so that you can return to work. She may be counting the months until she can go back to work herself, at least part-time, or she may be on "kid overload" and not want the responsibility of another baby to care for even during the day. Your mother may share your joy at the impending arrival of the baby, but that does not mean she wants to be on twenty-four-hour-a-day backup babysitting call.

Not surprisingly, many single mothers find themselves strapped for cash and consider borrowing money from their families. This is not necessarily the most promising start to an independent life, but it is not unusual. Many married couples rely on family members for financial support during the first few years, particularly if there are unexpected events like pregnancy or job layoffs. If your parents or other family members need convincing that your decision to become a single mother is the best one, you might want to investigate other loan sources before asking your family. If you must borrow money from your family, make a businesslike arrangement with them. Agree upon the amount, method of payment, payment schedule, and late charges, if any. This arrangement allows your independence and keeps you in control of your own life.

Don't Resent Couples

A number of women who were in relationships that came to an abrupt halt because of the pregnancy find that they often look at couples and wonder why their own partners couldn't handle pregnancy and parenthood. Combined with the early rush of pregnancy hormones, insufficient time to grieve the lost relationship can contribute to feeling angry or resentful

of other apparently thriving relationships. Since we hold so dear this image of the overjoyed new mother blissfully residing with her adoring husband, it's difficult to think realistically about the quality of the relationship the couples we spend so much time envying really enjoy.

Many couples are not as happy as they seem. In fact, a great number of women may actually resent the freedom you are enjoying in addition to the blessing you have brought into your own life with the expected arrival of your new baby. Rather than waste energy resenting couples whose happiness and contentment you envy, make the study of these couples a project. Decide what it is in their relationship that you envy or at least find desirable. Are these the very qualities and features that were missing in your previous relationships? Very likely. Decide then that you too deserve what you are witnessing and resolve to seek out these qualities in future relationships.

LETTING GO OF THE DADDY FANTASIES

I can't believe my baby's father isn't around during my pregnancy. He decided he couldn't handle it and left when I was barely in my second month. I get so depressed watching those baby food and diaper commercials and think of all that he is missing out on—the pregnancy, being part of the birth, holding the baby. How do I begin to deal with these feelings in a beneficial and productive way?

You need to be concentrating on yourself and not on how much fun the father is missing. He may be so much on your mind because the end of your relationship was so abrupt. Feelings cannot be shut off like water from a faucet.

Maybe what you should do is get together with some girlfriends and give a good, old-fashioned wake to signal the final goodbye to your ex. Wakes are designed for tears and laughter; so you'll want to cry while remembering the good times and the bad times and laugh at some of the silly times. Some types of wakes are notorious for great food. Eat and drink (sorry, no alcohol for you) and get rid of gifts he may have given you or things he didn't bother to take with him. You will want to keep some special mementos for you and your baby to share. The purpose here is to express your sadness at his departure, say what is in your heart, and then say good-bye. You need this ritual to allow you to go forward. A wonderful and exciting new part of your life is just beginning.

Your Changing Lifestyle

Naturally you are going to have concerns and worries about how the baby will affect your day-to-day life. This means you've thought realistically about how being a mother will profoundly affect every aspect of your life. If you are thinking of motherhood on your own, you need to be prepared and eager to embrace major lifestyle changes. Does this mean only coffee with the girls and never again any all-night parties? Will your conversations with your girlfriends change from talking about men to the best way to burp a baby? Will flannel nightgowns worn in celibacy replace romantic weekends in lingerie? No! What motherhood will

mean is that to have what you want you must prioritize and form a plan. Obviously, your baby is a priority and so is your work or career. But day-to-day priorities can shift, sometimes as often as hourly. Like other single moms, you can learn to be superorganized—a talented manager who is fast on her feet. Don't expect to be perfect or a superwoman! Since humans are incapable of perfection, no child has ever been raised by a perfect mother—and that's probably a good thing.

Worrying about Being a Good Mother

Almost all women worry about this. If you had a super relationship with your mother and believe she did a terrific job raising you, then you may worry that your abilities won't meet the standard she set. If your own mother was neglectful or uninvolved, you may worry that without a role model you will flounder. You may dread the "like mother, like daughter" scenario where you feel doomed to repeat her mistakes or, worse, magnify them.

True, there is no better teacher than good example, but keep in mind that your mother or whoever raised you lacked many of the resources we take for granted today.

If your mother or primary parent was neglectful or abusive, you've no doubt thought about how her behavior has influenced your life and, particularly, how you feel about yourself. Having this baby may partially be your attempt to right the childhood wrongs done to you by providing your child with the guidance and nurturing you never had. It's a worthy goal to incorporate these hard-won lessons into your parenting skills, but be sure to seek guidance, too, if you believe that you can create the happy family you never had and thereby magically erase the pain you experienced growing up.

I'm due in a few months and desperately pray that I can be a better mother to my baby than my alcoholic mother was to me.

Put your aspirations and hopes for this new life in perspective. If you haven't come to terms with the effects of your mother's drinking on your life, join Al-Anon or seek out a therapist experienced with situations like yours. It's never too late to begin healing and renewing your life. In fact, you may benefit more now than you would have when you were younger, when you may not have been as motivated.

HANDLING LAST-MINUTE ANXIETY ABOUT YOUR DECISION

I'm about to become a single mother in a few weeks. As my due date approaches, I'm becoming more and more anxious. I don't know whether I made the right decision or why I couldn't work things out with the baby's father. I alternate between feeling depressed and elated and am now worrying about the kind of mother I will be. I knew I did not want an abortion at thirty-six, knowing it might be my only chance to have a child, but now I'm confused. What's wrong with me?

Nothing is wrong with you. New mom jitters are normal and are part of every healthy woman's first experience of motherhood, whether she is married or not. Any major life-changing event challenges us to question whether or not we are capable adults. You would have reason to worry more if you didn't experience these feelings and didn't place much weight on the importance of becoming a mother. Remember those unpredictable hormone fluctuations early on? Well, they leveled out for a while, but now that you are preparing for childbirth, you can expect those same unpredictable feelings as your due date approaches. So relax; it's not all in your head! Lighten up on yourself for not working things out with the father. There is no way that you can control the feelings and behaviors of someone else.

YOUR PREGNANCY AND CHILDBIRTH OPTIONS

You have many choices when choosing a practitioner to accompany you during your journey through pregnancy and childbirth. But not all choices are good for all women. Choose what works for you financially, emotionally, and practically. Keep in mind that your confidence and ability in childbearing can be greatly enhanced by choosing the right care provider and place of birth.

Home, Hospital, or Birthing Center

You should have your baby wherever you feel safest and most comfortable. The benefits of feeling safe go beyond the obvious, as a strong correlation between fear and painful birth has been established. Most women in the United States have their babies in hospitals, where equipment is available for every contingency that might threaten the survival of mother or baby.

However, medical research shows that, if there are no medical complications, independent childbirth facilities, which will have backup support at a nearby hospital, and home birth are safe options and lower your risk of interventions such as episiotomy and Cesarean section. (Home birth, of course, is only safe with the attendance of a qualified health care provider, which may not be available in your area.) Many hospitals and medical centers today, in an attempt to minimize the clinical aspects of pregnancy and childbirth, offer maternity wards and birthing centers with all the comforts of home. Studies show, however, that these improvements may only be skin deep; if you are deciding between an independent birthing center and a birthing center in a hospital and you want a noninterventionist birth, you can compare the rate of episiotomy at both places and/or the rate of transfer from the independent birthing center (although many transfers may not lead to surgery) with the rate of Cesarean section at the hospital. Investigate the options available in your area, as well as which options are covered by your health insurance.

Obstetrician

Some soon-to-be-mothers feel they receive more qualified care from a board certified obstetrician. An obstetrician is considerably more trained in pregnancy and childbearing than a general practitioner. You certainly want to consider an obstetrician if you have a high-risk pregnancy. The only drawback is that this may be a new relationship, and you may or may not feel as comfortable with this doctor as you do with your familiar physician. You may have to shop around. Some obstetrical practices rotate who you see. You might see the same doctor throughout your pregnancy but then be delivered by whoever is on call. If this setup bothers you, you might want to look for an obstetrician in solo practice, although there is no guarantee that any doctor will be available to you at the precise moment of your delivery. Your gynecologist might also be an obstetrician, but don't assume that this doctor delivers babies just because he or she has provided your gynecological care.

Certified Nurse-Midwife or Certified Midwife

Out of the four million births averaged yearly in the United States, most occur in hospitals with an attending physician. Increasingly, some women are choosing a certified nurse-midwife or a certified midwife for their prenatal care and delivery. In fact, hospital births under the care of midwives increased nationwide.

The personal touch of a nurse-midwife or a midwife is appreciated by many mothers. Most women using midwives feel they have the added support of someone who can take the time to answer all their questions. Both types of certified midwives share a basic philosophy of watchful waiting and nonintervention during normal processes. Midwives endorse appropriate use of interventions and technology for current or potential health problems. Midwives also collaborate and refer to other members of the health team. Log onto *www. midwife.org* for further information.

The potential drawback of using

a certified nurse-midwife or certified midwife comes when a routine delivery takes a turn for the unexpected and complications arise. You want to make sure that an obstetrician is available instantly should you suddenly need care the certified nurse-midwife or certified midwife cannot provide.

Other Labor Companions

In providing support throughout a woman's pregnancy and labor, labor assistants and birthing doulas provide much of what was traditionally the role of a midwife but is not possible in most U.S. hospitals today. These professionals are remarkably effective in speeding labor, reducing interventions such as episiotomy and Cesarean section, and reducing the need for pain medication. As a single woman, you may benefit even more than a partnered woman by the support of such a professional if you don't have anyone who can be absolutely certain of being present for your baby's birth.

Although doulas are not medical professionals, they are trained to provide information on the birth process and offer labor assistance through emotional and physical support, which may include massage and aromatherapy. Doula comes from the Greek word describing the head servant in ancient Greece who helped the lady of the house through childbirth. A doula is a woman experienced in childbirth who provides continuous physical, emotional, and informational support to the mother before, during, and just after childbirth. Unlike medical procedures such as epidurals, the cost of a doula is not commonly covered by health insurance. But an improved birth experience and potentially easier recovery from birth may be highly worth your money.

CHILDBIRTH METHODS AND CLASSES

If you elect to hire a doula or labor assistant, this person may provide the instruction you need. Otherwise, childbirth classes are a must, whether you want to experience childbirth with or without pain medication. Above all else, these classes teach you what to expect and how to comfort yourself. Don't worry that the class will be crowded with cooing couples. Hospitals and childbirth educators report single mothers attending classes in record numbers. You should choose a childbirth companion—your mother, father, brother, other family member, or a male or female friend. Taking a childbirth class can empower you to trust your natural wisdom, make informed choices, and take responsibility for your health.

Many childbirth classes do not focus on a specific method but draw on the following methods. Books about birthing, however, which can be a powerful supplement to a childbirth class, generally do come from one or another of these methods.

The Bradley Method

This method of natural birthing was created by Robert A. Bradley and was dubbed by him as Husband-Coached Childbirth, which may be forbidding to single mothers. However, there's no reason to let the bias of the method's creator prevent you from considering this method, which includes learning about exercise, diet, advanced techniques for labor and birth, complications, Cesarean sections, postpartum care, breastfeeding, and caring for your new baby. Your coach can be anyone you choose—your mother, brother, cousin, friend, doula, nurse-midwife, or other labor and childbirth assistant.

Lamaze Classes

The goal of Lamaze classes is to increase a woman's confidence in her ability to give birth. According to Lamaze International (*www.lamaze.org*), these classes help women realize intuition they already have for giving birth. Part of the Lamaze philosophy is that women have the right to give birth free from routine medical interventions. Simple coping strategies for labor stress focused breathing but also include techniques such as movement and positioning, labor support, massage, relaxation, and hydrotherapy. Lamaze instructors discuss the pain that accompanies childbirth and teach mothers how to respond using techniques that shorten labor time and increase comfort.

Hypnobirthing

Based upon the work of the late English obstetrician, Dr. Grantly Dick-Read, hypnobirthing teaches the mom to use deep relaxation, guided imagery, and self-hypnosis techniques to help release the fear and tension associated with pain and a long labor. Although hypnobirthing doesn't claim to free a mom from all pain, many women report experiencing a safe and often pain-free birth.

Two popular methods are Hypno-Birthing—The Mongan Method and the Leclaire Hypnobirthing Method.

Both hypnobirthing methods employ breathing patterns and relaxation techniques to help the body release endorphins, the body's own natural painkillers. Both also work to shorten labor and reduce fatigue.

FOR WOMEN ONLY

I'm due to have my first baby in a few months and am really nervous. The father with whom I had a long-term relationship decided parenthood wasn't for him, and he left. Although this is probably for the best in the long run, I get so depressed when every half hour I see a commercial for our local hospital's birthing unit. They always show an impassioned father devotedly coaching his tearful yet happy wife through labor. Why do I think this is the only right way to have a baby?

You are watching too much TV if you've seen your local hospital's spot more than once. You don't need to be coached by a mate. In fact, research tells us that the presence of women during labor helps to facilitate an easier birth. You probably have more women than you realize available to you on this momentous day. Think about having your sister, your mother, or your best friend accompany you. If you have no one to help you, ask your doctor or certified nurse-midwife to help you find someone to provide the emotional and physical support you will require. By all means, you should also select a birthing coach so that you are well prepared to participate fully in this most miraculous "women's only" experience. But even if your birthing coach is your brother, father, or male friend, he can be a great source of comfort to you.

TELLING YOUR DOCTOR ABOUT PREVIOUS ABORTIONS

I had two abortions in the past five years, but I have not told my doctor. I already feel uncomfortable being a single mother and worry that he will misjudge me as promiscuous or irresponsible. Should I tell him in case this could affect my pregnancy?

Most likely, having had two abortions, if they were performed properly and early in the first trimester, will have little or no effect on your pregnancy. However, it is best to tell your doctor so that he will have a clear picture of your medical history. Additionally, now is the time to learn whether this doctor has the compassion, patience, and understanding necessary to be what you require in a physician. If you feel he is judgmental of your lifestyle or disapproves of decisions you have made, then you should find another doctor, one with whom you feel comfortable and are able to be honest. Trust your feelings. You will be sharing one of the most precious periods in your life with this person. For the next few months, he will become very important to you, and it is essential that you have a rapport with him.

IF YOU'RE A MIDLIFE MOM

Welcome to one of the fastest growing groups of single mothers, women over forty. A woman who postpones childbearing has often achieved goals like advanced degrees or enviable careers. Such accomplishments often give the older single mothers a financial cushion and greater degree of job flexibility. These assets, combined with well-honed organizational skills, give the typical older single mother great advantages.

Many such older single mothers report that the decision to choose single motherhood often means that career, hobbies, and travel have simply taken a back seat to a desire for the fulfillment and satisfaction of a child. The husband hunt may no longer interest or excite the accomplished single mother to be.

Despite the many advantages to postponing motherhood, there are certainly trade-offs. Fertility starts to drop after thirty-five; so getting pregnant may be more difficult than for a younger woman. Genetic screening, such as amniocentesis, is the standard recommendation for a woman over thirty-four. The older the mother, the greater the risk of complications in pregnancy and delivery such as gestational diabetes, high blood pressure, and kidney problems. Once, however, an older mother becomes pregnant and genetic problems have been ruled out, older mothers without preexisting health conditions usually do not require special prenatal care and can have healthy babies. In fact, recent studies have shown that the age of the mother alone is not as big a risk factor as had previously been assumed.

Women considering a later-than-usual-in-life pregnancy should do some advance planning. See your physician for a thorough checkup to identify and treat any medical conditions that could interfere with a healthy pregnancy and delivery. Make every effort to get yourself in peak physical condition. Of course, stop smoking. Take the recommended prenatal vitamins and folic acid supplements while trying to conceive. Discuss all options with your doctor as part of your pregnancy planning.

Prenatal Diagnosis

There are a variety of specialized tests your doctor may order if he or she has reason to be concerned about possible genetic defects. You may also request tests that you feel are warranted given your personal circumstances and private concerns. Make sure that you give your doctor a thorough health history so that you two can determine together the right course of action for you.

Sonogram or Ultrasound

This initial test uses sound waves bouncing off the uterus and fetus, allowing visualization that is far safer than X rays. Used widely on women of all ages, ultrasound can verify a due date by pinpointing the age of the fetus, in addition to seeing if you are going to have twins, diagnosing fetal size and movement, and determining the general condition, health, and sometimes even sex of the child.

Ultrasound is performed by lightly massaging a clear gel onto the abdomen, after which the doctor moves a metal device around the area until an image of the baby is seen on a nearby monitor. This is a painless procedure.

Maternal Serum Alpha-fetoprotein (AFP) Screening

A simple blood test that is often done before recommending amniocentesis, this screening detects elevated levels of AFP in the mother's blood, indicating a possible neural tube defect (spina bifida) or brain deformities. Extremely low levels can suggest a risk of Down syndrome. However, because this is a screening only, don't be alarmed if the results are abnormal. This could simply mean that further tests need to be administered. AFP screenings are usually performed around the sixteenth week.

Amniocentesis

This is usually performed on mothers over thirty-five, primarily to determine if the fetus has Down syndrome. Amniocentesis can also identify neural tube defects, metabolic disorders, and genetic and inherited disorders including hemophilia, Tay-Sachs disease (found mainly in Ashkenazi Jewish couples whose ancestors can be traced originally from Eastern Europe), and sickle cell anemia. Tay-Sachs, cystic fibrosis, and sickle cell anemia traits call for matching gene pairs—that is, one gene from the mother and one from the father. They are rarely passed on; so few babies are born with these disorders. Testing for these diseases is recommended only if either or both parents have a good chance of testing positively, if you've already had a child with genetic defects, or have close family members with hereditary disorders.

This is how amniocentesis is performed. A long, slender, hollow needle is inserted through the abdominal wall directly into the uterus, where a small amount of amniotic fluid is withdrawn.

To avoid poking the baby, the doctor is guided by viewing the image generated on a TV-like screen through ultrasound.

Your doctor may perform amniocentesis as early as fourteen weeks into your pregnancy and as late as the nineteenth or twentieth week. Earlier testing is currently being analyzed and refined because the cells from the test require about four weeks of cultivation. If defects are found and the mother wants to terminate her pregnancy, this allows her to terminate the pregnancy at an early stage.

Chorionic Villus Sampling (CVS)

This test is usually performed between the eighth and twelfth week of pregnancy. It is becoming more widely used than amniocentesis because it allows for an earlier and, therefore, less potentially traumatic termination of pregnancy in response to the detection of birth defects. CVS can detect thousands of disorders caused by defective genes or chromosomes. Hopefully, it will be performed more and more in doctors' offices, but presently it is performed in medical facilities such as hospital outpatient centers.

Depending on when you have the procedure, it can be done transvaginally (through the vagina) or transabdominally. In the transabdominal method, a guide needle is inserted through the abdomen and uterine wall to the placenta, where another smaller needle passes through the guide needle, withdrawing a sampling of fifteen to twenty cells to be examined. A local anesthetic is used, and as in amniocentesis, ultrasound imaging is used to determine the exact location of the fetus. Although not risk-free, if performed at a good testing center, the test is almost as safe as amniocentesis. The transvaginal procedure is done the same way, except that the cells are taken via the cervix rather than through the abdominal wall.

New tests are being developed constantly. Your doctor will advise you of the best route to take.

FIBROIDS AND AGE

I have always had fibroid tumors but was told since my early twenties not to worry because they usually only affect older women who are trying to get pregnant. But now I am thirty-six and pregnant with my first child. This is adding to my fears that maybe I am too old to have a baby.

You are not too old to have a child and most likely will have no problems. Most pregnant women with fibroids carry to term successfully. Fibroids occur most often in women over thirty-five, and because so many older women are now opting to have children, fibroids during pregnancy are reportedly becoming more common— almost two in every 100 pregnancies. Occasionally, certain developments can occur; it is best to discuss this with your physician and alert him or her to any treatment you may have previously had for fibroids. Generally, the worst thing most women can expect to endure is discomfort or pain from the pressure of the fibroids around the abdominal area. This usually is not a reason to worry, but you should still report every symptom to your doctor, particularly if you notice any irregularities such as spotting.

WHEN THERE'S NO MAN TO DUMP THE LITTER BOX

This sounds silly, but one thing I worry about since my partner left is who will clean the cat litter box while I am pregnant. I heard that cats and cat litter cause a disease that can harm the fetus. My partner gave me the cats, and now that he is gone, I don't want to have to give them up, too, since they're part of my family. How would I know if I have the disease?

You don't have to give up your cats, but you do need to exercise caution, even though your chances of contracting toxoplasmosis, the name of the disease in question, are low. First of all, if you have lived with your pets awhile, you have probably already contracted the disease (more than one-half the population of the United States has been infected) and most likely have built up immunity. Also, less than one woman in 1,000 gets the disease while pregnant. However, toxoplasmosis can cause serious fetal damage, and prevention is the best cure.

♦ Try to delegate the cat care chores to a family friend, relative, or neighbor. If you must remove the cat litter yourself, wear rubber gloves and be sure to wash thoroughly afterward.

♦ Change the litter daily, and be sure that if the cats go outside that you don't allow them to defecate in sandboxes or garden areas.

♦ Better yet, don't let the cats out because other animals can cause

your cats to contract the disease.

♦ If you'd feel better, have the cats tested to see if they have a current infection. If the results are positive, board the pets or have a friend keep them for the duration of your pregnancy.

♦ If your cats tested positive and you feel you need to be tested, call your physician right away. But remember, your chances of having toxoplasmosis during your pregnancy are slim.

♦ Remember that toxoplasmosis is also transmitted through uncooked meat and unpasteurized milk. Avoid these, and be particularly sure when eating out that meat is well-done or at the very least medium-well done. Save the steak tartare for a future dinner date!

IS IT SAFE FOR ME TO USE AN ELECTRIC BLANKET?

I told a friend recently that now that my partner and I have separated that I'd have to buy an electric blanket to keep my toes warm this winter. I was sort of joking, but she was pretty serious about my not using an electric blanket while pregnant. Why?

There are three reasons not to use electric blankets. First, they have been linked to potential fetal damage or miscarriage that scientists believe is caused by the electromagnetic field they create. Second, electric blankets and even heating pads can increase your body's temperature, a factor that is associated with fetal damage. Finally,

SEVEN SECRETS FOR A HEALTHY PREGNANCY

1. *Seek quality prenatal care.* If you are over thirty-five or have special medical problems such as diabetes or high blood pressure, be sure to choose an obstetrician who has experience with your particular condition. Even if you are the perfect picture of health, be sure to start spoiling your child now by getting the best prenatal care possible.

2. *Eat right.* Whether or not you suffer from nausea or are starving every second, it is important to maintain a diet high in complex carbohydrates, green and yellow vegetables, fruits, calcium-rich foods, and a moderate amount of protein and iron-rich foods. Although you need more calories when you are pregnant, your general eating patterns should be the same as your basic healthy eating plan. It is not difficult to add an additional 300 to 400 calories daily, but be sure these are not empty calories. Seek the advice of your prenatal practitioner.

Especially if you are overweight, underweight, or very young and still not fully developed yourself, be sure to follow your practitioner's instructions for the right amount of daily caloric intake for you. Always be sure to drink at least 64 ounces (2 quarts) of fluids daily, preferably water, to flush out toxins and waste, help reduce the chance of urinary infections, and minimize bouts of constipation.

3. *Lose the image of the perfect pregnancy.* Don't buy into myths that all pregnant women are happy, fulfilled, or have a certain glow. Be open to having good days and bad days, such as you or anyone else who is human would experience.

4. *Rest.* There comes a time in life when you simply won't be able to get everything done. It's called "motherhood," and pregnancy is a practice run. Stop trying to accomplish everything you think must

who needs the cords and extra energy usage? Why not get yourself a plump down comforter instead? You can also try warming the bed with the electric blanket first, but be sure to turn it off before getting in.

SEXUAL DESIRE DURING PREGNANCY

I'm seven months pregnant and all of a sudden am feeling particularly frisky, but not in the athletic sense. Why do I feel such strong sexual desires when there is currently no one in my life and the last person in the world I would want to reconnect with is my baby's father, who disappeared the minute he learned I was going to have a baby? I'm looking forward to having my child, but I'm concerned that I'm having these feelings because I haven't had a love interest for so long and may be missing male attention. Also, would masturbating cause any damage to the baby or me?

(continuation)

get done and start focusing on yourself and your new baby. This means giving up the idea of being superachiever-career-mom and relaxing a little into the role of normal pregnant woman!

5. *Keep in shape.* Avoid gaining weight too fast, and consult your prenatal practitioner about beginning an exercise program. If you've never exercised before, now is a good time to get started. Walking, cycling, and swimming are good picks for a novice, and be sure to pick up a good exercise video or book for expectant mothers. Unless you are proficient at some rigid workout routines, never start an exercise program during pregnancy that includes rigorous training such as jogging or weightlifting.

6. *Beware of your responses to feeling abandoned by the absentee father.* Worrying excessively about him can make you emotionally susceptible to a difficult pregnancy. You're having this baby without him, and you will do just fine!

7. *If you are addicted, get help, now!* If you suffer from a serious addiction, seek help through a twelve-step program such as Alcoholics Anonymous or Narcotics Anonymous. Attend meetings that are smoke-free. Never use a nicotine patch to quit smoking while you are pregnant. Never replace any drug with another substance unless it is approved by your doctor.

If your smoking, drug use, or drinking is chronic and/or if you refuse help from qualified experts, twelve-step programs, or certified alcohol or drug treatment centers, then you would be wise to consider postponing childbearing until you have this disease under control.

Masturbation will not cause any harm other than rocking the baby, since orgasm causes the uterus to contract. But don't worry; it won't be enough to induce labor. Still, if you are concerned, talk to your doctor. There is no question he or she has not answered many times before. Do not worry that your doctor will be shocked or think less of you.

Your feelings about missing male companionship might be why you are feeling amorous, but most likely it is physiological. During pregnancy, the hormonal changes that occur cause increased blood flow to your pelvic region. This results in engorged genitals, which can be responsible for the heightened sexual desire you are experiencing. Conversely, women who have had sex during these stages of pregnancy sometimes report a feeling of incompleteness due to a bloatedness that persists after orgasm, leaving them feeling they didn't quite have an orgasm. The pressure on the bladder caused by the baby's position is another reason for that sensual feeling you and many other women report.

SPECIAL CONCERN: IF YOU MISCARRY

If you start to miscarry or suspect that you are about to, you should call your doctor immediately. At this vulnerable time in your life, it is also crucial to have someone with you. Most doctors will give your body a chance to complete an early (first trimester) miscarriage on its own before intervening. However, you can lose a dangerous amount of blood during even an early miscarriage and may end up needing emergency medical attention. If you can't have someone with you, your best bet is to go to the hospital.

FEELING LESS ALONE ON THE BIG DAY

Although I realize that motherhood is a lifelong process, right now I'm concerned with making the big day, meaning the birth, as stress-free and pleasant as possible. Is there any way for a single mom who has a lot of family support but still feels alone to feel less alone?

This may sound as though it is coming out of both sides of the mouth, but in a sense you are not alone and yet you are. Even though childbirth is experienced by billions of women, binding them to one another in an enormous spiritual sisterhood, other emotions that accompany this process are yours alone to feel. Aside from the level of pain (and don't let anyone kid you—if pushing out a baby were painless, childbirth would be an activity that could be accomplished while napping), the flood of feelings that can gush out along with the baby can be as individual as is each new life's fingerprint.

The one issue that may make you and other birthing single mothers feel alienated, particularly if you are giving birth in a hospital or medical facility, is not being the better half of the happy, cigar-offering new dad in the waiting room. With the introduction of men in delivery rooms more than twenty years ago, this image of the happy father seems more apparent. But there must be many women giving birth without men in the delivery room. Around 53 percent of all first births are to single women, and if you combine that with the number of military wives giving birth and with those who separated early in pregnancy, millions of women in this country give birth each year without the assistance of a husband. In fact, millions of women in the United States have given up on having the obligatory male who is ready with suitcase in hand and a ride to the hospital. Many modern-day women take a taxi or have a friend or family member drive them and send someone to their place later to collect all the necessities.

MANAGING YOUR LABOR AND DELIVERY

I'm terrified that I will have contractions in the middle of the night with no one around to help me and I'll end up having the baby alone or, worse, dying alone during childbirth. I chose single motherhood, but I sure envy those who have a man around to pack the bag and get them to the hospital on time!

Relax

Even if you begin having mild yet inconsistent contractions in the middle of the night, you have a long way to go

before you approach active labor, when the contractions are strong, occur three to four minutes apart, and last for up to a minute. Besides, if you have been to childbirth classes, you will know that the first stages of labor, called early or latent labor, can last a few hours or even a couple of days. Rather than panicking and calling everyone you know, follow these simple steps:

◆ Try to go back to sleep because, most likely, this will be the most rest you will get for awhile, and you need it. If you can't fall asleep but feel comfortable and can get some rest, do so. Watch TV in bed or listen to music. Think pleasant, dreamy thoughts about your new baby.

◆ Do something relaxing or positive. If your bed feels like it's made of live wires, rather than lie there wide-awake timing your contractions and watching the clock, get up and make a cup of tea and review your pregnancy and childbirth literature. If that makes you too anxious, try reading, putting last-minute touches on the baby's room, or organizing your postpregnancy wardrobe.

◆ Put your coach on alert. When a reasonable hour approaches and you know your childbirth coach most likely will be awake, call to give her a status report, but don't make her drop everything and come running. Plan how and when you will stay in contact over the next few hours, and be sure you both have clear signals on how to reach each other.

◆ Know when to begin to time your contractions. If your contractions begin coming a little closer than ten minutes apart within a half-hour time span, you should begin timing them.

How to Know When to Go

If you experience mild to strong contractions that range from five to twenty minutes or more apart and last up to one-half minute, you are probably entering the second stage of labor, or active labor. The second stage of labor is when you should contact your doctor or nurse-midwife and let her know how far apart your contractions are, how strong, and the duration of each contraction. If you are with your labor coach, have her help you gather up your last-minute belongings and head to the hospital or birthing facility if the doctor says it is time. Even if your contractions are sporadic and not that strong, if your membranes rupture, it is time to go to the hospital or birthing facility.

You should be in the birthing facility or hospital by the time your contractions are about three to four minutes apart and last up to one minute. Have your labor coach begin assisting you in your breathing exercises. Try to remain calm and patient; because even though the rest time between these contractions grows less and less, this stage can last up to an average of three hours and in many cases a lot longer.

What to Do When You Get There

If you are not preregistered, you will need to do this now. You will be asked to fill out forms, sign routine consent releases, and answer a number of questions about when you last ate and how far apart your contractions are. This is the time to tell the staff that you are a single mother and introduce your coach or friend or relative who is accompanying you. If you have no one with you, be sure to ask if you can talk to a nurse who can remain with you during your labor and delivery. In fact, talk with the nurses at the nurses' station and see with whom you feel most comfortable and who is available to assist your doctor.

The Transitional Labor Stage

This is the most exhausting phase of labor, with contractions that can be overwhelming. You should already have had medication (if requested) before this stage, but nevertheless it's not unusual to feel that you are becoming unglued, frustrated, literally maddened, or insane. Hang in there, listen to your coach or birthing companion, maintain your breathing pattern, and, if at all possible, try to visualize relaxing images and think about how lucky and close to finally having your baby you are!

Here Comes Baby!

A flood of feelings accompanies the actual birth of a baby, feelings that may be so new and strange that you may be overwhelmed by them. You may look at your newborn and experience sensations beyond comprehension. The intensity of the emotions surrounding what went on with your former mate—love, hate, loss, grief, or relief; the intimate connection to a man you've never met if you were donor inseminated; or the unexpected passion you may feel for your doctor are normal, common feelings expressed by nearly all single women at the moment their child enters the world. It's okay to feel overwhelmed, and you have permission to react by crying, laughing, remaining motionless, or doing whatever else you feel compelled to do. It's okay, too, not to feel anything or to experience conflicting feelings. Don't be disappointed if you don't feel an overwhelming surge of love for your new baby such as you may have seen in the movies. Many women don't experience this; so don't worry.

Congratulations, Mom. You've done it, and you've done it well!

BANKING ON CORD BLOOD

Typically, after the birth of a baby, the umbilical cord and the placenta are discarded. Some alternative birth practices, following ancient spiritual rituals, even suggest that mom bury the cord and placenta in the earth near a garden or under a tree. A more modern use today for the umbilical cord is to collect and store the cord blood—the rich source of stem cells that produce all white cells, red cells, and platelets—as insurance for the future. These stem cells can help your child, a sibling, or even yourself if ever faced with certain diseases or disorders. This is a relatively simple and painless procedure. However, there are pros and cons you should weigh before making such a decision.

First, it can be expensive. The initial collection fee can range from $225 to $1,800, plus cord blood banks charge around $50 to $100 for the yearly storage fee. Public cord blood banks will store the blood with no cost to you, but there is no guarantee that another recipient won't get it first should the need arise. You are essentially donating your baby's umbilical cord blood. Although the stem cells can treat certain cancers and diseases such as sickle cell anemia and immune system disorders, if your child winds up with certain blood disorders, like leukemia, his or her own cord blood contains the same cells that may have the potential toward malignancy and therefore would not be used. However, researchers are excited about future therapies for cord blood including the treatment of Parkinson's disease, Alzheimer's disease, diabetes, MS, spinal cord injuries, and more. Another benefit for the single mom is that since cord blood cells don't need to "match" exactly as bone marrow (a source of stem cells that is painful to retrieve, may not be readily available, and can result in an increased risk of rejection), you don't need to search for a missing father who may be the only "perfect match." Still, the likelihood that you will need these cells is 1 in 20,000, unless your family has a genetic predisposition to certain diseases. In that case, you should consult a genetic specialist during your pregnancy. Ask your doctor for more information. Visit the Cord Blood Registry at *www.cordblood.com.*

WILL CESAREAN BIRTH LEAD TO LESS BONDING?

I feel like such a loser. First, my baby's father left because he "wasn't ready for this." Then, after months of trying to prepare myself for motherhood, there I was in the delivery room with coach, video camera, and support only to find that I had to have an emergency C-section. It's not so much that I didn't experience "natural" childbirth. I worry that my child and I won't bond as completely as we would have done with a vaginal delivery.

A baby does not have to travel through the birth canal to bond with its mother. Mothers who were under sedation while giving birth, those who have adopted infants, and women who have undergone C-sections have been able to bond successfully with their babies.

Try to remember that bonding is a process that develops over time, not something that is accomplished in minutes. In fact, many experts believe that real bonding doesn't occur until late in the baby's first year. It takes time for you to accept and feel warm toward this little stranger who made his grand entrance in such an attention-getting manner. Keep in mind, too, that the concept of bonding was introduced to mainstream culture sometime during the 1970s. Does this mean that people who had children before the 1970s never bonded? Surely mothers and children have bonded successfully for millennia before this word became popular and regardless of the events surrounding the birth.

Your dreams of the perfect child you were carrying for nine months would normally culminate in the perfect birth, but you need to stop thinking that it didn't go right. Look at the positive side of C-section. For one thing, babies born via C-section don't emerge with squishy, funny-shaped heads as many do who travel through the birth canal. So start thinking that the perfect birth is one where mother and child survive to come home to a new life together.

If You Give Birth to a Baby with Physical or Developmental Challenges

The birth of a baby with serious medical problems suddenly thrusts you into an unfamiliar, intimidating world. In fact, a number of women have reported that they became single mothers right after their baby was born because the father was unable to deal with the challenges that lay ahead. The best way to rise above the confusion and crisis is to arm yourself with knowledge. Learning all you can about your child's condition is also a way to cope emotionally with the feelings attached to having a baby born with medical problems whether or not you were prepared.

FILLING OUT THE BIRTH CERTIFICATE

Most hospitals will ask you to sign the birth certificate only hours after you have given birth. As if you didn't have enough to worry about, now you're wondering how to fill in the space asking for the father's name. For most women giving birth, this can be an extremely emotional time, particularly if the father has fled.

If the father filled out legal documents acknowledging paternity before the child's birth, you can put his name on the birth certificate even if he is not at the hospital. Many hospitals, following laws in their states, forbid you to place the father's name on the document without his being present or without your furnishing a legal, notarized document stating

that this man is indeed the father.

Just because you cannot legally put the father's name on the birth certificate without his agreement is no reason to go to pieces if the space is left blank or the word "unknown" is printed there instead. You know who he is, and it really doesn't matter what it says on the birth certificate. Your child has the same rights as anyone else. Don't ever let anyone tell you any different.

ESTABLISHING PATERNITY

Even if your child's father has offered little or no support and probably will remain uninvolved in your child's life, you would be wise to get him to acknowledge paternity if you plan to seek child support. You should not try to establish paternity if you are sure you do not want the father involved in your lives, emotionally and financially.

The least traumatic way to deal with establishing paternity is to have a talk with the father of your baby months before you are actually faced with signing documents. Under the best of circumstances, he will acknowledge that he is the baby's father and feel comfortable with this information. Ask him if he plans to take some responsibility for this child and to what extent. If he's hesitant to respond, say that you will give him some time and suggest that you talk again. Assure him that you realize this is a big load to drop on him at this time and you can understand that he needs time to get used to it.

9

It's Me and You, Kid—Starting Out

Regardless of how your journey into motherhood began, the first few weeks and months are destined to be filled with many unexpected challenges. No matter how much reading you've done, there isn't much short of plain and simple experience that can quite prepare you for the demands of this job.

Care of your infant may be your first real experience with sleep deprivation. You soon find out that the "all-nighters" you pulled in high school or college were child's play compared to the relentless demands of a crying infant at 2:00 A.M. It is a strange and humbling experience to be awake and functioning at an hour when the rest of the world is asleep.

Then there is the advice. Naturally, you heard your share during the pregnancy. Now you find that everyone has an opinion about something. Perfect strangers feel free to tell you that you are doing something not quite right or, more likely, disastrously wrong. Some of this unsolicited advice can be quite helpful, of course, but other little tidbits can make you wonder if you're up to the challenge of motherhood.

Although you've most likely prepared for the first few months after childbirth, you may have overlooked some things that need attending to now. Potentially tough decisions like establishing paternity need to be considered now, as do other simpler yet equally important parenting decisions such as how you will feed your newborn and if you want your baby to use a pacifier. Whatever you can do to make the first few weeks with your new bundle more enjoyable, do it now.

HOMEWORK HELP

If you can find a way to afford it, consider hiring domestic help for your baby's first weeks or months. Having someone come to your home and perform tasks such as light cooking and cleaning and perhaps even help you care for yourself and your new baby is worth it if you can fit it into your budget. New parents often expect this kind of care to be intrusive, but people who try it often find it's highly worth the cost. Many labor assistants and coaches, such as doulas, also come to your home during the postpartum period to assist with such needs.

THE NAME GAME

While many new mothers are thinking of cool names for their babies, unmarried moms are wondering what last name they should use—their own or the baby's father's.

Legally, you can't put the father's last name on the birth certificate as the father without his consent. Depending on case law in the state where you live, you may not have the right to give your child her father's last name if you are not married to him. Even if you do have that right, here are some reasons for using your birth name.

♦ Men have their greatest contributions named after them. Bridges, cities, airports, highways, buildings, and schools are often named after the man or men whose vision inspired the project. You contributed the most work in bringing your child into the world—carrying and caring for him or her for nine months, going through labor and childbirth, and accepting the full responsibility for parenting. It only makes sense that your greatest accomplishment should be named after you.

♦ Consider what happens if you get married in the future. Families become confusing when a woman remarries and has another child with her new partner. There are families today in which one mother has several children, all with different last names.

♦ In some cultures, having your mother's name is the norm, such as the Navajo. There's nothing better about our tradition of giving children their father's surnames.

♦ If you are raising your child as a single mother, most likely your child will have more contact with your relatives, whose name he would share, than with his father's.

♦ Giving your child your last name does not mean that your child can't have his father's last name as a middle name. Remember, whether or not a child has the last name of his father has nothing to do with the father's rights, his obligation to pay child support, or any other responsibility toward the child.

CHECKLIST OF MUST-HAVES FOR BABY'S FIRST YEAR

Be sure you have everything you need on hand before you return home with your new bundle. You'll want to make the transition from single-with-cat to single-with-child as smoothly as possible. Scrambling around for last-minute necessities is something you don't need to be doing. Here are items that you should have on hand:

♦ **Snugglesack, Sling, or Papoose Carrier:** A must-have—you're a single mother who will not have another pair of arms available to her as often

as your partnered counterparts. Slings and cloth carriers that strap the baby to your body are not only comforting but also will free up your hands to take care of immediate needs.

♦ **Car Seat:** Hospitals and birthing centers will not discharge the baby to you if you don't have one because child protective car seats are mandated by law.

♦ **Bassinet:** If you can't find an affordable crib right away, a bassinet is perfect, particularly if the baby will be rooming with you for awhile. But shop around or seek a loaner—some bassinets are so fancy that you might end up spending more than you would for a standard crib. Babies outgrow bassinets quickly!

♦ **Baby Bed:** Make sure that the crib you use meets all current safety standards, particularly if it is a hand-me-down or a garage sale find. If you are buying a new crib, investigate the kind that later converts into a child's bed. Visit juvenile furniture stores or look through catalogs to get ideas.

♦ **Playpen:** Find one that is as portable as possible. If you introduce your baby to a playpen early for brief periods, it can provide a welcome respite for both of you.

♦ **Diapers, Creams, Changing Supplies:** Consult your pediatrician or health care provider about the products and procedures he or she recommends. Ask for samples, if available. Keep a stash on hand, but try not to use too many unnecessary preparations.

♦ **Layette Items—Blankets, Undershirts, Sleep Sacks, and Simple Shirts:** You will probably receive many of these newborn items as gifts because people enjoy buying them. Newborns are changed frequently; so you will want a supply on hand. Friends will also offer hand-me-downs since babies grow out of these items quickly. Accept what is offered to you. You can always return or pass on what you did not use.

♦ **Pain Reliever/Fever Reducer:** Open a bag and tell your baby's doctor to load you up with samples of recommended products. This doesn't mean you will use them all, but they're nice to have in an emergency.

♦ **Thermometer:** A rectal thermometer is a must. Every phone call you make to the pediatrician will begin with the question "What is your baby's temperature?"

♦ **Bottles, Breast Pump:** If you plan to breastfeed, a breast pump is a must. If you will be working and breastfeeding, you'll need an electric one, or you can rent a hospital grade one. If you only expect to be separated from your baby for up to a few hours before you wean, a cheaper manual model should be sufficient. You'll also need bottles for you or a babysitter to feed your baby the milk you pump.

IF YOU HAVE A CESAREAN SECTION

The number of births by Cesarean section has risen steadily in the United States.

If you have a C-section, you will be in the hospital for a couple of extra days, need more medication, feel more tired, and generally be more uncomfortable than you expected. You will need to take extra care of yourself; so it is important to enlist the help of a friend or relative. Here are some tips for getting through the first several weeks:

• Find some way to get help with household chores, such as shopping or cooking. These may be too difficult while you are recovering from a C-section.

• Continue to walk as they had you do in the hospital. Try to walk even just around your living room, even on your first day home. Mild exercise like this will speed your recovery.

• Breastfeeding is an especially good choice for you. Keep the baby right beside you and enjoy the convenience of not having to prepare or heat formula. Save your energy for important activities like cuddling.

• If you would have preferred a vaginal birth, take the time to mourn. You may feel especially alone and sad following a C-section, particularly if your partner left you. Online support can be helpful. Post a message, if you need to connect with women who have shared your experience. Ask your doctor or contact your childbirth instructor about support groups that might be right for you.

BREASTFEEDING BENEFITS

The benefits of breastfeeding for the baby are well known, but did you know that:

• Breastfeeding will help you lose those pregnancy pounds. About ten pounds of the weight a pregnant woman gains is to support milk production after the baby is born. Breastfeeding uses up those fat stores.

• Breastfeeding flattens your tummy. The hormones involved in breastfeeding stimulate uterine contractions so that your abdomen regains its prepregnancy flatness more quickly—good not only for your self-confidence but also terrific for helping you fit back into your "prebaby" wardrobe.

• Breastfeeding reduces your risk of breast cancer.

• Breastfeeding is convenient and cheap. Your breasts are always with you, and when you go out, you don't have to bring anything. There is no formula to buy; even if you have to spend the maximum on a breast pump, you could purchase a lot of nursing clothes with the money you'll save on formula!

• Breastfeeding helps you relax by releasing certain hormones. You can rest better, too.

• Breastfed babies get sick less often, and you know you have no time for your baby to get sick!

• Breastfeeding will benefit you and your baby even if you are only able to do so for a short while.

Contact La Leche League at *www. lalecheleague.org* for advice about pumping, breastfeeding in public comfortably, and more.

Even though pediatricians encourage breastfeeding for as long as possible, only 29 percent of U.S. mothers breastfeed longer than six months, according to the U.S. Department of Health and Human Services. The reason may be that Americans really prefer to see breasts as sexual objects.

It's funny how the "Hooter's breast buffet" and sexy cleavage on TV is okay, but nursing isn't. Twenty-eight states currently protect your right to breastfeed in public, but you may find people treat you in a hostile manner. Remember that your baby's time at the breast is short, but the benefits last a lifetime.

WORRYING ABOUT DOING THE RIGHT THING

I am getting a lot of advice from neighbors and friends about caring for my newborn son. Even though I've read every book on infant care, they act as if I can't hack it because I couldn't stay married. So now I'm always worrying that I will make a mistake and not do the right thing.

Don't worry about making mistakes. Accept the fact that you will make mistakes. An important part of being a good parent is the ability to learn from both your mistakes and your successes. It doesn't matter whether you are married or not. People love to give new mothers advice; so don't take it to heart.

SINGLE MOM OF NOTE

Maya Angelou

She speaks six languages, lectures worldwide, is a best-selling author, and since 1981 has been Reynolds Professor of American Studies at Wake Forest University in North Carolina. But Maya Angelou also had some wild jobs when she was younger, mostly to help raise her son Guy, born to her outside of marriage. She has been a dancer, actress, writer, waitress, civil rights activist, even a madam, in what she calls her roller-coaster life. At the request of Bill Clinton, Maya wrote "On the Pulse of the Morning" for his 1993 inauguration as the forty-second President of the United States.

Following in his mom's footsteps, Guy is also a writer and has published two books.

Your most important source of information is your baby himself. He will be your best and most trusted teacher. When you are on the right track, he will be relaxed, and his face will be calm and content. If you are on the wrong track, he will thrash around. His cry will be breathless and piercing. He may turn red, and his limbs may stiffen. All these signs will give you a message, and in a short time, you will know exactly what the message is. The "right" answers come not from a doctor or a book but rather from your baby.

BABYPROOF YOUR HOUSE NOW!

Many single mothers like to make their home safe for baby as part of their preparations during pregnancy or may already have taken some safety steps, especially if their house is a welcome destination for the children of friends and relatives. Begin immediately if you have not already made your home safe for baby. Start by sitting on the floor of each room so that you can see your home just as your baby does. This will open your eyes to many potential hazards. Remember to use common sense. There is no substitute for supervision, and if something seems dangerous, it probably is. Be sure to:

- Install safety latches on all low cabinets and drawers.

- Put plastic wrap and plastic bags where your baby cannot find them. Plastic bags can cause your child to suffocate. Get into the habit right now of tying your plastic bags from the dry cleaner into knots before disposal.

- Get rid of the water and the buckets. Babies are fascinated by water; never leave a filled or even partially filled bucket unattended. A baby can drown in one inch of water. Toilet seat latches are a must.

- Review your house plants. Many household plants are poisonous. Dispose of all poisonous plants.

- Small items are a big worry. Babies put everything in their mouths. This is how they explore the world. To prevent choking, keep small knick-knacks, bowls of candy or nuts, and anything else with small parts away from the baby's reach.

- Keep window blind and curtain cords and even long telephone cords out of

the reach of your baby. These can cause your baby to strangle. Tie these cords securely out of your baby's reach.

- Cigarette lighters should be banned from your home. Babies and young children are fascinated by these devices. They are colorful. A wheel turns and makes sparks, and fire comes out. What's more, lighters fit easily into little hands. Ask your guests to leave their lighters at home. Smoking around young children is a serious health risk; make your home a "No Smoking" zone.

IDLE WORSHIP

You've heard the advice zillions of times: Slow down, take it easy, and get some rest. Sure, we know it's easier said than done, but it's often guilt that keeps moms from stopping to smell the roses. Learn how to take quick midday naps by imagining you're a cat curled up in a cozy chair. Even if you don't fall asleep, the pleasant imagery can make your day more manageable. Plus, splitting the day up like this makes mornings go quicker and afternoons seem less looming. If you don't like cats, come up with your own image of relaxation, or pick up a copy of *How to Be Idle* by Tom Hodgkinson.

BE PREPARED FOR EMERGENCIES

Find out from your pediatrician which hospital you should take your baby to in case of an emergency. Make sure you know how to get there because, most likely, you will need to rely on yourself to drive.

Babysitters need to be able to reach you at all times; so be sure your cell phone is fully charged and turned on. If you don't have a cell phone, suggest this idea to friends who want to buy you a baby gift.

Leave written authorization with babysitters that allows your baby to be treated by medical personnel if you cannot be reached. Some state laws do not permit a child to be treated without parental authorization. Given that you are the only parent, this is especially important.

Record on paper and leave with all babysitters any allergies your baby might have, the immunizations he has received, and any medication he might be taking. Carry this record with you also at all times.

HELPING YOUR BABY LEARN TO SLEEP THROUGH THE NIGHT

By about four months of age, most babies do not need a late-night feeding. You can probably enjoy a six-hour break, more or less, when your child begins to skip her nightly feedings. As important as not needing a late-night feeding to sleep through the night is, your little one must also be able to cycle between deep and light sleep several times. This development will be especially welcome if you are back at work or are just anxious to have things in your life settle down a bit.

Sleep experts have found that all of us cycle between deep and light sleep, coming up to a state of light sleep called REM (rapid eye movement) every ninety

minutes or so. Every three to four hours we come into a more active state, closer to waking.

Most babies can settle themselves during the ninety-minute stage of REM. It is at the three- to four-hour cycles that the baby has a harder time getting her behavior under control. Some babies cry out as if in fear or pain. They aren't awake, but sometimes their own activities awaken them. If you become part of the process by which your baby comforts herself back to sleep, it will be more difficult for your child to develop these skills independently. If you rush in and pick her up every time she whimpers during the night, it is unlikely she will sleep through the night any time soon.

One of the biggest complaints single mothers have about going it alone with an infant is not having someone else to get up when the baby awakens all through the night. But if you keep in mind that it is mostly mothers, married or not, who arise with the sleepless baby, particularly if they are nursing, you'll realize that lack of sleep plagues all new mothers.

IF YOUR BABY CRIES ROUND-THE-CLOCK

Sometimes when my fussy baby is crying nonstop and nothing I do is helping, I have fleeting thoughts of abandoning the baby or wish I had never had her. Of course, I would never actually leave my baby for an instant. I am so thankful to have her, but I'm so burned out from the hours of crying that I can't help thinking such bad thoughts. Is something wrong with me?

Nothing that uninterrupted rest and relaxation wouldn't cure. Howling babies can make even the most patient mother have feelings of intense frustration. Only a dishonest mother would never admit to having thoughts of getting rid of the baby.

Single mothers don't have the availability of another set of arms to help comfort the child and may find constant crying especially hard to tolerate. Don't feel guilty about such thoughts because it is your very honesty in facing these feelings that is working for you. Researchers have proven that excessive infant crying affects everyone around him by causing many common symptoms of stress such as quickening pulse, a rise in blood pressure, faster heartbeat, and holding one's breath.

To survive what may at times seem like round-the-clock crying with the least amount of stress, you need to understand why babies cry and find methods of comforting not only the baby, but also yourself.

Why Babies Cry

Crying is the first form of baby talk. This is the only way babies can communicate their needs. Sometimes babies have crying spells for absolutely no reason at all. In time, you will learn to interpret when your baby's cry means he is hungry, needs changing, or is simply tired or colicky. Most newborns will cry for up to one and one-half hours daily! So don't take it to heart if your baby seems to be crying a lot. It's probably nothing with which to become overly concerned. But if crying is constant where no source of relief is in sight or baby appears to be in pain, call your pediatrician.

WAYS TO MANAGE THE CRYING

Answer the call. Remember, your baby is talking to you. See what she wants, even if it is just to be cuddled.

Determine the Cause

Is baby wet or uncomfortable being swaddled in too many blankets? Is she simply hungry? Maybe your newborn needs burping or gentle rocking to relieve him of a colicky tummy.

Assess Yourself

Are you tense or upset? Babies can pick up on the emotions of the mother; so take a moment to regroup and relax. Chances are this is exactly what you both need.

PROTECTING AGAINST SIDS

Sudden Infant Death Syndrome, otherwise known as SIDS, causes seemingly healthy infants to cease breathing, almost always during sleep, resulting in death. Mounting evidence has linked SIDS to a stomach-down sleeping position. Let your baby sleep on his back. Your pediatrician is always your best source of guidance and information. Never, ever put soft pillows or stuffed animals in a baby's crib!

Be Consistent

Feedings and changing times should be at the same time every day, if possible. Sometimes a break in routine can cause excessive crying.

Rock Together

Rocking can soothe you both. The motion of rocking back and forth in your favorite chair is very sedating for both mom and newborn.

Seek a Change

This means for you and the baby. Hand the baby over to another person, grandma or grandpa, friend, neighbor, other relative, or babysitter. Get a little fresh air and take a walk.

DEALING WITH POSTPARTUM DEPRESSION

Nearly two-thirds of all new mothers experience the blues, or postpartum depression (PPD), after childbirth. Sometimes the depression starts within days; in other instances it doesn't kick in until a few weeks later. Often the postpartum blues can last up to a couple of months. In the most severe cases, 2 in 1,000, severe depression requires intensive professional help.

Depression reduces your capacity for nurturing, which may have lasting effects on your baby. Your primary care physician may not be qualified to diagnose PPD. Prevention and knowledge is always the best medicine. Risk factors for PPD include:

- A personal or family history of depression

- A history of acute premenstrual syndrome, including irritability or depression

- A complicated pregnancy or a difficult labor and delivery

- A childhood history of sexual abuse

Stress such as unresolved feelings about the baby's father or about single motherhood could also contribute to your likelihood of experiencing PPD. Being prepared for the emotions you might experience right after childbirth can help you understand that many women experience the symptoms of PPD and the effects are not lasting. For example, it is perfectly normal not to feel bonded to your baby from the first instant or even not to feel immediate love for your newborn. It is also perfectly normal to feel a little disappointed that the baby looks somewhat lopsided or is an unappealing shade of red. You might have secretly wished for a girl and feel deeply disappointed about not having a daughter.

The guilt and anxiety over these feelings are sometimes enough to trigger a period of mild depression for some postpartum women. These debilitating symptoms can include uncontrollable crying, feelings of self-doubt, guilt, anxiety, insomnia, persistent nervousness, and lack of concentration. Knowing what to expect is often sufficient preparation to ride out a brief postpartum storm.

If you experience any of these symptoms of PPD, talk out your feelings with a trusted friend or family member. When you are depressed, it is difficult to muster the energy you need to seek out help. Family members and friends can help by giving the support and direction needed.

If your symptoms are unbearable and you are having persistent difficulty meeting the demands of daily living, get help promptly. Don't be ashamed to ask for help. You are not the only woman who has felt this way. Don't worry about mild symptoms of depression that last less than two weeks. However, if more time passes and you feel there is no hope of ever returning to the old you, you need to see a mental health professional. Treatment may include progesterone therapy, psychotherapy, antidepressant medication, and/or attending a support group.

If you feel like hurting your baby but have not become abusive, call a parents' hotline in your community. There will be counselors to talk to you and reassure you that you are not alone in your feelings. If you feel you might hurt your baby, call a child abuse hotline or go to the nearest neighbor for help. Seek immediate counseling at your local mental health center. Don't be ashamed of your feelings; this is not the time to worry about what others think but about the potential for hurting your baby. Those who seek help fast avoid

the possibility of compromising the relationship with their baby and regain confidence as a good mother.

WHEN THE WORKING MOM HAS A PROBLEM WITH SEPARATION

I have returned to my full-time job after being home with my six-month-old son. He seemed to handle the separation well. I am a wreck. I find it difficult to separate from him and am reluctant to put him down for the night. Any suggestions?

Having been away from the baby all day, it is natural that you find it hard to separate from him at night. It is okay that you need your baby at night. It means you love him and are attached to him as mothers should be. Many working mothers find that a warm, intimate ritual at night, such as rocking in a favorite chair and singing a cherished lullaby, and setting aside special time in the morning for snuggling and cuddling helps. You feel like an emotional wreck because you are dealing with so many different feelings now. Concentrate on savoring every delicious moment with your precious baby boy.

COPING WITH THE NIGHTTIME BLUES

Should you have a "family bed," in which your baby sleeps in your bed? Should you let your baby cry herself to sleep? Should you have your baby in a crib or bassinet in your room or in her own? These issues are extremely contentious, and you could read a stack of books if you wanted to fully understand the debate. The bottom line is that you should do what is best for your family. No matter what you do, your baby is going to interfere with your sleep schedule! The issues you will want to consider in deciding how to cope with the nighttime blues are:

* Safety—What do you think is the safest choice for your baby? Your pediatrician is a resource on this issue.

* Your emotions—If letting your baby "cry it out" makes you feel like a bad mother, don't do it. If failing to give your baby a very consistent schedule makes you feel like a bad mother, don't do that. Some single moms report that they've been reproached for refusing to let their babies cry

on the grounds that they're projecting their own loneliness onto their babies. Every mother identifies strongly with her baby—that's very normal. Resist the urge to second-guess yourself when you're tired!

* Your sleep—Which option will get you the sleep you need to function? You can expect the first six months or so to be difficult, and it isn't abnormal for babies over one year to have trouble sleeping through the night. But try to do what makes you the best mother you can be—what gets you the sleep you need.

Trust yourself. There wouldn't be so much disagreement on this issue if the answer was obvious or if one size fit all families.

THE DO'S AND DON'TS OF STARTING OUT WITH YOUR NEW BABY

* **Do** carefully consider your options regarding paternity and custody and act accordingly. Delay may subject you and your child to danger, hassle, or interference. Know that in many cases the decisions you make will be final.

* **Do** accept the help that is offered to you. Just because you are a single mother does not mean you have to be isolated. In fact, your first lesson in successful single motherhood will be well learned if you find yourself increasingly comfortable asking for the help you need.

* **Do** plan ahead of time and purchase or obtain the baby items you will need.

You have no idea now how complicated a trip to the store becomes when you need to take the baby with you.

* **Do** make your pediatrician your trusted guide to issues related to your baby's health and development.

* **Don't** take all the advice and criticism too seriously. Listen to what is said, take what you can use, and disregard the rest. Remember, however, that the most valuable parenting skills and advice are often gotten informally from sources you might least expect.

DON'T WORRY WHEN BABY SAYS "DA DA"

I am a single mother by choice in the sense that I knew that the baby's father was not going to remain in the picture. He did visit a few times after my son was born but has not been around since. Now my baby is gurgling his first words, and I can't understand why he is saying "Da Da." Does this mean that my baby is looking for Daddy? I'm confused and wonder if all babies know that they should have a father.

Don't worry. This is one of the first stages in normal speech development. The babbling sounds you are hearing are your baby's attempts at communication and have no meaningful association to your baby. They are just easy sounds for him to make because they involve simple movements of the tongue. So relax and enjoy conversing with your chatty baby.

10

Taking a Closer Look at You

One of the big messages contained in this book is that the real expert on living successfully as a single parent is you. The day-to-day challenges of ordinary living supply the substance of real life, no matter what your circumstances. Every day you are parenting, growing, and working at your career brings new learning experiences. Yet as single parents, we get so caught up in the mundane details of our own lives that often one activity, responsibility, or chore seems to blend into another, leaving us to wonder if there is any time for us. This section deals with creating a framework or a foundation from which to make more selective choices about how we choose to spend our time and about evaluating how effective these choices have been.

IT ALL BEGINS WITH CONFIDENCE

As we face our individual life challenges, it is natural that we look about and try to find common truths—or maybe just practical lessons to help us improve our lives and make the most of the opportunities before us. We may look for role models or simply look more closely at lives we admire. Through the achievements and successes of others we hope to learn new lessons and gain greater understanding about how best to win at the game of life. Of course, winning looks different for everyone. The priorities and values that fuel our daily efforts reflect our individual beliefs, values, and interests.

Rosabeth Moss Kantor, a Harvard Business School professor and noted author, has used examples of winning from sports teams and corporate boardrooms in her latest book—aptly titled *Confidence*—to demonstrate how important confidence is to winning. Dr. Kantor believes that the expectation of success is more important in gaining success than talent, knowledge, or intelligence. Not that talent, knowledge, and intelligence aren't helpful, but confidence is essential.

WHAT EXACTLY DOES CONFIDENCE MEAN?

Confidence is the belief that persistence and hard work will yield results. This is different than self-confidence, which is a belief that you cultivate within yourself that you can make things work out. Confidence nurtured by others is the key to winning the game of life. Confidence is not arrogance or conceit, which can lead us to sit back and wait for things somehow to magically get better.

How does a single mom facing lots of life challenges and, perhaps, feeling particularly isolated go about getting that confidence nurtured by others?

Get Out of the House and Be with People

Sitting alone at home with only your children for company and support is not going to help you. If your work situation is less than ideal and your girlfriends are in perpetual crisis mode, participate in an activity at which you excel. You will then meet people to nurture your confidence. It really does not matter what this activity might be. It does matter that you give yourself the opportunity to excel and be recognized. Support to build confidence can often come from people you do not know.

The more confident you become, the more you will be able to become an integral and visible part of your community, significantly lowering the "isolation factor." Consider adding community volunteer efforts to build your confidence. Helping others creates a win-win situation: your confidence gets bolstered, enabling you to give more, and so the success cycle continues.

Celebrate the Small Victories

Small victories increase our odds of bigger victories later on. That is why so many confident, emotionally healthy people typically give themselves little

rewards or treats to acknowledge their accomplishments. Try it yourself. Even simple things like patting yourself on the back or scheduling some extra private time to read a magazine or go for a walk can increase your belief that persistence and hard work does pay off. Maybe you are not sure that you will climb to the very top of the corporate ladder but do celebrate that glowing performance evaluation or latest salary increase.

Pick Your Friends Carefully

Surround yourself whenever possible with emotionally generous and secure people who will not hesitate to boost your confidence.

Remember That Victims Are Never Winners

Don't think of yourself as a victim—you will only sabotage your own efforts. Don't get bogged down by holding on to what evils your former partner might have inflicted. Why give anyone the power to define you? Keep your actions directed on the future—whether that's finding a new partner, new career, or new hobby.

Realize That Life Is a Long March

Don't expect to leap past obstacles and bypass challenges. Every day is another opportunity to make progress toward your goals. You are not going to suddenly wake up one morning and find that your life is magically what you hoped it would become. Progress toward your own goals is much more satisfying than trying to blame or extract revenge on your former partner or your less than supportive family. If you have made mistakes, like everyone else on the planet, take responsibility, don't repeat these mistakes, and move on!

YOUR PHYSICAL AND EMOTIONAL HEALTH

Your health is your most important asset. Although heredity plays a part in determining whether or not you are predisposed to a certain illness, basically this is an area of your life that you can largely control through proper diet, adequate exercise, routine medical checkups, and stress management. Given all the media attention focused on health issues, research studies with conflicting results that confuse us, or the latest exercise craze or fad diet, it is natural to feel uncertain and overwhelmed. Don't let every new finding or fad influence you or cause you to abandon healthy habits that have worked well for you.

Watch What You Eat

Is there a library big enough to store all the information that has been written even in the last couple of years about diet, nutrition, weight control, and energy? In addition to all that has been written about nutrition, the complicated relationship that many people, particularly women, have with food is becoming increasingly recognized. It's the same set of choices as with drugs or alcohol. If food or other weight-related issues are controlling issues in your life, get help fast!

But even if we don't fall into the "need-help-with-food" category, many of us, given the hectic schedules and multiple demands we face, still need to be reminded of a basic fact: Food fuels our bodies. Eating "empty calories" will not get you very far. There are people who aren't particularly emotionally involved with their automobiles but still are very careful about the quality of fuel they put in their car. Yet, how many of us know of similar types who wouldn't think twice about wolfing down candy bars and pastries during the middle of a time or energy crunch?

You Are Not a Garbage Pail. There is something about being a mom and not wanting to waste that seems to make our hands magically gravitate to our children's uneaten food. Whether it is the half-eaten peanut butter and jelly sandwich or pizza slice, the couple of spoonfuls of macaroni and cheese, or half a syrup-soaked pancake, it all seems to wind up in our mouths. If you think it will go to waste if you don't eat or drink it, then that makes you a garbage pail. You are more important than a garbage pail. Weight gain and other troublesome health problems are often the result of thinking we need to dispose of those inevitable leftover french fries or fruit juice by putting them in our bodies. Bottom line: what the kids don't eat belongs in the real garbage pail. Protect your health so that you will be around to take care of your children.

Resign from the "Clean Plate Club."

Many of us are unconsciously eating more calories than we need. The Clean Your Plate message is a big reason why U.S. waistlines are expanding. Portion sizes, particularly in restaurants, are ballooning, but we still feel we must eat it all. The "clean plate" came to prominence most recently when Americans were urged to not waste food after World War II. The real message to Americans was "eat only what you need," and that message is more important now than ever before.

Strive for Balance in Your Overall Eating Patterns.

There are many healthful and beneficial food choices that are actually cheaper than unhealthy, processed, or ready-to-eat foods. Simply stated, water is better than soda. Fresh fruit is better than juice drinks. Fats are not always "bad" and are, in fact, necessary for your health—hence the term "essential fatty acids." Carbohydrates are not all unhealthy. Make the distinction between unhealthy carbohydrates, such as white sugar, and complex carbohydrates, such as vegetables and whole grains. These complex carbohydrates provide vital nutrition and fiber to aid digestion. Legumes, beans, and grains are far better and cheaper than fatty meats and dairy products.

Taking control and balancing your eating habits are especially important to single mothers. We need to be a shade more attentive than other parents, particularly those in a two-income household, because our financial and time constraints can lead us to make poor food choices. The fast-food outlets can seem a welcome haven to the weary single mother. Processed and prepared foods can seem a blessing when, in truth, they offer us very little of the nutrition we need. Make a point of trying to avoid eating on the run and actually try to sit down when you eat.

Make Exercise a Part of Every Day

The benefits of exercise are almost too many to mention. According to the American Academy of Family Physicians, regular exercise reduces your risk of heart disease, high blood pressure, osteoporosis, diabetes, and obesity. It keeps your joints, tendons, and ligaments flexible so that it is easier to move around. Exercise reduces some of the effects of aging and contributes to your mental well-being and helps treat depression. Stress and anxiety are often relieved by regular exercise. You sleep better and your energy and endurance are increased by regular exercise. Only thirty to sixty minutes per day of moderate physical activity is all it takes to supply us with all the benefits we need for our physical and emotional well-being.

Despite these astounding benefits and the fairly short time we need to spend exercising each day, many single mothers don't make the time to exercise regularly. Time pressures often make taking this valuable time out to care for ourselves seem an impossibility. Making a commitment to exercise can begin by just making deliberate efforts to simply move your body. Start with simple life changes, like parking your car in the parking spot that is farthest from the mall or work entrance. Instead of spending ten minutes looking for a convenient parking spot, enjoy a brisk walk. Are you carrying a heavy tote or other essentials? This added weight only improves the exercise benefit. Always take the stairs. Take them two at a time for an extra challenge. Don't be surprised if you meet your boss or other higher-ups. Successful people have long mastered using time efficiently. They are also trying to squeeze some exercise into their work day.

Regular exercise does not mean a fancy gym membership or a schedule like an Olympic athlete. The best exercise is the one that you will do. Walking is considered one of the best choices because it is easy, safe, and cheap. Brisk walking can burn as many calories as running but is less likely than running or jogging to cause injuries. Walking does not require any training or special equipment, except for good shoes. Old-fashioned calisthenics like the ones your high school gym teacher used to make you do are also effective. No matter what kind of exercise you choose, an added benefit, if you miss adult companionship, is exercising with a buddy with whom you can chat. Ask other moms in the neighborhood about joining you for early morning or evening walks. Just be cautious about where and when you do this. Stick to public places that are well lit and safe.

Work Out with Your Kids! Physical fitness is not only a prescription for enhancing your physical and emotional well-being, but also greatly benefits your children. Moms who exercise are more likely to have kids who exercise, helping them to have better long-term health. The best approach to family fitness is the "play-approach." Present exercise activities as opportunities to play. Imagination and creativity can go a long way to turning exercise into

play. Throw a Frisbee, do cartwheels on your way out to the car, or dance in the kitchen to a favorite CD. Rent exercise videos and work out with your kids in front of the television, or take a brisk evening walk after supper. Some single moms take their children along to the local track or park. While mom runs or power walks, the children can play, and she can still keep her eyes on what they are doing. The point is that you can find some activity to share with your child while benefiting from exercise, if you make family fitness a priority.

The Secret to Jump-Starting Your Day

Wake up before the sun and do whatever it is that feeds your soul. Sound impossible? Or just plain crazy? Well, it works, and here's why: when we try to carve time out of our day to fit in personal prescriptive routines such as working out, meditative exercise or prayer, bathing and primping (and we don't mean a quick shower), or studying or creating art, the knowledge that this activity needs to be performed lingers long and hard in our brains. Emptying our brains of tasks to be done by recording them on paper has always been a terrific stress management tool.

But imagine how accomplished you can feel not having to check a calendar or appointment schedule to see when private time can be slotted in because this has already been done and your day is now ahead of you.

There is no question that those folks who walk five miles in the dark morning, meditate while the moon is still out, or write the great American novel (or self-help book) while the kids are still asleep are the ones who get their goals met. Feeding your soul at 5:00 or 6:00 A.M. or even earlier, if necessary, makes you feel that the day hasn't gotten ahead of you. When the sun comes up and you've already coddled yourself with those extra, but oh so necessary, perks, you'll be ready to meet the challenges of your daily life head on, with a concentrated, intense dedication that is found in the attitudes of those who live fully in the present.

So go to bed early tonight, and wake up one step ahead of the rest of the Earth!

Stress Management

This section won't elaborate on popular stress reduction techniques (biofeedback, yoga, reflexology, deep breathing, and visualization) because we are bombarded with this information in every magazine and self-help book that deals with living in the modern world. Also, this information is not any different for single mothers than for those who are married or divorced, male or female, or gay or straight.

What is unique to single mothers is that their stress seems so built in, so inherent to their lifestyle, that the thought of taking time to learn how to reduce stress can cause more stressful worry. Tell a group of single mothers that you have discovered the latest stress management technique, and they will collectively refrain, "But where will I find the time?" So first, before we deal with stress, we have to understand our stress. Because we think of our stress as coming at us from every direction—job stress, money stress, parenting stress, family stress, and relationship stress—the sources seem endless. The more the sources of stress, the less possible it seems that we can begin to grapple with this fundamental life issue. Managing stress, however, is really a matter of "knowing your enemy." When you realize that stress results from having too many demands on too few resources—in other words, everyday life—you'll realize that all stress, no matter what the source, is essentially the same.

Following are common symptoms of stress, along with some simple cures:

Constant Fatigue. Make sure you get enough sleep. Some people require only six hours of sleep a night coupled with a twenty-minute catnap during the day, while others require a full eight hours or more at night. Figure out what sleep pattern works best for you, but remember that the quality of sleep is more important than the amount of hours actually slept. Most people find that sticking to a sleep schedule, going to bed about the same time and rising about the same time each morning, is of great benefit. If you have bouts of insomnia, ask a health care professional for some tips on how to improve the quality of your rest.

Just as your children need time to relax and make the transition to bedtime, so do you. Find out what works for you. Some mothers enjoy a relaxing cup of tea or the opportunity to read uninterrupted. Even five minutes of slow, steady, deep breathing while sitting up or lying down is beneficial, since it slows your pulse rate and adds to your general feeling of well-being. Organize for the next day before bedtime, but never, ever take your problems to bed. The one thing everyone deserves to have is deep, dark, delicious sleep.

Frequent Illness. Be sure to eat nutritious foods and stay away from energy zappers like sweets and highly processed foods. Limit consumption of heavy or rich foods and alcoholic beverages. Don't smoke and avoid smokers, since exposure to secondhand smoke is deadly.

Diet Deficiencies. Discuss with your physician whether you should be taking a daily multivitamin. Keep in mind that antioxidants are very important in your diet since they have been proven to combat the risk of getting many diseases, especially cancer. Eat lots of foods rich in beta-carotene (dark-green leafy vegetables such as collard greens, kale, spinach, turnip greens, mustard greens, and Swiss chard and yellow-orange fruits and vegetables such as carrots, pumpkins, sweet potatoes, cantaloupes, peaches, mangoes, and papayas) and rich in vitamins C (asparagus, broccoli, cabbage, brussels sprouts, cauliflower, green peppers, melons, oranges, tangerines, and strawberries) and E (almonds, hazelnuts, peanut butter, vegetable oil, sunflower seeds, and wheat germ). The best part is that most of these foods are inexpensive!

Depression. Daily exercise especially in sunny weather will not only give you more energy but also can ward off depression, since the brain releases endorphins when the heart rate is elevated for that length of time. In addition, exercise can help prevent you from coming down with common ailments such as colds and helps keep your immune system functioning optimally.

If depression persists, despite eating properly, taking vitamins, and exercising regularly, seek out a support group or talk with a counselor, friend, or family member. If your depression seems overwhelming or you alternate between depression and extreme hostility and anger, see a psychologist or psychiatrist. In addition, most cities and counties have resources and services for women through hospitals and community agencies. Check the listings in the local phone directory.

Anxiety about Time Constraints. Deal with conflicting or competing demands in a realistic manner by prioritizing and compromising. Never rely on your memory to remember chores or tasks that must be completed—write everything down for daily or weekly scheduling. Learn how to say no! Establish a routine that is highly organized, even if it borders on rigidity. You'll avoid retracing your steps and other timewasters like searching for your child's lunchbox or looking for your shoes or stamps. The occasions when you break the routine to indulge in something frivolous will seem like an exquisite pleasure. Teach your children how to manage and organize their time.

Understanding Chronic Stress

The stress of living with children can be all-consuming when you are not getting emotional support from friends, family, and community.

Don't take this statement as a message that it is unhealthy to have

children, when the message of this book is that children can be the greatest joys of your life. But it does mean that single mothers in particular need to learn how to manage their stress by first understanding that they may be at a greater risk for higher levels of chronic stress. Secondly, it is especially important for single mothers to learn techniques that will work for them to help control the chronic levels of stress most of us will experience.

Insidiously, stress and guilt go hand in hand. They feed off one another, gaining strength from each other in a self-defeating, debilitating cycle. Knowing what to do to stop this guilt-stress cycle seems simple enough. It's actually doing it that seems impossible. There is so much about which single parents feel guilty. Moreover, single parents genuinely feel that this guilt is deserved. We often feel powerless in the face of circumstances surrounding what we believe to be our own unique "guilties." To tackle stress, which is nothing more than too many demands on too few resources, we must recognize it as a fact of everyday life. Coping effectively with stress involves not so much isolating its sources but, more importantly, looking at stress in a global way and trying to increase the resources

available to cope with its inevitability.

Guilt is a far more insidious enemy than stress. Guilt is private; guilt is not easily talked about. Guilt can even be viewed as deserved because we made poor life choices in the past.

You may already have learned how to sort out your feelings surrounding your reasons for becoming a single parent and discovered that much of your guilt was unearned. As each day presents you with new challenges, you must remember to remain aware of the two types of guilt—earned guilt and unearned guilt.

Simply put, unearned guilt is the unnecessary one—we feel guilty because we don't make much money, we don't have a designer home, or we didn't become the person our mother thought we should be. Earned guilt is conscience. In other words, it's okay to feel a little guilty if you helped yourself to your friend's best lipstick and then lied about losing it. It's even okay to feel a little guilty because you consciously changed plans at the last minute and caused someone special disappointment. But it's also okay not to feel guilty if you take some private time by reading instead of watching your child show you for the fifth time that day how she does ten cartwheels in a row. Saying, "Mommy needs to do something for herself right now and doesn't want to watch you" is no reason to succumb to the "I'm-a-neglectful-mother" guilties.

If you're divorced or widowed and still plagued with guilt about the kind of wife you were or are a single mother outside of marriage and doubt your ability to handle the choice you made because you worry you are not good parent material or you got what you deserved, go back and reread the chapters dedicated to you and your particular life circumstances.

TIME MANAGEMENT

If I read one more "how to organize" article in popular women's magazines—you know, the ones that advise "take a bath and get your husband to take out the trash"—I'll hit the roof! Any advice on time management for those of us who forgot the husband?

Assess your time investment. Figure that there are 168 hours in a week and see where your time goes. Keep a log for one week and jot down everything you do. Then see what time bandits you can get rid of. Don't forget the staring, daydreaming, and distracted-by-TV time. Everyone gets the same amount of time, whether you are rich or poor, married or single. Decide what your priorities are and spend your time accordingly.

Here's a simple but effective tip: invest in an inexpensive kitchen timer. The uses are endless, particularly when used as a handy helper for managing kids. Here's how:

◆ When you need private time, set the timer for fifteen or twenty minutes, and concentrate on attacking or completing one special project or at least a segment of a job until the timer goes off.

◆ Use the timer when putting your preschool child in time-out. Experts advise one minute for each year of age. Avoid going over ten minutes.

◆ Set the timer to give your child undivided attention. Set the timer for about thirty minutes and let him know that this is his time and that

when the timer goes off that you are going to do something else. Rely on voice mail or simply let the phone ring. Allow no distractions.

◆ Set the timer for approximately twenty minutes daily to give yourself some private time. Relax, exercise, laugh, or write in a journal. Obviously, this is not possible when your children are infants or toddlers. Let your older children know, however, that this is your time and you are not to be interrupted.

YOU ARE LIKE A WAREHOUSE—STOCK UP NOW!

Suppose you are part of a group of single-parent employees at a major financial corporation sales incentive meeting. The speaker asks the audience of approximately sixty adults, "How many of you think that being a good parent means putting your child first?" Hands shoot up so fast that there is no time for anyone to think that the second part of this query might be a trick question. Would you be one of the handraisers? But wait. The speaker follows immediately with, "And how many of you believe that you, the parent, are number one?" Would you glance around to see if the others would recoil in horror, noting perhaps two women and one man hesitantly raising their hands? Where would your hand be if the speaker shot back, "Right you are!" to the minority who got it correct?

Look at it this way. You're like a warehouse. If you're not well stocked with inventory, how can you possibly give to anyone else? By making yourself number one, you will have on reserve a supply of "nurturing" that you can readily lavish on your children. Thinking about this for a minute, don't you agree that it is a pretty logical concept?

COMMIT TO YOURSELF

Believe it or not, the essence of being a good parent is putting your own needs first. Instead of endless self-sacrifice and denial of your needs, you should focus on making yourself the best person you are capable of becoming. It is this determined focus on yourself as a complete human being that creates the life energies vital to parenting, which is simply the process of supervision and guidance that allows children to emerge as independent beings. It is from your growth and development that your child grows and develops. After all, who arrived here first, you or your child? Just as the earth revolves around the sun for life-sustaining energy, your child thrives on the nurturing, caring, and warmth that you provide. You are the nucleus of your family, just as one day your child may become the nucleus of his or her family.

This commitment to self does not mean, however, that your children are left to their own devices while you pursue Zen meditation in some distant location. This commitment to self also does not mean giving yourself permission to accept a job in which sixty-hour work weeks are typical and expected. Simply stated, commitment to self does not give you permission or license to abandon, minimize, ignore, or in any other way compromise your responsibilities and duties as a parent. What this commitment to self does mean is that you also have the responsibility to develop your own unique talents and

skills to their fullest and not use your children as an excuse for not moving ahead with your own life. This idea of commitment to self shouldn't just pop into your mind every so often when you read magazine articles recommending occasionally pampering yourself in a hot bath. Commitment to self must be a priority and must be evident in all you do every day for both yourself and your children.

Demonstrate your commitment to yourself by completing the Partnership (with Self) Contract. As with any other important document, review its provisions carefully and know that you are making a promise to yourself when you sign it. Review the provisions of this contract often. Make it your guide to more joyful living in the present for both you and your children!

THE ART OF PRIORITIZING AND COMPROMISING

Coping with stress is usually a daily activity and often can be an ongoing battle. Successfully fought battles have two components: strategy and planning. The strategy is to decrease the demands and increase the resources. Planning is simply putting the strategy into action.

How in the world do we go about decreasing demands when everything around us seems so pressing and urgent? If there is, indeed, any one trick to reducing stress, here it is: set your priorities and make compromises. Which priorities will be set and what compromises will be made are yours to decide and are unique to you. Is it really necessary to have a floor you can eat off of or

PARTNERSHIP (WITH SELF) CONTRACT

My name is _____. I am a single mother who is committed to self-discovery and to furthering my joy and growth as a remarkable woman with my new best partner—me.

I agree to the following ideals:

I don't have to be mom and dad to my child(ren). I just need to be a loving, guiding parent.

Allowing myself time for my feelings to emerge has been a wonderful cathartic for me. I promise to allow a few minutes every day to express my feelings, no matter how great or rotten I feel that day.

If and when I remarry, I promise to continue to nurture myself above anyone else and not to stop growing because I am in a relationship. If I find that I can't grow because of the confines of a restrictive relationship, I will change that.

I will listen to and learn from my child(ren) as well as teach.

When people tell me how scary it must be to be a single mom, I will show them my bravery.

When people misjudge single mothers in my presence, I will educate them to the truths.

When people question the legitimacy of children whose birth certificates don't bear a man's signature, I will correct them gently but pointedly.

As a single mother, I have discovered how creative and resourceful I am. Within the next three months I will have chosen _____ as an outlet with which to explore myself more fully. _____ and _____ are two other interests I hope to pursue that I might not have considered had I not been a single mother.

I have chosen a friend, support group member, relative, or spiritual teacher named _____ to contact once a week if for nothing else but a reality check.

In the course of raising myself and my children, I have learned that this is not a transitional time until another husband or father for my child(ren) comes along, but rather a time that encourages me to deal with the here and now. The task is not so much to get through each day, but rather to appreciate the joy that is in the process. To that end, I agree to the above commitments, which have no specific time goals, but I agree to begin this new journey with myself on the following date: _____.

_____

(Signature)

a spotless kitchen? Is it critical that you get to the dentist? Trade off and put off chores that are not urgent. Move to the top of the list an evening exercise class or an afternoon of roller skating with the family. Plus, make sure you enlist the help of your children in performing chores they are capable of doing. For instance, five- and six-year-olds can help set the table or put away laundry and feed pets.

Don't wait for the opportunity to find the time to do what you need or want. Life can change in the blink of an eye. Time is never found, altered, hastened, or slowed down. You can only take charge of it. A few tips for staying on top of the stress:

♦ Don't jam your head with repeated thoughts of how much you have to do and how you will never get it done. This trap often happens when you are in a place where you have no choice but to wait.

♦ Write down things you must do or remember. Never keep anything that needs doing locked up in your brain. Think about saving up the many short errands and jobs for a once-a-month marathon.

♦ Ask yourself, "Will something terrible happen to me or my children if I don't do this right now?" If nothing terrible will happen and you are stressed and tired, you can save the task for later.

Keep this basic premise in mind: Whatever today's priorities are can be just for today. Very little is cast in stone. Flexibility is important. Remember, too, that it's the little things that tend to wear us down and cause us to experience debilitating stress. Knowing what little things drain us is critical not only to coping with stress but also to our overall sense of well-being.

DECIDING WHAT'S IMPORTANT

I'm a recent single mother of two teenage boys. How do I go about setting some priorities? It seems everything I need to do is so different from all the other families in my neighborhood. I mean, I work, my kids are involved in numerous activities, I'm taking a nursing course at night, and my house is one giant dust ball.

You set priorities based on what is important to you and your family and not on what others are doing. It sounds as if you are doing a very good job of that; so don't let guilt stress you out over a job well done.

For some single moms, clean clothes come first because they are hard to fake. Their children's tidy appearance is a priority for them. For others, the little things that get to them are a dirty bathroom and clutter like overflowing trash bins, dead flowers, two-day-old newspapers, and junk mail. If you would expend your last breath taking out the garbage rather than look at it, then most likely your kids and you know this and will typically respect the need for, if not a clutter-free house, at least a clutter-managed one.

But if older children's rooms are another matter, where overlooking the destruction is a very big compromise for you, then closing the doors and walking away might help, although not always. Messy bedrooms might frustrate all other parents as well, but you need to recognize that as a single parent you have a finite amount of emotional energy and time. Remind yourself that there are bigger parenting issues during the teenage years than dirty clothes on the floor.

Hoping that your children remember what you taught them about honesty and integrity rather than your monologues about bathtub ring or the value of organized dresser drawers is a healthy compromise. Your time together as a family will become increasingly precious as your children grow older and more independent.

Two for the Road

It's time to get rid of insensitive words or phrases that make most single moms bristle when they hear them. Here are two that should hit the pavement and never be heard from again:

* *Broken home*—Oh please! Too many mothers live in two-parent homes numbed by emotional distance, riddled with abuse, and marred by the constant threat of violence. Leaving this kind of situation actually creates the chance for a peaceful and loving home.

* *Illegitimate child*—There's no such thing! Why not just call kids kids? Why not instead teach others to adopt a more gentle term for a baby born outside of marriage as used by some South American cultures: "niño natural," which means "natural child"?

"DOES COMPROMISING MEAN I HAVE TO BE A MARTYR?"

I'm a never-married mom of twin boys and have found that compromising has definitely been a plus in reducing stress. But sometimes I hear from my family and friends, particularly the childless ones, how I shouldn't have to compromise and that I don't have to be a martyr. So now what?

Nonsense. Compromising is such a sophisticated negotiating tool that those who are successful at it may seem like martyrs to unsuspecting fledglings who don't know the difference between compromise and selling out.

If you are able to overlook dust as well as waxy yellow buildup in exchange for seeing that you get your nursing degree or that your kids are in the kayaking club, then clearly you are on the right track. However, if your children are allergic to dust, then again, only you can decide what stays and what goes.

INCREASE YOUR RESOURCES

At first, increasing our resources seems like an almost impossible task. Most of us are struggling with the double burden of too little time and too little money. It often seems that the more we are linked by technology like television, which can take us anywhere and show us anything, the more isolated we become from the families around us and from the resources in our own communities. It's a mistake to assume that because you are a single-parent family that you shouldn't network and seek support from other types of people and families. Whether it's the single woman down the block, the married couple next door, the retired couple across the street, or school-age individuals such as a friend's teenage son, you can expect to discover resources, allies, and support if you search carefully enough.

This search for resources begins with your willingness both to give and to receive help. Look around you with keener eyes. Do you live near a college or university? A student may need cheap housing. Maybe you have a spare bedroom in exchange for low rent and child care at night so you can attend a class yourself. Do you have a skill such as bookkeeping, word processing, or hair-cutting that you can barter in exchange for plumbing, cleaning, or home repair?

Is there a community bulletin board at your child's school, day care center, pediatrician's office, local hospital, or athletic club? Why not post your name and a note stating that you would like to get to know other parents who would be willing to exchange rides to or from school or other activities? Naturally, you would first need to be entirely comfortable that a responsible, dependable adult will transport your child safely. But once you have this assurance, think of the advantages. For instance, another mother may need to work late one or two nights a week. If you offer to pick up her child on those late nights, she may be happy to take your child to a scheduled activity such as piano lessons or swimming. Don't be afraid to reach out and include anyone in your community, married or not. The worst possible answer might be an occasional no. But isn't it exciting to consider the possibilities that could come from yes?

Decide what is important and what

you and your children need to gain some control over in what is for everyone a hectic, unpredictable world. Priorities and compromises do not take away from what we need. Rather, they give us less stress, less guilt, and more of what we all deserve—increased happiness and peace of mind.

Feel as though you cannot afford a social life because of the high cost of babysitting? Think about organizing a babysitting co-op, which is nothing more than each parent banking hours of babysitting toward receiving equal hours of babysitting. Begin with parents you know and trust. It does not matter whether you recruit single parents or married ones. In today's unpredictable economy, almost everyone would welcome such a venture. This is also a terrific way to network with people in your community.

If your group grows large, consider using a centralized system to keep tabs on babysitting schedules and hours.

LIVE IN THE HERE AND NOW

Any activity can be fun if you allow yourself and your children to enjoy it. Don't know how to do this? Take this advice from Alcoholics Anonymous: start acting as if you're happy. Better yet, start acting as if you're successful, as if you're fulfilled, and as if you're sitting on top of the world. These attitudes soon become your beliefs, and sooner than you realize, this is exactly how you will feel for real.

Copy this idea and hang it on the refrigerator, bathroom mirror, or any place where you can refer to it. Do another single mother a favor and make her a copy, too.

THE DO'S AND DON'TS OF TAKING CARE OF YOU

- **Don't** waste time regretting failure and feeling guilty. Give up all rescue fantasies.

- **Do** pat yourself on the back often.

- **Don't** attribute every crisis or problem your family faces to single parenthood. Every family has its own set of difficulties and has a rough time now and then.

- **Do** relish your independence. It's nice to make your own decisions. Remind yourself that there are many advantages to being a single parent.

- **Do** keep a determined focus on making yourself the best person you can be. From your life energies will come the energy to enable your children to grow and thrive as independent human beings.

- **Do** keep your personal warehouse stocked. Make a daily determined effort to nurture your physical, emotional, and spiritual needs.

- **Don't** let stress rule your life. Learn how to compromise and be flexible enough to know that goals and priorities will often change from day to day.

- **Don't** limit your support network to single-parent families only. Seek and give support to all kinds of people and families.

- **Don't** give in to your child's every whim. Single parents who are guilty of giving that extra toy or candy bar to replace the missing parent spoil their kids in the process. Spoiling children leads to more and more time-consuming battles over control. You are the parent, and your word is final.

11
Money Matters

There is no denying that the strongest force in our society is the power of money. Men have known this far longer than women, who are still faced with emotional obstacles that can sabotage asset-building efforts. Historically, men had mentors to lead them into the world of banks and boardrooms, while women were denied access to this world and taught to believe that financial matters were not part of their role or life responsibilities. Women were instructed that their only real contribution was to home and children. While women's roles have greatly changed and the responsibility for financial matters is now part of everyone's life role, many women still cling to self-defeating myths and assumptions. Emotional obstacles only partially understood plague many women. Addiction is one form of emotional obstacle, whether it is a dependency on a relationship, food, chemicals, or shopping. Myths with messages like "good girls will be taken care of" and "nice girls don't discuss money" are also serious emotional obstacles for many women. You will undermine your money management plans, no matter how well-laid, if you don't acknowledge these myths, assumptions, and emotional obstacles and eliminate them from your thinking.

CHANGE THE WAY YOU LOOK AT MONEY

If you have let some of these obstacles get in the way of managing your money, you need to change the way you think about money before you can become financially responsible. Whether you are currently getting a divorce, entering a new relationship, or pregnant and want minimal involvement with the child's father, you need to avoid situations where you will not be in control of your financial future. The first step in managing your finances is to take charge of your economic situation, no matter how bleak it looks.

Falling prey to all too common financial pitfalls can sabotage your efforts to become financially fit. All these traps that many women have found themselves in could be avoided by learning the difference between money matters and money myths. Just because you may be an investment banker from nine to five during the week doesn't mean that you are viewing money realistically when it comes to going in together on a condominium with your boyfriend or keeping joint checking accounts with your husband.

It's also important to have a clear understanding of the meaning of money as control when it exists as a dominant part of the male-female relationship. For example, your partner may feel he works harder than you because he earns more money and therefore leaves you solely responsible for cooking and cleaning. Clearly distinguishing emotional issues from practical ones and negotiating "house rules" early in the relationship can resolve many of these issues.

This is not to say that you shouldn't ever get involved romantically with a man unless every financial aspect of his life is up front. However, you should recognize that, in general, men and women have fundamentally different views of money. It is also important to understand the role money can play in empowering a man's life and how your financial independence frees you to make decisions that are in your best interest, too.

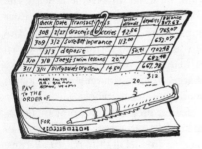

THE TRUTH ABOUT THE THREE MAJOR MONEY MYTHS

MYTH #1: *Money is synonymous with love and commitment.* Money is a medium of exchange. When we have certain needs and wants, they are satisfied through money. Money is how we measure our achievements in the workplace. However, many women report having trouble equating money with business. When control of money

instead is connected to an "I'm just not good enough feeling," nagging and persistent doubts can follow. Women who feel that they can't offer much in a relationship other than money often wonder, "Does he love me for me or for the money?" Feeling good about yourself never happens for women if they create situations where money substitutes for personal qualities they feel they are lacking.

MYTH #2: *He doesn't control me, only my credit.* Wrong. Too many women think that because their former partner or husband handled all the family finances that he should continue to do so even after a divorce. Wives who were not a major part of the financial decisions during a marriage often relinquish too much power to their spouse during a divorce.

Financial entanglements often signal not being able to let go. Severing money connections is an important step toward disengaging yourself from a dead-end relationship. Remember—the one who pays is the one who makes the choices.

If you are getting divorced, be sure that what appears to be your seemingly fair split of the debts includes not only totaling up the dollar amounts, but also looking at what debts are outstanding and in whose name. Make sure that money coming to you comes directly to you. Do not accept terms in a separation or divorce agreement whereby the former spouse agrees to make mortgage or credit card payments or any other type of loan payment.

MYTH #3: *It cost me nothing!* You've heard the expression: there is no such thing as a free lunch. Because money is a symbol of power and control, be cautious before agreeing to an arrangement in which someone else pays your bills, such as maintaining your auto insurance or paying for your child's swim club membership or child care. There will be a price to pay in some form, whether in blood, sweat, or tears. It is up to you to determine what that will be and if you are willing to pay. Weigh the advantages against the disadvantages of any economic agreement. Ask yourself, "What do I have to gain not only financially, but also in time, convenience, and peace of mind?" More importantly, ask yourself, "What do I have to lose in terms of time, convenience, and peace of mind?"

COMBINING ASSETS DOESN'T NECESSARILY MEAN COMBINING HEARTS

My significant other and I had wanted to escape the rat race of New York and open a New England bed and breakfast.

I guess I saw this venture as the end of our "dating years" and the beginning of real commitment, including marriage and kids. I saw the combining of our assets as proof positive of commitment and did not insist on drawing up legal, binding documents. The bed and breakfast succeeded, but the relationship failed. Had I kept my finances and heart separate from the beginning, with the financial obligations spelled out, I would have at least been in a financial position to move on from this failed relationship. But doesn't a business attitude seem to diminish the romance?

Money is not love and needs to be kept separate from it. In other words, don't allow unmet emotional needs to color your money management decisions. Money is not commitment nor can it make you feel good about yourself, in spite of its ability to purchase many material things. It is so important to remember that money is business.

In fact, the quicker you get the business side of dealing with money out of the way of new relationships, the more intense the romance can become because you never have to worry that you owe or are owed anything.

YOU NEED TO BE THE DECISIONMAKER

In a situation that is fairly common, a couple had long been divorced—kind of. The wife was deeply hurt and confused by her husband's announcement that he wanted out of the marriage. They had two young children, and she felt overwhelmed by the responsibilities that lay before her as a single mother. Fortunately, or at least so she thought at the time, her ex, following the divorce, showed no signs of abandoning his responsibilities, financial or otherwise, to the kids. She and the kids were allowed to live in the house, which had been a wedding gift from her mother-in-law, until both children were out of college. Having owned a home for awhile, the newly single mom was no stranger to the many expenses that come with home-owning, over and above the mortgage and taxes. She insisted in the divorce agreement that her ex take some responsibility for expenses like home repair.

That can work out just fine, depending on what type of agreement you may have. But if you have an elaborate agreement by which your ex has to pay a proportional share of home repairs and anticipated expenses—only if he agrees that the repairs are necessary—you're in for a run for your money. Your ex-spouse may get to choose the painter, contractor, or whomever and has to agree to the cost of the repair. Initially, you may be satisfied with this type of arrangement because you're glad that you are not going to be paying all the home repair costs. But in cases like this, especially if your ex is something of a control freak, he is going to have a lot more than just some say-so in the situation.

"MY EX-HUSBAND WANTS TO PAY MY MORTGAGE DIRECTLY TO THE BANK"

I'm getting divorced after many unhappy years of marriage. I had little say or control over the family finances during our marriage, and so I did not raise any objections to the suggestion by my ex that there be a provision in my divorce settlement that he would make the mortgage payments directly to the bank. After all, I'll have enough on my hands with two teenage boys to look after. Why should I have to go to the trouble of depositing his check and then turning around and writing a check to the bank as a house payment every month?

It's not that much trouble, and if you don't do it that way, you may find yourself in worse trouble. Consider what happened to one single mother who agreed to a similar arrangement. She changed her way of thinking after she received a notice from the bank that she was three months in arrears on the mortgage. The bank was demanding immediate payment or foreclosure proceedings would begin.

Like her, you would be stunned. You would need to spend more money on attorney fees once you discovered that your ex may have simply grown tired of writing that check every month. Most men who originally agree to such an arrangement later on admit, "Why should I be paying for a house I'm not living in? The divorce was your idea and your fault. You are the one who wanted out. You want to take care of yourself. Go ahead."

True, it is not written in stone that your ex will renege on his promises. But if, like many before him, he does, it can take a lot of scrambling, borrowing, and overtime for you to hold on to your house when you find yourself in this predicament. Other women have not been so lucky. Judges tell women every day, as they are about to foreclose on their homes, that the court can do nothing to enforce family court orders requiring former spouses to make mortgage or other types of payments. Work out the settlement differently so that the money is in your control, not your ex-spouse's.

"MY EX-HUSBAND IS MY HANDYMAN. . . ."

My ex has agreed to help me from time to time by paying for certain repair and maintenance bills, as long as he selects the handyperson or contracting help and determines what really needs to be done and when he can do it. I don't think this is so bad. It's not like he's intrusive or anything. Besides, there is no one else in my life right now to help me, right?

Think again. Some women in your situation have found that they were still a little angry and confused and wanted their ex around assuming "husband" responsibilities. Sometimes, the presence of that person in your home can enable you to remain in denial that your marriage is over. Do you ever think about reconciling your marriage? Maybe deep down you feel that as long as he is around the house for any reason that he will see what he had thrown away and reconciliation is possible. Maybe there are other things going on, but you still find yourself emotionally entangled. Your ex may be more than willing to agree to the home repair conditions because his needs for control are satisfied that way and he, too, is emotionally entangled.

If he is the one who initiated the breakup, he may be the kind of man who had few or no regrets about leaving his partner but feels rotten about leaving his kids and the home he considered to be his. He may just need something to do to occupy his unwisely utilized time. There is always something to do around a house, and home repair responsibilities might give him the perfect excuse to come and go in the house as he sees fit. Consider whether you would like to have unannounced inspection tours or risk having him march through the house like a commanding general issuing orders about everything from the CDs left scattered on your daughter's bed to the kitchen floor that he feels needs mopping.

At first, you may welcome these visits. But if you have any desire to build a life for yourself and your family, it won't take long for you to see his unannounced visits for what they are—intrusive, controlling, and unnecessary. You may be able to let go, but he is not.

"JUST ONE LAST REPAIR BEFORE I CHANGE THE LOCKS. . . ."

My ex has remarried and divorced, all in the course of eighteen months. His newest ex resented his coming here to help me around the house sometimes. Now he is living alone, but he has a girlfriend who can't stand that he still comes by my home just to check on things. The truth is that I'm sick of his coming by, but I haven't told him because it was easier to let his girlfriends and ex-wife do that. I'm thinking of changing the locks, but not until he fixes a leak that I just discovered in the roof. Is this a bad idea?

It would be more appropriate to have a talk with this man and ask him to please call first, before just walking in. Of course, if he doesn't comply, changing the locks is a good idea. However, don't proceed too hastily. It's not going to be hard to guess what might

happen next if you try to get him to repair your roof while distancing yourself from him. Knowing that you are serious about changing his "entry requirements," he may stall or look for excuses to postpone working on your roof. He may offer to come by, but only at a time when it would seriously inconvenience you or when you would have to take off from work.

Rather than continuing this emotional entanglement or putting up with a leaky roof, it might be best to come to some sort of negotiation where he pays you so that a roofer of your choice handles the repair. If that still presents problems, find a reputable company to temporarily patch the roof and repair it when you are able to pay for it without involving your ex.

TIME IS MONEY

I had a long relationship with a married man much older than myself. For a long while, his other life did not bother me all that much. I had a promising career and good friends and did not wait by the phone. As my thirtieth birthday approached, I began to feel that inexplicable longing for a child. Later, I found myself pregnant and was delighted. When the baby's father realized that his life would go on uninterrupted, he, too, seemed pleased that I was going to have a baby. I thought it best to plan for the baby as the single mother I was, without reliance on the father, although his offer to pay the baby's educational expenses was irresistible. He kept his promise to pay my daughter's educational expenses, but he chose

a private school to his liking. This school was close to his office because he does occasionally like to go to school plays and science fairs and that kind of stuff. It's a fine school, but it is located very far from my home and office. I wish I had never agreed to this because I am paying every day in time and inconvenience.

People most often will do what is good for them. Your daughter's father is doing exactly that. He wants his daughter to have a good education and wants to participate in the most convenient way possible for him.

You have a couple of options. You can tell him that you no longer wish him to pay for your daughter's schooling, thereby giving you the right to enroll her where you please. Denied the opportunity to manage your daughter's education, he may decide to seek greater control and even sue for partial custody. Of course, he may do nothing and simply retreat further from your daughter's life. So instead of seeing her father at least at school events, her contact with her father may diminish. This change may be good for you, but it would not be in the best interests of your daughter.

There is always the future to consider. The cost of a college education is enormous. His ability to provide a free college education for your daughter would be no small advantage in life. There is no denying that, for now, his control over where your child attends school is an inconvenience, using up both your time and energy.

What would you be doing with this time if your daughter was enrolled somewhere closer to home? One thing you might be doing is working extra hours, perhaps in part to help save for her education. Why not consider the time you are spending back and forth to her school as just that—a part-time job the earnings from which you will use to finance your daughter's education? Your daughter's father's offer to finance her education should be in writing. There should also be provisions as part of his estate planning to enact this agreement should he die before your daughter's education is completed. This is just good, sound business sense.

GETTING YOUR FINANCIAL HOUSE IN ORDER

The first step to getting your financial house in order is to put your financial goals in writing. Be as specific as possible. Saying "I want a lot of money" is not clear enough to be a specific goal, but stating "I want to provide my child with one half of his college costs" or "I want to buy a house" or "I want to own my own business" is a specific goal. It may seem confusing to write down goals when you aren't really aware of the condition of your financial house. But deciding first on your goals leads you to the second step—finding out where you stand—and ultimately to a plan of action.

Some people give up before even attempting the first step, believing that meeting their goals is impossible, especially after they learn what it costs to buy a house, send a kid to college, or retire. During this step, no one is asking you to pay for anything. Just write down your goals. Don't wait to find time to write down your goals; make time now. List as many realistic goals as you can. "Realistic" means leaving out

the magical thinking such as "After I win the lottery, I will buy a racehorse!" Whether you have three major goals or twenty, you must be specific, write them down, and keep them in a file labeled "Finances." Put the file away for a few days, if you are overwhelmed, and pull it out when you are ready to proceed to the next important step.

Establish an Operating Budget

It's critical to find out how much money you owe and how much you are spending to establish an operating budget. This critical step is often ignored because it is painful to take a hard look at how limited your resources might be and how much debt you really might be carrying.

It is especially important that single mothers keep a record of income and

---

SINGLE MOM OF NOTE

Cora Millay, Mother of Edna St. Vincent Millay

Edna St. Vincent Millay paid tribute to her single mother and Cora Millay's hard work as a wigmaker in her poem "The Ballad of the Harp-Weaver." Cora may have been poor, but she provided her three daughters with lots of books and the love of music, poetry, and independence. Although she dabbled in writing like her famous poet daughter, Cora supported her family by working as an overnight nurse and making wigs. Edna St. Vincent Millay credited her mother for much of her success: It was Cora who urged Edna to enter her first great poem in a contest that paved the way for her literary career.

outflow on a weekly or monthly basis since getting control of spending is crucial to managing money. Begin by keeping track to the penny of all the money you spend in one week, including that vending machine purchase or other small change outlay. Look at your discretionary and fixed expenses. Do you really need to buy so many books when the library is right around the corner? Is HBO really worth it? List all your income on the opposite side of the page so you can get a clear picture of your financial situation. Remember that child support at best is a temporary source of income. If you are relying on child support to meet rent or mortgage payments, you need to consider what your options would be if child support payments were interrupted or how you will manage financially when these child support payments stop.

If you find you need to take this hard look but feel you lack the skills or just can't face it alone, this is a good time to ask for the assistance of another single mom who might possess some savvy money skills. Most mothers going it alone understand financial problems, and there is no reason to feel embarrassment at your predicament. The calculating eye of another person who has taken hold of her finances might be just the incentive and role model you need.

If you're having problems paying bills, you may want to contact a credit

counseling service. Nonprofit organizations in every state counsel consumers who are in debt. Counselors try to arrange a repayment plan that is acceptable to you and your creditors. They can also help you set up a realistic budget. These counseling services are offered at little or no charge. You can find the office nearest you by checking in your telephone directory.

Establish an Emergency Fund

This is more important than saving for your kid's college, paying off debt, or saving for retirement. If something bad happens, such as you lose your job or get sick, you will need emergency funds to pay day-to-day living expenses. Ideally, you should have $10,000 to $15,000 in emergency savings. Try to set aside a percentage of your monthly budget for this crucial emergency fund. Need help? Contact America Saves at P.O. Box 12099, Washington, DC 20005-0999 or at *www.americasaves.org*. The Web site provides an online enrollment option.

Get Yourself Out of Debt

You risk far more than a damaged credit report when you fail to pay your debt. Once ignored consumer debts are a focus of a booming business that profits from bad consumer debt. Credit card issuers and businesses ranging from health clubs to utilities traditionally didn't hound debtors for more than a few months. The rules have changed, and creditors are selling their bad debt as a source of revenue. Don't let this hardheaded look at your financial status discourage you. Getting yourself out of debt can seem to be a slow, painstaking process, but well worth the effort.

Step 1. The first step is to get a credit card with the lowest rate possible that will allow you to transfer your other outstanding balances to that card. Many credit cards are still charging an annual percentage rate (APR) as high as 29 percent per year. Watch out for cards with expiring teaser rates and other fees, especially if you are worried you might miss a payment. If you pay your bills on time, negotiate. Call your credit card company and ask them to consider lowering your APR. If they refuse to lower your rate, ask for a time frame in which it could lower the rate and let them know that after that point you will close the account. Consolidate all your bills into one low-interest monthly payment, if possible.

If you have no credit in your own name, establishing credit should be a first priority. Begin by obtaining a secured credit card. In this case, you deposit a certain amount of cash with the credit card issuer in return for a credit line of the same size. If you default on your credit card payment, the bank can seize enough money from your deposit to cover your debt.

Step 2. Cut up all your other cards, saving one or two for dire emergencies only. Notify all the credit card companies (except for the one or two cards you saved) to close your account. This is a smart idea; even if you have no outstanding balance, the credit line existing for these cards might be so large that it prevents you from getting other types of credit such as a mortgage refinance or car loan. Having too many credit cards can seduce you into spending money that you don't have. Credit cards are best left at home. Most credit card debt comes from impulse purchases, not planned large expenditures.

Step 3. Pay your bills on time. A late payment on one account could cost you higher rates and fees on all your accounts—from your credit cards to your auto insurance. Credit card companies are looking for reasons to increase rates. More and more companies are peeking at credit reports regularly to justify raising insurance rates or increasing credit limits. A single late payment charge could ripple through all your unrelated accounts. Keep a list of your credit cards, due dates, balances, and credit limits. Get into the habit of paying bills as soon as they arrive, if poor organization has prevented you from making timely payments in the past.

Step 4. Stop using your automated teller machine card (ATM). Most of the time we do not record how much we withdraw and how we spend the money, and we are not keeping track of our spending. Instead of withdrawing money from the ATM several times a week, put yourself on an allowance. Give yourself the amount you can afford at the beginning of the week, and when it runs out, it runs out.

Step 5. Take advantage of direct deposit at work. Avoid standing in bank lines to deposit your paycheck or—even worse—stop using check cashing outlets that charge huge fees.

Making Your Money Work for You

After you have made provisions for an emergency fund and your high interest credit card debt is paid off, start an investment program. Again, it is important to write down specific goals. These goals will be influenced by your age and the kinds of responsibilities, assets, and resources you already have. What is it that you really want? Are you interested in saving money for retirement, or do you have more immediate goals? How much risk can you handle?

Some women begin by investing in mutual funds. Investment programs like this can often begin with as little as $50. Remember that no one investment plan is right for everyone. If an investment opportunity sounds too good to be true, warning bells should sound loudly in your mind. Remember that bulls and bears make money; pigs don't. How you invest your money is ultimately your decision, however, because it is you who will reap the reward or suffer the loss. Enlist the help of a financial planner, take a course or attend a seminar in financial planning, or check out investment publications at the public library. Learn what's out there and what investment vehicles might be right for you.

Investigate the opportunities for investment that may be available through your employee benefit package. Are you taking full advantage of the flexible benefits plan? Does your company offer a 401(k) or 403(b) plan? These plans allow you to set aside before tax dollars into investments whose earnings are tax-exempt until withdrawal, which is usually at retirement. Many companies are willing to match the funds the employee sets aside in these plans. Find out what kind of pension, if any, your company offers for which you are eligible. Use that information to plan your career moves and possible job changes more wisely.

Tax Planning Is Essential

Understand what your deductions are and plan carefully to minimize your tax liability. Know the tax consequences before you make major decisions such as purchasing a home or selling off investment assets. Keep receipts and other supporting documents in a safe, accessible location. Ask your tax adviser how long you should keep records and copies of your returns. Even if you don't make a lot of money, carefully file your tax returns promptly every year.

INCREASING YOUR ASSETS

PENNY-PINCHING PARENTING

Parenting will make you poorer, no matter how much you started out with. Why not take penny-pinching and turn it into a project? Instead of worrying about bills and fretting over what you don't have, learn ways to live better on your shoestring budget. Check out:

- *www.savvy-discounts.com*
- *www.thefrugallife.com*
- *www.stretcher.com*

Here's something to ponder: one of America's self-made millionaires attributes his wealth to thirty years of brown-bagging peanut butter and jelly sandwiches for lunch.

Entrepreneurial women are starting one-half to two-thirds of all the nation's new businesses. You can increase your assets if you market a special skill or talent. Here are some best bets for starting your own business, either full-time or part-time.

Start a Word Processing or Web Business

The investment for a home word processing business is around $1,500, including the computer, modem, and word processing software. When advertising your services, be sure to emphasize a specialty such as evening and weekend work for small businesses or another selling point such as free twenty-four-hour delivery.

For another $500, you can start a Web design or development business. Although there's a lot of competition, the world is running its business on the Internet; so this could be lucrative.

Drive New Vehicles to Dealerships

Manufacturers deliver new cars to dealerships by way of truck. Large specialty vehicles, such as RVs, schools buses, vans, ambulances, and limousines are driven to dealerships. The pay runs about thirty-five cents per mile, plus air transportation home for drivers once deliveries are made. Trip lengths vary from quick 100 mile trips to cross-country drives. You do not need a commercial driver's license to be a driver, but some states require a chauffeur's license, which you can get after taking a simple written test. You must, of course, have a clean driving record. This is a potentially terrific opportunity for single mothers with consistent visitation schedules and whose children spend extended time with their dads, particularly during summer vacation.

Be a Professional Organizer

Got a thing about being organized? Can you bring order to piles of paper or stacks of unsorted mail? Professional organizers also plan sales and auctions for individuals, whether they are managing an estate or simply want to bring garage and attic sales to a professional level. Some professional organizers tackle out of control closets and garages. Professional organizers typically charge $40 to $200 per hour. The National Association of Professional Organizers (*www.napo.net*) can advise you on the legal steps you need to take to get started and provide information about bonding and licenses that are necessary to protect yourself. If you would rather be a second pair of hands to someone, then offer your services as a personal assistant. You may be asked to schedule appointments, meet repairmen, pick up dry cleaning, or make travel plans. You can let your own skills dictate the kind of service you offer. Check out the American Errand Runners Association (*ErrandInfo.com*) online discussion groups for ideas and information.

Walk a Dog

Dog walkers typically earn $10 to $15 per hour per dog; so this is a great way to earn quick cash and get some exercise, too. Of course, you need to be certain that you can handle a pack of dogs on city streets. If you love animals, also consider pet sitting, aquarium maintenance, dog and cat grooming, or maybe a part-time receptionist job at your local vet's office.

Be a Personal Chef

Many double income families with more disposable income than spare time are relying on personal chefs for convenient, fresh food. Search "personal chef" on the Internet for a host of sites with helpful information on how to get started. You do not have to be a culinary school graduate. In most cases, you work with a client to set a mutually convenient schedule. You may wish to begin by advertising a single specialty, like homemade soup, on local bulletin boards or in newspapers. Single moms with flexible work schedules, like teachers, real estate agents, and freelancers, find becoming a personal chef a particularly good source of extra income.

Be an Event Planner

Almost every organization sponsors major events for fund-raising, issue awareness, and membership drives. Activities such as dinners, musical entertainment, trips, tournaments, and contests need to be thoroughly planned. Event planners are not on staff but are usually hired on a freelance or contractual basis. A knowledge of promotions, publicity, and public relations is a plus when dealing with newspapers and local television and radio stations.

Provide Courier and Personal Services

Today's working parents have very busy lives. They often need someone to do the most basic yet time-consuming errands. Some courier services are franchised, but to zero in on a more personal target for your services, a small personal service business might be just for you.

Be a Music, Art, or Exercise Instructor

If you have a particular talent or skill in a specialized field that does not have

too many regulations, offering tutoring, piano lessons, personal training, or kids' jewelry-making classes can be a great way to supplement your income. If you can find enough business, full-time classes can become your sole method of making money.

Try Lawn Care or Landscaping

If you have always enjoyed working outdoors and are able to buy the basic equipment, this could be a terrific way to earn extra money. Some single mothers with a creative flair and a green thumb have created thriving businesses caring for lawns, gardens, window boxes, or flower beds.

Be a Medical Transcriptionist

A medical transcriptionist takes the notes doctors dictate after performing operations or examinations and transcribes them to the written word. Typically, training takes about six months part-time. After completing the program, a medical transcriptionist is able either to set up shop at home with her own computer and printer or to work in a physician's office or hospital. The hours can be flexible, and the pay is quite decent to start. Medical transcription is needed everywhere, and jobs are plentiful.

Try Decorative Painting

House painting or interior painting is a familiar job. There has been a great revival recently in decorative painting with techniques such as stenciling, trompe l'oeil, rag painting, sponge painting, and a variety of other styles. Most people apprentice themselves to established painters and learn the techniques on the job. Your own home or that of a friend could be your best advertisement.

Provide Cleaning Services

As long as there are people living, breathing, and making a mess, there will be always be jobs for people willing to clean up. This is where a resourceful single mother can create a profitable part-time or full-time business. Offices, large and small, as well as homes are all possible job sites. Be prepared with references and know that cleaning is hard, demanding work.

Work at Home Opportunities

The basic rule of thumb is that if something sounds too good to be true, beware! The Federal Trade Commission says work at home rip-offs are one of its ten most common complaints. Most of these flyers advertise fabulous money for doing very little and without ever changing out of your nightgown. The people who typically make money from these supposed opportunities are those who get unsuspecting people to invest in a home business with the promise of easy money. If you are tempted by one of these offers, stop and ask the important questions. How many hours must I work before I will get paid? What are the total start-up costs? Will I be paid on salary or commission? How much money must I spend per month for materials and phone costs? Check out the offer with the Better Business Bureau and your state attorney general's office to see if there are any complaints against this organization.

Want more ideas? Let your imagination work for you. Ask yourself what you really enjoy doing? What are you good at? You may end up creating beautiful hand-knit sweaters, decorating Christmas trees, tending houseplants, boarding pets, making simple home repairs, or even doing a little data entry, if that's what you love and do well.

Scale Down!

Not only is scaling down your lifestyle necessary, but it is chic to live simply by reusing and recycling. Here are some rich ideas for cheaper living to help you start spending less while living better. When you are feeling poor, you should sit down with paper and pencil and figure out exactly how much your new scaled down choices are really saving. Use this saved money to add to your emergency fund account, savings for a special need or project, or your investments.

- *Walk instead of ride.* Two dollars per day saved by walking to work rather than taking the bus can add up to $500 per year in savings, in addition to the added health benefits of daily exercise. Instead of spending money to travel to your cubicle, how about putting this money into a vacation fund so you can go somewhere you really would like to see?

- *Vending machines are traps.* Vending machine purchases are costly, impulsive purchases, which typically give our wallets and our waistlines trouble. Bring along healthy snacks and water to combat those midday cravings.

- *Brown bags can be your smartest accessory.* Brown-bag it at work and rack up significant savings. Time spent waiting on line at crowded lunch counters or restaurants can be better spent on errands so that your weekends are less hectic or just catching a few minutes just for you. Your control over what you have for lunch will no doubt result in healthier choices, as well as money saved. Get your kids in on the action, too—school lunches are sadly seen as a significant contributor to the rise in childhood obesity. Your children do not need a daily fix of French fries, mystery meat, or fruit swimming in heavy sugar syrup. Plan your carryout meals from home with your child and allow these meals occasionally to be your child's choice. Money saved will be considerable. Develop a family plan for how this money will be allocated to insure greater cooperation.

♦ *Bottled water and expensive coffee drinks are not life essentials.* Carrying your beverage of choice from home can save significant money as well as time spent waiting in line. Take the time to figure out how quickly these small changes can add up to real savings!

♦ *Never go grocery shopping when hungry.* Use coupons, but only for those items you normally buy. You can let your kids cut out the coupons while helping you with your shopping list.

Plan menus and don't be swayed by packaging or TV advertising.

♦ *Make healthy food choices.* Buy rice, beans, potatoes, pasta, and legumes in bulk and save even more. Remember that these foods are located at the perimeter of the store and never at eye level, which is all the more reason to bring the children along to retrieve those items on the bottom shelves. Store in airtight containers. Avoid expensive meats and prepared foods. Seasonal markets are your best bets for fresh fruits and vegetables. Join with other families and buy in bulk to increase your savings and enjoyment. Simple vegetables, soups, and stews are cheaper and far healthier than processed food. Be on the lookout for healthy recipes and create opportunities for exchange with other single mothers. Boredom often leads to unhealthy and expensive food choices.

♦ *Consider shopping at discount high-volume stores* that offer substantial discounts on institutional size containers of food, over-the-counter medications, paper, and dry goods. Depending upon where you live, some stores also have large selections of meat and prepared foods in commercial sizes. Some savvy discount store shoppers report stocking their shelves and freezers with items they normally couldn't afford because they cost two or three times as much elsewhere. But be wary of overstocking with limited space and appetites. It is better to go in with several friends or a couple of family members or you may wind up busting your budget and ultimately throwing out your savings. Stay away from impulse purchases.

Stick to your shopping list. Avoid the "siege mentality." No home needs fifty rolls of toilet paper on hand or twenty-five pounds of peanut butter, "just in case."

◆ *Have a cooking marathon one day every weekend* and store extra portions in meal-sized serving containers in the freezer. Use powdered milk in recipes instead of fresh. Collect recipes, learn to use leftovers creatively, and grow your own herbs. Join with other single mothers who cook in quantity and trade a pot of stew for a pot of chili. Your children will learn to try new things and be offered more variety, and you'll have less hassle and save time in the long run.

◆ *Avoid the fast-food frenzy.* Time-crunched single parents tend to frequent fast-food restaurants more than they should. Next time you go out to dinner, find a family restaurant with discounts for kids. Be sure to choose small restaurants with simple menus. These places often need fewer people to make and serve the dishes and therefore often have lower prices. The typically less frenzied atmosphere is also a welcome change.

◆ *Control the clutter.* No matter how gracious your home, clutter can make it seem dirty and disorganized. Store similar items together. Categorization is very important when you're getting organized. Keep all bill paying supplies in one place. Gather all of your craft supplies in a basket. Keep what the kids need to do their homework in one plastic bin. When you need to work on something, everything will be easily accessible. Be meticulous about finding uses for outgrown toys

and clothing, as well as other household articles you no longer need. Organize a neighborhood garage sale and use the proceeds to buy something your family may need or enjoy. Be careful not to bring home more stuff than you contributed. Remember, you are striving for a simpler life.

◆ *When visiting your doctor, ask for free samples of everything you might need at some point.* Say that you are a single parent and on a strict budget. Stock up on over-the-counter remedies such as ointments, pain relievers, diaper creams, and decongestants, and don't forget those latex gloves. Besides cleaning, they're great for those of us who color our hair. Additionally, latex gloves should be worn when administering first aid to visiting children or anytime you come in contact with blood or fecal matter. Staying healthy saves money and lives!

◆ *Don't buy too many cosmetics or perfumes.* Request these items as gifts when reminding indecisive friends about your birthday or Christmas. Better yet, window shop at a large department store, and request free samples of everything the cosmetics department has to offer. Indulge yourself, and use the extras for little gifts or stocking stuffers.

◆ *Offer yourself and your children as hair models for beauty school students.* You can get a nice haircut, styling, and sometimes coloring (just for you, of course, and stay away from anything that requires too much upkeep) for practically nothing. Just be sure to keep your style simple—something that is versatile and keeps its shape with minimal care.

- *Learn to sew or swap skills with a single mother who does.* Many children's clothes, like shorts and simple tops for toddlers and preschoolers, are easy to make, even for the amateur. Your child will enjoy picking out the fabric. Even teenage girls who are notoriously picky about clothes will enjoy a cozy flannel nightshirt hand-made by mom.

- *Think swap and not shop.* Organize and find other single mothers with skills to barter. Some women are fabulous cooks and terrible housekeepers; other women are just the reverse. Could a swap of services benefit both? Absolutely. Be clear about the rules and keep careful records. Not only can this be a big money saver, but it also can lead to wonderful new experiences and opportunities. Many successful small businesses have begun by women swapping or bartering their skills and discovering just how valuable other people found these talents to be.

- *Give up or at least cut down on some of your bad habits.* Cigarettes are a deadly and expensive addiction. Cutting back just four canned soft drinks a week saves you $200 annually. Give up smoking altogether and replace sugary drinks with water (much healthier than soda), and you'll have quite a nest egg to show for it, not to mention the added years to enjoy it.

- *Don't buy magazines at the checkout counter.* Just love keeping up with the latest magazines? Do you always grab for the latest fashion magazine or tell-all gossip newspaper at the supermarket checkout or newsstand? Consider looking for bargain subscriptions and swapping with other like-minded readers to keep your pleasure reading costs down.

- *Don't shop till you drop* unless it is at garage sales, flea markets, and consignment or thrift shops. Never buy expensive toddler outfits for your young ones because after five minutes of wear they are as used as anything you can pick up second-hand. At the rate that kids grow, you wouldn't be able to keep up. Also, believe it or not, toddlers and infants simply don't care about making fashion statements.

- *Find the discount movie house in your neighborhood and sneak in your own popcorn.* Matinees are always cheaper. For a day of fun, rather than spend a bundle at a theme park, take the pack to a park, zoo, or historical site. In fact, some peanut butter sandwiches, a dog, and a kite can make for an invigorating day for under a couple of bucks.

- *Don't overlook the library as a source of family entertainment.* Take advantage of their free activities, including films and video series, storytelling and puppet shows, poetry readings, and guest speakers. In fact, you probably wouldn't have enough time to take advantage of all their classes, workshops, and special programs if you did nothing else.

FASHION TIPS FOR THE MONEY CONSCIOUS

- *Stick to one color family for your work clothes.* For example, buy work clothes that can be accessorized with black—shoes, handbags, belts. Maybe brown is your color. The point is that sticking to one color family allows you to afford better quality and longer-lasting items because you have to buy fewer things.

- *Buy classic styles that do not easily become dated.* Basic jackets, traditionally tailored shirts, the little black dress, and classic skirts and slacks can be combined to create dozens of looks from just a few basic pieces. For fun and to look fashionable, rely on well-chosen accessories like scarves or costume jewelry. Quality matters; buy the best you can afford.

- *Respect the unwritten corporate rules when choosing clothes for the office.* Take special note of how your boss dresses. If she never wears pants to the office, then perhaps dresses and skirts are your best get-ahead bet. If you work in a more trendy, casual place, then the corporate suit with matching pumps will look out of place. Men have known for years the importance of the corporate uniform. Smart women who get ahead also know the importance of image. Your chances for promotion will improve if you look as though you already have the job.

- *Indulge yourself in color and style for your casual clothes.* Casual wear costs less, and during your time away from work, you really are free to dress as you like.

- *Keep yourself and your clothing meticulously clean.* Hang up your work clothes and let them air out when you get home. The more quickly you air out your things, the fewer times expensive things will have to be dry-cleaned or laundered. Fewer dry cleaning bills and longer clothes life will save money. Repair loose buttons and make other small repairs promptly. There is nothing like a missing button on the front of a blouse at precisely the wrong moment to ruin a day.

- *Avoid purchasing too many items that require dry cleaning.* Stick to fabrics that are easily laundered and do not easily wrinkle.

- *Take advantage of discounts on items like panty hose and buy in quantity.* Order with girlfriends and increase your savings.

- *Be wary of shopping outlets* and avoid the temptation to buy simply because you are there. If you would not have paid full price for it, it is probably not a bargain no matter what the tag reads now.

- *Catalogs and online shopping may save you money in the long run* if shopping around for bargains takes you away from your job and the potential for earning money, not to mention the costs you incur for gas and parking. Time is as valuable as money; so if catalog and online shopping works for you, go that route. Get on the mailing list of discount clothing catalogs and take advantage of their special sales for regular customers. Just be sure not to overspend simply because you have a credit card in one hand and a phone in the other. Remember, online shopping can be particularly enticing. Keep a calculator on hand and monitor the total cost of your purchase carefully. Remember, it is fun to watch the shopping channels, but these celebrities and hosts are paid lots of money to make everything they are trying to sell look irresistible.

- *Buy your work wardrobe carefully.* Your appearance will affect how others judge you on the job. Unless you have unlimited resources, careful planning is essential. Make no major purchases on impulse without giving thought to how this item will fit into your wardrobe-building plan. The purple and fuchsia jacket may have instant appeal in the store, but it will never give the service that the well-tailored basic black jacket will.

- *Many large department stores have personal shoppers who will help you select clothing for no additional cost.* You are under no obligation to buy, and often these shoppers can show you many ways to mix and match so that you can get maximum mileage out of your minimal clothing dollar. This service can be a real blessing for the time-crunched single mother who hates to shop.

- *Organize a single mothers' clothes swap.* That teal and magenta jacket that one woman is sick of, the scarf that goes with nothing, the dangling earrings that annoy you, or the wool coat that causes one mom to have an allergy attack might be just what someone else is looking for. Everyone gets something new and the chance to socialize. Every item is considered

an even exchange. What doesn't get exchanged gets donated to charity.

- *In bigger cities and towns, there are exchanges run by women's groups that help women trying to get back into the workplace.* Many of them offer gently used business clothes for little or no cost. Investigate these by calling your local women's commission or the library or just ask around.

- *Seek out secondhand clothing stores or consignment shops,* particularly for items to fill out your wardrobe or for special occasion items you will wear only once. Make friends with the owner or manager, and she may contact you when something terrific in your size comes in. Keep in mind, too, that if you have a special event to attend that requires formal dressing that you don't have to purchase an item that you will never wear again. Consider renting a formal from a store specializing in this. In fact, many of these places also rent jewelry and accessories.

BANKRUPTCY

If you are considering filing for bankruptcy, remember that creditors are often willing to negotiate with you. This possibility should be explored first. In general, legal advice is essential. Bankruptcy law is complicated and varies from state to state; you need an attorney with expertise in this area of the law. Recent federal legislation limits debtors' use of provisions in the bankruptcy code, which allowed credit card or other unsecured loans to be wiped out. Income-based tests for measuring a debtor's ability to repay debts have also been created. People in bankruptcy may now be required to pay for credit counseling. Overall, legal requirements for debtors in the bankruptcy process have been stiffened, and paperwork obligations have increased enormously.

Be sure you know where you will stand financially after you file for bankruptcy and what effect this filing will have on your credit history and for how long. Generally, filing for bankruptcy will greatly limit your ability to obtain a mortgage or car loan, often for many years. Bankruptcy is a last choice option.

IF YOU NEED PUBLIC ASSISTANCE

Regardless of your circumstances or reasons for becoming a single mother, if you find yourself unable to take care of yourself and your children adequately because of a severe lack of funds, you should apply for financial assistance.

As the result of the major overhauling of our welfare system, aid to families is now the responsibility of individual states rather than the federal government. Rules and procedures differ from county to county and from state to state, and even program names may vary. Depending upon which state you reside in, different time limits and guidelines may also be set. Your best resource for seeking financial aid is through your Department of Social Services (DSS). Look under government listings either located in a special section or in the beginning of your phone book for the phone number and address of your local DSS.

Ten Steps for Requesting Assistance with Dignity

Familiarize yourself with this ten-step plan first to increase your chances of successfully obtaining benefits.

1. Keep in mind that you will encounter caseworkers who will try to dismiss you because that is their job, regardless of what you are told. The more requests they can deny, the better it is for the Department of Social Services. Remember, too, that every state will have a different set of standards; so do your homework first.

2. When you go to DSS to fill out the many applications required to apply for aid, be sure to bring every document you can think of, including everyone's birth certificates, death certificate (if spouse died), divorce or separation papers, monthly expense and income statements (including gas and electric bills and canceled rent checks or receipts), and anything else that shows you have substantial need. Because there is the risk that states will be required to deny benefits to children where that state has failed to establish paternity, be sure to bring proof of paternity or request that an action be started to establish paternity.

3. Don't be intimidated but do expect some unwelcome behavior on the part of the caseworker. These people are inundated with caseloads and can barely muster up the enthusiasm to keep their mouths from frowning, let alone smiling. Be sure to take a pen or pencil and

paper with you so you can take notes. Nothing gets a caseworker's attention more than a potential recipient who writes down everything the caseworker says. Above all, be sure to note his or her name and ask for the correct spelling. For some reason, the intimidation process seems to reverse itself when you are poised with pen in hand and a look that says, "I'm ready when you are!" Never forget that knowledge is power.

Note: If you encounter abusive behavior on the caseworker's part, don't let him or her see you cry. Maintain your composure and explain that you have a legal right to this information and would prefer that it be given to you in a straightforward, no insults manner. (It is by no means the case that caseworkers are abusive monsters, but many women who have been through this procedure have met with unpleasantness.)

4. You mustn't give up. Moms seeking welfare benefits often fall prey to discouragement, humiliation, and intimidation. Keep these three common feelings in mind and don't let them force you to give up. In some cases, it might take four or more visits to DSS and even more telephone attempts to finally collect what you are entitled to.

5. Don't avoid applying for food stamps (a separate program) because you are not receiving cash assistance. Food stamps are based on your income compared with your shelter costs, which include rent and utilities. If your shelter costs come to more than half of

your total income, you are usually awarded close to the maximum amount of food stamps. Remember that the amount is determined by the state. People receiving Social Security or disability benefits, the elderly, and even employed persons are eligible to receive food stamps based on the comparison of income to expenses.

6. Don't assume you are not eligible for benefits because you own a house or a car. You can own a house as long as you live in it. Your car's value may not exceed the amount set by your state. Also, if you have a savings account, find out the maximum dollar amount allowed. Unfortunately, because some women have a little nest egg in case of emergency, this may cause a denial of benefits. Be informed of the maximum assets you can claim.

7. If the caseworker suggests that you are not eligible, make certain that you ask for the denial in writing. Some caseworkers will change their tune at this request—either way, documentation will benefit you.

8. Always ask for the address of the hearing office so that you know where to request a hearing whether or not you are immediately denied benefits. If the person responds by telling you that the address is on the forms, ask again, saying that you don't see it and you would like to make note of it immediately.

9. If you request a hearing, do so in writing at the state level. Your local

DSS office will give you the address and telephone number of the state's social services department. Be sure to keep your request brief. You are not arguing your case, simply requesting a hearing. Saying, "I was denied (specify the type of benefit) because . . ." is enough. Note the date, name of caseworker, and address of office where you were denied. Chances are that you won't need a hearing because most caseworkers will do their work once they learn that you are asking for a hearing. If you do require a hearing, keep in mind that if the state receives your request for a hearing before the date of termination of benefits, reduction of payments, or whatever you are being threatened with, you must continue to receive your benefits at the current level until your problem is resolved. Don't accept anything else and, if necessary, go to a Legal Aid office for help.

10. If you are still getting a hard time from your caseworker, insist upon the names of all supervisors in the department. Go to the higher-ups, office heads, and even the director of the agency, making sure that copies of every document are sent to them and that your caseworker knows that you have sent these copies. Additionally, send copies to the media, politicians, and your representatives at all three levels—state, county, and federal—and also send copies to local and national women's organizations. You can call your local election commission to get the names of your representatives in state and federal government.

If you run into problems such as lateness with checks or reduced amounts or are just told that you will have to wait, be persistent. Keep calling and repeat, "I did not receive my benefits." You may sound like a broken record, but that's a great way to get someone to intervene. Never forget that the squeaky wheel gets the grease.

SEEKING OTHER SOURCES OF HELP

Keep in mind that there are several programs that are made available through government agencies and nonprofit organizations that can assist you in making ends meet while you are gaining marketable job skills.

Medical Insurance Programs

The Department of Social Services has a federal Medicaid program that provides health insurance for low-income families. If you do not qualify for this particular health coverage, ask a DSS caseworker to give you a referral to other agencies or the local health department for other types of health insurance for low-income individuals.

Food Programs

DSS also has a food program. Food stamps are food coupons that are allocated on a monthly basis for low-income persons to use at the grocery store. However, these coupons are limited to the purchase of certain foods. Alcohol, tobacco, and other nonfood items are excluded. The WIC (Women, Infants, and Children) program provides food coupons for specific food items from your local supermarket to benefit pregnant women, infants, and children up to two years of age.

Local nonprofit organizations also have food supplement programs (and sometimes cash aid programs as well). The following national organizations (listed in your local phone directory) can refer you to help in your area:

United Way, Salvation Army, Catholic Charities, and Food Bank. Area churches, Jewish community centers, and homeless shelters can put you in touch with programs providing food and other assistance.

PROVIDING FOR YOUR CHILDREN IF YOU SHOULD DIE

Because the future rests with those who will experience it, the responsibility of all adults is to see that their children, then their children's children, and so on will have a safe planet, where they are protected from unnecessary suffering and where they all start out with an even chance at success. These responsibilities rest largely on the shoulders of the individual parents. It would be nice if all children had access to funding for college, creative endeavors, and health care, but for now, it's up to you to take care of these things.

Here's a story to which many single moms can relate, particularly if they have very young children.

A woman was waiting for her doctor to examine her for what she complained was serious cramping, backaches, and fatigue. She was frantically struggling to wrap herself up as gracefully as possible

in the sterile white hospital gown but wasn't having much luck. The perky little nurse, whom the woman decided had no idea what a stretch mark looked like and had never experienced an unwanted body hair, popped her head in the examining room and reminded the woman that the gown snapped in the back. Whatever dignity remained was now waning.

When the elderly doctor entered the examining room, the woman, who was in her late thirties and obviously quite distressed, tried to appear composed but was unsuccessful at mustering up even a hint of decorum. Ignoring her feeble attempts to calm herself, the doctor was busily scribbling on a chart when he asked, "So why are we here today?"

"We have ovarian cancer," blurted the woman.

This got his attention. "What makes you think you have ovarian cancer?" he said, looking up slightly disturbed.

"The Internet! I entered all my symptoms into an online questionnaire: bloating and swelling, constant lower backache, and sudden fatigue—and the results said I could have ovarian cancer."

"Wait a minute," said the doctor, who was getting noticeably annoyed. He started thumbing through the charts. "Weren't you here just six months ago claiming you had a brain tumor?"

"Look," the woman said. "I never had a migraine before and didn't know what it felt like, okay? So sue me!"

"Wait a minute." He was furiously flipping pages. "Nine months

before that you insisted you had lupus or Lyme disease and then a couple of years ago . . ." the doctor continued.

The woman started sobbing. "Look, I'm sorry. It's just that I'm a single mother, and I worry every time something is wrong with me that it's terminal and I'll die. I can't help it. I worry about who will take care of my child if something happens to me."

The doctor softened a bit. "Listen, you don't have any indication of ovarian cancer. All your tests from your last visit look pretty normal. In fact, everything is fine with you, except maybe you could use some peace of mind. You want my advice? I suggest you get some kind of will, make plans for your child's future—just in case."

Worrying about who will take care of your child in the event that something happens to you is a common thread that binds single mothers, following a close third after guilt. (Never having sex again has been running neck and neck against guilt in a tight race for second place, and lack of money is still number one.)

Chances are that you will live a long and healthy life if you don't make yourself crazy with worry. But it is definitely a good idea to get certain things out of the way—for example, planning for who will raise your kids if something should happen to you.

Having a plan gives your children a double gift—first, your peace of mind, which will allow for less stressful parenting and second, a safety net in the event that something happens to you. Peace of mind allows for a healthier outlook both physically and mentally, and what

better start to longevity than that?

FIRST THINGS FIRST: GET LIFE INSURANCE

The most important thing to remember about buying life insurance is to get the coverage that fits your needs. Decide how much life insurance you need, for how long you need it, and what you can afford to pay. Premiums for all types of insurance can be paid monthly right along with your other bills. Keep in mind that the major reason to buy life insurance is to cover the financial repercussions of your unexpected or untimely death. Life insurance can be one of the ways, however, that single moms also plan for the future. Speak to a general insurance agent who represents many companies. Learn what kinds of policies will meet your needs and pick the one that suits you best. Finally, choose the combination of policy premium and benefits that emphasizes protection in case of early death, or benefits in case of long life, or a combination of both.

You may already have life insurance. If you decide to replace your policy, don't cancel the old policy until you have received the new one. It can be costly to replace an insurance policy. Much of what you paid in the early years of your current policy paid for the insurance company's cost of selling and issuing the policy. You may pay this type of cost again if you buy a new policy. If you are older or your health has changed, premiums for the new policy will often be higher. You will not be able to buy a new policy if you are uninsurable. You may also have valuable rights and benefits in the policy you now have that are not in the new one.

You need to determine how much life insurance coverage you need. As part of the decision about how much life insurance to buy, keep in mind that Social Security benefits are certainly not a guarantee for the future. Know what Social Security benefits your children might currently be eligible to receive in case of your death but consider these benefits only as a possible extra. You cannot build security for your family based upon benefits that could be greatly curtailed or entirely eliminated. Make a rational decision about how much life insurance you need and can afford. Be careful not to be influenced by irrational fears. Ask yourself how much of the family income you provide. Would you like to set aside money so that your children can complete their college education in the event of your death? Are there other people, like your parents, who depend upon you financially? Remember that you may also have other assets, such as real estate, savings, and investments. You may also have group insurance where you work.

Basically, there are two types of life insurance: term insurance and cash value insurance.

Term insurance generally offers the largest insurance protection for your premium dollar and typically has lower premiums in the early years. Term insurance does not build cash value that you can use in the future. Term insurance covers you for a term of one or more years. It pays a death benefit only if you die in that term. You can renew most term insurance policies for one or more terms even if your health has changed. Each time you renew the policy for a new term the premiums may be higher. Ask what the premiums will be if you continue to renew the policy. Ask if you will lose the right to renew the policy at some age. For a higher premium, some companies will give you the right to keep the policy in force for a guaranteed period at the same price each year. At the end of that time, you may need to pass a physical examination to continue coverage, and the premiums may increase.

Cash value insurance is a type of insurance for which the premiums charged are higher at the beginning than they would be for the same amount of term insurance. The part of the premium that is not used for the cost of insurance is invested by the company and builds cash value. You can use this cash value in a variety of ways. You may borrow against a policy's cash value by taking a policy loan. If you don't pay back the loan and the interest on it, the amount you owe will be subtracted from the benefits when you die or from the cash value if you stop paying premiums and take out the remaining cash value. You can also use your cash value to keep insurance protection for a limited time or to buy a reduced amount without having to pay more premiums. You can also use the cash value to increase your income in retirement or to help pay for college tuition without canceling the policy. To build this cash value, however, you must pay higher premiums in the earlier years of the policy. Cash value insurance may be one of several types. Whole life, universal life, and variable life are all types of cash value insurance.

Generally, it is not a good idea to insure risk (your death) with risk (factors that cannot be predicted or controlled). If you do decide to buy a policy for which cash values, death benefits, dividends, or premiums may vary based on things which cannot be predicted, like interest rates, get an illustration from the insurance agent that helps explain how a policy works. This illustration will show how the benefits that are not guaranteed will change as interest rates or other factors change. This illustration will also show you what the insurance company guarantees. It can also show you what could happen in the future. Study everything carefully and do not make a hasty decision. Nobody has a crystal ball. You should be ready to adjust your financial plans if the cash value doesn't increase as quickly as shown in the illustration. You will be asked to sign a statement that says you understand that some of the numbers in the illustration are not guaranteed. Remember, if you don't understand, don't buy it!

FIND A QUALIFIED ATTORNEY

The counsel of a well qualified attorney is essential to insure that the custody of your children and the distribution of your property are handled in the manner of your choosing. It is critically important to have a will to provide for your children. If you die without a will, state laws will largely determine what happens to your assets and who becomes your children's guardian.

Attorney fees are unlikely to be exorbitant, especially when you consider that you are purchasing peace of mind for your children's future. If you are unable to locate an attorney by referral, try logging on to *www.findlaw.com* to find a qualified attorney in your area. When you speak with the attorney who will draw up your will and draft your two Durable Powers of Attorney (more on them following), speak candidly about the situation with your former husband

or partner and about any unusual family situations that might exist. Do not be too embarrassed to be as open and honest as possible. If you have other legal matters now unresolved, make sure you inform this attorney. This is not the time to hide anything. Remember that everything shared is protected under attorney-client privilege. Unless this attorney graduated from law school yesterday, there is probably nothing you could say that would be new or surprising.

What Is a Durable Power of Attorney (DPOA)?

No matter how limited your financial circumstances, it is crucial that you have two DPOAs in place. These are two separate documents. A DPOA is a legal document in which you appoint someone, called an agent, to act on your behalf in the event that you become too ill or incapacitated to make decisions for yourself. The DPOA allows your agent to handle your financial matters, and you can specifically define how much or little authority your agent may have in these matters. A DPOA does not give your agent the authority to make medical decisions.

The DPOA for health care (also known as a health care proxy or medical power of attorney) spells out whether you would want to be put on life support.

It is hard to think about a time when you might not be able to care for yourself and your children. Think about the peace of mind you will have knowing that it would be so much easier for your loved ones to handle your affairs knowing that they are doing exactly as you would have wanted. If you have reason to believe that other family members may argue with your agent, bring all individuals involved together so that they can hear from you directly why you are making the choices you have specified.

SELECTING A GUARDIAN

Typically, when one parent passes away, the other parent assumes guardianship of any minor children. It is far simpler to make contingency plans when you can count on the other parent. Some single mothers, however, must make alternative arrangements in the event of their death if their children's biological father is not willing or able to assume custody. If this is your situation, some of the unique concerns are discussed here. Talking to your children about your death will be more challenging than if you could expect the children's father to fill the void.

I wasn't married to my child's father, and he's seen my four-year-old daughter only once. Could he ever get custody of my daughter if something happens to me?

It is possible that a long absent father could get custody of the child. A biological father has rights, whether or not he was married to his child's mother. It does not matter how little contact he has had with your child. Courts almost always appoint the surviving biological parent as guardian. Even if you appoint a guardian for your child in your will, this does not eliminate the rights of the surviving biological parent. It is essential that you consult with an attorney and do what is necessary now to make sure that your daughter would be taken care of as you wish in the event of your death. It is possible for the biological father to waive his parental rights and agree to custody by the guardian you appoint. These uncomfortable matters need to brought up now and taken care of legally. The peace of mind will well compensate for your efforts in time and money.

My ex-husband would try every trick in the book to get custody of the children as well as the money and property I want to leave to my son and daughter. I feel overwhelmed just thinking about talking with a lawyer. How do I begin to even think about all the horrible possibilities?

Stop focusing on the worst and think about what you can do now to help insure that your wishes are carried out in case of your untimely death. Unless you made prior provisions in your divorce agreement allowing you to appoint a guardian for the children, your former husband will most likely be named guardian by the courts. Only convicted felons are unlikely to be named guardian as the sole surviving parent of a child.

You may wish to go ahead and appoint a guardian for the children who would petition the courts for custody in your will. This individual would need to clearly understand the situation. If you feel that your former husband would not be an appropriate guardian for the children, try to discuss this matter with him now. For the sake of the children, he may be willing to waive his rights to guardianship and endorse your choice of guardian. Do not initiate this conversation, however, until you have fully discussed your particular situation with your attorney.

Guardian of your children, however, is not the same as guardian of your property. Trusts can be created that allow your money and property to be left to your minor children. Creation of a trust means that you appoint a trustee, or guardian of your property. This person would follow your specified wishes as to your estate. Laws and procedures differ from state to state. The trustee should be someone with financial knowledge and in whom you have the utmost trust and confidence. It is better to name an attorney as trustee, if you have no one in your life you can trust with this tremendous responsibility.

Don't choose the same person who you wish to be guardian of your child. This can create too much temptation. Besides, you want to ensure that the guardian of your children and the trustee keep a check on each other.

How to Choose a Guardian

First, talk privately with the person you would like to appoint as your child's legal guardian. Ask this person if he or she is willing to assume this important responsibility. If the person says no, accept this and understand that he or she has good and valid reasons for the refusal. Never try to talk anyone into accepting this responsibility. You do not need to choose a blood relative. It is not important whether the person you choose is male or female, single or married, or childless. It is only important that your child's prospective guardian would be able to care for your child in a loving and capable manner. Consider the changes that might be necessary like leaving a familiar school, neighborhood, and friends. Most importantly, however, you are looking for someone with similar values who would promote the same expectations and standards

you have tried to instill. This person would need to make major life changes to suddenly and unexpectedly accommodate the needs of a grief-stricken child. Consider if this person has these emotional resources and would be willing to literally change his or her life at a moment's notice. Don't disregard asking a lifelong friend with whom you feel close, even if that person has not spent a lot of time with your child. Whomever you select, obviously, needs to be someone who has meaningful time with your child. How terrible to think about a child losing her mother only to be placed in the custody of a virtual stranger.

Make sure that you have serious no-holds-barred discussions about the assets that would be available to provide for your child and any anticipated legal problems that might arise from actions by your former husband or partner. Your family needs to be made aware of your wishes. Any potential disagreements or conflicts need to be aired and ironed out now.

Talking to Your Child about Your Death

You can obtain real peace of mind by allaying fears your children may harbor of losing their only parent. Remember—this is about allaying their fears, not creating fears where none existed. It is probably necessary to have this kind of discussion with a young child only if you are seriously ill. Otherwise, it is probably not necessary to bring up this subject until the child asks, which is typically not until they are school age.

If you feel you need to discuss this subject with your child or your child asks, say that you plan to be her mommy for a long, long while but if the time comes when you can't be that the guardian you have chosen would love to take care of her. Keep these conversations age appropriate. Reassure children that having this kind of "backup mommy plan" is something that all good parents do and that you are not planning to go anywhere. If you have teenagers and anticipate that your former husband or partner would seek custody despite your wishes to have another person assume these responsibilities, let your children know these facts. Assure them that the court will take their wishes into account. Tell them also who would be the guardian of your property and how they would be provided for in case of your death. This conversation will likely only have to

---

THE DO'S AND DON'TS OF MONEY MANAGEMENT

Money management is essential for your survival as a single mother. Some things to remember:

- **Do** remember the golden rule: He who has the gold rules. The person with resources is always the person with choices.

- **Don't** allow or expect others to make financial decisions for you. You can enlist the aid of an adviser, but only you can decide what and how much you want to invest in something. Remember, too, if something sounds too good to be true, it most likely is.

- **Don't** invest in anything you don't understand, and never make financial decisions in haste.

- **Don't** let emotional obstacles get in the way of managing money. Feeling guilty because your relationship fell apart is not a reason to refuse what is financially yours, such as part of the proceeds from the sale of a house, car, or boat or even accepting spousal support if your job was taking care of your family.

- **Do** remember that money is not commitment, love, or attachment. Money is just business.

- **Don't** be afraid of money or sabotage any moneymaking efforts because you think you are acting in too masculine a way or it's not important enough to you. Money is genderless.

- **Do** remember that control of your credit is control of your life.

- **Don't** overlook the total costs of what is offered you. In other words, nothing is free—time and energy are also costs.

- **Do** start today to make a financial plan. Think about your goals and how to achieve them. Above all, write them down.

- **Do** investigate your employee benefits package. Understand all the benefits available to you and make the best possible use of them.

happen once or twice. Remember that it is likely you will live to a ripe old age and can look forward to spoiling your grandchildren!

Another way to feel as though you have your house in order is to make a videotape or write a letter for your child to open in the event that something happens to you in the future. In fact, it is a great idea, whether you live to be thirty-five or ninety-five, to have personal messages prepared for your child to open at different stages of her life—for instance, one when she has her first child and another when he has his thirtieth birthday. Leaving a loving part of you is a wonderful gift of reassurance for your children and rewards you with a great amount of comfort as well.

12

Home Economics —Affordable, Comfortable, and Practical Living

Finding adequate housing when you are on a shoestring budget can be an enormous task. Not to mention the ever-increasing prices on real estate. Sometimes, it's too easy to overextend yourself when you're not sure how much you really need to be able to afford your own home or condo, comfortable apartment, or other rental property. Affordability, as defined by the U.S. Department of Housing and Urban Development (HUD), means a household spends no more than 30 percent of its annual income for housing. If you pay more, it is considered that you are "cost burdened and may have difficulty affording necessities such as food, clothing, transportation, and medical care."

In today's "fear and consume" world, all types of uncertainty make it hard to feel secure. But, who doesn't want a nice home? The home embraces the family—it tucks you in.

If you're having trouble finding affordable housing, you're not alone. Affordable housing is a national concern and a frequent topic of debate. It's obtainable, however, if you're flexible, practical, and realistic about your housing needs.

Finding adequate housing when you are on a shoestring budget is a difficult task.

CHANGING YOUR LIFESTYLE

Perhaps you've already planned for this. You and baby are in a cozy apartment, or you and your brood of three teens have moved into a smaller but still comfortable house. Aside from the financial considerations, there are others factors that must be considered to decide what kind of housing arrangement will work

177

best for you and your children, particularly if you are recently divorced and can't maintain your previous residence or if you are single in a studio apartment and need a room for the new baby. Think beyond your present location. If you don't have ties to a particular place and want to seek out new horizons, do some research. If you are a widow, these decisions can be even more difficult because your grief makes it difficult to tackle the realities that must be faced.

Fortunately, today's single mother has options, such as sharing a residence with another single-parent family, living with relatives, or scaling down from a house to an apartment (which means no more mowing the grass or rebuilding your own place from start to finish). With some flexibility and careful planning, you may be surprised to find that you like your new living arrangement more than you did your old one.

SIMPLIFY YOUR LIFE

Like many other suddenly single mothers trying desperately to cling to a past lifestyle, you may find that maintaining your past living habits is not working out very well either emotionally or financially. If you're divorced, for example, and living in a busy city where the cost of keeping your car garaged is almost as much as the rent on your apartment, can you forgo car ownership? Why not take public transportation and bank the extra money?

One divorced mother recalls her change of lifestyle as feeling like she was "going from the country club to the welfare line." This was an exaggeration, but she had been so accustomed to her previous lifestyle that she did temporarily imagine that she would be destitute. Cutting

back does not necessarily mean you are in crisis. You can learn to simplify your life to your advantage.

Your emotional outlook has a lot to do with how smoothly the transition from one lifestyle to another is made. You don't have to become a totally different person, but it's healthier to accept that single people have different (and sometimes more enjoyable) living habits than married people. Redefine your living style to suit a more independent you.

FACING THE FEAR OF HOMELESSNESS

Many Americans fear homelessness. Even those who chose motherhood after doing some serious financial planning worry that they could lose their jobs or their health and end up homeless. If you visit a homeless shelter, chances are you will find someone who claims they never imagined being there or hear a story about a person who had all the trappings of a successful life until everything went wrong and they lost it all.

For most single mothers, the fear of homelessness is exactly that—an irrational fear. True, your life may change significantly, and you may have to reduce your standard of living somewhat. But moving to a smaller place, eating in more often, and clothing your kids from the local thrift shop hardly mean you are headed toward homelessness.

On the other hand, if you do find yourself homeless due to a sudden change in circumstances, you are not alone, and you are not a failure. It is difficult but critically important not to let yourself fall into the "I'm poor, therefore I'm worthless" trap. Let your children know, too, that although they may not have four familiar walls to call home, that home can represent your dreams and values that will one day be realized. For now, however, you need to find temporary housing either in a shelter or through a crisis assistance center, if you can't find living arrangements through a friend or a relative. If you find yourself desperately needing assistance, the Welfare Warriors have provided information to fight poverty for nearly twenty years (*www.welfarewarriors.org*).

STAYING OR MOVING?

One of the biggest issues newly divorced or widowed single parents face is whether or not to remain in the same house that they lived in when married. The decision of whether to keep or sell your house, condominium, or cooperative apartment certainly should not be rushed, but neither should you avoid a decision for too long.

Make a realistic assessment of your new expenses and income. Determine if keeping your current home is even affordable. A basic rule for determining whether you should reside in any living space is to calculate what percentage of your monthly income your house payment represents. If you're paying out one-quarter to one-third, then you're okay. But if your mortgage eats up well over 30 percent of your total income, your best bet would be to look for something more affordable.

Don't kid yourself into thinking that you will magically be able to afford this house some time in the future. Be realistic. Do not rely on child support payments to pay the mortgage. You never know when the payments will stop, and even though you may take legal action

to enforce the child support order, any delays could cause your lender to foreclose on your property. If you can afford to stay where you are, you can then ask yourself whether this is what you want. Even if you can afford to keep the house, if you want to start fresh somewhere else, do so. Don't let yourself feel guilty about staying put for the sake of your children. Unless the change would be an immediate and serious educational disruption or cause them to miss out on important milestone events, remember that children are adaptable and resilient and may welcome the change.

GETTING ANSWERS TO YOUR MORTGAGE QUESTIONS

I'm getting divorced and want to keep the house, but my husband and the co-owner of the property won't explain the details of the loan or answer my questions about it. My husband has always handled these details, and now I have no idea what is going on. However, he says that if I want to buy him out that it's okay with him. Where do I start?

If you find yourself in the middle of a split from a person with whom you jointly own a home, contact the current mortgage holder and ask questions. You have a right to any information concerning the loan's terms and payment schedule. Learn about your repayment options. Don't be afraid to keep asking questions until you understand. Find a lending officer with whom you feel comfortable.

Banks seem to work hard at maintaining an aura that often intimidates us or makes us feel as though we are somehow intruding, with our silly little questions and our piddling amount of money. Nonsense! Banking is still a service industry.

Some bank personnel act as if they are doing you a favor, when actually it is they who should be grateful for your business. You are entitled to the information regarding the services the bank provides and to more specific information regarding your particular loan or account. Loan officers should welcome your business.

My child's father, who was my housemate, wants to move out of state. He says we should sell the house we bought together and split the proceeds, but I don't want to move. I love this house, and it is perfect for raising a child. The payments are just too high for me. Do I have any options?

You might consider refinancing and using your share to buy out your former partner's share. By extending your terms—in other words, refinancing for fifteen or thirty years, depending on what's left on your mortgage—you can make smaller monthly payments. You can also pay off your former partner and maintain the same payments you have

now by getting a housemate to share some of the costs.

Cut the Interest on Your Mortgage Payments

Most people don't realize that, although they can deduct the interest on their mortgage to reduce their taxes, the amount of interest paid out over the years can be enormous. For example, let's say you have a 30-year loan at 7 percent interest. In the first year of paying off your mortgage, you will pay $7 toward interest for every $1 you paid toward principal. In short, a lot of money goes toward interest. Of course, by the time you get to the end of your mortgage-paying years, you will be paying less interest and more principal. So how do you shorten the life of your mortgage? Usually, just refinancing your home at a 15-year term would make your monthly payments too high.

Here's what to do to easily cut the interest on any mortgage. Simply make an extra payment once a year along with your regular mortgage payment and designate it to go strictly to principal. By "tricking your mortgage" (perfectly legal, but rarely suggested by lending officers, since mortgage holders love getting that interest), you can cut the time on a 30-year mortgage almost in half and avoid paying thousands of dollars of interest.

REASONABLE RENTALS

If you're already in an apartment that isn't quite as large as you'd like but you have a dining area or sleeping alcove that could serve as a nursery, by all means do this to avoid a rental increase. However, if your current rent is too high and your building has other rental apartments available for less than what you are now paying, check with the landlord about getting something a little cheaper or see if he will reduce the rent in exchange for your painting the apartment or performing certain maintenance tasks.

If you definitely need to look for a place, you should be aware that finding a reasonable rental for you and your family is a little trickier than it used to be. A number of state housing departments maintain a Directory of Affordable Rental Housing. Your local real estate association, newspaper, or county chamber or business association usually list available rentals on the Internet, which is a good place to start.

In some cities, the tactic among those in the race to find the most desirable apartments is not to search the classifieds but to read the obituaries and see where a recent "vacancy" has occurred. Less drastic techniques include calling a rental agent daily at a place where you really would like to live. One of the best ways to find out about available rental units in an apartment complex is to talk with the residents already living there. Searching the classifieds, being on the lookout for yard signs announcing a vacancy, and checking listings and notes posted on community bulletin boards at your local college or university, post office, or health and human resource agencies are other ways to apartment hunt. Don't overlook posting a message online or running an ad in your local newspaper or apartment guide. Enlisting the aid of real estate agents is another good idea because often these people sell homes to people exiting from apartments. Some of these agents will also charge you a fee; so be sure to ask about possible costs up front.

Retirement homes can be another source of information on affordable apartments because many of the residents may be giving up their apartments to live in a place with health care professionals on staff. Ask the director of the home if you can post notices in the recreation room announcing your need for an apartment. Often residents may know of others moving into the retirement home who may give you a lead on an available apartment.

SUBSIDIZED HOUSING

Your Department of Social Services can refer you to subsidized housing programs that are provided by local housing authority departments. These programs can assist you in finding a place to live and even provide some financial relief with your rent. Keep in mind that most housing assistance programs require you to pay a portion of your monthly income. If you're required to contribute, for example, one-third of your income toward rent, they will pick up the remaining balance of your rent.

You can also contact your local housing authority for a list of subsidized and HUD (Housing and Urban Development) housing in your county. These housing developments base their rentals on a sliding scale, but you may also find low-rent apartments in higher rent areas. Since there is usually a huge waiting list for these apartments, you might want to move into a nonsubsidized unit. By doing so, you can get to know the landlord or building manager, prove what an exemplary tenant you are, and often move up the waiting list faster for a subsidized rental when it becomes available.

HOMESHARING

Homesharing—two or more single-parent families maintaining one residence—is gaining increased popularity. Basically, homesharing usually consists of two mothers sharing an apartment with their children or purchasing or renting a house together. Networks like Co-Abode: Single Mothers Housesharing (*www.co-abode.com*), help single parents find others who may be looking to share an apartment or rent out part of a house.

One single mother, who was a teacher, feared that she wouldn't be able to afford the house that she had previously shared with her spouse. A friend of hers introduced her to another single mother with one daughter who had to give up her apartment because the building was going co-op and the woman could not afford to purchase her apartment and pay the monthly maintenance fees. The teacher rented out a portion of her house to her new friend and her daughter. Both greatly benefited from this arrangement because the woman who lost her apartment had always wanted to live in a house in the suburbs and the homeowner did not have to lose her house since she was now able to make her mortgage payments.

BUYING A HOUSE WITH ANOTHER FAMILY

A few months ago I met a young woman at my son's karate class, and we've become fairly good friends. She's a single mom like me and has always wanted to buy a house but couldn't afford it. We've discussed going in on some real estate together, not only as an investment, but also so we can have more living space and our children can attend an excellent school. Even though I'm fed up with my tiny apartment, I'm a little worried. What happens if we don't get along or if one of us loses a job or gets transferred? What happens if one of us decides to get married and move out? What do we need to know about buying a home together?

B uying a home together can work well if you consider all the pros and cons of joint home ownership before making this commitment. Many single-parent families are successfully sharing living space, and based on your forethought and your intelligent, thoughtful, and realistic questions, it's clear that you are doing your homework first. Weigh the advantages against the pitfalls of joint home ownership.

SINGLE MOM OF NOTE

Beverly DeJulio, Handy Ma'am
"If you can use a hand mixer, you can use a power drill!" says the first lady of home improvement, star of a PBS television series, *HandyMa'am with Beverly DeJulio*. A single mother of four children, DeJulio found her mission one day when her overstressed washing machine caused a near flood. She passionately believes that just about everyone has the ability to handle just about any home-based challenge and offers detailed step-by-step instructions in her user-friendly book, *HandyMa'am: Home Improvement, Decorating, & Maintenance Tips & Projects for You and Your Family*. DeJulio also urges moms to get their children involved in home improvement projects.

Buying a home can be a lot easier today than it has been in the past. Interest rates have been low the past few years, and through certain programs offered by some lenders, down payment requirements have dropped to as low as 5 percent or even less. Years ago, not having a husband's signature on the mortgage document was very uncommon. Today, more than one-fourth of all home buyers are unmarried, and more and more of these individuals are pooling their resources and purchasing properties together.

Joint home ownership can be complicated, since all the factors that need to be considered when you individually purchase a home are now twofold. You may prefer an area with a fabulous elementary school, but it has a problematic high school. If your co-owner or partner has older children, this may present a problem. Additionally, the location of your jobs, family, and friends may appear to be at opposite ends of the earth when you are considering these factors in your decision-making process.

Joint home ownership is first and foremost a partnership, not unlike being in business. As in business, you should be informed of all the possible liabilities. Be aware of the responsibilities of home ownership and know all the details of the financing. Being informed means that you are headed in the right direction.

The best thing to do initially is to sit down with your prospective partner and talk about possible problems and workable solutions. Because any kind of joint ownership—whether involving a married couple or two single mothers who have pooled their resources—invites certain problems, severe financial disruption can be avoided, if a realistic plan is devised.

Next, it is wise to seek the advice of an attorney before even seeing a lending officer. An attorney can best advise you whether or not the agreement you have discussed is workable and alert you to any possible complicating factors or unforeseen situations you might not have considered. Tax planning will also be important here. You will need to decide, for example, how deductions will be apportioned. Your attorney will also outline costs, such as additional legal fees or special types of insurance coverage, which you will need to factor into your decision-making. Carefully review all the information provided so that you can make the best informed decision about whether or not this housing arrangement is right for you.

If you decide to proceed, your attorney will draw up an agreement, not unlike a prenuptial agreement, in order that both of you will have your rights protected in the event of a dissolution of the partnership. At this stage you may wish to be represented by separate attorneys so that each of you is equally protected. As in any partnership, your individual interests may conflict, and such conflicts need to be ironed out early. Although the benefits of joint ownership are many—the ability to afford a larger down payment, lower monthly mortgage and maintenance expenses, and the joys of gaining an extended family—knowing what to do in the event that one person opts out of the partnership is most important.

WHEN ONE FAMILY DOES TOO MUCH

My teenage daughter and I live with another single mother and her young daughter. This woman schedules everything, right up to how we spend our weekends, but sometimes I want private time with just my daughter. My housemate's three other young children will begin summer vacation soon. My housemate thinks that my daughter will be in charge of caring for them. I don't think it is fair for her or a good practice to be tied up taking care of all the young kids in this household (who are not even family related) and miss out on being with her friends. What should I do?

When you say "not even family related," you are shortchanging yourself on the definition of family. Family is defined as a place where love is shared and a place that feels safe. One of the reasons you probably entered a homesharing situation was not only to save on bills and expenses, but also to create a sense of extended family. However, you are right that a teenager should not be expected to be the caretaker of all the youngsters in a household. A certain amount of responsibility is necessary and important for all teenagers to help them make the transition from childhood to adulthood, but resentment can occur if they are expected to do too much.

How to Make a Homesharing Arrangement Work

Hold regularly scheduled family conferences, including the children, if they are old enough to participate, to review any changes and allocations of responsibility. Children feel good about themselves when they are allowed to participate in the decision-making. Ask each of them what household tasks they like to do best and what tasks they feel should rotate. Allow your teenagers to voice concerns about excessive babysitting responsibilities or any other similar problems.

All your children will learn valuable negotiating skills and will get firsthand practice in how to compromise for the common good.

You and your housemate will also need designated times to meet away from the children to discuss finances, pay bills, or discuss any home repairs or other joint decisions that must be made. Just as in any type of partnership, communication skills are critically important. Not only do you live with this person, but she is also your partner. Use your business manners and avoid name-calling or losing your temper. Make every effort to discuss your shared interests reasonably and with respect for each other's feelings. Insist on similar treatment in return.

Remember that all collaborative efforts are shaky in the beginning and need an extraordinary amount of cooperation for success. Things will be tough at the start, but the outcome will make all your efforts worthwhile.

Define responsibilities clearly by putting up a chore chart on a wall in the kitchen. You and your partner should assign everyone chores. Older children and teens can be responsible for preparing meals, cleaning, and shopping.

Even younger children can pitch in by setting the table, putting laundry away, keeping their toys picked up, and helping to cut coupons (using safety scissors, of course) for grocery shopping. If one of you has more members in her clan, she should have to absorb a larger share of the cleaning duties.

Make sure to reward extra effort and cooperation. In exchange for extra baby-sitting time, teenagers will appreciate receiving that extra ride to the mall or to a friend's house. Even when they are legally allowed to drive, many teenagers are unable to afford a car; so borrowing the family car can also be a big incentive.

What if the homesharing arrangement is not working out? Incompatible business partners terminate their relationship. If this is your home, after giving a reasonable notice to your housemate, you can start looking for another single-parent household to share living space and expenses. If the house belongs to your housemate, then you must begin the search for a new place to live. Ways to search can include posting notices at work, local schools, churches, universities or colleges, real estate and rental agents, women's shelters, community centers, day care centers, and/or online bulletin boards such as Craigslist. You should also investigate other types of housing options to ensure that you make the best choice for yourself.

COHOUSING

Cohousing is a concept that began in Denmark in 1972. It consists of private apartments or houses that form a small-scale community around shared common facilities such as playrooms, kitchens, dining rooms, and laundry areas.

Today in the United States, there are over seventy finished communities and more than 5,000 people now living in cohousing (*www.cohousing.org*), with 150 other neighborhoods being planned and built. This lifestyle lets families know all the neighbors. Many families get together in the community-owned Common House several times a week to share meals and catch up on each other's lives. In the summer, residents enjoy working together in the community vegetable garden, while their children play within earshot on the neighborhood playground or ride bikes around a pedestrian path that links the homes and the Common House.

Cohousing neighborhoods emphasize diversity of age and family makeup. Retirees enjoy the extended-community roles of grandparents, single moms find supportive neighbors, and people without children become adopted aunts and uncles, available to read a story or lend a hand when needed. What makes cohousing particularly appealing to single parents is that the other adults in the community provide companionship and often pitch in on child care and food preparation. It is economically advantageous because the lending, sharing, or shared ownership of seldom-used items such as sewing machines, video cameras, or camping equipment is encouraged so that you can borrow and use such items without going to the expense of purchasing them.

MOVING IN WITH YOUR PARENTS

It is not uncommon for single working men and women, single-parent families, and young married couples to move back

home to live with their parents.

Since residing with your parents is in all likelihood not the living arrangement you would choose first, it is easy to forget that this represents a major adjustment for them, also.

Your image of one or both of your parents as caretakers and providers may not have changed, but it is likely that since you grew up and left home, they have changed. For starters, they probably enjoyed the changes that came with an empty nest. They were able to set their own schedules and priorities. They may have enjoyed having company more often and taking spur-of-the-moment vacations. If one of your parents is deceased or single, it is likely that this parent has made a fine adjustment to the post–single-parent life. He or she probably enjoys many activities and friendships and is doing his or her best to live joyfully in the moment.

Your arrival with the children will probably cause your parents to have some mixed feelings. On one hand, they are probably glad to be able to help you and sad that things have been tough for you. In addition, it is a blessing to be a real part of their grandchildren's lives and to be able to share with them important events and exciting changes. On the other hand, their lifestyles will most certainly be disrupted. There will be noise, sticky fingerprints on everything, toys with a million pieces, and requests for a snack at all hours. There might now be a line at the bathroom, where before your parents had the luxury of privacy. There will be added expenses like bigger water and utility bills and generally more wear and tear on the house and its contents.

Establish Some House Rules

Before you and your parents come to an understanding about the details of daily living, you must recognize that your parents are sacrificing and compromising on your behalf. They may be more than happy to do so, but if you are going to retain your grown-up status, you must gratefully acknowledge the adjustments your parents have made. It is also critically important that you work out businesslike financial arrangements. In all likelihood your financial resources are quite limited—otherwise, living with your parents would not have been your first choice. Try to pay them something no matter how small an amount. As your financial situation improves, increase your contribution to the household proportionately.

Decide who is responsible for food or shopping and how the cleaning chores will be divided and discuss curfews, loud music, allowing guests in the home, and babysitting arrangements. Formal agreements will make everyone's roles and responsibilities more defined and help ease the transition.

When Living with Your Parents Is Difficult

Knowing that your parents have compromised still may not be enough to enable you to deal effectively with how you may be feeling. A little communication might go a long way toward solving any problems you might be experiencing. You may want to write your parents a letter. After you write it, review it and either throw it away if it contains too much anger or edit out the accusatory parts and rewrite it and give it to your parents. Ask if all of you could sit down quietly away from the children and discuss what is expected of you and what all of you see as appropriate roles in the day-to-day care of the children. Ask what might be making them uncomfortable with their current situation.

Because of financial strains, I had to move back into my parents' home, and let me tell you, my mother is driving me crazy. Don't get me wrong—she's a wonderful lady—babysits, feeds the kids if I'm late getting home from work, and cares for them when they are home sick from school. I know that she loves us. But, if I so much as attempt to discipline my kids (without spanking), she says I'm being ineffective. Before I go out on a date, she gives me the third degree. She often waits up until I get home. I'm thirty-four years old, not fifteen. Why does she treat me like a child just because I'm not married?

Although moving back home is an economic necessity for many new single moms, one of the major issues cited by women who have moved back with their parents is that of being treated like a child again by one or both of them.

Some mothers, particularly mothers of the baby boom generation or earlier, were themselves raised to believe that a woman's success was measured by how long she could hold a family together and not so much by how she felt about her-

self or her ability to create her own life. So these moms often feel responsible for what they see as their daughter's failed relationship or marriage. If you try and see things more from your mother's perspective and understand where it comes from, you will cope more effectively with your current living arrangements.

Acting like a grown-up will also go a long way toward helping your parents treat you as one. You might simply say to your parents some version of "Thank you for being here for us. You're really helping me save money I couldn't afford to spend on a higher rent or mortgage elsewhere. If I get a place for myself and the children, I'll always know you helped make it possible."

Another tip: Do choose your battles carefully. If your mother wants to tell your son that socks and underwear should never be placed in the same drawer, so what? But, on the other hand, if she makes constant ethnic or racial slurs, abuses substances, or hits your children, you need to work these issues out because this is not an acceptable or healthy way to live. You will want to come to an immediate understanding about who will discipline the children and what means are acceptable to you and determine mutually agreeable house rules.

Here are some more tips to help you live peaceably with your parents:

♦ Don't expect your parents to give up or alter lifetime habits just because you and the children are now living with them. Insisting that they do so will diminish their own feelings of security and confidence and maybe cause disruption in everyone's lives. You have the capacity for greater flexibility, and you may need to demonstrate this skill more consistently than will your parents.

◆ Remember that your parents' energy levels are not as high as yours. A trip to the grocery store to buy a carload of supplies may be routine for you but might be exhausting for your mother. From simply a fairness perspective, heavy chores should be your responsibility.

◆ Help your parents to locate resources that might make their adjustment to this situation easier. You may want to get them books or videos that describe parenting ideas for grandparents or materials that have influenced your parenting choices. But don't present these materials in such a way as to suggest they are less than wonderful grandparents. Say something like "I know how hard it has been and how wonderfully you've tried to deal with our living here, and so I thought this book might help make it a little easier."

◆ Simple gestures can also go a long way toward making life more pleasant for everyone. How about getting up a little early one weekend to make your parents a special breakfast? Why not complete that extra chore that makes the house look especially nice? Have you considered hiring a babysitter and taking your parents to a movie or to some activity that they might really enjoy?

◆ Keep in mind that sharing a home with your parents will be a temporary solution to your housing problem. However, if it turns out to be successful through your combined efforts, welcome the knowledge that you and the children will have the privilege of living with all the benefits of an extended family under one roof.

◆ Always pay something toward rent or barter or trade in exchange for living with your parents. Have a written contract that is agreeable to all of you.

◆ Be open to change. Your parents may decide they need to live in a warmer climate or nearer to their friends for part of the year. Be prepared for any change in your living arrangements by having a backup plan.

FENG SHUI FOR SINGLE MOMS

Pronounced *fung shway*, this 5,000-year-old Chinese art of creating balanced and harmonious environments to achieve better health, productivity, and relaxation doesn't cost much to practice.

A Feng Shui expert would find centers of energy (ch'i) in various locations throughout your home and suggest different furniture and accessory arrangements to maximize the effects. Wind chimes, fountains, mirrors, stones, and natural products are used.

Before you hire an expert, try these tips:

◆ *Lose the clutter.* Positive energy occurs when you can move easily around your house.

◆ *Make pleasant sounds.* Running toilets and squeaky hinges interfere with your home's life force. Indoor fountains, quiet music, and even CDs of the ocean surf or rain falling softly can reflect the seasons, bring you closer to the elements, and calm fussy children.

◆ *Bed down right.* Feng Shui practitioners warn against placing your bed against a window because your ch'i could escape. Headboards facing north promote better sleep. To symbolize motherhood, paint your southwest wall a shade of yellow. Pictures or vases of peonies in your bedroom can attract good men to your life!

- *Reflect your kitchen.* The kitchen is the most important room in a home because this is where body and soul are nourished. Many Feng Shui experts believe that food tastes bad if the cook is startled or interrupted. A mirror helps you see who is nearby while you're slicing and dicing. Tables should be rounded because experts say sharp edges invite negative energy. If you're not convinced at least you know your children won't be bumping their heads on sharp objects.

- *Feng Shui the children.* Good ch'i and a balanced home environment help children grow. Practitioners say if you position your child's bed so her head is in the "wisdom" direction, her grades will improve. Although no study has found that "A" students used a compass when positioning their bed, it doesn't hurt to create a peaceful environment in your child's bedroom.

PART 3

RAISING GREAT KIDS WITH CONFIDENCE AND COURAGE

13
Child Care Basics

Most moms don't have the luxury of a sizeable income earned on a flexible family friendly schedule, a spouse's generous paycheck, or lucrative investments. Those moms who need to work at a job outside the home find headlines like "Stay-at-Home Moms Under More Stress Than Working Moms" quite comforting. They're true. Even career women who left dream jobs to stay home with their children for awhile often ask themselves (after they return to work) "What on earth possessed me to give up my job?" In fact, in article after article in magazines and newspapers, many mothers talk about how their illusions about the joys of being a stay-at-home mom were shattered by the day-to-day reality of being home full time. The days spent baking cookies or drawing together just didn't happen as they had imagined. Their confidence took a nosedive without their work routine and the rewards that accompany productivity. These moms discovered what many stay-at-home moms already know: raising children full time means having almost no private time. Even moms who can afford to stay home often put their children in some kind of child care program or hire a child care provider because they know the importance of attending a fitness class, meeting friends for coffee, or simply feeding their own souls by visiting

museums or art galleries. Research indicates that high-income families use the largest amount of child care.

Leaving your kids at a day care center or under the care of a babysitter is one of the hardest things single mothers face. We are not alone. Parents of every description often feel overwhelmed as they seek reasonable and affordable child care. However, with more and more women entering or already in the workforce with children at home under the age of six, the need for child care is greater than ever before. There are many resources to answer these needs, and you have a number of options when seeking quality care. Plus, study after study is showing that children who spend time in a good child-care situation develop better social skills than those who don't. Begin your efforts by shaking some of the old myths that have surrounded child care.

THOSE CHILD-CARE MYTHS

MYTH #1: *Day Care Means Someone Else Is Raising Your Child.* Single moms seem particularly prone to this guilt-inducing myth. You are the parent. It is your values, beliefs, and standards that will raise your child to adulthood. No one in your child's life will ever be a more important role model than you. Leaving your child to earn money or to further your education creates opportunity and security for your family. This is going to be very difficult at times, but a big part of love is doing responsibly what needs to done. Your daily efforts to reach your educational and career goals demonstrate to your child in the strongest possible way what commitment, reliability, and perseverance are all about. Tune out the rhetoric of ultraconservatives and the misinformed who loudly proclaim that child care causes children irreparable damage. Imagine the idea that having a chance to use your imagination, draw pictures, play with friends, count to a zillion, sing songs, take field trips, read books, and laugh together could be harmful to a child. Experts say not so. They say that a quality child-care center can actually improve a child's language and academic skills as well as teach the valuable social skills we all need to live successfully in the real world.

MYTH #2: *The Next Best Thing to Mom Is Grandma.* Those who are guilty of watching too many *Andy Griffith* reruns may have the idea that the ideal single parent's child-care provider is a full-time grandma who stays at home. Not every child's great-aunt or grandmother is an Aunt Bea. A child care provider who is stable, loving, and consistent in his or her routines and expectations of the child can promote confidence in the child of a working single parent and also teaches young children that there are many caring adults who can be trusted. Proper training is even more important in caring for children than "old-fashioned" experience. Warm, loving, attentive caregivers provide the best environment for young children.

MYTH #3: *Day Care Can Lead to Long-Term Insecurity.* On the contrary, a stable environment that offers structure yet permits the child to advance at his or her own rate of learning can be a boon to a child's sense of well-being and security. As stated previously, not only is the caregiver's relationship to the child not an important factor, but also a group setting offered by professional day care centers can be emotionally and intellectually stimulating for children. Research proves that toddlers and preschoolers who have greater interaction with other children excel in verbal and social skills, enabling them to gain an increased sense of independence.

MYTH #4: *Your Child Won't Be Sure Who Mommy Is.* Nonsense. Your child may feel like he has a number one mommy and a number two mommy (the child care provider), but there is nothing wrong with a kid thinking that there are many adults who care for him. It's simply impossible to care for a child too much. You may feel sad if you are not there when your child experiences major breakthroughs such as taking his first step, losing his first tooth, or eventually mastering the potty-training challenge. You may berate yourself for having to work or even for choosing to work and think that if you could be a stay-at-home mom that your child would thrive better. But staying home is no guarantee that you will be focused on your child's every move. In fact, some studies suggest that stay-at-home moms share less than thirty minutes more one-on-one time each day with their children than working moms do.

REVIEWING YOUR CHILD-CARE OPTIONS

What is the difference between a preschool, a day care center, and a child care center?

Actually, most places that keep children for a fee before the child is eligible for public school are referred to as child care facilities, whether or not they have particular preschool programs and activities. Day care is another term commonly used to describe an environment where children are kept while the parents are at work. Here is a description of the most commonly available child-care options.

In-home Care

This includes nannies, au pairs, roommates, babysitters, housekeepers, and friends or relatives. In-home care is ideal for the new mom with an infant because the baby stays in his own environment, receives individual attention, and does not run the risk of picking up infections from other children in a busy day care center. Because babies need special care the first few months, a one-on-one relationship with a care provider is preferable to that of a

---

ANIMAL SINGLE MOMS HAVE LARGER BRAINS

When comparing species with three different parenting behaviors, researchers found that species such as raccoons, bears, and small felids in which the females receive no help from mates or other animals in caring for their young have larger brains than those who exhibit biparental or community care. Researchers credit the difference in brain size among the groups to the higher cognitive and perceptual abilities required of independent females. These moms must do everything from finding a den site and gathering food to protecting their young from predators and teaching them to hunt. No difference was found in the male brain size proportional to body size among the studied species. (Zoologists only studied animal mothers. No bipedal moms—even those eating meat for dinner and then getting on all fours scrubbing the floor late at night—were included in this study.)

---

facility where there are many providers. Yet due to the controversy stirred up by the film *The Hand That Rocks the Cradle*, many new moms think the only safe nanny is a grandmotherly type who only changes diapers and sings nursery rhymes all day. Actually, the ideal in-home provider might be a younger woman with a lot of energy who sings the latest pop songs.

Family Day Care

This is the oldest and most widely used form of child care. It attracts many women who not only need child care but also are considering their own at-home child-care service. Many women with young children who either can't afford child care or simply do not want to return to the corporate workplace until their children start school have found this to be an ideal solution. It's a way to earn money while caring for their children. One advantage of family day care is that there are fewer children in this kind of environment because licensing may often be easier for a small home care business to acquire than a larger center. In addition, this type of arrangement may be more affordable than larger centers. However, certain drawbacks exist. For one, the home care provider may not be experienced in child care or may not be prepared for unexpected crises. Additionally, this person may become burned-out, decide to return to an office job, move away, or close down her business for a number of other reasons.

Workplace Child Care

Imagine being able to take your coffee or lunch break to be with your child, who is only minutes away from you when you are on the job. As ideal as this situation sounds, it is still evolving too slowly to satisfy the needs of the majority of mothers in the workforce. Yet, more and more corporations are realizing the benefits of having child care that is conveniently located to their employees. To find out if a company has on-site child care, contact the chamber of commerce in the area where the company is located. Also, pick up a copy of the annual *Working Mother* magazine's "Top 100 Companies" issue. This feature provides information on places that offer on-site quality child care.

Franchised or Private Preschools or Child Development Centers

Like all child-care environments, professionally run day care centers have their pros and cons. One problem many mothers encounter in this kind of environment is too rigid a structure. For example, because preschools and child development centers prepare young children for kindergarten, children are moved from activity to activity at a pace for which some may not be ready. Also, you may not find the flexibility you need if your job demands you stay late at times or if you have erratic hours during a seasonal crunch. These centers usually open and close at a fixed time and charge costly late fees, while an individual caretaker or in-home center may be willing to work around your schedule. The bright side of franchised or private child care facilities is that the staff is usually well-trained and the facility is equipped with state-of-the-art children's play and learning equipment and furniture.

Nonprofit Day Care

Usually affiliated with churches, synagogues, or community service agencies, these child care settings offer reasonable rates, trained and licensed providers, and a host of activities to keep little ones occupied. Like many professionally run for-profit businesses or day care franchises, nonprofit child care facilities may also offer preschool programs. One thing to keep in mind when considering a church or neighborhood-run nonprofit child care arrangement is that often these places have long waiting lists. Be sure to sign up early in your pregnancy to ensure a slot in this type of facility. Check with your local YWCA, community Head

Start program, or local United Way agency for help.

Employee-Run Child Care Co-ops

One of the brightest solutions for the future of child care is the on-site employee-run co-op. Many small- to medium-sized businesses are opting for this arrangement for two reasons. First, they are not large enough to offer employees company-owned child care nor are they able to provide benefits or credit toward outside child care.

Second, as with larger businesses, most medium-sized corporations know that a happy worker is a productive one. Because the workforce consists of a majority of women with small children at home, the needs of this group simply must be met to ensure production in the future.

The employee-run co-op is a child care arrangement in which company staff using the facility donate hours to help run it. In a sense, it is like job sharing because you trade off with other employees to help manage the cooperative, plus you share job tasks

---

THE DO'S AND DON'TS OF FINDING CHILD CARE

♦ **Do** research your child care options long before you need them. For example, if you are pregnant, plan for child care now.

♦ **Don't** let headlines make you paranoid about every child care facility you visit. The majority of child care situations are safe. Be cautious, but not panicky. You'll be more apt to make good judgments if you are calm.

♦ **Do** ask questions, and then ask more. Then ask and check the answers again! You can never investigate a child care provider or center too much or exhaust a list of questions too soon.

♦ **Don't** dismiss male providers because you think they pose too much of a threat or risk to your child. (You should thoroughly investigate the person regardless of gender.) Even though this chapter refers to caregivers primarily as

"she" and males are not as readily found as women in this field, qualified young or mature men who have elected to provide caring, activities, and enrichment for children often bring to the job a sense of adventure, creativity, and a different point of view.

♦ **Do** check licensing requirements for providers in your area. Even though having a license is no guarantee of quality child care, if your state requires a license for a home with five or more children and the caregiver has six children with no license, be wary. Likewise, if a center is licensed and has significantly fewer children than the allowed staff/child ratio, be cautious, too. Maybe other parents know something that you don't.

♦ **Do** keep at it. With perseverance and research, you will be able to find a workable solution.

with others on days when a company position is unfilled because that employee is working in the co-op. To present a proposal such as this to a prospective employer, you need to have a detailed plan of how this arrangement would operate. Remember, the bottom line to your employer is how this situation can improve overall production on the job. Don't forget to look at other concerns about starting an on-site child care co-op. Investigate the licensing requirements in your state and ask an attorney about any legal ramifications.

School-Age Child Care

School-age child care includes almost any program that regularly enrolls children from kindergarten through early adolescence during the times when schools are traditionally closed. This includes programs operated by schools, family day care providers, recreation centers, youth-serving organizations, and child care centers. Also known as extended-day programs, before- and after-school programs provide enrichment, academic instruction, recreation, and supervised care. An array of drop-in and part-time programs also serve an ad hoc child care function.

HOW TO FIND CHILD CARE

Finding child care can be a formidable task. Parents often don't know where to turn for help and quickly become overwhelmed by high costs, varying quality, the confusing array of programs, and the shortage of openings. Most working mothers seek child care that is convenient to their home or office, has extended hours, is affordable, offers a

SINGLE MOM OF NOTE

Maria Montessori,
Educational Theorist

Maria Montessori was the first woman to graduate from medical school in Italy, where she became an influential researcher and educator in special education. It was there in her late teens that Maria had an affair with another doctor and discovered that she was pregnant. The couple never married, and Giuseppe Montesano eventually married another woman.

Maria was the creator of the Montessori Education Method, but it was her son, Mario, who is credited with developing the curriculum used in Montessori schools.

highly trained staff or individual, and, above all, provides parental peace of mind. Following are some ways to go about seeking quality child-care.

Talk with Other Parents

Because first-time mothers, particularly single mothers, have not been in the mainstream of "parent talk," finding referrals from friends and neighbors may not be the easiest method of locating an ideal placement for their child. But referrals are one of the best ways to find a child care arrangement because not only are you being pointed toward places you may not have known existed but also at the same time you are getting information about the quality of child care. Get a list of mothers in your neighborhood who have used the services of a day care center or preschool and call them to ask questions. You'll want to know where they found desirable arrangements, what the going rate is in your community, precautions to take, and if they know of any openings.

Read the Ads

When you can't find anyone to recommend a good child care environment, check the ads in your local newspaper. Don't overlook the free parenting publications now becoming popular in most cities and larger communities. These freebies rely on ads targeted toward those interested in anything to do with children, families, and parenting. You could also place an ad in these newspapers or magazines stating exactly what it is you are seeking.

Post Notices

You can also post notices in your local supermarket, Laundromat, post office, elementary school, children's store (if allowed), hospital and community health bulletin boards, and apartment complexes (where notices are permitted) to announce your search for a child care provider.

Use the Phone Directory

Larger centers that are professionally owned or operated will be listed under child care in your phone directory. Some in-home centers and church- or religious-affiliated child care programs may also be listed in the Yellow Pages of your local phone book.

Use Referral Agencies

All methods for seeking child care should be used, but if it is available, be sure to seek the advice of resource and referral agencies who can help you find a child care facility that is right for you.

Dependent Care Reimbursement Accounts

Your company may offer dependent care reimbursement for its employees. This means that as part of your job's benefits, your place of business may pay part or all of your child care costs. Check into this by speaking to the director of human resources or the work and family coordinator at your place of employment.

INTERVIEWING A NANNY

Some key questions to ask when interviewing an in-home child care provider:

♦ Even if you are using an agency, don't leave it up to them to investigate a nanny's references. Find out why she left her last job and ask if her former employer would hire her again.

♦ Ask the agency how long they have been in business and their process for screening their nannies or babysitters. For example, did the agency check her criminal and medical records?

♦ Don't hire a caregiver until after an extensive interview, with and without your children present. If your kids feel uneasy around this person, go with your gut feelings and do not hire her.

♦ Always ask about the caregiver's feelings on discipline. If she shows signs of impatience or rudeness or confesses that she makes children stay in a corner or on a chair for extended periods of time, say "No, this one's not for me."

• Ask the caregiver how she would handle a situation such as when a child refuses to listen or if the child yells and throws things in the house. If she responds sensibly or shares her successful experiences with these matters, you may be looking at a possible hire.

THUMBS UP

Here are six signs that your child is receiving quality care:

1. Your child shows you lots of artwork or projects on which he has been working. Not only does this mean he's busy, but also it means he's being supervised.

2. Your child is so involved in what he is doing that he doesn't want you to take him home.

3. The provider asks you numerous questions: where you can be reached, who your child's doctor is, what kinds of allergies your child has, whether your child requires a special diet, and so on. Also, the provider is not necessarily being nosy if she queries you about your relationship with your child's father. Smart babysitters don't want a disgruntled, estranged ex scouting around their property. (Be sure you feel comfortable enough with the provider to disclose your situation.)

4. The child care center has the following combination: low staff/child ratios, small group size, recommended

caregiver qualifications, and well-planned activities and enrichment programs.

5. You feel you have established a rapport with the caregiver. Because a single parent does not have the other parent as a backup, the most important backup person in your daily life is the caregiver. It's a good sign when you and the caregiver are able to work together.

6. Television is used as a learning tool only, and the set is only tuned in to a public television station or a cable channel specifically geared toward kids.

CHILD-CARE CAUTION

Following are nine warning signs that may indicate a problem:

1. The babysitter makes you drop off or retrieve your child at her doorstep. The day-care center does not allow drop-in visits.

2. The television set is always blaring (most likely in in-home care centers).

3. The children look tired, forlorn, confused, or sad.

4. The place has an unpleasant smell or is dirty and cluttered. True, children should be able to have their things visible, but there should be a reasonably warm and tidy appearance.

5. There seem to be few toys, play equipment is broken, or play areas are unsafe.

6. The staff is smoking or chatting among themselves rather than interacting with the children. If your child stays in a babysitter or caretaker's home, make sure there are no domestic issues. Your child should not be in a situation where the provider's spouse has a drinking or drug problem or where domestic violence occurs.

7. The routines for hand-washing and overall cleanliness are less than perfect. Pay particular attention to where and how diapers and other soiled clothing are changed.

8. Your child acts differently around the in-home nanny or babysitter or responds negatively to the provider at a child care center. A baby who screams every time the caregiver appears is showing fear or dislike. If children complain frequently about a caregiver, it's more than an adjustment phase.

9. You notice changes in eating and sleeping patterns. Watch for unexplained bruises, cuts, burns, or other injuries.

THE COST OF CHILD CARE

Not only do single parents pay the same child care costs as married or partnered parents but also more often than not single parents pay higher fees. The reason is that the child-care provider has to back up and support the single parent in the same way a second parent would and has become someone upon whom the solo parent has come to rely. However, because of the dual earnings in a two-

parent family, which allow more choices in child care, the single parent often has to make do within her budget. Generally, full-time child care costs range anywhere from $100 to $250 weekly, depending upon what part of the country you live in and the quality of care.

DEALING WITH SEPARATION ANXIETY

Leaving a child at the babysitter's or a day care facility the first few times can be extremely upsetting for a new mother. However, if you can accept these temporary separations in a matter-of-fact manner, the separation will go more smoothly for you and your child. In fact, if you treat the subject like any other routine that is part of your day-to-day parenting activities, you'll find that your child will learn to separate from you more easily. Although some experts disagree as to whether it is best to discuss the separation beforehand (many discourage any discussion, saying that it creates more problems), most agree that you need to reassure your child that "Mom is going to work now and will see you later." Try not to

stress your child by telling him or her to be good or to behave. Rather, wish your child a good or fun day, and always let your child know that you love him.

PARTING WITH LESS SORROW

I have a three-and-a-half-year-old son. Suddenly, he is clinging and crying every time I leave him with his regular babysitter to go to work. Forget telling me to leave him with anyone else—now he's afraid of everyone, including his grandmother, whom he usually adores.

Assuming the caregiver is someone in whom you can place a lot of trust, this is probably separation anxiety. Separation anxiety means fear of losing the bond to the parent as an individual. Sometimes separation anxiety manifests itself as a fear of "outsiders," a category that includes not only strangers but also everyone who does not live in the house—even close relatives like grandma. A child dealing with separation anxiety isn't so much afraid of the outsider as he is of the possibility that the outsider might come between him and his mother. All children experience separation anxiety to some degree. It is a normal response.

Talk about what you will do together when you return—the more specific, the better because your child will have a sharper picture left in his mind. Just make sure that you live up to your promise and do whatever you promised as soon as you return. Create a ritual way of leaving and returning. Say the same special good-bye phrase every time you leave—preferably make it the last thing you do—and the same hello phrase every time you return—preferably the first thing you do. This predictability and special attention will be reassuring to your child. Expect some distress—you cannot eliminate separation anxiety entirely. Be careful about communicating that what he is experiencing is wrong or upsetting. It's okay to comfort your child and reassure him the first couple of times this happens, but then pick yourself up and say good-bye and leave.

I have just taken a great job. Previously, I was temping for an agency, so my four-year-old daughter was in a part-time day care program only a few times a week. I now have her in their wonderful all-day program, but she seems to be having a harder time with my new job than with the old one. Now I feel like this new job was a bad idea since I'm having such a hard time leaving her. Is something really wrong?

Sounds like you both have a touch of separation anxiety. It is natural to miss your child, but don't allow your own separation anxiety to feed hers. Don't make a big deal out of how much you'll miss your child. Parents are especially likely to experience separation anxiety of their own when the tables are turned and their child leaves them for an extended period of time, such as to go to nursery school or day care. Avoid making the transition more difficult for your child by putting off leaving your child behind, oversentimentalizing the occasion, or behaving differently from the way you normally behave.

THE DO'S AND DON'TS OF SEPARATING WITHOUT ANXIETY

♦ **Do** plan ahead. Have all of your child's belongings packed in one bag ready to hand to the caregiver so you won't be dragging out the event.

♦ **Do** be quick and straightforward about the separation. When it is time to leave, do so without hesitation and without giving your child reason to worry. Don't hug and cry excessively, or your child will suspect something is wrong with the whole scenario.

♦ **Do** have a few practice runs if parting is difficult for you. For instance, ask a friend or relative if you could drop your child off at his or her house a couple of times until you and your child become comfortable with the idea. You don't have to stay away long—maybe grocery shop, take a walk, or get a manicure. Make each time a little longer. In only a few weeks your child will be secure knowing that the routine always means mommy is coming back.

♦ **Don't** call your child at day care every time you get a break or at lunchtime, asking if he misses mommy. It's okay to call once a day to say "Hello, hope you are having fun," if you can handle this, but be sure that the time you call is okay with your child care provider.

♦ **Do** develop a ritual for saying hello and good-bye. For example, leaving your child with a lipstick kiss is a constant loving reminder of your presence. Cover your lips with lipstick and then kiss your child on the hand or wrist where she can see the lipstick imprint. Long-wearing lipstick works best because it does not wash off easily. Let your child keep a family photo in her bag or knapsack.

♦ **Don't** show how upset you are at leaving your child. Remember that children take their cues from their parents. Try to handle the separation in a confident and upbeat way. If you do well, chances are that your child will do well, too.

♦ **Do** consider making audiotapes or videotapes for your child if you are going to be separated from him for more than several days. These tapes can be played to reassure your child of your presence and, more importantly, of your continuing love. Try reading a favorite book on tape, telling a family story, or talking to your child about what you are doing while you are away and what you will do together when you return.

14

Parenting Those Ages and Stages— The Early Years

While parenting is one of the most difficult challenges any woman can face, it also is supposed to be among the greatest joys in life. Often it is, when a parent cannot only guide and teach her children but also learn valuable lessons as well during this lifelong process. However, for the single parent facing this challenge alone, the task seems more intense than it does for two-parent families.

Yet, when the real goal of parenting is more closely examined—that of raising a child to go out into the world as a productive, participating, and caring member of the human race—we find that all families in our country face pretty much the same child-rearing issues, such as providing a quality education; dealing with behavior and discipline problems; balancing work and family; and teaching kids to avoid drugs, crime, and heartbreak.

You can raise a child successfully with one parent or two, as long as you build a network that connects your family to the rest of society by engaging others to serve as models and mentors, either directly or from a distance. Not everyone welcomes children as the gifts they truly are and appreciates the fresh perspective their innocent eyes offer. But there are people who can become part of your community if you are willing to look. It's important to remember that you can't have too many adults loving a child. America's favorite "daddy," the late Fred Rogers, of *Mr. Roger's Neighborhood*, agreed: "Here's what I think: the roots of a child's ability to cope and thrive regardless of circumstances, lie in that child's having had at least a small, safe place (an apartment, a room, a lap) in which, in the companionship of a loving grownup, that child can discover that he or she is lovable and capable of loving in return. If a child finds this during the first years of life, he or she can grow up to be a competent, healthy person." Letting your children know that they were meant to be here means you have already started off on the right track.

YOUR BABY

Here are some of the issues that you may face with your new baby.

Feeling Unloved by Your Baby

My baby is acting different. She was so cuddly and sweet the first year, but now she screams, fusses, and seems generally uncooperative. I feel like she doesn't love me as much as she used to. I've been working outside the home since she was four months old, so it couldn't be because I can't stay at home with her all the time, could it?

Maybe the "love affair" that new mothers and babies experience during the first year has ended, but this doesn't mean that a stronger, more unconditional love can't flourish. It certainly isn't that your child is mad at you because you have a job.

Babies don't do too much during the first year; so there are few problem behaviors. But now your child is ready to move ahead toward greater independence. When you have had a cooperative, easy baby, this burst of independence and negativity comes as a shock! Try to ride with the changes, as these are all a natural part of your baby's development in trying to explore her world while lacking the wherewithal to deal with it. Coping is a skill children develop as they grow.

"My Baby Won't Let Me Touch Her. . . ."

My baby doesn't want to snuggle as much as she used to. In fact, she yells when I grab her and she doesn't want to be held. She gives me grief when I try to do anything with her. I get embarrassed thinking people will judge me a bad mother because my child doesn't want me to touch her.

Infants of this age have a fear of being invaded. Intrusions into her personal space by staring too intently or standing too closely are typically met with shrieks or screams of protest. This is only your daughter's self-protective instincts at work. Embarrassing for you, but perfectly normal and to be expected from her!

Your baby seems irritable and gives you grief over the simplest requests because she is at the beginning of her journey toward independence. You have not created a monster but are merely entering a whole new phase of your child's development. All this is good news because it means your baby is moving ahead developmentally in the appropriate and expected way. Remain calm and go with it. This stage won't last forever, and before you know it, other stages will bring new challenges.

Overcompensating for Father's Absence Can't Spoil Baby

My baby is beginning to act up. I feel I may have overcompensated for her not having a father and in the process spoiled her during her first year. I'm afraid I've made a mistake by "overparenting."

Put aside your fears because it's pretty difficult to spoil a young baby. An independent one-year-old is not spoiled. The behaviors we call "spoiled" are simply children's ways of asking for what they instinctually know they need—limits. Spoiled behavior occurs when a child does not know his or her limits or when to expect limits from you or others. Consistent handling and setting limits will help your child, but this does not ensure relief from the turmoil brought about by the changes occurring at any stage of growth. The beginning of your child's second year will be cause for even more change, and your child can become confused by what's happening. Maintain consistency by letting your child know what is acceptable and what isn't. Things will improve, but you need to hold on because this is what the motherhood ride is all about!

TODDLERS

Here are some of the challenges you may encounter during the toddler years.

Changes After the First Birthday

My sweet little girl's first year was blissful. She ate and slept well. She smiled and laughed. I knew she was happy, and I felt like I was doing a good job. Right after her first birthday, I began to notice changes. She screams when anyone looks at her. She wakes up every four hours all through the night. Every time I want her to do something, she resists. She seems irritable. What is causing these changes? What have I done wrong? Will I ever sleep again?

What actually is happening is that your sweet, cooperative baby girl is growing up. All the behaviors you described—including being up every few hours at night—are normal, anticipated behaviors in one-year-old children. Disturbances in sleep patterns typically occur whenever the baby achieves a new developmental motor milestone like walking. More acceptable sleep patterns will return. What you do need to do is have faith that one day you will sleep through the night again.

It's Okay to Sleep with Your Child After a Nightmare

Last week my eighteen-month-old must have had a terrible nightmare or something. He woke up screaming. I was so tired myself that half-asleep I carried him to my bed, and we both fell asleep. I told my mother what had happened, and she warned me that I was ruining him. What is so terrible about sleeping with your child for part of the night every so often?

Nothing. There are few issues about which mothers are made to feel greater unwarranted guilt than bringing a young child into their beds every once in awhile. We have enormous taboos in this society about children sleeping with their parents. Single mothers seem particularly suspect as awareness of child abuse sometimes crosses the line into witch-hunting. All parents—even your mother—have comforted a child in their own beds from time to time. The key question is whose needs are being met. In your case, your son woke up crying hysterically, and you comforted him in your bed. You did not wake up your son to comfort you. If you are the one needing comfort, then it is your needs being met, not your child's. In such circumstances, you need to look for more appropriate means of comfort.

You are not a terrible person if you need comfort, but your child should not be expected to comfort or take care of you.

Child Acts Up for Mom Only

Not that I expect praise because I think this is what I should be doing and what I want to be doing, but I make incredibly complicated arrangements to spend the most time possible with my eighteen-month-old son. I think about him all day and look forward to a loving reunion at the end of the day. When I pick him up, he lies on the floor kicking and screaming. The caregiver at the day care center says he never behaves that way for her.

The caregiver is right. He does not behave that way for her because she is not his mother. An emotionally healthy toddler saves his most intense feelings for his mother. This means that it is to be expected that when you pick him up that he will scream or cry pitifully. He will not cooperate in efforts to dress him to go home. His behavior will lead you to believe that he hates you and that you are the last person he wants to be with. This is not true. As part of the normal developmental process, your child must let negative as well as positive feelings surface. Otherwise your son will become passive and confused.

As your child grows older, these same patterns persist but in more subtle ways. Simply stated, children save the bad stuff for mothers because they are most closely connected to us emotionally and with us they feel safe. If we understand this, it puts things in perspective and helps us feel much less defensive and confused when we observe how many strong emotional messages from our children have only our names on them.

The best way to handle these strong reunion messages is to realize that your child needs to be comforted, not reprimanded. It is also helpful, no matter what the age of your child, to establish and stick to routines so that your child knows what to expect when you arrive to pick him up. These routines will help him learn self-control and establish trust. Don't try to accomplish too many domestic chores when you first arrive home. Your child needs your full attention and comfort. Having things as organized as possible when you get home at night and keeping things like dinner menus simple are lifesaving ideas.

It is important to remember that just as there is sometimes unconscious competition between mothers and fathers, there is sometimes the same

SMOOTH OUT MORNING MADNESS

Frustrated with rushing around in the morning trying to get your toddler to eat and winding up late for work anyway while half her breakfast is still on your clothes? Your blender plus fresh fruit mixed with juice, milk, soymilk, or yogurt can supply you and your child with the nutrition and taste to smooth out what could be a hectic morning. Save more time by making it the night before and putting it in the freezer. When you get up, take it out of freezer, let it thaw a bit, and press high for a tasty breakfast smoothie.

kind of competition between mothers and caregivers. It would have been much more helpful if the caregiver had told you that your son had been waiting for you all day, rather than give you the impression that your son's behavior was directed to you in some kind of negative way. The caregiver might have wanted to reassure you that your son had been happy and well cared for. When you are feeling vulnerable and frazzled, however, it is hard to interpret her message as other than a put-down.

TOILET TRAINING

Toilet training should be an accomplishment for the child, not for the parent. All mothers tend to want to rush this stage because it's such a noticeable milestone in their child's development. Moreover, many day care centers and preschools like children to be potty trained at around two and a half to three years, which makes single mothers particularly vulnerable to the potty-training rush. Many single moms, however, fail to realize that even though there is a policy that it's rarely rigid. Many children quickly train when their classmates call them "baby" because they are wearing diapers.

Preschool children also enjoy being part of things in a group. Children not yet toilet trained quickly observe that they are not part of the "bathroom routines" at day care or preschool.

Don't Rush Potty Training

Because tight budgets are often common in a single-mother household with young children, the temptation to skimp on diapers looms large, steering moms into trying to potty train too quickly. Don't cave in to it. You may want to consider cloth diapers, which are the cheaper alternative and certainly the best bet for the environment. Buy cheaper diapers and purchase in bulk packages. Pushing a child too soon will only result in wasted effort and frustration for everyone.

Potty Training Hints

- Many diaper manufacturers are reversing years of diaper engineering to make diapers less absorbent. These less absorbent diapers are geared to smooth the way for toilet training by holding a small amount of liquid close to the skin so your child feels the wetness. These diapers and others marketed to be transitional for toddlers are very expensive. These kind of disposable diapers give the child the feeling of being a "big kid" wearing underwear without the messy consequences if the child wets or soils. Many mothers feel that using disposables like these prolong toilet training because children cannot feel they are wet. Pediatricians generally believe that children must be unhappy about having a wet or soiled diaper before successful toilet training can begin. Given the cost and the possible delay in toilet training, some moms opt for underwear. Your choice depends upon your personal preferences, child care situation, and tolerance for accidents. If you have concerns, your pediatrician or health care provider is your best source of information.

♦ Begin slowly with fewer expectations. Many moms begin by allowing the child to flush the toilet when a soiled diaper is cleaned. Praise his "flushing success" and then use this success to try sitting on the potty chair or toilet. Do not brag to others about what your child has accomplished nor complain when he is less than successful. Toilet training is a process, not a competition.

♦ Many children are fascinated with the new underwear that accompanies potty training. Certainly less cumbersome than diapers, "big boy" or "big girl" pants are often a terrific incentive to use the potty. Make a big deal out of this new clothing and stress how these items signify "big kid" status. Your child will not only have fun but also may actually look forward to using the toilet, rather than diapers!

♦ Resist the urge to do extraordinary things to reward your child for using the toilet. Your child will sense your frustration, stress will escalate, and a battle for "who is in control" can easily overwhelm both of you. Do not give your child rewards like stickers or candy for using the toilet. When the time is right for your child, a "good for you" or a high five will work just fine.

♦ Nighttime training usually takes much longer to accomplish than day training. Expect to use diapers for overnight for awhile even after your child is dry during the day.

Can My Son Learn Potty Training Without Dad Around?

Whenever I pull out the potty chair, my two-year-old son balks. My helpful but nosy neighbor thinks it's because there is no man around to show him how to do it. She says I'd better hurry and teach him before it's too late. Why is my son so disagreeable?

Many parents get well-meaning but inaccurate advice about when a child should be completely potty trained. As for not having a father around to teach your son to use the potty, that is totally unrelated to why your child balks.

Several developmental steps will need to come together before your child is ready to be toilet trained. Negativity is a hallmark of this age, and it tends to come and go. The closer your child is to three, the less likely the natural negativity of this stage will prevent successful toilet training. Your child will be more ready to be trained when he is ready to understand concepts like "this is your potty chair" and is able to follow two-step commands. Your child needs to show curiosity about the toilet before potty training can be successful. He needs to be over the excitement of walking and ready to sit down. Many children after their second birthdays show great interest in imitating adults, and this interest in imitating can be used to spark their interest in toilet training. Children ready for toilet training are beginning to understand orderliness and putting things where they belong. The desire to put things in their proper place can be transferred usefully to urine and bowel movements.

PRESCHOOLERS

Besides toilet training, other issues will commonly arise as your child moves from toddler to preschooler.

Biting, Hitting, and Other Worries

My three-year-old son is in a play group. One of the other children bites, and I overheard the mothers say that he's acting out because his dad recently left. I felt personally offended because I'm a single mother, too. Will my child act out? Also, I was afraid to speak up when I saw one of the parents biting the child back to prove how this hurts.

Children normally communicate with each other and imitate one another, and often behavior like biting or hitting is included. However, blaming it on the dad's absence is simply a way for others, well-meaning as they are, to find an answer to a question that could just as easily plague them. Don't be surprised if your child doesn't act out at all. Do keep in mind that biting or hitting another child back is never acceptable. This overreaction sets a pattern for more of such behavior, rather than eliminating it. Children bite, hit, or pull hair at this age when they are overwhelmed and lose control. They are frequently as horrified and shocked

as the child who got bitten or hit. The intent was not to hurt another child. Never bite the child back so he knows how it feels. Not only is this degrading to both, but it also reduces the adult biter to a toddler level of behavior.

Instead, comfort both the biter and the child bitten. Tell the child who bit that "No one likes to be bitten. Next time you feel that way, please use your words. I will help you." Give the child an acceptable substitute, such as a toy to punch or a rubber dog bone to bite. The less adult interference, the more quickly children learn the give-and-take skills necessary to all relationships.

Teaching the Joy of Accomplishment

My almost-three-year-old son loves to be helpful. Is it too early to begin to teach him to do simple chores?

Absolutely not. Teaching your child to do useful things is a wonderful gift. As a single mother you will appreciate the help, and your son will bask in the glory of his accomplishments. It is important to keep the tasks appropriate to his age, such as putting his toys and books away. If you're having company for dinner, perhaps he could put the napkins through little wooden or plastic rings. The time that you spend teaching your son to do his assigned chores will be richly rewarded. Responsibility and trust well earned are key to building healthy confidence. You could not be spending time in a more productive or useful way.

SLEEPING

*I'm exhausted at night and
can't stand the bedtime battle.
Any ideas for promoting a more
hassle-free, less fearful bedtime
for a four-year-old?*

Around the age of four, a child is sufficiently independent in spirit to appreciate having a big bed and an emotionally satisfying bedroom environment. Make the child feel safe and reassured by giving him special bedclothes (for the financially strapped, this does not mean fancy—recycled T-shirts are great) or a favorite sleep blanket. Preschoolers need separate routines for day and night. Arrange the furniture in the child's room to help create distinctly different areas for playing and sleep. Limit TV watching before bed. Sometimes even a "kid friendly" show can be too overstimulating before bed. Try switching to a CD of bedtime songs or read a bedtime storybook together. Bright lights can also delay sleepiness. About half an hour before bedtime, try dimming the room lights. Also, add to the sense of security by leaving the door slightly ajar, having the radio playing softly, or keeping a night-light on.

Nightmares Don't Mean Emotional Disturbances

Nightmares are perfectly normal, even once or twice a week. Each specific nightmare should be taken seriously because that approach will help the child resolve any real-life issues that caused the nightmare. If the child has the same nightmare a number of times (more than six) in close succession, you might want to speak with a mental health professional experienced with young children who can help you sort out what your child is experiencing. Whether or not the cause of a child's nightmare is a troubling issue or event in daily life, the effect of the nightmare all by itself can be very emotionally upsetting.

When your child complains about a nightmare, here are some steps you can take to alleviate its effects and possibly eliminate its cause:

1. Allow your child to wake up naturally. Try not to jolt her awake—that can be as upsetting as the nightmare. Jolting her awake may prevent your child's dreaming mind from reaching its own creative "solution" to the nightmare. A nightmare that is strong enough to cause moaning and thrashing will usually provoke a child to wake up on her own.

2. Don't play fantasy games. Don't pretend that you chased the monster out of the closet or the wicked elf out from under the bed. This technique will reassure your child for the moment, but it will come back to haunt you because the monster or the wicked elf could always come back. Otherwise why would you

have chased him away in the first place? Instead, show your child that there is no monster in the closet, or let her look under the bed to make sure there is no wicked elf. Do not suggest or deny that there ever was one in the closet or under the bed.

3. Do not insist that the nightmare was not real. To your child, the nightmare was very real. Assure your child calmly and reasonably that she is safe and that what happens in a nightmare can never really hurt her or bring harm to anyone.

4. Encourage your child to describe the nightmare in as much detail as possible. If your child is allowed to talk it out without being distracted by your reactions, chances are the nightmare will lose its power to terrify. Asking her to draw a picture of what was scary in the nightmare is a great idea. Also, you will learn about how your child's dreaming imagination works, what scares your child, and what may have triggered the nightmare in the first place.

5. Ask your child to describe what she could do to make things better if the same experience was to occur again. This request will cause your child to rehearse coping strategies, both consciously and subconsciously, that will help her to manage this specific nightmare if it happens again, as well as similarly upsetting nightmares and real-life situations.

6. If your child wakes up from a nightmare and is especially upset, consider letting her sleep the rest of the night with you. It's perfectly okay.

The Difference Between Nightmares and Night Terrors

I'm a single mother who is going through tremendous guilt wondering if something happened at day care because my child has terrified me a couple of times with night terrors. Actually, they may be nightmares. How can I tell, and what should I do? I feel like such a lousy parent.

Night terrors (also called delta parasomnia) are not psychologically induced, but can be dangerous, since some children sleepwalk while having them and can hurt themselves or get lost.

The way to tell if a child is having a night terror rather than a nightmare is that during a night terror he will not respond appropriately to outside stimuli even though he looks awake. Thus, your child may be screaming "Mommy, Mommy, where are you?" even though you are holding him and reassuring him that you are there.

Here are six tips to follow if your child has a night terror:

1. Don't wake him up unless it is absolutely necessary. The episode will last a few minutes, and your child might return to normal sleep with no ill effects. If you wake him up, you will panic him.

2. Hold your child gently and do not resist any strong efforts to break free. Remember, your child does not realize you are there. If your child gets out of bed, follow him and do what is necessary to prevent accidents.

3. If you can and he does not resist, pick him up and put him back in his bed. Obviously, if you think he is going

to hurt himself, wake him up. This is the exception to the don't-wake-him-up rule. Wake him up gently—a warm washcloth on his face is good.

4. Your child will not remember having a night terror after awakening. Remain calm. Night terrors are developmentally okay at this age. They do not mean that you are a bad mother or that your child has deep-seated emotional problems or has had a trauma.

5. If you feel that your child's night terrors are dangerous, talk to your health care provider about how your child's difficulties might best be handled. Some physicians recommend avoiding caffeine at night by eliminating snacks of chocolate or soda.

6. Stop telling yourself that you are a lousy mother and instead pat yourself on the back for following these steps. You did the right thing.

EATING

My daughter used to be a hearty if somewhat messy eater. Now, my four-year-old is finicky about certain foods, refusing to eat and misbehaving while eating. Are these behaviors signs of an early eating disorder like anorexia?

Not likely. Children younger than six seldom suffer from eating disorders with psychological roots such as anorexia or bulimia. Children do have a wide range of responses to eating on a schedule, food choice, and adults' attitudes about food. Each child has a unique set of eating habits and tastes.

It is impossible to make general statements about what is normal, when to expect problems, or what to do in troublesome situations.

I worry that my child is poorly nourished because he sometimes refuses to eat anything, at home and in day care. What's more, I'm concerned that others will think I'm neglecting my child because I already feel scrutinized by my neighbors as a single mother. They are always hinting that I probably am too busy to feed him. Yet he seems so active and healthy.

First, you don't owe your neighbors any explanation other than that you appreciate their concern, but since your child is giving every other indication of good health, he is probably getting proper nutrition. That is probably the best guideline. Remember, too, that after the age of two that most children experience a natural reduction in their appetites. If you really are worried, however, write down everything your child eats for one week and ask the caregiver to do the same. Consult your child's health care provider and listen to his or her judgment.

COPING WITH FOOD ALLERGIES

Food allergies occur most often in infants and children, but they can appear at any age and develop suddenly to foods that were previously eaten without any reaction. Approximately two to four percent of children have allergic reactions to food. Food allergies happen when the body sees a food as harmful and causes the immune system to release massive amounts of a chemical called histamine. This release of histamine triggers the allergic reaction. Eight foods cause 90 percent of the food allergy reactions in children. These foods are fish, shellfish, tree nuts (such as pecans and walnuts), wheat, eggs, soy, peanuts, and milk. Children often outgrow allergies to eggs, milk, and soy, but allergies to other foods often last a lifetime.

WHAT SHOULD YOU DO?

Food allergies cannot be prevented but can be delayed in infants by breastfeeding your child for the first six months of life, withholding solid foods until your child is six months old, and avoiding cow's milk, wheat, eggs, peanuts, and fish until a child is two years of age.

Even if your child never develops food allergies, encourage your child to eat only food at school or at the caregiver's that you provide. Swapping or letting other children have a taste of their lunch or snack may be harmful to children with food allergies. Sharing should usually be encouraged, but with severe food allergies on the apparent rise, eating only what your mom has provided should be the rule.

If your child's father has visitation rights, as part of the visitation routine, each parent should make sure that the other parent is aware of foods that should be avoided. If a child is exposed to a new food during or immediately before visitation, the other parent should be notified. Without knowing what a child has eaten, a pediatrician or other health care provider can misdiagnose a sudden rash, vomiting, diarrhea, or other far more serious symptoms.

Guidelines for Feeding Your Child

1. Avoid serving your toddler hot dogs, marshmallows, grapes, raw celery, large slices of apples, whole raw carrot slices, popcorn, and peanut butter by the spoonful. All these and any other food that does not readily dissolve in a toddler's mouth can be a choking hazard. Be particularly careful if you are using medication to ease gums during teething. These medications can interfere with a toddler's ability to chew normally.

2. Be patient and avoid making a big deal out of children's poor eating habits, such as picking at food or pushing away vegetables. If children get a lot of attention—even negative attention—the poor eating habits will be reinforced, which means they will persist and get worse.

3. Determine at what times and under what circumstances your child eats best. If your child eats better after a bath or a story, feed him then. Maybe breakfast is the big meal; so play up this healthy habit. See when you can devote the most time and energy to meeting this need, even if it isn't

your own best eating time. Toddlers should be fed sitting down to minimize the possibility of choking and to encourage sociable eating habits.

4. Take note of when and what your child eats when under the caregiver's supervision. This information will help you to ensure good nutrition by knowing what "gaps" need to be filled in by meals at home. For example, if your child refuses to eat fruit with the caregiver, you need to make sure he eats fruit when he is home.

5. Some children do best eating alone, away from others. Mealtimes should not last longer than thirty minutes. Children should learn to eat meals when they are served. Try to provide a calm atmosphere.

6. Introduce new foods singly and in a pleasant, low-key manner. Don't be overly enthusiastic when introducing a new vegetable. Children notice and appreciate when food is presented in an attractive way. Fruits and vegetables presented creatively not only make food look more appetizing, but also will encourage your child to try healthy foods. Nice-looking eating utensils and manageable-looking portions can go a long way in getting a child to eat. Even if you are a time-stressed single mom who serves lots of pizza, cut the portions out with cookie cutters in the shapes of dinosaurs, stars, or triangles. Not only are the portions the right size and very appealing, but you could also throw in a few words about the differences between geometric shapes.

7. Do not force your child to eat against her will. Don't override a "no" by shoving the food into her mouth. This will only aggravate the problem. Give the child a set amount of time to eat most of what is on her plate. However, if an hour goes by and only half the meal is eaten, don't make her sit there the rest of the night to clean her plate.

8. Do not offer your child dessert until she has eaten something of more nutritional value. This is an effective, time-honored technique—do not abuse it. Use this technique only once a day, at the meal where the most nutritional value is offered. Always stick to the bargain without theatrics on your part.

9. Do not worry about table manners until your child is around five or six—table manners are a sophisticated skill. Don't make the table a further battleground by insisting on good table manners before the child is ready.

FEARS

Why is my five-year-old so fearful? It makes me feel inadequate that my child doesn't feel secure with me as her mother.

The child under the age of six lives in a world so baffling that it is difficult for adults to understand. Everything is new and potentially unsettling—capable of causing fearful reactions. It is hard for young children to differentiate between what is real—the death of a pet, for example—from what is not real—the death of a character on a television show. Children of this age are well aware that they are small and powerless, and they routinely feel shocked, puzzled, and surprised by what is happening. Naturally, children of this age experience many different fears as well as individual incidents of fear. Big message: this is normal five-year-old behavior. Second big message: parents should not overprotect in the face of fears at this age. Fear teaches. Fear of dogs teaches a child to develop safer, more respectful, more appropriate ways of treating all animals. Fear of separation can teach a child to appreciate being taken care of, to manage anger, and to feel empathy for others.

Managing Your Child's Normal Fears

- Listen respectfully to what your child is saying, but do not respond with a shower of concerns. That not only rewards being afraid with attention, but also scares the child more.

- Do not belittle or dismiss the fear either. Then your child will not discuss fears with you, and what remains unexpressed will hurt your child emotionally far more.

- Be patient and allow the child to confront and overcome fear at his own pace. Help your child devise constructive ways to cope with his own fears.

- Praise his efforts, even if they consist only of petting the senile dog down the street in his first attempts at overcoming a fear of dogs. Honestly reassure your child about his own coping skills. Say that "I have seen you pet that big dog down the street, and you were not afraid."

- Encourage physical play, drawing, painting, and performing small tasks—all activities that demonstrate to children that they can exercise control and master their own little worlds.

- Set a good example by not communicating your own anxieties to your child. Perhaps you were afraid of bugs as a little girl, but your child may find them interesting if you don't project your fears.

- Anticipate frightening situations and prepare for them. This is not the same as overprotection. For example, if your child is afraid of scary-looking faces, it may not be a good idea to have him greet the trick-or-treaters who come to the door. Better yet, politely ask the ghouls and goblins to take off their masks and show your apprehensive five-year-old their real faces underneath.

Could Fears Be Related to Not Having Dad at Home?

My kindergarten child always has one fear or another. Now he is very reluctant to go outside because he tells me that bugs will get him. His teacher reports the same fears at school and wonders if he is excessively frightened because we have no "daddy" at home to protect us. Could she be right?

It's very unlikely. A more probable explanation is that he generally needs to explore things with reassurance. It's good that he talks about these fears. Ask your child what kinds of bugs he fears. The next step would be to find a simple book or video about insects and ask him to indicate which ones are scary and which ones are okay.

Another possibility is that your child is very creative. Like Calvin from the comic strip *Calvin and Hobbes*, he imagines these critters changing into "megamorphasaurs" or whatever and needs help putting the fear into perspective.

Trap a few of the kinds of insects your child fears in a drinking glass, and let him look at them safely from a distance. Arming your child with this new understanding will go a long way toward eliminating this fear. Let the teacher know that you appreciate her concern but feel very capable of protecting your family whether or not a father is present.

DISCIPLINE

My five-year-old daughter is making me a frazzled lunatic. You wouldn't believe the scenes she makes in front of other people whenever I take my eyes off of her, even for a second. It's like she wants to be the center of attention. I give her everything she asks for and spend a lot of time with her (although sometimes I'd like to hop a freight train and leave), and yet she complains incessantly that I never do this and I always make her do that. I don't have a moment to myself! Don't tell me to let her visit her father. He's been out of the picture since birth.

Your daughter is the center of attention and will remain there as long as you allow her to behave this way. Right now, you need to decide that you are going to make time for yourself because your life needs to revolve around you.

You were here first, you are the mother, and you get to make the decisions. Ask yourself, too, how anyone as little as a five-year-old can drive you nuts. Children can't make us crazy unless we let them play on our guilt.

Why on earth would you want to give your daughter everything? Won't this be setting her up for some future shock when she has to mature and meet the real world?

Stop spoiling her now. But remember that it took awhile for her to get like this; so be patient.

Invest in a kitchen timer. Announce to your daughter that you will spend, for example, thirty minutes of uninterrupted time with her. While you're together playing or reading, don't answer the phone or allow other distractions. Let her know that this is her time and she is to make good use of it. If she wastes it, that is her choice.

After you've spent some quality time together, set the timer for another twenty minutes and explain to your daughter that now it's your turn for some private time. Make sure she has a quiet, safe activity and inform her that she is not to bother you until the timer goes off.

If she balks, give her a choice of either coloring or reading books. If she keeps acting up, send her to her room and tell her to have her tantrum in there.

I feel so guilty every time I punish my four-year-old son because I feel not having a father (he left right after our son was born) is punishment enough. But he won't go to bed when I ask, throws tantrums in public if he doesn't get everything he demands, and is generally driving me loony. Is it too late to unspoil him?

It's never too late to unspoil a child, but first you need to figure out why you equate "loss" with "punishment."

What you may see as a gain, such as giving in to your child's demand for candy or staying up late, does not necessarily replace a particular loss, such as a parent leaving. Loss is the way we learn to grow, and it cannot be avoided by anyone, whether it is the loss of a loved one, job, limb, or even a dream.

One particular way of looking at this comes to mind through the writing of single mother and author Anne Lamott. In her book *Operating Instructions*, which is a journal of her son's first year, Lamott laments that her son, Sam, does not have a father to toss him in the air or teach him manly things like fixing the toaster. At the same time, she's thinking of friends who are expecting a boy named Sam in a few months who will be born with only one arm. She pictures the two baby Sams hanging out together while she and the other Sam's father are teaching a workshop. Her Sam is studying the other Sam and says, "So where's your arm?" The other baby shrugs and replies, "I don't know; where's your dad?"

The point here is that loss is not punishment. Loss is loss. One kid doesn't have a father, the one across the street doesn't have a pet, the little boy on the corner doesn't have his own room because of the new baby, and the little girl in the neighboring apartment has a health problem. There is no perfect person, perfect family, or perfect life other than what is falsely depicted on television. But we can all strive for the best for ourselves. First, accept that this is the way things are and then go from there. Stop spoiling your child by trying to provide everything because you think he is deprived. You will be giving him more by setting limits and saying yes less.

I've yet to go through a grocery checkout line without purchasing gum, candy, and other junk for my hysterical, demanding daughter. Should I just stop taking her shopping and avoid seeing friends and doing other things? I work all week and must accomplish shopping and other errands during the weekend. Plus, I don't have extra money for babysitters and really don't feel right being apart from her just to go get the dry cleaning, and so on. I'm beginning to dread weekends and wish I were back at work, but I feel guilty there too, thinking that if she had a father that she wouldn't need so much.

It's true that if she had a father, you would have someone to take her when you need a break, which is why work on Monday morning looks so appealing. But having a father at home does not guarantee that she wouldn't be spoiled or demanding—that is based upon what you have allowed her to get away with.

As for making the errand time run more smoothly, try this: ten minutes before you leave for the store, discuss the purpose of the trip and what kind of behavior you expect from her. This will give your child enough information so that she gets into the right mood. You might say that "We are going to the grocery store to buy milk, bread, and onions, and you may choose the flavor of ice cream we are going to buy." Your child then has a limited opportunity to control some aspect of the trip.

If your daughter pulls a stunt at the grocery store after you have given her two warnings, simply put all the items back on the shelf and leave the store. You may think this is inconvenient, if not impossible, but it works, especially if you say "I will not take you shopping with me if you behave that way again." If she behaves well the next time you go out, encourage her efforts with praise.

Remember that toys, gifts, and candy do not a father make! Break the cycle now and don't expect results overnight. Be consistent and patient.

COPING TOOLS FOR DEALING WITH ANGER

While parenting is one of the greatest joys in life, it can also be stressful. This goes double for single parents. If you could use some suggestions for releasing family tension or expressing negative feelings in a controlled manner, read on.

1. Learn how to communicate your anger in nonjudgmental ways. In other words, rather than telling a child who has misbehaved that "I'll wring your neck" or "You are a rotten kid for doing that," try saying that "This has made me very mad" or

---

THE DO'S AND DON'TS OF DISCIPLINE

* **Do** discipline with consistency and fairness. The punishment should fit the crime and should not change or be arbitrary. If timeout is how you handle throwing things or no television is the result of failing to do chores, then stick to these.

* **Don't** spoil your child to overcompensate for the lack of the second parent. Purchasing candy at the checkout line in the grocery store does not make up for a missing parent.

* **Do** try to remember the benefits of single parenting, particularly if you came from

a volatile household where you spent much time arguing. Don't continue this communication style with your child. Instead, teach negotiating skills and be grateful for the peace that you've acquired.

* **Do** take periodic breaks so you don't overreact to something minor. If you're stressed out, things will seem worse than they really are.

* **Don't** forget that there is no greater gift you can give your children than the ability to live in loving cooperation with others.

"I don't like what you are doing right now."

2. Put your child in a time-out chair or send older school-age kids to their rooms or a special time-out place. For toddlers and preschool children, experts advise estimating about one minute in time-out for each year of their age.

3. Don't return hurtful feelings by saying "If I die, no one will care for you" after your child may have screamed "I hate you, I hope you die!" All children get these feelings every now and then. Remember, it's okay for your child to have feelings of anger, rage, and "hate," but it is not okay to express those feelings with physical violence or abusive words.

4. If your child really needs to "feel those feelings," put her in a safe place—her room, a play area, or a "tantrum tent" (made by throwing a sheet over a couple of pieces of soft furniture). Explain that she can grovel on the floor like a wild thing if she wishes, but you prefer not to watch. Never strike or punish your child for having feelings.

5. Encourage your child to take a run around the block, do jumping jacks, or throw a ball against the side of the house. These are coping strategies that he will be able to use both now and in the years to come to handle negative feelings appropriately.

SINGLE MOM OF NOTE

Pauline Trigere,
Fashion Designer

A Parisian-born, Jewish fashion designer, Pauline Trigere fled the Nazis and arrived in New York in 1942. With little money and donations of materials and supplies, Pauline made eleven dresses for her start-up business. She elegantly suited and dressed such legends and royalty as Bette Davis, Josephine Baker, Hattie Carnegie, and the Duchess of Windsor, all the while raising her sons Philippe and Jean-Pierre. She said, "I brought up my boys alone—not one half penny from their father. He left me because I wanted to work, be myself." Pauline worked up until her death at ninety-three.

IT'S HEALTHY TO BE SELF-CARING

Think the best parents are the ones who dote excessively on their kids? Think again. Single mothers who have an interesting, active personal life are actually setting a more positive example for their children.

No one feels the pressure of the supermother syndrome more than single working mothers. Not only do single moms think they have to devote twenty-four hours a day to entertaining, stimulating, educating, and caring for their children, but they also think they have to do this with double the gusto. Because they've also been led to believe that their children are "at risk" for all sorts of emotional and academic problems, they erroneously assume that they must provide more attention and perform these child-rearing tasks exactly as would two parents. Nothing could be further from the truth. Single mothers deserve a break. You know that, but a break never seems to be in sight.

Harness the Power of Laughter

See who can laugh the loudest and longest. In fact, just smiling can bring with it positive physiological changes because of the number of facial muscles that are pulled into action.

If a little one is acting horribly and filled with miserable discontent, try "squeezing the meanness out of her" with firm but gentle hugs. Tell her you'll stop when you get a giggle. When all else fails, a little tickling works wonders.

Do Your Kids a Favor— Ignore Them a Little

Unless you tend carefully to your own needs, some of your children's needs won't get met as optimally as they should. Now you ask: "But what need of mine could possibly be more important than feeding when hungry, warming when cold, and bathing when not clean, not to mention what goes into providing an education and the constant watching and worry?"

Children who have mothers who pamper themselves actually learn how to take the needs of others into consideration and understand that they are not always the priority or the center of attention. Let's face it: nothing is more annoying than an adult who whines, attempts to manipulate, and genuinely feels that the world should accommodate him or her at all times. So, the next time you worry that you're doing your child a disservice by not being

there for every whine and whim, think about this. The more attention you pay to yourself, the more your child will realize that you are worth paying attention to.

Seize the Moment— Take a Nap!

There are plenty of single mothers, from Hollywood to the housing projects, who paint simply for the joy of it, have taken up piano, do crossword puzzles, and, yes, actually nap while getting their nails done! One single mother, a nurse, worked a ten-hour shift, after which she picked up her children and a neighbor's daughter from day care and school promptly at 3:30 P.M. every day. She learned that she needed a nap every afternoon at 4:45 P.M. when she fell asleep on the couch one day in spite of trying desperately to stay awake. Even though she awoke refreshed and ready to deal with what the evening had in store, she still felt a little guilty until she realized that her children looked forward to these moments, which they affectionately referred to as "Mommy's night-night."

The Family Primal Scream

One way to get bottled-up anger out of your system and help your kid express negative feelings while under control is to organize a "scream." This really works if you find a special place for this. One single mom who lives in a rural community rounds everyone up in the car and cruises an uninhabited street or country road. Then she rolls up the windows, and on the count of three, she and her daughter and son simultaneously scream, with the dog howling in harmony.

The first time you do this, your child may look at you like you're nuts. Just say that "Mommies get angry, too," and then have a contest to see who can scream the loudest.

Make a Game Out of Rest Time

It started when her seven-year-old son asked what was wrong when Mom collapsed on the couch, and she replied that she was just too tired to move. He saw that this was not the moment to ask her if she wanted to play a game. He knew she would probably tell him to do his homework anyway, which he was supposed to do before supper. When his precocious four-year-old sister and her five-year-old friend asked if the weary mother was dead, she looked into their little faces and whispered, "Almost." The little neighbor girl's face lit up as she delightedly exclaimed, "Let's play funeral!" Mom was instructed to close her eyes and lay still while the two little girls proceeded to the backyard and lovingly picked dandelions from the lawn. They laid them carefully on the now-sleeping mom's chest, put kitchen towels on their heads, and marched around the couch quietly humming. While the "procession" mourned, Mom, who was having no trouble holding up her end of this game, was deeply relaxing and rejuvenating herself. As long as she kept her eyes shut and did not move, the girls were happy. In fact, the older one commented on what a nice mommy she was because "You are such a good dead person!" In the meantime, her son was doing what he was supposed to be doing, and her daughter was playing happily. This thirty-minute

mininap soon became a family ritual. During the winter months, single sheets of toilet paper became the substitute for fresh flowers, but no one objected. Even though the children are now grown, the phrase "playing funeral" has retained a special meaning for this family because it reflects the intimacy of a shared experience. This is what being part of a family is all about!

Sure, there will always be another room to dust, a load of laundry to be done, and a kitchen counter to be wiped. Your child will always be ready to say yes to one more story, ten more minutes at the playground, or just one more round of her favorite board game. Children are typically marvelous negotiators and will not hesitate to demonstrate this skill. You have that same privilege, and so why not learn from them?

SPECIAL CONCERN: TEACHING HERITAGE TO MULTIRACIAL CHILDREN

I recently became a single mother when my daughter's father left me a couple of months before I was due to give birth. I am white, and he is black. I am uncertain how to bring cultural richness to my biracial daughter's life. I have another dilemma: my mother refuses to have anything to do with me or the baby. I feel like a single mom dealing with a double whammy. Any ideas?

Single parents in similar circumstances suggest seeking out local churches, schools, and community centers.

Although your daughter's father has chosen to be out of the picture, his family doesn't have to be. Establishing a relationship with a member of your ex-boyfriend's family—aunts, uncles, cousins, grandparents, siblings—cannot only help teach your daughter about her cultural heritage but may also provide you with some emotional support as well. They may very well want your daughter to be a part of their lives, but you'll need to make it clear to them that this isn't an effort to get your ex-boyfriend back. Deal with him directly, if you choose to obtain child support. Your mom's inability to give herself to the grandmother role may change with time. Her attitude may improve with each visit.

But if this doesn't happen, you have time to prepare your child to face her grandmother's feelings by explaining that your mother's ideas about race differ from yours, which is, remember, your interpretation of your mother's actions.

When your child is old enough to understand racial differences, you might say that "Even though my mother raised me, she has different ideas about race than I do." It's important that your child know that she was not the cause of her grandmother's shunning her.

HELP YOUR CHILD BECOME A CITIZEN OF THE WORLD

◆ Educate yourself. Reading books such as *40 Ways to Raise a Nonracist Child* by Barbara Mathias and Mary Ann French and subscribing to magazines geared to specific cultures can teach you a lot.

◆ Expose yourself and your child to a variety of literature, theater, and films. It's important for you both to see a broad spectrum of culture and talent, but don't stop there.

◆ Get out and make friends. Create a supportive community of friends of many different backgrounds. By inviting people into your lives from many diverse backgrounds, you can enrich your life and your child's future with tolerance and acceptance.

◆ Consider how you talk about beauty in your household. Do you typically admire only European or Anglo features? Then your child needs to hear praise regarding the appearance of other types of beauty.

◆ Keep maps and globes in your house and let your child see just how vast and varied the world really is. Geography interests many young children who naturally enjoy learning different facts about faraway places. Use these interests to reinforce how each culture is to be respected and admired for its uniqueness.

◆ Frequent restaurants or shops that specialize in food or other items from different parts of the world. You will not only broaden your world but also these shops and restaurants can be an opportunity for the budget-stretched single mom. Time-hassled moms often turn to franchise fast food when stressed. Knowing what is available from around the world right in your own neighborhood can often help you feed your family for less. Give your child the opportunity to see just how much the world has to offer—if you just make the effort!

15

As Your Child Grows

As your child grows, parenting doesn't get easier; it becomes, as many mothers say, "different." Demands that young children make are no longer placed upon you, but new challenges arise. Your child's needs are not any less or more important, but they have evolved to a new level. For example, you don't have to remember to feed them all the time because they are quite capable of knowing when they are hungry and fixing themselves a snack. But they may need guidance and reassurance about making decisions regarding school, friends, and others and becoming comfortable with who they are along the way. They are becoming young adults, people who are beginning to show responsibility for their actions.

There are so many ways for gauging your child's success according to a variety of different child development experts. Some say if you raise a child who is liked by other people besides you, you've done a fine job. But one single mother found the following in an old newspaper column and has shared it with others:

You can use most any measure
When you're speaking of success.
You can measure it in fancy home,
Expensive car or dress.
But the measure of your real success
Is the one you cannot spend.
It's the way your kids describe you
When they're talking to a friend.

—*Martin Buxbaum*

WORKING WITH YOUR CHILD'S SCHOOL

It is the responsibility of all types of families to work conscientiously to make sure that their child receives every possible benefit from the educational opportunities available.

Each of us, no matter what the family background, will meet with situations less than ideal for our children, and it will be our responsibility to negotiate around and through these circumstances. The difficulty is that these less-than-ideal circumstances can take many forms. It is virtually impossible to prepare parents for each and every situation that may come along.

HELPING YOUR CHILD ACHIEVE SUCCESS IN SCHOOL

Every type of family feels challenged when it comes to helping their children in school. Single mothers are no exception. Channel that "worry energy" positively by focusing on ways you can help your child succeed in school. Remember that single mothers are not more likely to have children with problems in school, just as growing up in a two-parent home is no guarantee of school success.

- *Stay organized.* The notices found nearly every day in your child's book bag are your communication link. Check the book bag daily. Develop a system for keeping track of field trips, book fairs, and other special events. Monitor your child's school supplies and replace as necessary. This daily routine emphasizes your commitment to success in school and teaches your child the valuable organizational skills critical to success in every area of life.

- *Let your child know that you value education.* Research indicates that a parent's encouragement is more important to a child's eventual success than family income or background. Show your child that you think learning is important every day by reading together, watching educational programming, and helping her with her homework.

- *Talk positively about teachers in front of your child.* Teachers are the key people in your child's school life and almost always valued allies. Most teachers are dedicated, hard-working professionals making the best

of few resources to meet a dizzying array of individual needs. Your child needs to know that her mother and the teacher are a team. Children are experts at divide and conquer. If you disagree with a teacher, whether it is about an assignment or about a way a particular matter was handled, keep this difference of opinion between the adults. Undermining the teacher's authority and credibility is particularly harmful to a child growing up in a single-parent home. Your child may already be struggling with contradictory expectations and demands from parents living in separate households.

- *Reward your children's efforts, not just the results.* When your child tries to read a more difficult book than usual, praise him for this new interest. Do not criticize him for the words he is stumbling over, but emphasize all the new things he is learning. If your sports-minded son suddenly picks up his sister's watercolor paints and tries his hand, don't devalue his first efforts and thereby give him the message that he should stick to football. Children who are praised only for their successes can become afraid to try new tasks. They might try only once and give up. This kind of behavior is very discouraging to teachers.

- *Encourage communication.* Children who have learned to express themselves at home with parents and siblings have an easier time talking with their teachers. This means taking the time to listen and not interrupt. Tell your child that you respect his feelings or point of view and demonstrate respect by being a good listener. The best way to help your child be a better communicator is to encourage a home atmosphere where everyone's feelings are accepted and respected. It does not work to set aside time for family meetings if nobody talks to anyone else at other times. Shouting, name-calling, or deliberately hurtful remarks have no place in a home where respect for one another is valued and certainly will not be tolerated in the classroom.

◆ *Practice good manners at home.* Children must not only be encouraged to express themselves but must also be taught to have good listening skills, follow directions, and work cooperatively in a group. These skills are best mastered by children whose experiences at home incorporate these expectations. Start to teach these skills well before your child begins school. For example, when your baby is sitting in his high chair watching you cook, say out loud the steps you are following to make that pot of spaghetti. Routines at home are also important. Tell your baby the plan even if you feel a little silly reciting a list of errands or chores to a three-month-old. Working cooperatively in a group might begin with simply letting your toddler watch older children work or play together. Tell your little one what is going on by saying something like "See how nicely Joey and Philip are working together building that sand castle" or "Look how Sally waits for Jessie to finish before she takes her turn." These kinds of experiences alert early on what the expectations will be when your child begins school.

◆ *Teach your child how to wait his turn.* Teachers cannot always give

immediate attention, and so learning to wait your turn is an important school skill. Give your child the opportunity to know that everything in life is not instantaneous. Many teachers complain that children reared in the era of video games and TV come to think that everything should happen right now. Life does not work that way. Provide your child with the opportunity to learn patience. Grow plants from seeds. Do jigsaw puzzles together as family projects. Share with your children activities such as arts and crafts or needlework, which require time and patience. Create and display proudly a family collage that each of you adds to as the years go by.

◆ *Get involved at school.* Involvement in parent-teacher organizations is not just for stay-at-home moms. There are ways you can assist these organizations without stepping foot in school during your hectic workday. Your involvement allows you to stay connected with other concerned parents and gives you another opportunity to meet and get to know other single parents.

FILLING OUT SCHOOL REGISTRATION FORMS

School will start soon, and I dread registering my children in school. I had a long and messy divorce, which ultimately resulted in a need for the children and me to move from our old neighborhood to one we could better afford. I am worried about what the school is going to ask and just do not know how to respond to the questions.

My husband died of cancer when our baby was one year old. It was a terrible struggle, and I still miss him very much. I have since moved to be nearer to my family. Enrollment time at the local pre-school is fast approaching. I do not know how to answer the questions I know they will ask.

Every time you register your child for day care or school you will be handed a mountain of forms to fill out. This is routine for every parent; so try not to take it personally. No one reviews these documents with a particular interest in passing judgment about your family's circumstances. Consider your particular feelings and decide before it is time to fill out those forms how you are going to handle these standard questions. Here are a few tips to help you get through this the next time you have to fill out those inevitable questionnaires.

Face Your Feelings

You may be sensitive or sad about some of the information you provide like a change of address made necessary by rocky finances. You may feel shaken by not being able to write Mr. and Mrs. Seeing the word "father" on the registration form may remind you of your loss or make you feel that you are different or that you are the only single mother in the world. You are certainly entitled to those feelings, but these are your issues and not the school or day care's priorities or concerns. Acting defensive or indignant when these routine questions are posed does not get you or, more importantly, your child off to the best start. Remember, it is highly possible that the school or day care secretary is a single mother. Try to

remember that these forms are geared to all families and are not a test but simply procedure. School and day care officials as individuals have had their share of life experiences and are not interested in prying into your private life. Some other tips for school or day care registration:

♦ Be aware that you must produce a birth certificate whether or not the father's name is on it to register your child for school. Some school districts require proof of residency, such as a copy of your lease or utility bill. Save time and energy and come prepared.

♦ Decide ahead of time what information about your home situation you are going to share with the day care or school.

♦ When asked for information about the father—date of birth, name, place of employment, and so on—feel free to leave this space blank.

MAKE A PLAN

Prepare for the inevitable. Single mothers do not have the built-in backup that two-parent families often enjoy. Without warning, a fever, vomiting, diarrhea, pink eye, or other contagious condition will mean your child needs to stay home from school. Asking your child to "tough it out" with over-the-counter medication is just not appropriate. If your work situation is inflexible, line up last-minute backup care options now before the emergency arises. Acutely sick children need the attention of a parent or parent substitute whose judgment you can completely trust. More often your child is just under the weather or needs that extra day or so for the antibiotic to kick in. Consider a retired neighbor, graduate student, or person with a similar schedule who may be able to take care of your child at the last moment. Money is seldom refused, but if your budget is already stretched, consider barter. Your willingness to provide transportation, tackle home improvement chores, or prepare home-cooked meals might just be your ticket out of some last minute child care problems. Let your child know the backup plan so that there will be no added stress on a day that your child is sick. Keeping a sick child home from school assures school authorities that you are the capable and responsible parent you strive to be.

Critical Information

Your child's school and/or day care needs to know how to reach you in case of emergency. They will also need to know name and telephone numbers of several backup people to contact in case a parent cannot be reached. Emergencies can include sudden weather changes and unexpected school closings, as well as sickness or injury. Be prepared with the information when you enroll. Work out any complications or disagreements with your child's father as a priority.

Once your child is old enough, make her a partner in the plan because, in case of emergency, she needs to know what to do. Schools typically require picture identification before they release a child to anyone, including a parent. Make sure you and your backups always carry photo ID. Make arrangements so that your child can contact you once she is situated at the backup place, if you are unable to pick her up from school. When things happen that are truly unexpected and maybe even quite

upsetting, it is especially important that your child has the reassurance of a telephone call from you.

Make Allies of Stay-at-Home Moms and Dads

Single parents tend to distance themselves from stay-at-home moms and dads when, in truth, there is much each can do to support one another. Arrangements with stay-at-home parents are a terrific option when your child needs to be picked up from school with a sudden illness or school closes or begins late. Single mothers sometimes secretly envy the stay-at-home parent who does not seem to have the incredible logistical problems or conflicting time demands single mothers face everyday. This envy can blind us to the ways we can be of mutual benefit. How about offering to keep their children for a Saturday night into Sunday so they can actually enjoy a night out, blissfully sleeping late in the morning? Can you do some extra car pooling on the weekends? Are you a sewing whiz or a gourmet cook?

Even if a miracle occurs and the whole school year goes by without having to call upon your backup or stay-at-home parent ally, meaningful thanks are still in order. You are acknowledging the peace of mind, and of course, you are hoping to keep the same arrangements.

HANDLING INSENSITIVE OR UNEXPECTED REMARKS AT PARENT-TEACHER CONFERENCES

My seven-year-old son is entering second grade. Last year, he entered first grade shortly after my partner and I split up. Because my son is energetic and restless, he has trouble sitting still and paying attention. His first grade teacher blamed this on his being from an unstable home. She says this behavior is common among "fatherless boys from broken homes." Aren't there other reasons besides changes at home that could account for my son's behavior?

Despite the fact that less than one-quarter of the households in the United States are made up of married couples with their children, some teachers who are inexperienced in dealing with single-parent families often rely on the quickest explanation for a problem, suggesting that the blame lies with the facts of the child's home life. While this is not really your immediate concern, some teachers may be in the throes of a personal crisis. Maybe this teacher had a traumatic upbringing, and these carelessly chosen words reflect his own unresolved issues. Maybe the teacher is considering separation, and the comment about "broken homes and fatherless boys" reflects her own worries and fears. Words like "broken home" or "dysfunctional family" mean nothing. Your only real concern is to try to figure out what your child's behavior at school may truly indicate and what you can do cooperatively with the school to make things better for your child.

Reasons for your son being fidgety might include that he is still too physically immature to sit still for long periods. He might have certain allergies, need more sleep, or simply require more exercise. Perhaps a combination of all of these may be the cause. These are things you can look into now. Discuss your concerns and observations with your health care provider, if you need advice and help determining what may be causing problems like this at school.

Set boundaries between your personal life and your son's education, but at the same time, strive for cooperation between school and home. Not only will you be helping your son but also your own example of successful single parenting just may help to educate the teacher.

My son, now nine years old, did not get along well with his teacher last year, and neither did I. I feel she overreacted to fairly typical "boys will be boys" behavior and was quick to ask how I felt the divorce affected my son. He can be a handful, but things do seem better with maturity and some changes I have made at home. I want to work more cooperatively with the teacher this year. I got pretty upset at some of the conferences last year. Any advice?

YOU'RE THE POSITIVE INFLUENCE YOUR CHILD NEEDS

No matter what you're heard, seen, or read about the effect single parenting has on a child, keep this fact close to your heart. There is absolutely no evidence that being a single mom has a negative effect on children. Moreover, the idea that single moms produce high-risk kids in school is inaccurate, too. A study by Cornell University researcher, Henry Ricciuti, released in 2004, points out that favorable maternal characteristics—mom's ability, education, her positive expectations of her children, and to a lesser degree, income and home environment—are what counts, whether married or not. "Single parenthood in and of itself [is] not a risk factor for a child's performance in mathematics, reading, or vocabulary, or for behavior problems."

Before meeting with your son's teacher this year, be prepared. Inquire about the exact reason for the conference, if the teacher asks for the meeting. Ask if other school personnel, such as the school psychologist, will also be attending. Don't schedule the meeting on an already hectic day. Take the time to jot down beforehand some questions you have for the teacher. Conference times are limited; it is critical to prepare for the conference. Share what you are currently doing to help remedy your child's problems. For example, tell the teacher that you are limiting your child's' television time and enforcing rules about snacks and bedtime. If you are adding more opportunities for physical exercise and play, these are also important to mention.

Don't assume this year won't be much better—this year's teacher may have a far greater tolerance, for example, for restless children and movement around the classroom. Start a new school year with a fresh perspective and give this year's teacher the benefit of the doubt. Don't make assumptions that may turn out to be unwarranted. It is very possible that the new teacher may be a single mother!

MORE ABOUT YOU AND THE TEACHER

Respect the Limits

Your family circumstances may be especially challenging, and you may wish your child's teacher could be a ready source of aid and comfort. Teachers are not psychologists or referees. Your focus is solely on your child, and your child is just one of many in the classroom. If you need to reach your child's teacher, write her a note. Expecting a teacher to call you more than once or twice, particularly after school hours from home, is not reasonable.

Red Flags

However, if your child's teacher calls you frequently, this is a red flag that your child is experiencing serious academic or behavioral problems. Talk to the teacher in person and figure out what you can do together to straighten things out. Give your child's father copies of the notes sent or simply alert him to the difficulties taking place, if appropriate. This will go a long way in insuring cooperation once a solution or strategy is attempted.

Resist the Urge to Tattle

Decide what you think the teacher must know to understand your child and meet his needs most effectively. The teacher does not need to know the dirty details of your former spouse's affairs or how your finances went south after the breakup. Let the teacher know what role your child's father is playing in your child's life. If you have a demanding work schedule, particular challenges at home, or money is especially tight, share the simple facts.

Problems with the Teacher

It is certainly possible that you will encounter situations with teachers that your best efforts cannot resolve. Some teachers and some children are just not a good mix. It is possible that a child could be singled out for undue criticism from the teacher because he is from a single-parent home. But it is more likely that he could be given this dubious distinction because he may be more active or inquisitive than the teacher may be ready to accept or your child may remind her of someone from her past.

If you suspect that your child is being singled out for any reason, ask for a conference with the principal and teacher. Be prepared with specific examples that illustrate your concerns. Be ready to listen as well as speak. If, after this conference, you feel that your concerns were well justified, ask that the child be transferred to another teacher. If you sense that the principal is not taking your concerns seriously enough or you are aware from other parents that this teacher has a similar history with other children, write a letter to the superintendent of schools or the principal's immediate supervisor detailing your

reasons for asking to have your child transferred.

The best strategy when your children encounter such hurtful people is to listen and to help them understand why the teacher may be behaving like this toward them. You cannot realistically run interference for your children with teachers once they reach high school. Hold the school accountable and make it clear that you will be an active team participant in your child's education.

CHILD CARE FOR THE SCHOOL-AGE CHILD

Changes in family structure and values have altered the way in which many children are cared for. Because more families are headed by single parents and fewer relatives are available to care for children, increasing numbers of families are looking for ways to care for their children in before- and after-school programs.

There are many options for school-age care. Each offers advantages and disadvantages, and none is right for all children under all circumstances. Some children may benefit from the slower pace and smaller environment of family day care, while others may need the larger physical and social setting of an after-school program. Children with special talents may enjoy a narrowly focused program that allows them to improve their skills, while other children may require highly varied programs that help them maintain their interests.

Advantages of after-school programs also include the use of community resources as much as possible. They usually provide indoor and outdoor space for active play and places for socialization and private time, not often available in someone's home. If you have the opportunity to select a school district, consider the after-school care opportunities different school districts might provide. A school district with a well-respected after-school program might be preferable to a school district in a comparable neighborhood that offers no after-school care. Consider relative costs as you budget for housing and child-care expenses.

Supportive Services for Self-Care or Latchkey Kids

In addition to adult-supervised child care programs, some communities offer supportive services for self-care. These include educational materials and curricula that provide information for latchkey children and their parents; telephone reassurance lines staffed by phone counselors trained to provide a friendly voice and occasional advice; and block parent programs using trained volunteers who make their homes available during after-school hours in case of emergency. These programs are designed not to address the day-to-day needs of children after school, but to reduce the possibility of serious harm befalling a child.

Unsupervised Latchkey Arrangements

Self-care arrangements do not meet the developmental needs of all school-age children. Because some of these children are still struggling to make the transition from childhood to adolescence, they need opportunities to make friends, play, develop skills and initiative, and receive attention and appreciation

from caring adults. Most children caring for themselves do best when there is a supervising adult on hand, but children who are not quite as mature certainly aren't ready for any kind of unsupervised self-care arrangements.

Is Your Child Ready for Unsupervised Self-Care?

According to the U.S. Department of Education, 19 percent of kindergarteners through eighth graders spend time before or after school taking care of themselves at least once a month. Other research studies estimate that nearly five million school-age children spend time without adult supervision during a typical week. While the American Academy of Pediatrics recommends adult supervision for children until they are eleven or twelve years old, numerous parents are forced to let their children fend for themselves at young ages, either because good child care and after-school programs were unavailable or too expensive or because their parents were isolated from other members of their community.

A good rule of thumb is that children below the fourth grade are not ready to be unsupervised at home. Setting absolute guidelines for older children is difficult because so many factors must enter into this important decision.

- How does your child feel about being left alone? Is your child afraid to be left alone, or does she have the maturity and initiative to assume this responsibility?

- Do you have neighbors upon whom you can depend in the event of an emergency?

• Is your child fairly obedient? For example, if you make rules about not turning on the stove or the computer, is your child likely to obey or will he have to test the limits?

• Is your child able to occupy himself in your absence with safe, quiet activities like watching television or, better yet, by reading or working on other independent projects?

• Does your child enjoy the quiet respite that comes with being alone, or does he find it scary and intimidating?

• Can your child give her full name, address, and phone number? Does she know your full name, the exact name of the place where you work, your telephone number, and any cellular phone or pager number you might also have?

Think through your own situation carefully. You might want to begin by orchestrating some trial runs during which you leave your child alone for short periods of time so you can determine how well he handles the situation and how closely he obeys the guidelines that you set. A few measures that can help if your child will be home alone after school:

• *Make the Rules Clear.* Evaluate your particular home situation and your child's maturity and capabilities to determine the rules of the house in your absence. Clear, specific rules are needed regarding having friends in the house, leaving the house once your child has come home, use of appliances, activities that are permitted, and whether homework must be done before you return home.

• *Children Are Always Hungry!* Prearranged, safely prepared snack foods are a must for those hungry after school hours. Teenagers and their friends eat practically all the time.

• *Review the "What If Emergency Plans" Often.* Make sure your child knows what to do in case of fire, sickness, accident, or other unexpected happening. Better yet, have important phone numbers entered as "speed calling" numbers on your home phone.

• *Get Caller ID.* If you are concerned that your child may tell unexpected or unwanted callers that you are not at home, caller ID can be an inexpensive protection. Instruct your child to answer from only "preapproved" callers, allowing unknown calls to be picked up by the voice mail or left to simply hang up.

• *Wear a Beeper.* Beepers can enable your child to let you know he is home safely or to alert you to call home immediately. Equipping yourself with a beeper is particularly smart if your workplace is less than "child friendly" about making or receiving personal calls. Consider using prearranged codes to convey specific messages.

Keeping Your Child Safe Online

The Internet has opened up new worlds of information to us. Many of us shop online and enjoy connecting by e-mail with family and friends. Seeing your child actively engaged at the computer often reassures us that our child is actively learning, particularly when she tells us she is working on a school project. When our child tells us she is chatting online, this way of keeping in touch with friends seems acceptable. We certainly remember the hours we spent on the telephone talking to our girlfriends once we started junior high. Many of us feel that a computer is an essential tool and wonderful convenience for our homes. Our work situations often demand that we have Internet access at home.

Many of our children have earned the trust of being allowed to stay by themselves until we return from work. The evening and weekend hours are always hectic. Seeing your child working diligently at the computer can give us a false sense of security.

The Internet Is Not Just Another Electronic Babysitter

Every one of us has used the television as a temporary babysitter when we needed a little time to get our act together at home. The Internet is not just a different kind of television. Think of the Internet like a telephone that allows your child to be in contact with strangers and, in fact, welcomes these strangers into your home. Just as you are preparing your child for the real world, you need to inform your child about the online world.

♦ Limiting your child's computer time is not enough. Establish guidelines and rules with clear consequences, if rules are broken.

♦ Know as much as your children about their Internet and computer use. Familiarize yourself with the programs your child is using. Consider Internet filters or blocks.

♦ Place the family's computer in the location that will make it easiest for you to insure that family guidelines on Internet use are respected. You would not permit your child to bring strangers into their bedrooms. Computers with Internet access need constant parental supervision.

♦ Alert your child to the benefits and dangers of the Internet to make sure your child is making smart decisions when online. Emphasize that people are not always who they say they are online. Make sure your child knows how dangerous it is to give out personal information online. Stress that it is never safe to arrange a face-to-face meeting with someone he first "meets" online. Chat rooms are a particular hazard.

♦ Make sure your child can put a face to every screen name on his buddy list. Explain that Instant Messaging (IM) is only for chatting with school friends and family friends who are approved by you.

♦ Be alert to cyberbullying. Many school administrators are reporting that the taunting and bullying that used to end at dismissal continues through e-mail and posting on Web sites. This seems especially prevalent during the middle school years.

♦ HDOP—Help Delete Online Predators. Visit *www.cybertipline.com* regularly to get updates and helpful hints. The list of chat abbreviations is a must-have for every parent.

WHAT CAN I DO WITH A SUMMER LATCHKEY CHILD?

Any ideas on what to do with a latchkey schoolchild who is home for the summer? Two hours a day after school was manageable—homework, talking with friends, and doing a little yard work or straightening up around the house occupied my daughter's time. She'll be thirteen soon and is pretty responsible, but I'd hate to see her wandering around aimlessly all summer or spending days watching TV. I can't afford these expensive camps that some of her friends are attending.

With a little ingenuity and some scouting around, you should be able to locate some alternatives to your daughter's just "hanging out" all summer. A good place to start is with your child's school. A number of school systems offer summer activities through after-school programs or in cooperation with your county's Department of Parks and Recreation. The difficult part might be the transportation factor—coordinating your working schedule with your daughter's plans. One way of handling this would be to organize a car pool. Exchange phone numbers with other parents whose children will be attending the programs you are considering. Early planning is essential. Worthwhile cost-conscious programs fill up fast. Right after New Year's Day is not too early to start looking into what your child might like to do next summer.

Here are some ideas to get you started:

◆ Many community arts centers feature courses and workshops in pottery, dance, painting, music, and acting. Don't forget to look into scholarships that these cultural centers and programs often make available to lower-income children.

◆ County parks, state and national parks, and recreation facilities usually have activities for kids and teens all summer long. Check in the government section of your local phone book. Also, community pools offer swim classes. Better yet, if your daughter is a good swimmer, see if she can qualify for free admission by working as a junior lifeguard.

◆ Day camps run by the YMCA, YWCA, or the Boys' Club of America are affordable and can fill your child's afternoons with arts and crafts, swimming, boating, and sports. Again, inquire about available scholarships and sliding-scale options, and consider your child's working as a junior counselor to earn her fee. Investigate the possibility of her earning school credit by either taking summer classes or serving as an apprentice in programs or camps that need helpers. Many churches and synagogues offer inexpensive summer fun. Your daughter might volunteer to help out during these planned events in exchange for available or free transportation.

- Public libraries not only host storytelling hours, film and video showings, puppet shows, lectures, and writing classes, but also have countless brochures, flyers, and other information on the various goings-on in your region during the summer months. The library's community bulletin board is a great place to advertise your car pooling needs. You'd be surprised at how many other parents are in the same situation.

- If your daughter is a Girl Scout, don't overlook the summer camps that might be offered in your area. The 4-H program is another excellent source of summer fun. Call your county's Department of Human Services to see what camps and activities are available for children of parents on a limited budget.

- Keep in mind that there is no rule that says kids should be completely and thoroughly entertained at all times. Sometimes a little boredom spurs creative behavior. Just remember to limit TV and Internet access and keep a large supply of books and other reading materials on hand.

- Contact your local chapter of AARP or a senior citizens' center. Elderly people who don't have relatives nearby often welcome the opportunity to

spend time with children. "Adopting a grandparent" could be a mutually rewarding experience.

THE TEENAGE YEARS

Until the twentieth century, there were no "teenagers." There were merely young members of farming households. The transformation of youth from members of farming households to teenagers occurred during the last hundred years and was ignited by several forces. Before the Industrial Revolution, youngsters went from childhood to adulthood. It was not uncommon to be married by fourteen, start a family, and work on the family farm where you had worked alongside your parents as a child. But then came child labor laws creating a class separating children from adults. Cities and public schools were built, men went off to war, and all sorts of major cultural changes were in the works. Slowly, there emerged a group between children and adults that had no name or identity. But little by little, they began to relate to things that neither children nor adults could claim.

Music like rock and roll and clothes that seemed to look good only on their bodies became their trademark. Still, they had no identity. Were they children, or were they adults? Their biological structure wasn't too different from their counterparts at the end of the nineteenth century, but they began to mature a little more quickly.

These are today's teenagers—a group of people making the transition from childhood to adulthood and living in a nether world of confusing expectations. Inadvertently abandoning teenagers to their own culture is seen by many as one of the social costs of our changing world. Teenagers may be difficult to understand not because they are rebelling or evading us, but rather because the adults around them have become absent. With the absence of significant adults, teenagers turn to unreliable sources for information, guidance, and emotional support.

BELIEVE IT OR NOT: THE TEENAGE YEARS ARE AN EXCITING OPPORTUNITY NOT TO BE MISSED

When your children are young, a moment of privacy in the bathroom is an unheard of luxury. A trip to the supermarket unencumbered by restless, demanding children seems the impossible dream. More quickly than you could have imagined, however, the toddler who never gave you a moment of privacy is now the sulky teenager who acts like she does not want to be seen with you. Your bathroom suddenly has real-man shaving equipment. There are more kinds of shampoo positioned around the tub than you ever thought existed. Instead of exhausting solo trips to the supermar-

ket, you have an eager young driver who would happily drive twenty miles for a loaf of bread. Your child is taller and stronger than you. Your child has skills you do not possess. Interests and activities are often separate from your own. Passionate beliefs are expressed that you do not share. Your child cares deeply about his friends.

It is so tempting to think that the hard work of parenting is now nearly complete. Being able to leave your child for significant hours during the day is a great relief to the time-pressured single mother. In addition, many single mothers report that having a teenager in the house prompts a midlife crisis. Regrets, self-doubt, and the desire to recapture our youth confront many single mothers as their children enter this defining life stage. Issues and goals in your own life may take on an accelerated sense of urgency. Even the most dedicated and responsible single mother may wish nothing more than to get out of the house, leaving behind the twenty-four-hour-a-day cares, demands, and responsibilities of raising children solo.

While no human being can be complete without dreams, desires, and goals of their very own, your children's teenage years are not the time to lessen your involvement and participation in your children's lives. Remember those years from birth to age two? Every day your child was growing, changing, and learning more about the world around him. The teenage years incorporate nearly as much physical, social, and emotional change as those first critical two years. The teenage years can be just as memorable, joyful, and rewarding as those unforgettable and endearing "baby times."

The teen years are your last oppor-

allow your child to schedule her own routine doctor and dental appointments so that she is able to take care of these needs when she no longer lives at home. Your teenager should be guided toward responsibly managing everyday chores like shopping, kitchen cleanup, and errands. Things will not always go smoothly. Resist the idea that it is easier and quicker just to do it yourself. When responsibilities are unmet or mistakes are made, sit down with your teenager and review what went wrong and how different choices would have led to a more successful outcome. Emphasize that with the privileges of growing up come added responsibilities. Actions, not words, demonstrate that your teenager is ready for a later curfew, greater access to the family car, a part-time job, or whatever your teenager feels he wants to do. A young man who protests that he can't figure out how to use the vacuum cleaner is obviously not ready to be trusted with the infinitely more complicated family car.

tunity to have a real and lasting impact on your child's life. Your teenagers need your time and attention. Just being there, your physical presence is the best guarantee that your children will make safe, healthy, and appropriate choices. Single mothers, who typically nourish closer relationships and more open communication with their children, should continue to use this well-earned advantage. We need to know what is really going on in our child's real life, not just what we think, assume, or hope their life is all about. No teenager is going to accept advice or guidance from any adult who does not have a genuine understanding of what really goes on day-to-day in his or her life.

Most importantly, teenagers need the gift of our time. Teenagers may not need us round-the-clock like a newborn, but they need us "on demand." Let your teenager know that, without meaningful exception, you are available for them at any time. Make it true even when you are dog-tired and can think of a thousand things (sleep number one) you would rather be doing at 11:00 P.M.

This is also a time when important life skills that will equip your child for a smoother transition to independent life can be taught. Time and money management are the keys to self-reliance. You, as a successful single mother, are a master of these skills. Share your knowledge directly with your child. Teach essential skills like check writing and keeping track of receipts. Under your guidance and supervision,

TEENAGERS NEED LIMITS: BE THE ADULT THAT YOU ARE

Your teenager requires firm limits. He will secretly appreciate the love and concern setting and enforcing such limits demonstrates. Set curfews and enforce them by staying awake until your child returns home. Keep informed about what she is doing and with whom she is doing it. If your daughter says she is at Sue's house, then dropping by Sue's house to check will be no big deal. If your daughter is not telling you truthfully where she is going, you need to exercise more control and greater supervision.

If a party is planned, call the host's parent to make sure that this parent will be home all evening to supervise. Remember that the last minute phone call asking to sleep over at a friend's house is most often the cover story for all-night partying or other rule-breaking activity. Insist that sleepovers

SINGLE MOM OF NOTE

The Crown Princess of Norway

Mette-Marit Tjessem Hoiby was a rebellious student attending private school in Oslo, Norway, when at twenty-four, she discovered she was pregnant with her son Marius. She worked as a waitress to support her son. Five years later, on August 25, 2001, in front of millions of TV viewers, Metter-Marit married Norway's Crown Prince Haakon, whom she met one year earlier at a concert.

In this liberal country where half the babies born are outside of marriage, most Norwegians didn't raise an eyebrow about Marius's birth, although there were some questions about his father, who was a drug dealer. The new princess successfully defused these questions, and the Norwegian Prime Minister Jens Stoltenberg called the wedding "a triumph for tolerance and respect for single mothers."

be planned a day ahead. It is important to be neither gullible nor intimidated. Practice saying "I'm not concerned about what the other kids are allowed to do. I'm concerned about you. These are the rules in this house." You are, after all, the parent. As much as teenagers act like they know everything, the truth is they do not have your hard-earned experience, maturity, and wisdom.

You are going to have conversations about topics never whispered or imagined about during your own teenage years. Be genuine about your own feelings. If you are confused, admit it; if you are appalled, say so. Your example is the strongest message. Tell your child what you believe about sex, drugs, and alcohol. Do not expect the school to do more than teach the facts. Your child's values and subsequent choices about sex, drugs, and alcohol will come largely from what you have taught and the behavior you have displayed.

What Teenagers Ask of Their Single Mothers

Like young children, teenagers may repeat the same questions over and over again, even though you have been openly discussing certain family issues for years. But their questions may mask the real issue: am I going to turn out just like my father? Very few teenagers have the insight to know and to express that this is really their deep-down worry. You need to say to your older children that "I bet you worry that along with those beautiful blue eyes that you also somehow inherited your father's tendency to hurt and disappoint." It does not matter what your child calls an absentee dad, but do not be surprised if your teenager stops referring to him as "Dad" and starts calling him by his first name. As your child grasps the degree of emotional distance, this may seem more authentic to him. Teenagers may worry about their own romantic relationships and ask themselves if they are holding on to an "over with a long time ago" boyfriend or girlfriend because they just can't handle another abandonment. Teenagers may need the experience of volunteering with younger children to prove to themselves that they can be of value to younger children. Often teenagers choose to volunteer with children who are precisely the same age as they were when their own father more or less left. This is an important healing experience and should definitely be encouraged. Tell your teenagers that their life experiences have only made them more sensitive and aware of the pain the kind of behavior they have experienced causes. They are less likely than most to repeat the mistakes both you and their father may have made. Tell them straight out—because it is true—that they are better, stronger, and wiser people for all the things they have experienced, survived, and, indeed, triumphed over.

RED FLAG: IF YOUR CHILD'S FATHER HAS A HISTORY OF SUBSTANCE ABUSE

If your child's father has a history of substance abuse, even if he is completely out of your lives, it is important to remember that his history may indicate that your child has a genetic predisposition to substance abuse. You need to instruct your child explicitly and with great care about the dangers of these substances. Set a good example by drinking responsibly and abstaining

from recreational drugs. Establishing routines and structure are key life skills for children whose hereditary makeup includes the potential for such serious problems. Your responsibilities may be greater than for other mothers whose children's backgrounds do not include such dangers, but it doesn't guarantee that your children will also abuse drugs or alcohol.

HELPING YOUR CHILD PLAN FOR THE FUTURE

It is incredible to every mother how fast the years go by. Before it seems possible, it is time to think beyond high school and look ahead to what will be the next step your child will take toward self-sufficiency and independence. A college education used to be the "magic ticket" guaranteeing a well-paying job and comfortable lifestyle. While college graduates may certainly have specific opportunities not available to others, it is no longer any kind of guarantee. College is simply not for everyone. Just as you have helped your child cope successfully with every transition and change, it is now time to help her face this new challenge. Your strong emotional bonds and insight into your child will be significant assets. As your child faces the big question "What am I going to do when I graduate from high school," you will be the same invaluable and constant ally who dependably stood by him during all the growing years.

How Am I Supposed to Know?

When our children were little, they all wanted to be firemen or ballerinas or whatever caught their fancy at that moment. Most often, however, they wanted to do something familiar or something they saw applauded and appreciated. While your child may still harbor fantasies of a professional sports career, the truth is that there are many careers with which your child is simply unfamiliar. This is why after-school and summer jobs can offer so much. These jobs give our children firsthand experience and responsibility. They can discover what they enjoy as well as what they absolutely detest. Job opportunities are available now in fields that did not exist when you were a teenager. The more your child has a chance to participate in the "real world," the greater the chance the first efforts after high school graduation will lead to job satisfaction and success.

School Resources

While we are always glad to hear that our child had a conversation with his guidance counselor about life after high school, it is important to "do the math." When you divide the number of students by the number of high school guidance counselors, you can see that your child is unlikely to get much of her time. Guidance counselors are your best source of information, however, about programs your school district might offer. Guidance counselors are familiar with the various standardized tests your child may have to take to qualify for college admission or other post–high school training programs, as well as the application procedures, including those critical deadlines. Guidance counselors can also provide important information about applying for financial aid. Teenagers are notorious for responding to the last gong they have heard, often changing plans and interests with

dizzying speed. Guidance counselors have much experience navigating these critical years and can help you understand what your teenager might be thinking or feeling.

Let's Talk

Conversation at home is critically important to help your child make realistic and thoughtful post–high school plans. For example, does your child hate his after-school job? If so, why? What would he change at this job, if he could, to make the job more to his liking? Does he prefer to work alone, or does he miss being part of a team? Does he like a fast-paced work environment, or does he find pressure stressful? Does he welcome routine, or does he like a job where the unexpected is expected? These answers give your child valuable clues to career options he might care to explore. What seems to be the common thread among the teachers he has respected and liked? Does he do best with teachers who have strict rules and procedures or better with teachers whose classrooms offer greater latitude and personal choice? Your child can be guided to think about career options that might more closely parallel classroom situations he enjoyed. Many high school students love their after-school jobs and find the world of work far more satisfying than time in school. Make sure your child has a clear understanding of what she enjoys at this job. What are her particular skills and interests that this job showcases? Maybe it is her "people skills" that really make her shine at this job? What can she take from this after-school opportunity and grow into a career?

But Mom, I Hate School!

Many children, for a variety of reasons, do not enjoy the traditional school experience. They may have found the classroom confining and the daily routine tedious. While you may have responded to whining and complaining about school with "Sorry, it's your job to go to school," you need to make it crystal clear that education past high school is very different. Whether your child chooses a traditional four-year college, two-year college, technical school, or some other vocational program, this will be a whole different kind of experience. Emphasize that post–high school education is his or her choice and will reflect his or her interests and goals. Skeptical teenagers may need help to network with older students enrolled in programs of interest to hear firsthand about differences between high school and this next educational opportunity.

The First Step Is All-Important

Single moms may have the advantage of a closer and possibly more insightful relationship with their teenagers. We know the kinds of activities at which our children excel or the experiences that our children enthusiastically embrace. We may have fewer financial resources, however, and typically have many competing priorities. For these reasons it is critical for single mothers to help their teenagers begin their post–high school plans in a timely way. Senior year is usually too late for a meaningful beginning. Letting graduation day pass without a plan in place can lead to much wasted time and potential family conflict as you correctly see your child floundering and without direction. Remember, all that needs to be accomplished is the first step. Career choices change, and new interests develop. You need to be the early voice of reason. If your son or daughter shuns physical challenge and strict routines, the military may not be an option, despite their offer of tuition and other assistance. Liking to tinker with automobiles every so often does not necessarily suggest auto repair training as an ideal first career step. If your child needed supervision and much extra help to complete every written school assignment, then college might not be the best next step.

Let your child fantasize about the ideal job and what she would be doing every day at work that she would truly enjoy. Ask the questions and help your child consider the answers. Make sure your child knows what he hopes this first step will accomplish and what options completion of this first step will offer.

WHEN IT IS TIME FOR A MOM TO HAVE THE BIG TALK

My daughter and I have discussed openly for many years that she was conceived well after my first divorce with a man I barely knew. Despite my lousy romantic choices, my daughter and I have created a happy, stable family life. It is now time to have serious talks about sex during which any good mother stresses responsible behavior and the need for careful choices. How can I possibly have these kinds of talks with my daughter when she knows my own behavior was the total opposite? I want her to avoid the mistakes I made, but I certainly do not want her to think that I feel she is a regret or a mistake.

It should come as no big surprise but many women, even those who end up happily married with 2.2 children, have sexual histories that they are less than eager to share with their own daughters or sons, for that matter. Most of the time, however, these mothers do not exactly lie but rather spread the truth differently about their own past or current sexual behavior. These women typically think of themselves as "good mothers." You should think of yourself no differently.

Glossing over certain things or spreading the truth differently is not an option for you. With just a few possible exceptions, the whole truth is your greatest ally in helping your daughter make the critical life choices ahead. It is likely that some of your less than wonderful choices were influenced by a lack of self-understanding. Tell your daughter how important it is to know what she is doing and why. Girls are often influenced to dress up their sexual appetites and activities in romantic clothing pretending that hormonally driven lust is really true and lasting love. Help her to know the difference. Now that your daughter is older, you can certainly discuss in a limited way not only the joys but also the heartaches of single motherhood. Your success as a single mother has involved compromises like any important life choice. Make your daughter aware of these compromises. You certainly want to stress the greatly increased health risks of sexual activity. Keep the lines of communication open. Our children expect us to be less perfect than our fear and confusion make us imagine. Make your experiences valuable teaching tools to counsel and guide your daughter as she enters the sometimes scary world of relationships.

TEACHING A RESPONSIBLE ATTITUDE TOWARD SEX

My son is starting to date, and I am concerned that he may treat young women badly because of behavior of his father's that he has witnessed. His father was a notorious womanizer, which makes me that much more worried that if my son copies him that he will risk getting AIDS.

Rest assured that very often children who have had the opportunity to see over time the results of boorish behavior of a parent or older brother or sister actually strive hard not to make the same mistakes. Your son, no doubt, is aware that his father was unfaithful to you and may have lost track of the number of girlfriends who spent the night while he was visiting his father. None of this was very appealing at the time and is probably an even less appealing lifestyle choice now. It is more likely that your son will want to take an entirely different path. It may even be that you will have to encourage him to date many girls before he gets too serious.

Encourage your son's participation in group activities and sports so that dating does not become the exclusive focus of his free time. Discuss drug and alcohol use with your son. Establish clear rules and enforce them. Remember that curfews are not just for girls. Remind your son of the need to practice safe sex. Make sure he has condoms, even if you buy them and leave them in his dresser drawer. Also make sure he knows that it's okay not to have sex if he doesn't feel ready. Thinking of our children as sexually active is always a jolt, but we cannot be good mothers if we are in denial about the realities of our children's world.

WHEN PETS BECOME ALL-IMPORTANT

During my son's freshman year in college, he adopted an abandoned kitten and named him Leland after his lacrosse coach. When my son moved into an apartment, he was more concerned about the apartment being right for the cat than right for him. He buys dry cat food in fifty-pound bags so that Leland can never go hungry. He has a special blanket for the cat and buys the cat toys. He takes pictures of the cat, which he carries in his wallet. He tells me that each meow has a different meaning, and if you listen closely, Leland meows "out" when he wants to go outside. I don't think this is normal. My son acts just like a proud father, but Leland is a cat, not a child.

Could this have anything to do with the fact that my son has seen little of his father since he was about seven years old? Should I worry that my son goes so overboard with this cat?

Obviously, some people really love cats, but more likely, your son is taking important steps toward healing the wounds caused by his father's abandonment. Along the way, your son has asked himself whether he has the capacity to be a loving and committed father. Your son has something to prove to himself. In taking such loving and devoted care of this cat, your son is practicing the responsibilities, joys, and, yes, drudgery and worry of parenthood. Every day your son is proving to himself that he can be the kind of "daddy" he did not have. It is probably not the time in his life when he should be assuming the responsibility of a "real baby," and so he has, in essence, done the next best thing by caring for Leland. Naming the cat after an important male person in his life is no accident. This choice of name signifies that the coach is an important role model in your son's life on and off the athletic field.

Perhaps you are not ready quite yet to be called grandma, but cherish the opportunity to watch your son preparing and practicing for the joys and responsibilities that parenthood will eventually bring to his life. Stop worrying and congratulate yourself for giving your son the emotional stability and courage to heal himself while taking exceptional care of one very lucky cat.

16

Who's Your Daddy?—What to Say about an Absent Parent

We know that the number of ways that women become single parents are many—from initiating a divorce to finding oneself abandoned; from accidentally becoming pregnant after a brief fling to personally choosing anonymous donor insemination; from staying in a relationship just long enough through the childbearing years to conceiving a child with someone you thought you knew better but realized you knew nothing about. Even though moms mothering without their child's biological father may express many different concerns, most place a pretty strong focus on one particular area: how to handle the inevitable and many "daddy" questions.

ARE YOU READY TO TALK ABOUT DADDY?

Make sure you are ready to discuss this vital topic with your child well before he brings it up. Know that his questions will come at the most unlikely moments—while you are waiting on line at the supermarket, dropping him off at day care on the day of your big presentation, or twenty minutes before your big date arrives for the first glamorous, romantic evening you have had in months. This is all the more reason to be prepared.

If you feel you are not ready and if the thought of discussing your child's father makes you angry or upset, then address your feelings first. Write down exactly what thoughts get you going or bring tears to your eyes. Better yet, write a letter to this person without the intent of mailing it, and state all

WHEN YOU KNOW YOU'RE A FAMILY

It may be subtle and sweet. It may hit you like an epiphany, but the realization that you're a family will come sooner or later. Here's how some moms completed the following sentence: You know you're a family when . . .

♦ "I woke up with my baby next to me and knew my life would never be the same."

♦ "I bought a ticket to visit my parents and answered differently when asked how many were traveling. This time it was 'my daughter and me!'"

♦ "I put my baby in the car seat for the first time."

♦ "I bought life insurance and listed my son as my beneficiary."

your disappointments, regrets, and sadness over how your expectations were never met. Keep in mind that you want to purge these feelings, not necessarily find fault with or blame this person. To add a healing, ritualistic touch, why not burn the letter, tear it to shreds, or continue a long-held tradition of bottling it up and sending it out to sea? If you find no relief on your own, seek help through a support group, friend, spiritual advisor, or a mental health professional. It will be difficult work sorting out these feelings and leaving the anger and otherwise destructive emotions behind you. But these steps will ensure success in answering any questions your child may have.

What to Expect

Most little ones begin asking questions about Daddy around the age of four or five. Before that, children think that all families are just like theirs. At the preschool age, children become more aware of the world around them and start to see themselves as part of that bigger world. Children also observe other kinds of families by participation in day care or by attending church or synagogue activities. We know that what children see on TV influences them greatly. Children also by this age become keen observers of simple day-to-day living around them.

How to Begin

Start your talks about Daddy by discussing the differences in families your child may have observed. Comment that a friend at school does indeed live with her mother, father, and both grandparents or that another friend has her married sister and her husband living with her. Take every opportunity to tell your child that these differences in families are to be celebrated. Talk about the positive things that happen, for example, when a grandmother might be living with a family. Mention that the grandmother can share stories of the family that others cannot remember or were not alive to see. Such celebration and acceptance of differences in other families sets the stage for your discussions of your own unique family and how you came to be. It also teaches children that diversity can be beautiful.

Remain positive, even upbeat, if possible. Especially if their father is neglectful or abandons his responsibilities to them in a major way, keeping your words positive will be emotionally demanding. Children neglected or abandoned will express rage, hurt, or anger. Comfort them as only a mother can. Say that "I know you are feeling hurt. I am sorry. I wish I could make things better for you." Resist the urge to say things like "Now you know why I left the bum!" or "What do you expect from a jerk like your dad?" This will require every last ounce of maturity and strength you have. Every time you succeed, your child will gain an added measure of happiness and confidence. Make this effort a life priority.

Every positive comment you make about their father becomes in the same way part of how your children view themselves.

Think about your words as sharp, deadly arrows. Protect your children from wounding words just as you would protect them from physical danger.

THREE TOUGH QUESTIONS

"Why did you and Dad split up?" Avoid statements suggesting that you "fell out of love." Then children may think that it is also possible for you to stop loving them. Let them know that this can never happen. It is okay to say that you and your child's father don't love each other as moms and dads should anymore. Assure your child that a mother is always a mother and that you will always be there for them.

"Will Dad ever come back?" Hope is the magic that sparks everyone's life in a positive way. However, falsely suggesting that a father who has no intention of returning will come back or stating that you would like a father to return with whom you have no

intention of ever becoming involved makes way for more loss. It's better to say that "I hope that you and your father can find happiness and peace together as the special people you are." But for now, he will just have to occupy a place in your child's heart, if he can't be there in person.

"Can I live with Dad?" This question has a totally different meaning when asked by a toddler and by a teenager. Older children may be thinking about living with Dad when their values and life plan are in place and they are able to take care of themselves. But when a little one asks, try not to feel threatened or unappreciated. Tell your child that it's okay for him to think about living with Dad when he is older. Just remember that in all likelihood this will never happen. But, again, a little bit of hope is a healthy feeling.

Keep in mind, too, that you wouldn't be the first single mom to have adult children develop a kind of friendship with a long-gone dad. If this remarkable event happens, your strength and loving spirit, which has enabled them to forgive the past, has helped make their father some small part of their lives. What a tribute and a triumph for you!

WHY THE DADDY TOPIC IS SO SCARY

Children learn their view of the world from the messages and values taught at home. If mommy says that some children live with both a mom and a dad, others live with either a mommy or daddy, and still others live with a grandparent or relative, children will accept this with little difficulty. The problems arise when children sense that Mommy is uncomfortable or anxious about their own situation. We know that children take their cues from their parents on any subject. If it is clear to children that we are comfortable with a discussion, our comfort will translate into comfort and reassurance for them.

Remember having a single mother is normal—whatever that means! The fact is there are more children today living in single-parent and blended families than there are those who spend their entire upbringing in their biological parents' home. Your children need to know this and should be encouraged to realize early that they fit in just as well as anybody else—whatever their family background. One mom, to give herself some moral support, taped a cartoon to the bathroom mirror that was captioned "Normal people from traditional, two-parent families." It shows an auditorium with a banner spread before hundreds of empty seats reading "Welcome Adult Children of Nondysfunctional Parents" and two self-conscious participants looking around to see that they are the only ones who showed up!

Another mom recalls a television sitcom where a boy wonders if on his first day at a new school whether he'll be the only kid with two parents at home. He cringes, hoping he finds another outcast! She reported that her attitude allowed for a bit of levity. When we can laugh at different kinds of situations, it brings a sense of normalcy to them. Stepfamilies, two-parent families, single-parent families, and adoptive families—their makeup, size, and structure may be defined differently, but they are certainly all "normal."

MISTAKES TO AVOID WHEN DISCUSSING DADDY

Sometimes we tend to jump in too quickly with words of reassurance or with too much information because we are trying to convince ourselves that everything is okay. But, by doing these things, we discourage our children from expressing their feelings.

♦ *Don't Change the Subject or Try to Avoid Listening to Your Child.* It's most important to allow him to express freely whatever feelings or thoughts are on his mind.

♦ *Keep Your Discussion Age-Appropriate.* We also sometimes forget that our explanations need first and foremost to be appropriate to our child's developmental level. For example, there is no way a four-year-old understands what commitment, trust, or intimacy means. The explanation that "Your father and I did not feel happy living together," rather than details about how he was never able to make a commitment to you, would be more easily understood by a preschooler.

♦ *Don't Give More Information Than Necessary.* Sometimes we are so apt to share every detail regarding our children's birth with them that we forget to keep our conversations age-appropriate. Surely you will recognize this new interpretation of a dusty old joke: A woman who had been inseminated with donor sperm was asked by her five-year-old son the long-awaited question, "Mommy, where do I come from?" Priding herself in being quite a liberal parent, this mother engaged in an elaborate explanation regarding eggs, sperm, basal body temperature, and so forth. The child's eyes glazed over, and after about fifteen minutes, he pleaded with her to stop. But being a no-nonsense kind of woman, she kept right on talking. Finally, he interrupted her with, "No, Mommy. I mean, Johnny comes from New Jersey. Where do I come from?"

The takeaway message? Stick to the basic facts and keep your explanations simple. Reveal more and more information as your child matures.

◆ *Don't Lie.* Lying to your children doesn't work because you simply won't be able to sustain the lies. The loss of a loving father will be compounded by the loss of their trust in you.

◆ *Don't Miss Any Opportunity to Be as Positive as Possible.* Let your children know that they don't have to repeat their father's unacceptable behavior or poor life choices. Look for opportunities to make truthful positive comments about their father.

◆ *Exercise Caution in Talking about a Father's Failure to Pay Child Support.* If your child's father doesn't pay child support, you need to be careful in the way you talk about this. Here are some tips:

1. Recognize that children are aware when fathers do not pay child support, if only because finances often become critically tight.

2. Consider different methods of answering questions about Dad's failure to pay. For example, if Dad's lack of support is due to sickness or unemployment, share these facts.

3. Point out that their father may be angry for a number of reasons, some of which he may not understand. However, point out that not paying support is a poor way to express these feelings.

4. Don't say that Dad's failure to pay is because he never really loved his children or that he's a lifetime member of the low-life club. These words will wound your children and will certainly do nothing to make the checks arrive any sooner. Better to explain gently that his behavior is sort of like a grown-up temper tantrum.

Why Do Children Ask the Same Questions Over and Over Again?

I am satisfied that I have answered my eight-year-old's many questions about her father, who left us while I was still pregnant, honestly and thoughtfully. Maybe I am wrong because my daughter tends to ask the exact same questions over and over again. What am I doing wrong?

In all likelihood, nothing. Children ask questions over and over again partly because they can't initially grasp all the information given them. Sometimes they are told too much too quickly, or their own learning styles prevent them from absorbing completely all that was told them. Remember, for example, you probably did not understand multiplication the first time the teacher discussed it. She reviewed it many times while you practiced. This is how learning takes place. Understanding of what has been shared about your child's father will be no different. It will take time and repetition.

Children also ask the same questions over and over again to see if the answer remains the same. Little ones take comfort in the security of repetition in the same way they like hearing the same bedtime story or eating some familiar food. However, the most important thing to remember is that if you are comfortable with your feelings about your single-mothering experiences, chances are your child will be, too.

SHOULD YOU EVER LIE?

You're told over and over again how important honesty is when talking to your child about why the other parent isn't around. But it can be terribly tempting to lie about a former partner, particularly if absolutely nothing positive comes to mind whenever you think of him. Maybe he considers prison a home away from home, or he's never seen a sober day in his life. Maybe you thought you were really connected to this person only to learn that he had a harem of others who felt the same way.

Do you gloss over certain painful parts when talking to your child or allow some little white lies to creep into the talk? It's okay to tone down the truth, but creating a whole fictional person, even though it seems

the kinder and simpler thing to do, just doesn't work. Don't do it, no matter how huge the temptation. You may think you are sparing your children the heartache you underwent, but fictionalizing means being untruthful. Being diplomatic and sophisticated in your choice of words is better. No matter what the circumstances are that helped create your single-mother status, don't stray too far from the truth.

IF YOU ARE DIVORCED OR SEPARATED

For divorced or separated single mothers, the challenge is that the daddy questions can change depending upon the circumstances or may simply focus on the same painful issues throughout your child's growing up. For some fortunate children, while divorce may mean some adjustments, not all of them easy, Dad remains an active coparent who is involved in their lives. For other children, their father is around a lot initially but then gets into a different lifestyle and may see them less and less. One or both parents may remarry or be seriously involved with another partner. Sometimes a father moves to a different part of the country, and the loss is devastating. The divorced single mother must be ready to answer a host of different questions in response to whatever life path the father of her children has selected.

Remember, being able to talk about things isn't enough by itself. Establishing a fairly predictable household routine is important for all families, but it is particularly helpful given a recent divorce or separation. Children need structure and a sense of order—from getting dressed in the morning to regular mealtimes and bedtime—especially since the usual household routine has already been altered or disrupted.

When Dad Acts Like He Still Lives with the Family

My husband was routinely unfaithful, and after a lot of therapy, I got my own act together enough to ask for a divorce. He readily agreed, obviously eager for his freedom. I did everything I could to make the transition easier for the children. Just as we were getting our lives together, we started seeing more and more of Dad. Apparently, freedom was not as much fun as the sneaking around. The children are asking me why Dad is around our house so much. What should I tell them?

A good question—why is he around the house so much? Part of getting your lives together is establishing boundaries and house rules. Boundaries in your case mean that your ex-husband is not allowed to come and go in your house as he pleases. It is not a good idea for anyone, particularly for the children. It is confusing and sends the wrong message.

Calmly tell your former husband that he is welcome to visit, if he calls first with whatever advance notice you feel is appropriate. If he balks, insist in a firmer tone of voice. Tell him you are sure he would not want you to drop by his new apartment unannounced, particularly on a Saturday night, and this is just how his intrusive behavior feels to you. Tell him it is confusing to the children, particularly since you are working so hard to help everyone get their lives back on track. Make sure you reinforce the importance of keeping his dating life—and his history of infidelity—

private. He may have regrets and conflicts and have a sudden urge to "come clean," but his children should not be a part of any emotional makeover. It might be a good idea to change the locks on the door and, for now, not to give him the keys.

When Dad Is Gay

My soon-to-be-ex has led a double life during most of our marriage. I thought we had a wonderful relationship—he was a great husband and a fantastic father to our son, who just turned eight. So imagine how shocked I was when he confessed to me that he was gay and had been having a relationship with another man he met at his health club. He said it hurt him to live a life where he was not honest with me and felt I deserved the truth. But I'm the one who was devastated—I had no clue that he found anything wrong with our marriage or me! What about our son? I haven't told him we're getting divorced let alone tell him the truth about his dad.

It's understandable for you to feel betrayed, hurt, and angry. Infidelity will cause turmoil, whether your husband is cheating on you with a man or a woman.

You're also reeling with confusion because you thought you had a wonderful marriage but was surprised to learn your husband didn't share the same feelings. It sounds like you did have a wonderful marriage. Your husband was good to you and your son. The problem was not with your marriage, and it has nothing to do with anything you did or did not do. Aside from your husband's infidelity, the problem was that your husband was not being true to himself.

Your husband and you both need to tell your son the truth—minus some details about the man from the health club. Together, try broaching this difficult topic by starting a conversation with your son about different families—how some kids live with a mom or a dad or both, some live with grandparents, and others live with two moms or two dads. This will give you the opportunity to explain your impending divorce—that it may change the family dynamic and that Mom and Dad won't be living together but "we're still your family."

Your husband's need to be honest may just provide the next opportunity to explain what being gay means. Talk to your son about the importance of being honest to oneself. Reassure your son that although Dad loves him and he is happy he is his son that he doesn't feel like himself being married to a woman because he is gay. He is more comfortable in a relationship with a man rather than a woman. This doesn't mean he doesn't love Mom. He does, but in a different way. Dad needs to be who he is in addition to being a father.

Your son's reaction may be unpredictable, but don't be surprised if he knows more than you expect. Kids are sheltered from very little today, and this may be a good thing when teaching tolerance and acceptance. One couple was taken aback by their daughter's response when they were struggling to explain that mom was a lesbian: "Yeah? Susie's mom has a girlfriend who makes the best mashed potatoes ever!"

Your focus, however, should be more on regrouping as a family in the face of your divorce. If you and your husband could get past the hurt, you could successfully coparent your child and provide the added benefit of teaching him that love and responsibility are what counts, not a person's religion, color, weight, sexual orientation, or any other form of difference.

When a No-Show Dad Breaks Promises

I try to give my ex-husband frequent and regular visitation. My children adore him. The trouble is that he is very irresponsible and often hurts their feelings by not showing up when he promised. I am often left with two crying, disappointed children. When I confront him about this, he just shrugs his shoulders and tells me that something came up. How do I lessen my children's hurt?

The best way to handle this situation is to prepare. The next time he is scheduled to take the children somewhere, talk to them about what the plan will be if their dad does not show up. Say very specifically that "Your dad is planning to take you to the movies on Saturday. He told us he would pick you up at 12:30 PM. What is going to be our plan for the day if he does not arrive?" To minimize disappointment, the alternate plan should probably be something more fun than vacuuming the car or washing a few windows. Suggest, for example, that you do a few errands and then see the movie later in the afternoon. If your finances are tight, decide together on a fun and low-cost activity like kite flying or a trip to your local museum. Do not let Dad have control of the day and of everyone's feelings when past experience has taught you that he may suddenly and for no reason decide not to show up.

WHEN YOU AND DAD ARE STILL FIGHTING

Child support and money for extras have always been provided for our two daughters, now both teenagers. My ex has never missed visitation. The problem is that he and I are still fighting, mostly about how he feels about my family. He refers to my mother, sister, and me as the "nut job triplets." When he picks up the girls, he never misses an opportunity to say something hurtful about my family and me. He tells the girls he is constantly afraid they will "turn out nuts like your mother." I think he is hurting the girls emotionally, and I am considering stopping visitation. Any advice?

The Court will not revoke visitation for his behavior, even though it clearly demonstrates his level of immaturity! Even if your children were much younger, the Court would not revoke visitation. In the case of your daughters, the decision is theirs.

Shielding our young children from any and all potential harm is a top priority. That maternal protection instinct could be what you are now feeling. Young children lack the critical thinking skills to put into perspective what they hear and experience. They need adults to make judgments for them about what is safe and what is dangerous. Your teenagers are developmentally ready, however, to make these judgments. Is their judgment always flawless? Absolutely not!

Unfortunately, you may not be the best person to guide your daughters' judgment at this point. Perhaps you are able to discuss your ex's behavior in a nonjudgmental way—if so, you are an unusually forgiving person! But even if you have that capability, your daughters will perceive you as being offended by his insults. Remember that they most likely love and need their father—even though he's a jerk. He's a part of them, and they may feel they have to defend him—even if they feel he's behaving badly. You and your family are a part of your daughters, too, and that's exactly why his behavior is so unacceptable.

You may want to discuss the problem with someone not related to you that your daughters trust and who can talk about the issue with them in a neutral and supportive way. You should also try to communicate to your ex—whether in person or via a letter mailed to him (never ask your children to be messengers)—your concerns about the damage he is doing to your daughters.

In any case, make certain that you do not stoop to anything like his level and begin insulting him to his face or behind his back when your children can hear. Blow off the steam with your friends!

WHY DOES DAD PAY MORE ATTENTION TO HIS NEW GIRLFRIEND?

My ex-husband is like a scene out of a bad movie. He had a midlife crisis of mind-blowing proportions. He has a new hairpiece and a girl-friend half his age that he showers with lavish gifts and nonstop atten-tion. The children are puzzled by their second-class status with him, and I suspect they are deeply hurt. He has not seen or spoken to them in several months. What do I say when they ask me why Dad likes his new girlfriend more than he likes them?

It will not help to tell them it just is not so when all the evidence points to her over them on their father's priority list. Begin by telling them that you certainly know and understand that they feel hurt. Explain that sometimes grownups have difficulty knowing what is most impor-tant in their lives and can get off track— just like when children "forget" to do their homework so they can watch TV or play video games. Further explain that this is someone with whom their father is fascinated because she is a different type of person than he usually spends time with or spent time with when you and he were together. No doubt that is true in more ways than one!

Tell your children that sometimes we just need to be patient and see what

happens. There are some things over which we have no control, and other people's behavior is certainly one of those things. Tell your children that, much as you would like to, you cannot make their father pay attention and spend time with them. This is some-thing he must want to do himself.

Remind yourself that midlife crises typically end with the big hangover of reality. It is likely that in your case things will be no different. He will wake up and realize that the girlfriend is gone, the children have moved along nicely without him, and he is not only lonely but also alone.

If Dad Is Getting Remarried

Few children are thrilled by Dad's impending change in marital status because it deals the deathblow to the cherished "reunion fantasy." You need to be alert that this news may impact the kids in a number of ways, but you may notice sadness or a sudden lack of interest in activities your child previ-ously enjoyed. They may also be "act-ing out," especially if Dad just blurts the news out or they stumble on wedding invitations carelessly lying around Dad's apartment. So be prepared first. If you suspect wedding plans are being made, ask your ex for the specifics about when and where and discuss the best way to tell the children.

Why Does Dad Lie to Me?

My children are ten and twelve years old. Their father has a long history with illegal drugs. I am sure he is now dealing to support his habit. He is an advertising execu-tive with plenty of income but, nonetheless, a cocaine addict. His visits with the children are few and far between, but when he does visit, he promises them all kinds of things. Sometimes he arrives with presents as though it were Christmas, giving them some of the things that he has promised in the past. For this reason, my children tend to believe his promises, although their trust and belief are wearing thin. What do I say when they ask me why Dad lies?

Your children have reached the age when they are very conscious of truth and the difference between right and wrong. Begin by telling your children that Dad has the disease of addiction. You will be supported in your explanation by the fact that children are being taught at school about substance abuse, and this information will not be new to them. Obviously, it is painful to discover that your own father is an addict. Explain his lying behavior in terms of his addiction. Explain that he is lying not because he does not love them, but rather because his addiction makes it impossible for him to behave toward them as he would choose to if he were well. Tell them that addiction

is like having a broken leg. It makes it impossible for that person to walk or run normally. That is what addiction does—cripples the addict and prevents him from being able to do things that would normally be expected of him.

Before their father visits the next time, remind the children that Dad will make many promises. Remind them gently to remember to put the words "I wish" in front of whatever their father tells them. For example, he may promise to take them camping or on a trip to the mountains. Your children should listen to his words and think to themselves that "Dad means he wishes he could take us camping or to the mountains." This is truthful. Their father does wish these things, but he is weakened by his own addiction. Moreover, lying is a defense the addict uses to avoid acknowledging his own addiction. In a sense, he is lying to himself intentionally but lying unintentionally to others.

WHY IS HE ALWAYS WITH DIFFERENT WOMEN?

My children, ages twelve, fifteen, and sixteen, see their father about once or twice a month on a schedule convenient to him. Every time they see him, he has a different woman with him whom he introduces as his girlfriend. This is nothing new to me. I left him because of his nonstop womanizing. The children are curious and ask me why Dad has so many girlfriends. What am I supposed to say?

Probably the most appropriate thing is to tell your children that this is a good question to ask their father. If they are uncomfortable doing so, tell them you can only guess at why there are so many different women in his life. Since your children are older, the point to make here is that you do not have all the answers to why anyone behaves in a certain way. Again, since they are older, ask them to try to guess why their father behaves the way he does. They may guess that he likes to be with different people, he has never found someone he wanted to be with all the time, and other similar responses. Any or all of these could be right, and you should tell your children so. Their observations and your discussions of the possibilities are a good lesson for them about the complexity of human behavior. These discussions can also open the door for you to further communicate your own values about the importance of commitment and honesty.

Why Does Dad Love His New Kids More Than Me?

My former partner is uninterested in the nine-year-old daughter who resulted from the twelve years we were married. He left several years ago, has remarried, and turned into Superdad not only to the child he fathered with his new wife but also to her three other children. What do I say when my daughter asks why her father loves his other children so much and does not love her?

This kind of abandonment is really heartbreaking. Begin by telling her that although adults seem to know how to do everything well, this is not always the case. Some adults learn to show love and concern in stages, just as people learn to play the piano a little at a time. When her father was with you, he did not have

the skills to show the kind of love that each of you needed. Explain also that he has probably come to realize that unless he behaves in a loving way toward others that he will never receive love in return. His new children are not in some way better or more lovable than your daughter but are rather on the lucky receiving end of changed behavior on his part. Simply stated, tell your daughter that her father has changed. She will ask, no doubt, why if he has changed that he cannot be different toward her. Tell her honestly that you do not know, but again these differences have nothing to do with her and everything to do with what her father is capable of doing. Tell her that you wish things were different, acknowledge and comfort her in the pain of rejection she is experiencing, and give her the extra measure of attention and support that she needs.

If you have any kind of relationship with her father, take the opportunity to meet with him and discuss the feelings your daughter is experiencing. He honestly could be unaware, immersed as he is in his new life. Encourage him to set aside some special time on a regular basis to spend just with your daughter.

WHEN THE CHILDREN ARE AFRAID DAD WILL RETURN

My former husband was physically and emotionally abusive. He terrorized me for years, but I finally got the courage to leave when he started abusing our six-year-old daughter while I was pregnant with our son. My former husband was jailed briefly after a particularly violent incident unfortunately witnessed by my daughter. He is

*reportedly living in another state
and gratefully we hear nothing
from him. My son is a thriving
toddler, but my daughter is terrified
her father will return and "hurt me
and make me live in a bad place
with no mommy."*

Your daughter has suffered emotional and physical abuse. Pretending these events did not happen or attempting to minimize her fears will only make her more frightened. Since what happened to her (repeatedly) was real, your responses must be real in the sense that she needs to see that you and everyone else take seriously what occurred. She needs to trust that everything possible will be done to make sure nothing like what took place ever happens again. At night, when fears and worries seem most real, bedtime rituals can include locking the doors and saying calmly that "We are all safe in our home." The words can be of your choosing, but what you are trying to create is a comfort phrase, which your daughter can repeat to herself when frightening or painful memories intrude.

You should definitely put safeguards into place at school to make sure your former husband does not attempt the ultimate power/control act—kidnapping your daughter. Share with your daughter that the adults at school know that she is only to go with you or someone you have specifically designated. You may wish to let the school principal, as well as her teacher, assure her that the adults in charge are well aware of her special circumstances and know what to do to keep her safe.

Try your best to maintain routines and keep things at home as happily uneventful as possible. Create new family rituals and explore new family activities. These should be as simple as making Wednesday special dessert night or finding a local park with a terrific playground. All these efforts signal to your daughter that life is moving ahead in positive and fulfilling ways. It is important that, if you chose to date, you keep these activities separate from both your children. Everyone is dealing with enough at home without introducing another adult and his needs and concerns into the mix. The last thing you need is more human drama!

Above all else, take care of yourself! Keep your own mental reserves and energy at peak levels. Make your best efforts to stay healthy. Keep life simple and try to minimize stress as much as possible. Seek out appropriate support groups, if you wish. Continue the counseling made available to you after your former husband's arrest as long as you feel it is necessary. Your child may not be ready to talk about what she witnessed or how she felt when her father was present in her life. Reliving these events as they are retold to a mental health professional may cause what happened to become more traumatic by the repetition rather than offer the comfort adults and older children typically experience. For this reason, counseling right now may not necessarily be the best option. While these events will always be some part of who she is, you want your daughter to see herself as the one with choices rather than framing her life in the role of victim. As your daughter matures, it is particularly important to recognize her accomplishments and the efforts she made to reach these goals. Feeling in control of your own life is empowering and can overcome the worst of childhood experiences.

You are to be applauded for the strength and bravery it took to break away from a horrible situation and do what needed to be done to make a new life for you and your children.

IF DAD LEFT AND HASN'T RETURNED

About four years ago, my children's father left one Friday evening and never came back. I am sure he will never return. My two boys, eight and ten, still talk about him and refer to him as their father. We were never married, and I am sure that is why he left. They still hope he will come back, and it breaks my heart. I do not even know where he is. How do I answer their questions about why he left?

In many ways, this is tougher than losing a father to death because his choice to leave is so final, like death, but is obviously his deliberate choice. Acknowledge what a terrible loss this is for your boys. It is okay to tell them that you do not know exactly why he left, but his decision was definitely not about them. He did not leave because they were bad boys or unlovable or in some way not good enough, but rather for reasons that he himself may not even understand.

Help your boys come to terms with the loss of their father. Transitions in life like marriages and death are commemorated in our society with rituals and ceremonies. This is what you need to organize for your boys. Choose a quiet evening. Give each of the boys an opportunity to give a little speech about their father—kind of a eulogy for the living. You can also talk about your good memories of their father. You can set aside photos and other mementos in a special place. Light candles and prepare special refreshments. Irish Americans would recognize this as a good old-fashioned wake with tears and laughter. Most importantly, there will begin to be some kind of closure. The loss will be acknowledged and mourned. This is critical for all of you. Your boys can hope that Dad will someday return. On his birthday, light a candle and express the hope that he will return but remember that these hopes cannot dominate any of your lives. The ritual of lighting the candle once a year keeps the hope in proportion to the probability of his return. Wish Dad well on his birthday as the candle is lit, but at the same time, tell the boys that it is time for all of you to move on with your lives just as Dad is moving ahead with his.

Will Dad Ever Come Back?

Life is meaningless without hope, and this is precisely the reason that children will continue to express the hope, long past any reasonable expectations, that Dad will return. Many children ask frequently if they will be able to find their father when they are older and go live with him.

Many single mothers find these questions deeply disturbing, for a number of reasons. Many of these long-absent dads have given their children nothing but disappointment, and mothers fear that their children's quest for these men will lead only to more heartbreak. Other mothers know that their former partner's addictions, habits, or deep personal flaws make it unlikely that their children will ever be able to establish a parentlike relationship. These are not men upon whom to depend nor are they appropriate for their children to trust. Many single mothers, weary from the conflicting and demanding roles of single motherhood, feel resentful that their children are so interested in a man who has provided nothing and lives responsibility-free.

IF YOU WEREN'T MARRIED TO YOUR CHILD'S FATHER

I feel a little guilty when I hear other single mothers who chose to become pregnant talk about all the soul-searching and planning they went through. My pregnancy was an accident. I chose to keep the baby because it seemed like the right thing to do, and it has been the best decision of my life. Do I tell my child he was an accident?

No. Tell your child he was a delightful surprise. Many single mothers report that their pregnancies were accidents, but many experts believe that there are fewer contraceptive accidents or failures than there are unconscious desires to have a baby. More than you may be able to understand or accept

now, your decision to have a baby may have been more planned than you realize. It may have felt like the right thing to do because in ways you still may not fully understand you were ready to become a mother. The best parts of life are often the delightful and unexpected events. For you, a seemingly unplanned pregnancy may have been one of these events. Emphasize with your child the joy and surprise. Save the word "accident" for events like crumpled fenders and spilled milk. Never forget that some people "plan" themselves out of a lot of joy. Don't be one of them.

Special Concern: If You Were Raped

My child was born as the result of my being raped. It was not an attack that occurred in a dark alley or in my home. I knew the person casually, and this took place as he drove me home from my job one evening. I have no idea how to talk about this to anyone.

If your pregnancy was the result of a rape, you cannot begin to discuss this event with your child until you are at peace with how this traumatic event shaped your life. Counseling has probably been an essential part of your healing. Even if your need for counseling support has long ended, it is now a good time to seek some professional assistance in helping you explore and discuss your child's violent conception as he begins to ask the expected questions about how he came to be brought into this world. This is especially important if your rape was publicized and members of your community are aware that your child resulted from this violence.

Didn't Dad Want Me?

*My child's father left when I was
pregnant. He lives nearby, although
we never see him. He is completely
uninterested in my son, who, frankly,
receives a lot of attention for his
handsome appearance and great
athletic skills. Now that he is twelve,
he is beginning to ask with more
seriousness why his father rejected
him. What do I say that I have not
already said a thousand times before?*

You have no doubt assured your son
that his father's lack of interest has
nothing to do with him and everything
to do with his father's limitations. Your
son has asked this question time and
time again because he has probably
thought about this a lot. Now that he
is approaching adolescence, you can
begin to give him more information
that you might not have appropriately
offered in the past. For example, his
father probably has a problem with
commitment in all areas of his life.
If this is the case, you might now be
able to say to your son that Dad has
real trouble committing to most other
people—not just him. As an athlete,
your son is familiar with what coaches
demand: dedication and commitment.
Emphasize that he has not inherited his
father's limitations. Give him examples
of how he has shown commitment and
reassure him that you are there to help
him develop into the kind of man he
wants to be.

"My Daughter Makes Up Stories about Her Father. . . ."

*Despite my best efforts to
positively and realistically discuss my decision not to marry
her father, who incidentally had
a major drinking problem, my
six-year-old daughter has created
elaborate fantasies about him that
are so far from the truth it's scary.
What should I do?*

Your concerns are shared by many
other single mothers who express worry
and fear when their children conjure up
detailed, unrealistic portrayals of their
biological fathers, even if they have
never met them. But don't become
overly concerned because it is quite
normal that fantasy plays an important
part in every child's life. Young children
have vivid imaginations that they use to
provide themselves with the entertainment and stimulation they need. This
is why children of this age may have
imaginary friends or pets or talk about
taking trips to places like the moon or
Candy Land.

Rather than immediately trying to
correct or change your child's story,
try adopting an interested and accepting attitude. When your child claims
that her daddy is an ice cream man
and drives all over town giving children
ice cream, respond with "You are pretending what a fun job your daddy has!
Wouldn't it be great to ride on an ice
cream truck all day long and get to eat
all the ice cream you want!" She doesn't
need to know for now that her father is
a CPA with so many drunken driving
convictions he's not permitted to drive
a car, let alone an ice cream truck!

As time goes on and your child
matures, her interest in fantasy
naturally becomes replaced with a
growing interest in day-to-day reality.
This is when your child will want to
learn more facts about her biological
father.

"My Daughter Pretends Her Father Was in a Car Crash. . . ."

I overheard my teenage daughter tell her friends that her father was killed in a car accident in California. We recently moved here from out of state, and everyone believed her. The truth is we really don't know where her bilogical father is. I doubt he has ever been to California. What would prompt her to make up a story like that?

There are probably many reasons your daughter told her new friends this untrue story. First, she is new in town and probably is trying hard to connect with her new classmates. Possibly she feels awkward and insecure. When the subject of her father came up, probably very innocently, she made up a story designed to quash any further questions on that topic, which proves what a quick thinker she is! Remember, too, that teenage girls have something of a flair for the dramatic, and this story certainly would rate four stars for drama.

Yet, you do not want to encourage her to go through life making up "interesting" stories about herself. At a quiet moment when you can be reasonably sure you will not be interrupted, talk to your daughter about what you overheard. Assure her that you were not eavesdropping, but you think that her new friends' questions probably surprised her and she most likely did not know what to say. Explain to her that these other young people probably did not mean to embarrass her—they were just curious.

Your daughter would probably welcome the opportunity to learn how to deal with this the next time questions about her dad arise. Tell her that many of her new friends are being raised in single-parent homes, and nobody would have been shocked or surprised by the truth. Help her rehearse or practice responding with something like "My mother and father could not stay together happily." Let her know that saying "My father has lived in a lot of places, and we really do not see too much of him" would have been perfectly all right.

You can also reveal more information as the opportunity arises. Your daughter might welcome knowing some new information about her father to feel more comfortable. Make sure you share what you can remember about his interests, early family life, or work life. This information will give her a feeling of connection—for example, when you let her know that her fabulous math skills obviously come from her father (particularly when you're still counting on your fingers to balance your checkbook).

Consider the possibility, too, that your daughter made up that story about her father being dead because she is really angry about him not being around. If, when you speak to her, such anger is apparent, you must help her find ways to come to terms with the absence of a father in her life. This may mean just talking it out quietly or having her speak with a counselor. Often, schools have staff-facilitated support groups that allow children to discuss their family situations or crises with their peers; check into this, too.

"My Son Pretends His Dad Died in the War . . ."

My six-year-old son told his teacher that his father was killed in a war far, far away. Absolutely not true.

I think he made this up from all the media coverage on the conflicts in the Middle East. I have never even mentioned his father to him because he has never asked. What would make him create a crazy story like this?

By not discussing his father with him, you have created something of an information void. Your son's story is his way of filling this void. He needs to know about his father, and since you have not brought the subject up, your son has tried to meet his need for information by creating what sounds to him like a perfectly logical explanation. Maybe now is the best time to start talking with your son about his father.

You might break the ice with something like this: "I'll bet when you go to Paul's (here you would name any friend who has a father living at home) house and his daddy plays football with you that you wonder about your own father." From this starting point, you can explain how you and your son came to be together as a family.

When Your Child Never Brings Up the Subject

My seven-year-old daughter has never once asked me about her father. He left us when she was a baby, and I was devastated. I try to bring the subject up because I know she must be curious. Why do you think she never wants to discuss her father?

Some children are not as curious about certain topics as others. Maybe because you've attempted to bring this up in the past, she doesn't sense any secrecy and has enough information to satisfy her. On the other hand, children are wonderfully intuitive, and your daughter may perceive that this is a painful topic for you. For this reason, she denies to you that it is important to her. Tell her, as you have been doing, that you know she must be curious about her father. Look for opportunities to bring her father into the conversation. For example, as you flip around the television channels, casually remark how much her father loved Westerns or football or whatever is accurate. These simple remarks let her know that it is okay for you to talk about Dad, that you won't burst into tears, and that it is definitely okay for her to have questions about him. Keep things as positive as possible, stressing his good qualities. She will no doubt ask why he left. Explain to her that raising a little girl is a big job and that her father was not ready to take on such an important job. He left her with you knowing that you would always love her and take good care of her.

Can't Dad Get Better and See Me Too?

My son is seven years old. His father is now living in a halfway house thousands of miles from us in recovery from alcohol and substance abuse. He met our son once several years ago, but his addictions have kept him from having any relationship with our little boy. I have explained to our son that his father's illness keeps him from being here for him. My son wants to know why Dad can't get better and still be with him, if only for visits?

This is a pretty logical question from a seven-year-old boy. He sees you doing many things even when you have a cold or the flu; so it just seems natural that someone could recover from addiction and still play video games with him or come to his soccer game. Explain to your son that addiction is not like the time you were sick with the flu and still packed his lunch and made sure his homework was done. Tell your little boy that addiction makes it impossible for adults to do the things they are expected to do and want to do. Recovering from addiction, it should be explained, takes every bit of energy adults have. Emphasize that his father really wishes he could be with him, but now he just cannot. Your little boy should be made aware that his father's residence in a halfway house is a hopeful sign that his father is trying to get well. Encourage your son to communicate with his father by letter, if this is possible. If not, your son can keep a box or scrapbook containing things he would like his dad to see or know about when the time comes that Dad is well enough to be some small part of his life.

When Children Want to Search for Their Birth Father

My sons' biological father disappeared about five years ago. He has many problems, including substance abuse. We have not heard from him since my younger boy was nine. Both my sons are suddenly obsessed with finding him, and they talk about this all the time. I don't know if I would want to find him if he even wants to be found or what the boys and I would do if, indeed, we did find him. What do you think is really going on in their minds?

More likely than not, your sons' interest in finding their father has more to do with curiosity and concern than anything else. They are both now at an age when they realize the hazards of their father's substance abuse and, with good cause, probably worry about his safety and health. They are also at an age when they are beginning to think of themselves as young men and are naturally curious to know more about their father as a man.

Anyone can search the Internet and discover a lot about any individual. It would probably not be too difficult to locate the boys' biological father, and frankly, if he were interested in finding you, this would also not be difficult. You also have a network of shared friends and family who are fairly certain where each of you may now be living. The problem is not finding their father, but rather what his reaction might be if the boys try to reconnect with him. Your sons could be hurt if you found their father and he was unable to see them because he was in treatment or incarcerated or unwilling to see them out of anger, embarrassment, or denial. Drug and alcohol problems may mean that their dad is really down and out and could look to your children for emotional and financial support. Your children have probably developed an idealized expectation of their father and may well be disappointed at finding that their image of Dad is quite different from reality.

All mothers, of course, need to monitor their children's Internet use, but you need to be especially vigilant. If they are teenagers and do search the Web without your supervision, you should expect them to at least attempt an Internet search, and you will probably need to discuss this and your concerns about it with them before they try it.

Compromise with your sons by contacting relatives or friends of your sons' father and asking if they know of his whereabouts and can offer some indication of his present circumstances. Do they feel he might be receptive to some contact with his sons? If his friends or relatives feel he would be receptive, perhaps it would be best if your sons wrote to him rather than trying to arrange a visit. If their father's whereabouts are not known to family or friends, you can at least alert these people to your sons' interest in a reunion of some sort. You can certainly assure your sons that if they still want to find their father when they are older that you will support their decision no matter what. But finding someone who may not wish to be found is an adult decision and one they can make only when they are grown-up and on their own.

When Your Child Calls Someone Else Daddy

My children's biological father drifts in and out of their lives. They call their biological father by his first name, Howard. They call my boyfriend, who has lived with us for the past three years, Daddy. This has just sort of evolved, and I am wondering if I should let well enough alone or whether I should insist that they stop calling him Daddy. It is not very likely that we will get married, although I think we will continue to live together.

Your children have given your boyfriend the name that probably best describes his role and place in their

lives. He is obviously more of a daddy to them than their absent, neglectful father. He is the one who tells them bedtime stories, plays with them, eats meals with them, washes their clothes, helps provide for them, and performs other "daddy-type" duties. You are right to be sensitive, however, to what this name might mean to them.

There is no reason for them to stop calling him Daddy, but do explain to them that this is a pet name for this very special person in their lives. In most situations, children call their biological father Daddy, Dad, or Pop. Calling your boyfriend Daddy as their pet nickname does not necessarily make him their father. Your boyfriend need not have a permanent commitment to you, but you should discuss with him whether he has a permanent commitment to your children—one he would honor even if you and he broke up. If not, it is important to tell the children that their relationship with "Daddy," although wonderful, might not last forever. You don't need to share the details of why your relationship may not be a lasting one. What's important is to let them know that if this relationship is not permanent then it is okay for them not to assume he will be a part of their lives forever.

Why Can't Daddy Take Care of Me?

I had a long relationship with a man who has a serious drinking problem. I left him for good after my son was conceived because I did not want this alcoholic chaos in my child's life. This man's life is still in a shambles, and he can barely take care of himself. When he is well and able, I encourage him to visit our four-year-old under my supervision. My son adores him and asked me the other day why his daddy cannot be around more and help take care of him. How do I begin to answer my son's questions?

Begin by telling your son how much his father cares for him and how much he wishes that he were able to spend more time with him. Inform your child that his father has a disease called alcoholism that makes him too sick most of the time to take care of a little boy. When your son asks if his father will ever be better, tell the truth by saying that you hope so but do not know for sure. Encourage your son to hope for his father's sobriety while at the same time reassuring him that you will always be there for him.

Why Doesn't Daddy Show Up When He Says He Will?

I am a single mother outside of marriage. The father of my child refused to have anything to do with me after he found out I was pregnant. I wanted a child more

than I wanted him; I kept the baby and dumped him. Now that my daughter is almost two, he suddenly contacts me and wants to see her and me. The first time we arranged a meeting at the local park, he never showed up. The next time he was an hour late. I would like my daughter to at least meet him and have some relationship with him. How do I handle his irresponsible behavior?

The best way to handle irresponsible or inappropriate behavior is to respond to it as responsibly and appropriately as you can. The next time your child's father calls, remind him of the importance of being on time as he promised. Allow him a thirty-minute grace period and then leave and implement Plan B. Plan B is whatever you decided to do ahead of time in case he did not show up or was ridiculously late. Try meeting him one more time. If he is a no-show but calls again, suggest that next time he call you from a nearby restaurant or coffee shop when he arrives. Then he can wait the five or ten minutes until your arrival. If you do not hear from him within a half hour or so on the day and time you both selected, leave your house and go enjoy the sunshine. Do not wait by the telephone for him to call.

When Dad Suddenly Appears

My child was conceived with a man who, despite my pathetic and desperate pleas at the time, left us for parts unknown. I had explained to my daughter, now age eight, that he was simply not ready for the big job of taking care of a little girl. Suddenly he appeared on our doorstep one day announcing that he was ready to be "everything a daddy should be." What do I do now? How do I explain when she asks why he has suddenly returned?

Before you explain anything, insist that you and your daughter's father meet alone and discuss exactly what he means by "everything a daddy should be." Assuming that you have established sole custody, his rights to spend time with your daughter are under your control. Your concern should be to allow him to develop a relationship with your daughter, becoming a special adult friend to her, without inflicting the double whammy of abandoning her again. He will need to understand that there may be now or in the future other men in your life who will also be important to your daughter. You have not been in suspended animation waiting for him to return. He will need to abide by the house rules and support the values you have been working hard to teach.

This relationship should begin with the three of you spending an hour or two together sharing an activity like visiting the zoo or seeing a movie. You need to know for yourself that this man is reliable in both his judgment and behavior before you allow him time alone with your daughter. In many ways, he is a

stranger, and you should exercise the same care you normally would if any other new person wanted to be part of your daughter's life. It is not unheard-of for fathers like this to decide to take ownership of their children and literally kidnap them. Better to be overly cautious than risk exposing your child to trauma and danger.

At the same time, you need to explain to your daughter that adults sometimes realize that they have made mistakes and try to correct those mistakes. In her father's case, he now feels that he made a mistake leaving her and is trying to make things right. Explain gently also that sometimes adults can know they made a mistake but not be able to fix it. Tell her that both of you will try together to build a relationship with Dad, but it is up to him to show by his behavior that he would like to be part of your lives. Make sure you also let her know that you are aware that she must feel quite confused and surprised by what has happened. Assure her that you understand and share her surprise, but at the same time, you will do all you can to make sure that she is well taken care of and protected.

IF YOU DON'T KNOW THE FATHER'S IDENTITY

My child was conceived during a time in my life when my behavior was not exactly exemplary. Fortunately for me, my three-year-old son was born healthy, and I am lucky enough not to have gotten AIDS or killed myself with drinking and drugs. But soon my child will ask who his father is. I do not know. It could be either of two men. What should I tell my child?

You need to decide for yourself who the father was and appoint him in your mind and heart as the "designated dad" before you can discuss this with your child. Presumably, your former sex partners are long gone, and the chances of one claiming paternity are slim. Maybe a good start is asking yourself whom you would have chosen as the biological father. If you spent considerable time with one man and had only one or two encounters with the other, it is most likely that your regular lover was the father of your child. Of course, without a test there are no guarantees, but based on your son's appearance and disposition, who is the more likely candidate? Does your son's sweet nature and pitch-black hair allow you to discard as the candidate the ill-tempered blond surfer with whom you spent one very unforgettable night?

Make your best decision and stick with your choice. When your son begins to ask about his father, tell him what you know about his "designated dad."

But add, too, that you and this person did not love each other the way grownups who parent together should. It's okay to say that you didn't know him very well. Assure your son that your meeting was special because your son was the result of this event, but point out that his dad was not destined to have a larger role in either of your lives.

When Dad Was a Forgettable One-Night Stand

I conceived twin girls with a man I met in a bar at a convention in Las Vegas very soon after my divorce. At the time, I was bored and a little down and thought I was treating myself to a little fling because I had no intention of

seeing him again. When I realized I was pregnant, I knew that I had not let this happen by total accident. I had real longings for children for many years. My girls are the greatest, but now that they are four, the daddy questions are starting for real. How do I explain to my children that Dad was nothing more than a pickup in a bar?

Begin with the most obvious—tell them how very much they were wanted. You can tell your girls that sometimes grownups do not know exactly what they want until it starts happening to them. Tell them you were far from home and feeling lonesome. You met a man and shared a very special adventure and made two beautiful babies together. Tell them that things in life happen for a purpose and that you met this man for one and only one purpose—to create the little girls you love so much. Discuss him more as a useful part of getting your heart's desire rather than the lounge lizard he most likely was. When they push for more information, it's okay to tell them that you really don't know that much about him. Do emphasize, however, that you know that the most important thing about him was the part he played in helping you to make them.

IF YOUR CHILD WAS ADOPTED OR CONCEIVED VIA DONOR INSEMINATION

My three-year-old daughter is adopted. I have used this word with her since the day I brought her home at nine months. When she asks me why her parents gave her up, what am I going to say?

All adopted children ask this question in one form or another many times over. At your child's age, simply say that some mommies and daddies are not ready to take on such a big job as raising children. This is a good beginning. Also, be sure to let your child know how important birth parents are and how they help those who are physically unable to have children become parents. Emphasize over and over that their help makes many people—especially you—very, very happy. But more importantly, because some adopted children were given up by single mothers, be sure to let your daughter know that you want to be her mommy always.

What Is a Father?

Many thoughtful single mothers have answered the question "Who is my father?" in unexpected ways. Yet most moms—whether donor-inseminated or impregnated by someone they know—reject the notion that providing sperm in whatever way automatically makes a man a father. To them, "father" is a title to be earned by love, devotion, sacrifice, and plain hard work. In response to the "daddy" question, some tell their children that they have no father. In answering the question "What would you say to those who think it's wrong to tell your child he or she has no father," one donor-inseminated mom suggested teaching a child the definition of the word "father." Then she would tell her that "I wanted you, this is what I went through to have you, and so this is what you've got. Be grateful that you are here and loved very much."

Others respond differently, depending upon the circumstance. For example, some refer to the child's grandfather as a father because he has been a loving, guiding, nurturing man in their lives and will continue to be until the day he dies. Still other women might tell their children that their new husband or partner is the children's father because this is the responsibility that he has freely chosen.

If you were donor-inseminated, it is important, just as when children are adopted, to incorporate this important piece of information into the fabric of your child's life literally from the day you bring the baby home from the hospital. You can never say too often or too early how much you love your child and how much you wanted him. Emphasize the planning and care that went into his conception.

Who Was My Daddy?

When your child begins to ask questions in earnest at about age three, tell him that you knew you wanted to be a mother more than anything else, and you went to a doctor who helped you have a baby by using the seed from a specially selected man. As your child grows older, you can give more information on the donor's background, which is furnished at the time of the insemination. Some donor inseminated mothers use special, affectionate terms for this donor like "miracle maker" or "special helper" when discussing with their children how they were conceived.

When the Donor Sperm Came from a Friend

My son was conceived using donor sperm from a friend of mine. There were so many qualities, not to mention good looks, which I admired about him. I wanted to have his child but knew we could not make each other happy as husband and wife. My son knows that Jake is his father as well as a special friend of the family. But now that he is eight, he is beginning to ask why Jake and I are not married. What should I say?

This is a perfect example of how practical and easy it is to tell the truth. Your son can be told exactly what you have just told us. There are many things about Jake to admire, and it is beneficial to your son to elaborate on these at every opportunity. Mention Jake's honesty, sense of humor, or whatever qualities you like best. Tell your son that you think Jake is a handsome man. Mention his terrific smile and big muscles. It is then important to explain that not all grownups who like and admire each other love each other in the special way husbands and wives do. Tell your son that both you and Jake knew that you could not make each other happy as a married couple. Tell your son also that you and Jake are glad that you realized this before you tried to be married and made each other unhappy.

"My Daughter Tells Me She Is a Freak. . . ."

I was donor-inseminated by an anonymous donor because I was ready to be a mother but had not found the right man to share my life and the big commitment of parenthood. My daughter, now age thirteen, has been told all of this over the years. Suddenly, however, she is very upset. She tells me she is a freak of nature, and she hates me for ruining her life.

Every mother who has ever raised a daughter has been told countless times for countless reasons that mom has ruined her life. The reasons range from not being allowed to get a tattoo to insisting that she do her homework. Forget the "ruining her life" barb. This is normal teenage girl stuff and is best ignored.

Just as you have let her know the facts of life as they relate to how she came to be, it is now time for a few more lessons in reality. Teenagers, like all children, need limits and boundaries. You need to tell her exactly how it is and not get caught up in the turmoil and drama many teenagers like to create.

Tell your daughter that having her was the most important thing in your life. You decided that donor insemination was the best way for you to bring her into the world as your child to love. This is how it is, and you are certainly not going to debate the wisdom of your choice or listen to her refer to herself as a freak of nature. Tell her straight out that she should just be glad that she is here. You certainly are.

I Want a Dad to Beat Up That Bully's Dad!

My seven-year-old came home from school very upset and sporting a black eye. The boys on the playground were bragging about whose dad was the toughest, and the bully said he'd beat up my son because he has no dad to protect him. Rather than walk away, my son went for him. Suppose there is a next time?

"Bully" is a good word to describe this kid, since this situation has little to do with your home situation. Use this as a learning experience for your son so he will know what to do next time.

Explain to your son that a bully is someone who feels unhappy or unloved, which makes him want to hurt others. Compassionate as your child may be, let him know that this still is unfair because the victim of the teasing or roughness could begin to believe that he or she deserves this treatment, which isn't so. No one deserves to be treated that way.

Rehearse with your son for the next time by letting him play the bully's role while you play your son. When he gets obnoxious, stare back at him fiercely and announce "Stop, now!" and walk away. Encourage your son to try reversing roles.

Don't turn this event into a major crisis, but you might want to add that "I wonder if that boy has someone in his life who is mean to him" to encourage empathy on your son's part.

IF YOUR CHILD'S FATHER HAS PASSED AWAY

Many single moms, especially those who have experienced an angry and nasty divorce, have fantasized about the death of their former partners. Part of this fantasy has to do with the dignity and respect shown a widow in contrast to the indignities many divorced women face. More of the fantasy is about the desire to live your life without the interference and rancor many ex-husbands or ex-partners still bring into our lives. Of course, the fantasy stops being "fun" when our rational minds consider the impact a parent's death would have on our children.

No event is more devastating to a child than to lose a parent. Even if the presence and care of that parent is already "lost" to the child because of substance abuse, emotional neglect, incar-

ceration, or simply personal choice, your child has lost even the hope that their father might someday be even a small part of his life. Loss of hope is always a terrible tragedy. Your child will need much added love and support to face this terrible loss. You will be shocked by how this man's virtues will be extolled and his memory enhanced by his passing. It may take much maturity on your part to keep quiet about this man's many heartbreaking shortcomings.

Your child's father may have been an active and integral part of your child's life. You may have counted upon his financial and emotional support as well as his "second set of hands" to help raise the children. Much as you will miss him and mourn his passing, you no longer are in love with him. Your children love him dearly, and his passing will mean significant unwelcome changes in their daily lives. You and your children will be in very different emotional places. You will be scrambling to figure out the practical everyday solutions to this new set of circumstances; the children will have suffered a terrible life blow. Resist your natural impulse to point out that you are still around, as always, to take care of them. This is cold comfort. Reassuring them that you will not die and leave them is not honest and simply flies in the face of the reality they have just experienced. This will be a time to reassure them that they will be taken care of if something does happen to you. More details about how exactly this would unfold in case of your death may now need to be shared.

The death of a parent, no matter what the circumstances, is a compelling reason to consider family counseling. Grieving is constant and without any schedule or timetable. Keep these suggestions in mind as you help your child face this loss.

If You Were Married

♦ Give your children a sense of their father as the person you knew him to be. If they had a positive, ongoing relationship with him, they probably already know he was a baseball fanatic or movie buff. Share with them what you know about the positive aspects of his character and beliefs. If you need to be selective, this is okay. His flaws are meaningless now anyway.

♦ Share the details of your courtship and marriage with your children in ways that make them feel the joy you both experienced. Include the mundane details like who wore what to the wedding. Aunt Sophie's purple chiffon dress or Uncle Milt's glow-in-the-dark tie are what family history is all about.

♦ Your children should have an age-appropriate understanding of how their father died. Give them socially acceptable ways to answer questions others might ask. Avoid telling the children that there are "family secrets," but stress that everyone does not need to know everything. Idle curiosity and genuine concern are two totally different reasons why people ask questions. Help your children recognize the difference.

♦ Emphasize that their father did not choose to leave them. Remember to say often how much their Dad loved them.

♦ Be prepared for occasional episodes of inappropriate behavior or outright defiance. Children often express sadness by acting out rather than by tears or silence. Encourage lots of active outdoor activity. Keep family routines stable and make sure their diet stays healthy.

If You Were Not Married

♦ Tell your children the reasons why you two did not marry. Brutal honesty is not required. True statements like "We were just not right for each other" or "We found we did not want to spend the rest of our lives together" are enough. Practice ways to answer questions that might come up about who their father was and how he died.

♦ Share with your children the happy details of your relationship. Talk about how you met and the kinds of things you enjoyed doing together.

♦ Don't portray their father as a complete loser even if he left you penniless or died in prison. This man is still your children's father, and it will not escape them that they are biologically half of him. They need a positive view of him; so try being generous and creative. Point out his most interesting or redeeming trait. If he had a dazzling smile, a knack for fixing things, or a terrific knuckle ball pitch, let your children know.

♦ Consider keeping something tangible to help the children remember their dad. For example, if he loved a particular singer or musical group, you might wish to keep a CD or picture of that artist or group in your home. Your children may find comfort planting a tree or flowers in his memory.

17

The Testosterone Challenge— Raising Boys with No Man Around the House

Most mental health professionals dispute the notion that boys require constant male companionship and male guidance to grow up healthy. These professionals believe that either parent can successfully raise boys. In fact, having a father at home who does not provide the necessary qualities of a healthy male role model can do more harm than good, according to the experts and authors Olga Silverstein and Beth Rashbaum. In their book *The Courage to Raise Good Men*, the authors write that "The assumption that the world is full of good men, or that any man is better than any woman to help a boy, is ridiculous. To saddle boys with the wrong kind of men will simply help create the kind of men we now deplore, men who are overly competitive and unable to form intimate ties."

THE MALE AGGRESSION FACTOR

My infant son and I spend lots of time in the park on weekends. I definitely see a difference between how the little boys and little girls play. The boys are so active! It is not unusual for the pushing and shoving to get out of hand. Often the mothers have asked them to stop, but sometimes the fathers need to step in and tell the boys to stop. Sometimes the fathers don't even have to say anything. They just walk closer to the group, and the boys seem to instantly get the message. With no dad in my son's life, how will my son learn what fathers seem better able to teach? Is my son at risk for acting out and getting into serious trouble?

Your son is not at greater risk for anything as the child of a single parent. Single mothers of sons need to be aware, however, that dealing with those expected bursts of male aggression, like the pushing and shoving on the playground, will be an integral part of your parenting responsibilities. Boys do behave differently. These differences are all about the Y chromosome and have nothing to do with being raised by a single mom. Without a father in the picture to rein in these "boy behaviors," your job is to set limits. Later on, your son will meet men who by example teach responsible and appropriate ways to deal with male aggression. Your parenting will set the stage so that your son is ready to learn this important life lesson from "fatherly figures" like coaches and teachers.

Start by making clear what is appropriate behavior in your home. Hitting, punching, and kicking certainly will be against family rules. Discuss alternatives to aggressive behavior so your son can make more positive choices next time. Spanking may work for the moment, but it certainly gives your son the powerful message that acting out your feelings is acceptable, as long as you are the one in charge. Limit exposure to violent games and media images. Take every opportunity to praise positive male role models and seek out opportunities for your son to spend time in organized activities directed by such men. Stress using words rather

SINGLE MOM OF NOTE

Chris Affleck, Mother of Film Star Ben Affleck

When Ben Affleck showed up for the Academy Awards where he accepted an Oscar for *Good Will Hunting,* guess who was his date? No, not Gwyneth, Minnie, J. Lo, or his latest costar. His mom, Chris, accompanied him to the ceremony.

Because of his father's drinking problem, Affleck's mom, a schoolteacher, raised Ben and younger brother Casey alone. Close to his mother and brother, Ben told a *USA Weekend* reporter how he credits his single mother for his "female side" and raising him to learn empathy, consideration, manners, lack of pretension, and humility.

"My mother was such a sweet, kind woman; it gave me a sense of responsibility for women," Ben says.

than actions to convey feelings. As your son gets older, explain that aggression only leads to more aggression. Help him acquire additional alternative ways of dealing with hostile feelings by inviting frequent conversations about what your son is feeling and experiencing.

THE OEDIPAL THING

My four-year-old son tells me all the time that he loves me and wants to marry me. Is it true that all normal boys go through this developmental stage during which they want their fathers to die so they can marry their mothers? How is my son going to get through this normal stage when his father is not part of our lives?

This is the oedipal drama, which is quite different from developmental stages like toilet training or weaning. Mental health professionals who believe in the importance of the oedipal drama contend that the conflicts a little boy experiences when he wants to marry his mother and somehow get rid of the father must be resolved. Competition between father and son during activities like "pretend wrestling" convince the son that he will never triumph over Dad. The son then turns his attention to other women and begins an emotionally satisfying romantic life. Research has not substantiated claims that an unresolved oedipal issue will lead to years of therapy.

It is also true that nearly every mom has been pledged the undying love of her preschool son. Play activities are how children grow emotionally. Little boys often pretend to be a warrior carrying Mom off to his secret kingdom or declare themselves the king and tell Mom she is now a queen. These play activities are often accompanied by smothering kisses and proposing marriage to Mom. These play activities result in getting Mom's undivided attention, which only increases the likelihood that these activities, as well as the hugs, kisses, and marriage proposals, will be repeated. The romantic behavior is nothing more than a little boy's attempt to mimic and try out behaviors he sees other men do. Young boys often see media images of kissing and hugging as well as proposals of marriage. Family gatherings as well as almost any public place will give a young boy ample opportunity to witness adult romantic behavior.

Your role as a mother is simply to reassure your son of your love, while making it clear that you love him the way a mommy loves a son. For a little boy, discovering that Mom will not be his wife is part of figuring out how the world works and what his place in the world will be. Coming to this understanding does not require a dad as a constant presence in your son's life.

ANY DAD IS BETTER THAN NO DAD

Nonsense. A bad father can do untold damage to a son by being a model of poor behavior. If his father would be neglectful, physically or emotional abusive, or just plain unloving, your son is better off without him. If you love and affirm your son and respect the fact that being male makes his life different from yours (just as, for example, being of a different generation affects both your son and your daughter), you will be a far better parent than a bad father. Of course, your son, like your daughter, will mourn his lack of a healthy relationship with his father—but this grief is unlikely to overwhelm him. We cannot offer our children perfection.

WHEN THERE'S NO REGULAR MALE ROLE MODEL

What happens when boys don't have one single, constant male to do things with and fashion themselves after?

This might actually be a good thing. Your son will not have just one role model, but the opportunity to have many. He will pick and choose and take for himself the behaviors, habits, and beliefs of the men he encounters during his growing-up years. The men from whom he selects will be influenced, in part, by the kind of men you allow into his life. Some men, like coaches and teachers, are the luck of the draw. Some will be friends you introduce to him.

If you are there to guide and support, the best parts of the men in your son's life will become part of your son, like a lovingly pieced-together patchwork quilt. Some of the pieces are tiny—like how your son's band teacher may be the one to teach him how to knot his tie. Other patches are part of a larger design where the influence of many men can be seen—like your son's respect for individual differences. This piecing together gives your son a richness of experience and opportunities that many men lack. Your son will be conscious of this process as he matures, although he may not talk to you about it. By the time he reaches the early to middle teen years, he will begin to share with you why he admires those who have impressed him.

WHAT A GOOD MALE ROLE MODEL DOES

Boys derive important benefits from the bond with adult men. Good male role models help teach boys to become respectful, caring, and productive men. Good male role models share these essential qualities.

◆ *Encourage independence.* Because men generally are bigger "risk-takers" and less protective than women, boys benefit from the opportunity for exploration and exposure to assertive behavior.

◆ *Broaden your son's world.* Male role models can be a link to the outside

world through their jobs, leisure activities, and interests or hobbies. A young boy's horizons are expanded when he gets the male perspective on issues and ideas.

◆ *Offer support to you.* Like any parent, sometimes you need a break. Your son's male role model may be one of the people who give you that time by yourself.

◆ *Look at life from the male perspective.* Based on their own feelings surrounding their experiences at your son's age, good male role models can provide insight into the complexities of male behavior. Unless you had lots of brothers, you will be amazed, for example, to discover how an otherwise restrained man can so instantly share the glee your son experiences making weird noises at random times.

WHERE TO FIND ROLE MODELS

Your community may have local programs where men can serve as mentors to young boys. While many men volunteer for such programs for all the right reasons, you need to investigate all programs and participants carefully before allowing your son to join. Big Brothers/Big Sisters has chapters in many cities and towns. Your local Y, athletic club, and community center are also good sources. Find out about school- or community-related activities where men help coach ball teams and sponsor other events. Let your son's interests dictate his outside activities. While physical exercise should be part of every child's daily life, participation in organized sports is not mandatory. Your son can just as easily learn the value of teamwork and sportsmanship by pursuing other interests, including music and art. The unique community you create for your family as a single mother is the best source of male role models for your son. Don't overlook friends, relatives, or neighbors who have something special to offer. Look to make your own "family community" grow. The man down the street who can fix anything could certainly teach your son valuable skills. The amateur pilot next door with the passion for flying could certainly be an inspiration to your young airplane enthusiast. Your retired neighbor who works so patiently with such outstanding results on his vegetable garden has life lessons to share which few men can match. Role models don't have to be constantly available to spend individual time with your son. Your son can learn much just by observing and, of course, having the opportunity to talk about what he sees and experiences with his most important and influential role model—you!

WHAT TO DO IF YOUR SON LIKES TO PLAY DRESS-UP

Playing dress-up is normal for preschool children; so you don't need to worry. However, if you'd like to keep your child out of your closet, take a trip to the nearest thrift shop or attend a yard sale and buy lots of big shirts, baggy suits, and ties for your son to play dress-up. Uniforms are great, too, especially because little boys love to pretend to be policemen or soldiers. For a few dollars, you can fill a box with stuff that will keep your son busy for hours.

While I am putting on my makeup for work in the morning, my two-year-old son stands next to me applying lipstick, powder, and anything else he can get his hands on. Do I need to be worried that he'll be gender confused or something like that?

Not at all. Your son is mimicking your bathroom routine in the morning—combing hair, brushing teeth, and, in your case, putting on makeup. All children do this at an early age because this is how they learn. By the time he reaches kindergarten, he will naturally outgrow this, even though it's not uncommon for first and second graders to find amusement playing around with Mom's makeup. However, if you want to get a head start on defining the differences between male and female secondary sex characteristics, try this:

◆ Explain to your son that little girls grow up to be women or mommies and little boys grow up to be men or daddies. Daddies and men don't wear makeup, but they do have "guy stuff."

◆ Set out a little basket of male toiletries for your son to use in the bathroom while you're fixing your face. Fill it with a mock razor, shaving cream, comb, toothbrush, and maybe a bottle of "aftershave" (two drops of cologne mixed with water). Place it on the sink or counter next to where you keep your cosmetics. Announce to your son that he is to use this stuff and not yours.

◆ Stop worrying and enjoy your child's antics. Besides, you never know if there will come a time when your grown-up son will be too busy to visit his mom and will need to be blackmailed with all those old makeup stories!

DON'T WORRY, HE'LL BE A STAND-UP GUY

Many single mothers report concern over their son's sitting down to use the potty. Not to worry. Chances are your child will outgrow this when he realizes that it's easier and more fun to urinate while standing.

HOW TO CONNECT WITH YOUR SON AS HE GROWS

Talking to your boy as he grows older can be challenging because he doesn't want to reveal his vulnerability. Our culture has taught boys to fear weakness, and so they try to solve problems on their own. We're advised to "leave him alone, he doesn't want to talk" and "let him shoot a few hoops, he'll be fine" and reminded that "boys will be boys," when we vent our frustration over the struggle to connect to our sons. Your son may talk to you in one or two-word responses only and then say that "I'm fine, leave me alone." Moms everywhere may shrug their shoulders and simply walk away. But this is the time when parents should do the very opposite. Here is where we should offer help and advice to build communication with our adolescent sons.

RAISING A HEALTHY SON

Here are some comforting and reassuring thoughts to help you raise a physically, emotionally, and spiritually healthy son.

1. No matter how hard it is for you to understand your son, accept your son's differences from you, such as the way he views things, plays, or responds to problems. Boys grow and mature at a slower rate than girls; be patient, too, about his development. Teach him your values, but let him express them uniquely. He's a male and will often respond to emotional situations somewhat differently than you.

2. Give up worrying about whether your son is missing out on anything by not having Dad around. Stop wishing his father or any father was around to see his antics, and start enjoying your baby, toddler, or school-age child now!

3. Believe in yourself as a strong and confident guide for your son. Your confidence and positive attitude are contagious.

4. Teach your young son that it is okay to be raised just by Mom. Reading to a preschool boy from the many children's books featuring animal families raised by mommy mice, cows, or chickens is an easy start. Look to connect in friendship with other single-parent families.

5. At the same time, try not to avoid "daddy stuff" totally. It's okay to read stories about all kinds of families to give your child a realistic world perspective and to encourage tolerance for diversity. It is also important to value by your words and actions all types of human relationships because we all must learn to live peacefully together.

6. Regardless of how you became a single mother, never make your son the "man of the house." True, you want to guide him toward manhood, but your son cannot be responsible now for things adult men are supposed to do. Your child is not your confidant, your knight in shining armor, or your rescuer. His job is to be a child.

    Especially important for the newly widowed or divorced is to correct others if they ask your son, "Are you taking good care of Mommy?" or "How does it feel being the man around the house?" Tell them quietly and privately that "Just because his father is no longer here with us, doesn't mean my son should take on any adult responsibilities. Children have a right to be children for as long as they can."

7. Try not to have negative attitudes toward men, even if you became a single mother under the most excruciating circumstances. Be sure you resolve any issues about men and relationships. If you are still angry at men, find an appropriate outlet to vent those feelings. When you look at your child and see his father's face, it's okay to get a little emotional. After all, if this man gave you anything of value, you're looking at him. Let your son know how important he is to you regardless of how you feel about his biological father.

8. Point out the positive qualities in men you see on a day-to-day basis. This means that if you're buying your son baseball cleats and the salesman is especially attentive, point this trait out by mentioning what a helpful person he is. Even if you can hardly find anything nice to say about your son's own dad, find something. For example, if you know that his father liked vanilla ice cream, you might mention something like "Isn't that neat that you like vanilla ice cream? Your father's favorite flavor is vanilla, too!"

9. Help your child learn about "guy stuff," but don't sweat the details. As long as you make sure you don't make him feel uncomfortable asking about jock straps or standing up to urinate, if something's important to him, he'll ask you—or a man in his life.

10. Role models are important and will be best found in the community you help create for your family. Help guide your son toward men who can teach him important life lessons.

As your child matures, investigate activities of special interest to your son. In strictly male activities, like Boy Scouts, don't be intimidated by sponsored events such as father-son boat races or picnics. Let the group leader know that with the number of single-parent families these days, it would be more appropriate if the organization sponsored parent-child events.

11. Make expressing your feelings an essential part of family life. Do not give boys the message that it is okay to shut people out. Do not disparage your sons when they tell you they are feeling frightened or vulnerable. Let boys cry when they feel the need.

12. Exercise is critical for all children, but many boys seem to have lots of extra energy. Remember, testosterone is an active hormone! If your child is really energetic, consider getting a chinning bar. Make sure you install the bar correctly to avoid accidents. Start low but raise the bar higher as your son grows. Inexpensive stair-steppers or even jump ropes are also wonderful alternatives to outdoor activities.

13. Limit TV viewing and exposure to violence in video games and movies. TV and movies tend to promote artificial values and questionable beliefs, which most likely are not in keeping with what you hope to instill in your son. Seeing too much violence on the screen or by frequently playing "killing and destroying" video games increases significantly the likelihood that your son will act out violently or aggressively. Constant exposure to media violence also desensitizes all children to the pain, terror, and trauma such actions bring and can influence children to believe that violence is the only way to resolve conflict. Reinforce by example and instruction appropriate conflict-resolution techniques such as negotiation and discussion.

18

Mothers and Daughters— Teaching the Gift of Self-Reliance

It's not uncommon to hear kids, particularly teenage girls, complain about their parents. But three decades ago, it was rare to meet a young girl who didn't insist that "There's no way that I'm going to grow up to be like my mother!" Many girls swore they wouldn't be caught dead dressing or acting like their moms, and many stated they were often embarrassed that their mother's position in the home seemed insignificant.

More and more often, however, experts who work with families are noticing a major change. Girls are no longer panicking at the prospect of turning out like Mom but rather are finding their mothers' lives interesting and exciting. Young girls are not only admiring and appreciating their mothers, but are also more likely to view their mothers as mentors.

PREPARING YOUR DAUGHTER FOR THE FUTURE

Raising a daughter to take her place in the world is a daunting challenge no matter what your family circumstances might be. It may be tempting to think of your job as infinitely more difficult because you are a single mother. Your perspective really depends upon your answer to the age-old question: is the glass half empty or half full?

HOW BIG A LOSS IS IT NOT TO HAVE A DAD AROUND?

Your daughter won't experience the support and validation that comes from having a loving father at home. She may have difficulty forging a close relationship with her father—especially if he lacks the emotional maturity or stability that good parenting requires. Yet, judging from the confusion many young women express today about topics ranging from career choices to sexual orientation, it is hard to believe that all the problems facing young women are somehow more easily faced and more quickly solved when their childhood was spent with Dad close by. Having a father at home, just physically present, does not guarantee that he will be a good parent. Some dads are just there like another piece of furniture or, worse yet, are emotionally demanding, uncaring, and in some cases abusive. So before you lose heart and begin to worry that your household is less healthy for your daughter than one in which both mother and father are present, be sure you are seeing things as they are.

WHEN DADDY DOES NOT SEEM TO BE MISSED

My ninth-grade daughter came home from a friend's house very upset the other day. At first, all she could say over and over again was how lucky she was not to have a father. Apparently, this friend's father is quite abusive verbally and really did a number on my daughter's friend with all her friends watching in terror. I am glad that she is not terribly sad about her father's absence from her life, but this is going a bit too far. How should I handle this?

First, tell your daughter that she is not lucky her father has chosen to be out of her life but that she is lucky she does not have a father in her life who behaves the way this father apparently did. As she describes what happened in greater detail, use the words "verbal abuse" and tell her the kind of damage this kind of behavior creates. Tell her that people's confidence and pride are often severely damaged by contact with abusive people. Use this sad experience to alert your daughter to the dangers of abusive relationships. This father is a "what to avoid" role model, and you should identify him as such to your daughter. Tell her that verbally abusive behavior should alert her that she is spending time with someone who can potentially hurt her a great deal—in short, not the stuff of which great boyfriends are made.

WHAT HAPPENS TO GIRLS DURING ADOLESCENCE

Any kindergarten teacher will tell you that when girls begin school they are miles ahead of boys. They are taller. They are better coordinated and much better able to hop, skip, and run than their male classmates. Their fine motor skills are also much better. Girls color, cut, paste, and learn to write much more quickly and certainly with greater neatness than boys. They usually learn to read more quickly. Girls more often bring home the proud-to-hang-on-the-refrigerator report card, while boys seem to need their mothers to come to endless conferences with the teacher to discuss the latest snag in a not-too-illustrious elementary school career. All told, little girls are the stars of elementary school, while it's not uncommon for little boys to struggle.

All these advantages seem to come to a crashing halt as adolescence begins. As one exasperated mother put it, "What happened to my daughter? One day she was the star of the sixth grade, and the next day she was a mess! Where did all these problems come from?"

This mother's lament reflects the changes girls experience as adolescence begins. It is not the bodily changes in and of themselves, but rather how society's expectations influence how girls view themselves as their bodies naturally change.

The confident, accomplished sixth-grade girl begins to grow and develop as does her somewhat less stellar sixth-grade male classmate a few years later. Abruptly, this once-confident little girl is subjected to a whole new standard—how she looks. Grades, interests, and accomplishments all take a back seat to appearance, particularly concerns with weight. It is society's obsession with appearance that makes the journey into adulthood so perilous for girls. For boys, however, who are applauded loudly for simply letting their bodies do what they are expected to do—grow taller and get heavier—the trip is much easier. The changes girls can expect naturally are not always changes society welcomes. Girls can expect a temporary awkwardness in movement, mild skin eruptions, and the inevitable addition of fat, which is necessary for menstruation.

To make things more difficult, television and other media exploit normal female adolescent concerns about body image and development. Impossibly thin actress after impossibly thin actress populates the television shows directed at young people. The message is clear: be pretty, and above all else, be thin. We harp on good grades and worry that they will not be able to go to a good college or get a well-paying job. Meanwhile our daughters are reading magazines geared for them that feature articles like "Rating Your Buns—How Does Your Fanny Compare?" or "15 Can't-Miss Ways to Make Boys Really Like You." There is little wonder girls are confused.

This confusion all girls experience as adolescence begins has less to do with the part their fathers play in their lives than with how suddenly their bodies are in conflict with society's unattainable ideal of teenage beauty—perfectly clear skin, waiflike thinness (skip the breasts and hips), and the grace of a ballerina. Perfect SAT scores as well as being president of the student council, head cheerleader, and part-time model would also be nice touches!

WHAT'S A MOTHER TO DO?

My fourteen-year-old daughter is really unhappy. She is going through that very awkward stage. Her skin is a mess. Maybe if her father was around, she would feel

better about herself. How can I help her? I am particularly concerned about the weight she has gained. I have always watched mine carefully, and I am nuts that she might get fat.

First, too many mothers are tempted to view their daughter's bodies as extensions of their own. Your daughter's body is not your body, and how she looks is not a reflection of you or under your appropriate control. If you choose to try to control your daughter's body through ridicule, nagging, or constant mention, the result will be that she will rebel even more than is typical. She may begin to show you how much she is in control by binge eating or by experimenting with drugs and alcohol.

As for her father, who is to say what part he would play if he was around? The point is that he is not around, and giving your daughter what she needs is up to you. According to a number of developmental psychologists, what your daughter needs is good old-fashioned maternal warmth. Daughters

need Mom to be Mom. Girls need their mothers to express their love with hugs and kisses. Girls need their mothers to be genuinely involved in their concerns and interests—from what they are now washing their face with to what they are planning to do for their science project. Maternal warmth means being there for them always and without reservation. Of course, you can always express an opinion or even forbid them from doing something. Maternal warmth simply means that always in your every word and action you are telling them that they are loved and accepted for who they are now.

LOOKING FOR ROLE MODELS

While girls are being shown physical role models who resemble survivors of a death march, they are also aware that life holds more promise, opportunity, and expectation for them than to be wives and mothers. As women's roles have expanded, ironically, the pressure has only increased. Now you need to be not only beautiful and thin, but also accomplished and talented as well. But who are today's young women supposed to look up to as models for how to fashion their lives so that they can take every advantage of the opportunities and expectations placed before them?

Looking First at Home

Whether you feel up to the challenge or not, your daughter will first look to you as a source of inspiration for her own life. You can be the inspiring woman she is looking for, despite what you feel to be your failings, shortcomings, and mistakes. Just as you are strong enough

---

INSPIRE CHANGE

Empower your daughter and yourself by both of you taking on today's issues. In *If Women Ruled the World: How to Create the World We Want to Live In,* a book edited by Sheila Ellison, 150 women share their stories and ideas for creating peace, compassion, and equality in our private lives and in the political world and challenge other women and girls to work to inspire change. Share these timeless essays with your daughter. Who knows? You may be raising a future president!

to appreciate all the uniqueness of your daughter, she is also, given the opportunity, strong enough to embrace your weaknesses, faults, and failures. Give her this chance to know and understand you better!

How to Be a Role Model

Honest communication is the key. For example, if you feel you married too young, short-circuiting what might have been promising opportunities in a career you loved, say so. This will not be interpreted as a rejection of what came to be your daughter's eventual place in your life, but an honest recognition of the costs any choice entails. If you feel you were influenced by what you felt everyone else was doing or what your parents wanted, tell her so.

At the same time, tell her about women who have influenced your own life in a positive way and why. Since there are so few complete role models for any of us, most of us wind up taking for ourselves selected characteristics or beliefs of people who have influenced and shaped our lives. Tell your daughter, for example, about your fifth-grade gym teacher, who taught you so well what real sportsmanship was all about. If you

admire someone now, share the reasons with your daughter. You may admire someone who is able to decorate on a shoestring or give terrific parties on a budget. Tell your daughter so. Point out women of accomplishment and discuss their contributions toward making this world a better place.

Sharing Your Goals

Not only is it important to share with your daughter your past, but it is also equally important to share with her your goals and aspirations for the future. Your goal does not have to be becoming recognized as a world-famous oil painter. It is wonderful enough that you would like to expand your creative side a bit and try oil painting. Perhaps you would like to go back to school. Your goal does not have to be medical or dental school to be worthwhile. If your plans begin with simply getting your high school equivalency certification, your daughter will be pleased to share in the events of your life and help you to plan. Involving your daughter in this way will give you a common bond of shared experiences and encourage her to share more easily her own thoughts, plans, and dreams.

Giving the Gift of Self-Reliance

Being able to take care of yourself and depend upon yourself, without question, is a priceless life skill. Self-reliant individuals, both men and women, have a great advantage over those more dependent, less confident types as life challenges and opportunities appear. People are expected to have more than one career and to juggle many different responsibilities simultaneously.

Single mothers are fabulous role models of self-reliance. Your daughter will remember how courageously you juggled many tasks, often with little to rely on but your own ingenuity and strength. Begin to give your daughter this precious gift of self-reliance by offering her the opportunities to develop the skills and the confidence to face any life challenge.

THE MYTH ABOUT GIRLS FROM SINGLE-PARENT HOMES

Despite what you might have heard or been told, there is no truth to the myth that girls from single-parent homes are more sexually active than other girls.

It is true, however, that girls from single-parent homes experimenting with sex may be more apt to discuss these activities with their mothers because trust and communication are long established. While discussing sex with their daughters is one area in which some mothers could still use some liberating, most mothers are bravely breaking new ground. Take a deep breath and

think before you respond to your daughter's latest revelation about her love life. Be prepared to talk with your daughter about the information taught in school about human sexuality. Helping your daughter make safe and responsible choices without threats and theatrics can be tricky. Familiarize yourself with community resources, if you feel particularly unsure or overwhelmed.

WILL MY GRANDDAUGHTER BE PROMISCUOUS?

I adopted my granddaughter after my own daughter passed away. Frankly, I was very promiscuous when I was my granddaughter's age. By the time I was sixteen, there had been too many men in my life for me even to count. Do I share these mistakes with my granddaughter? If I tell her that I was sexually active at her age, doesn't that just give her permission to be the same way now?

No, not necessarily. In fact, it actually may help you talk to your granddaughter about sex. You may want to tell your granddaughter that at her age you made foolish and reckless choices. You were fortunate back then that most of what it took to deal with the results of permissive sexual behavior amounted to nothing more than some visits to a health clinic for a few shots of penicillin. Today, such choices could be far more serious because of sexually transmitted diseases, including AIDS.

Tell your granddaughter your honest feelings. These sexual experiences were not exciting, satisfying, or even fun.

They were probably your way of finding affection and comfort in a world that was not offering you too much at the time.

Of course, no matter what you share, she may have to make a few of her own mistakes along the way. At the same time you are telling her of choices you regret, make sure you are telling her that, if she chooses to be sexually active, birth control and safe sex practices are musts. This information can and should come from you. Do not rely on her teachers or friends to give her the information she may need to save her life.

Where male sexuality is often a source of pride, it takes most women ten years or more of experience to accept themselves sexually. Take pride in knowing that you are one of the pioneers in bringing grandmothers and granddaughters closer by not keeping secrets and by allowing women of all ages to be open and honest.

SHOULD MY DAUGHTER KNOW I AM SEXUALLY ACTIVE?

I am unclear about how much I should share about my dating life with my eight-year-old daughter. I am concerned that she will become sexually active way before she is ready if I give her any indication that I have a lover now and have been sexually active my entire adult life.

You are right to be concerned. Your daughter does not need to know that you have a lover, but you certainly can let her know that you understand what it means to be curious about sex

---

SINGLE MOM OF NOTE

Mary Wollstonecraft, Early Feminist
Mary Wollstonecraft was a feminist writer in the late 1700s, the author of the feminist classic, *A Vindication of the Rights of Woman*. Mary believed marriage could only work if two people had strong identities and did not take advantage of each others' place in society. Her daughter, Fanny, was born out of wedlock, and Mary Wollstonecraft was a single mother for three years. Mary Wollstonecraft died only days after giving birth to Mary Wollstonecraft Godwin, who would grow up to marry poet Percy Bysshe Shelley and become the author of *Frankenstein*.

---

and that you understand what it feels like to be sexually attracted to someone. What is most appropriate to share with your daughter is that sex is a wonderful experience—for adults. Emphasize with her that becoming sexually active means being able to take responsibility for birth control and for protection from disease. Most children are really not interested in hearing too many details of your private life, but it is your job to teach the information your daughter needs to make safe and responsible choices in her own life. However, as she matures, keep the communication open and more honest. You may bring up the subject, for example, when you are getting ready for a dinner date by saying out loud to yourself, "I wonder if I should let him kiss me goodnight? He's such a great person, and I really like him." Your daughter may be speechless, but after a few more "talks," she may respond. Never burden her with your problems about men, but at the same time, you should let her know that she can discuss anything she wants with you.

WHEN YOUR LITTLE GIRL SEEMS TOO INTERESTED IN MEN

My six-year-old daughter seems to be obsessed with men. Her father has not been with us since she was two years old. She is affectionate with everyone but seems particularly interested in flirting with every man who crosses her path. Of course, she gets a lot of attention when she blows the postman a kiss or waves an enthusiastic goodbye to the gas station attendant. How do I know if things are out of hand?

Your daughter's behavior sounds like natural six-year-old stuff. Since she is getting so much positive attention for her antics, it is very likely that she will continue to blow kisses and wave. When people stop paying attention, she will lose interest.

What you might be worried about is whether or not her attention-getting behavior has something to do with her father not being around. It is possible that it does, but not necessarily in a harmful way. Your daughter wants male attention and is finding age-appropriate ways to get this attention. Her behavior should alert you to this possible need and suggest to you that she may need more male figures in her life. You might want to speak with the school principal and request, if possible, a male teacher for next year. You may want to seek out more male friends, not necessarily romantic companions for you, to

include in your extended family circle. Enroll her in activities like soccer or other sports where she gets to be with other children and their fathers. A male coach would be a terrific idea for your daughter.

WHEN TEENAGE DAUGHTER HAS DATES AND MOM DOESN'T

My daughter has started dating. Instead of being proud and thinking how my little girl is growing up, I feel resentful. I've been critical about the boys she picks and don't like anything she chooses to wear on dates. Could I be suffering from sour grapes because there is no one in my life at this time?

It is natural for you to experience some jealousy and resentment. Your daughter has more options than you do, and that is an enviable place to be. You have already taken the first big step by acknowledging these feelings. The next big step is not to let these feelings get in the way of your relationship with your daughter or cloud your vision when it comes to helping her navigate the treacherous teenage social scene. Much as you might regret the choices you made in your life, chances are that deep down you would not want to be a teenager again. The envy you feel is not the desire to relive the rejection and uncertainty, but rather wanting a chance to be part of things in a new way. This is a choice open to you. Happiness for a single person requires action. You need to build up your social support network and actively seek out intellectual challenge. Your daughter's maturity and independence give you added opportunity for just such positive actions.

Your daughter needs your guidance and support. If she does not get these things from you, she will seek sources of information elsewhere, and these sources of information may be nothing more than shared ignorance. If you have delayed talking to her about sex, delay no longer. Your daughter needs the facts about sexually transmitted diseases and birth control. If she is sexually active—and there is no use putting your head in the sand about this—she needs appropriate medical care. More importantly, you need to share your beliefs, experiences, and values with her.

19

If Your Child Has Special Needs

Raising a child diagnosed with developmental, physical, and/or neurological disorders poses unique challenges for single mothers—as for all parents! Single mothers of children with special needs may feel especially isolated, both by their children's special demands and by the differences in their lives from parents with partners and parents with children who do not have special needs. Rest assured, you are not alone.

TRAVELING AN UNEXPECTED ROAD

You may feel that your task is overwhelming. Yet, as always in single parenting, you are your own best ally! You will learn from your experiences, come to appreciate your child's uniqueness, allow yourself the frustration, grief, and sometimes anger that are only human for a single parent of a special needs child, and, most of all, celebrate the joy and love inherent in raising your family.

All these things come with time. While you wait, concentrate on doing what needs to be done today. Remember to maintain your sense of self. Almost all children require more from their parents than the parents can give without risk to emotional health; children with special needs may require even more. Without a coparent to share the load or a marriage to maintain, you are at particular risk of never making yourself the priority. Yet, being a single mother means that you have an even greater duty to maintain your emotional health.

You cannot define yourself only as your child's mother. Reserve time to indulge some small passion. Find time to savor those mystery novels you love, stay in touch with friends, and make the effort to keep a journal. Don't give up the things that feed your soul.

WHEN DAD CAN'T COPE

Some men leave their families because they are unable to cope with the intense responsibilities of raising a child with special needs. He may feel less macho or embarrassed for making what he considers an imperfect smaller version of himself. He even may feel guilty or somewhat responsible for the child's problems and secretly blame himself. Sometimes this apparent "bale out" is simply a stage of grief. Given time and understanding, Dad's relationship with his child may resume in a strong and positive way. These emotional crises leave the mothers, of course, to deal with their own feelings as well as do "double duty" under difficult and challenging circumstances.

Our three-year-old son was recently diagnosed with a developmental disability. I felt for a long time that he had serious problems. His pediatrician finally arranged for a comprehensive evaluation at the university hospital. When we were told the diagnosis, his dad and I were both devastated. His father became hostile toward the doctors and then very withdrawn. After a couple of weeks, he left for good, telling me that he just "can't deal with it." How am I going to get the medical treatments and educational services our son requires? How am I going to cope without the one person I thought I could count on? How could this man just leave his son who needs him now more than ever?

You have bravely made the first important steps toward helping your son. Early intervention is critically important for all children with special needs, and your persistence has made these opportunities possible. There are resources readily available to help you access the medical treatments and educational services your son requires. Online resources will provide you with valuable information as well as help you connect with other parents facing the same challenges. Search for online resources specific to your child's diagnosis. Reputable Web sites are sponsored by credible professional organizations and are constantly updated with the latest information. Be cautious about information from so-called breakaway groups whose political agenda may not help you effectively address your child's specific needs. Post to the message boards and attend support group meetings as frequently as you can.

These efforts will sometimes be daunting, and it is natural that you wish for the comfort and support of a loving partner. For today, your son's father is not able to be there for you or to be a meaningful part of your son's life. He cannot cope with this traumatic news and the shattered belief that his son was "perfect" (whatever that means). If you're in touch with Dad, encourage him to get some counseling or at least to attend support group meetings with you. Keep him posted on your son's progress. E-mail updates may be all you can manage now since your own feelings of disappointment and abandonment may make communication difficult. If your partner abandoned you, seek help and support from friends and extended family members. It's also not uncommon for paternal grandparents and some of your ex's other relatives to offer help when they consider that your son is part of their family.

HELPFUL RESOURCES FOR PARENTS OF CHILDREN WITH SPECIAL NEEDS

◆ Parents Helping Parents found at www.php.com is a good starting point to identify the resources and services your child may require.

◆ The Web site www.specialchildren .about.com provides a wealth of information on practical topics and links you to other related sites of possible interest.

◆ Your child may be entitled to certain Social Security benefits offered within two programs. Social Security Disability Insurance is paid to your child if you are disabled or unable to work or retire, even when your child is over eighteen years old. Supplemental Security Income (SSI) is a federal income supplement program funded by general tax revenue, not by Social Security taxes, to assist children with disabilities under the age of eighteen whose families have scant income and resources. Call 1-800-772-1213 between 7:00 A.M. and 7:00 P.M. Monday through Friday or visit www.ssa. gov for more information and to locate a Social Security office near you.

◆ The National Institute of Mental Health found at www.nimh.nih.gov is the lead federal agency for research on mental and behavioral disorders. Check this site for reliable information and for updates on new treatments and research findings.

WHAT IS SPECIAL EDUCATION?

Special education refers to specially designed individualized or group instruction or special services or programs implemented to meet the unique needs of students with disabilities. Special education services and programs are provided at no cost to the parents under the Individuals with Disabilities Education Act (IDEA). Special education services include early intervention services; if you have an infant or preschool child with special needs, do not wait until your child is ready for kindergarten to contact your local school district.

There is a prescribed process to access special education in the United States, which works like this.

1. Your child is referred to a multidisciplinary team called the Committee on Special Education (CSE) or the Committee on Preschool Special

---

CATWOMAN: GLAMOUR AND PURRS TO PARENTHOOD

Julie Newmar, the original Catwoman to TV's *Batman and Robin*, was first a star on Broadway and then television back in the 1950s and 1960s. She and her husband split up when her son, John, was six months. John has Down's syndrome and has been profoundly deaf since age two. Newmar has told reporters that "I love this wonderful person who just happens to be my son. I live my life with him, not in spite of him." She and her son, John, have traveled the world together, enjoy time in their home garden, and even attend black-tie dinners. "I want John's life to be as complete as possible. He fills my life with joy everyday."

Education (CPSE). You can make this referral yourself; community agencies, health care providers, as well as teachers and parents, can refer to CPSE/CSE. Contact the special education director at your local school district to obtain specific information about how to make a referral to the CPSE/CSE. The school psychologist is always a helpful resource when questions about special education arise.

2. The CSE or CPSE arranges for an evaluation of the child's abilities and needs. This individual evaluation includes any tests or assessment, including observations, given individually to your child to find out whether he or she has a disability and/or to identify his or her special education needs. The results of the evaluation must be shared in writing with you.

3. Based on the evaluation results, the CSE or CPSE decides if your child is eligible to receive special education services. Eligibility largely depends on documenting that your child's disability interferes with his or her learning to the extent that special education services are needed.

4. If your child is eligible for services, the CSE or CPSE develops and implements an appropriate Individualized Education Program (IEP), based on evaluation results to meet the needs of your child. Based on the IEP, the CSE or CPSE must determine your child's placement, ensuring that services are provided in the least restrictive environment (LRE) meaning that, typically, services are provided within your home school district.

5. The CSE or CPSE will review the IEP at least once a year to make modifications and revisions as required. The student has a reevaluation at least once every three years to review the continued need for special education and to revise the IEP, if appropriate.

HOW TO BE YOUR CHILD'S BEST ADVOCATE

♦ Special education programs and services have restraints and limitations. Strive to work within the system. Make every effort to attend all CSE or CPSE meetings and annual reviews.

- You are entitled to bring anyone you choose to your child's meetings. Many single mothers bring a friend to these meetings to take notes so that none of the important information shared is missed or just to feel that extra measure of support. This is a good idea, especially if you feel overwhelmed or can get easily upset or flustered.

- Save copies of all evaluations, IEPs, and notifications received from your school district. Store them in a binder or large file so you can always find the information you need.

- Read carefully the information booklets made available detailing your legal rights under state and federal law. Join the special education PTA, if one is available in your school district. Make allies of school personnel who generally strive to provide adequately for a wide diversity of special needs.

- Remember that the special education system is not flawless. Sometimes things don't fall into place as quickly as you would like. Choose your battles carefully. Bring your "business manners" to all meetings, remembering that everyone present shares your concerns about your child's progress and well-being.

WHAT IS A 504 PLAN?

Section 504 of the Rehabilitation Act of 1973 guarantees the right of persons with mental or physical disabilities not be excluded from participation in or denied the benefits of or be subjected to discrimination under any program or activity receiving federal financial assistance. This means that a child with a disability that is a substantial limitation on major life activities may qualify for typically reasonable accommodations to enable equal opportunity. This includes access to education including all the school's programs, activities, and services. Examples of reasonable accommodations include assistive technology, preferred seating, and modifications in the administration of a testing instrument. These accommodations are set forth in a 504 plan. If accommodations are written into a 504 plan, the school district has made the legal commitment to provide them.

If you feel that your child may qualify under Section 504, contact the Section 504 compliance officer in your school district to request a Section 504 meeting. Expect a written response from the school district. Under federal law, school districts must respond to your request. A meeting will typically be scheduled within thirty days to determine eligibility and to develop a plan. Your child may be eligible for a 504 plan if he or she is no longer eligible to receive special education.

CONSIDER A SPECIAL NEEDS TRUST

A special needs trust, also known as a supplemental needs trust, is a critical part of planning for parents of children with severe disabilities. People with disabilities are not eligible for public aid, such as Medicaid and Supplemental Security Income, if their assets exceed $2,000. By setting up a special needs trust, your child can accept gifts and inheritances without jeopardizing access to governmental programs. This trust enables a child with special needs to enjoy lifestyle benefits, like attending movies, owning a computer, and taking vacations, as well as get medically related equipment and receive extraordinary health care without disqualifying them for government benefits.

A special needs trust can be established for a child with severe disabilities from birth through age sixty-five. It is important to consider opening a trust well before your child is eighteen so that experience and familiarity can be gained with the various regulations and related laws. It is advised by many experts to consider such a trust before opening a bank or brokerage account in the child's name, especially a 529 plan or a 401(k) plan. Grandparents and others need to know not to put financial vehicles in the name of the child, but to make gifts only to the special needs trust.

There are numerous legal issues connected with government benefits. Approval from the Social Security Administration requires specific language. Regulations vary from state to state. Drafting the special needs trust document should be done by an attorney with special expertise and experience. Referrals to a member lawyer of organizations such as the Special Needs Alliance or the National Academy of Elder Law Attorneys are the best options.

HOW TO HANDLE LOOKS AND COMMENTS

My ten-year-old son wears a leg brace and ambulates with crutches. He also has some facial paralysis. People say the most astounding things to me. I have been told my son's difficulties are a blessing, part of some cosmic plan, or the fault of his doctors. Virtual strangers tell me that I must be a saint to cope with my son's disabilities! How do I respond to such statements?

People typically have a hard time accepting that sometimes things just happen. People are often afraid to admit that there may be no rational reason, no one to blame, and no way to change undeserved events. Comments that attribute your son's physical challenges to divine intervention or medical malpractice comfort these people because it helps them defend against their own feelings of vulnerability and helplessness. After all, if there is no

---

IF YOU CAN'T SAY SOMETHING NICE, LET IT RIP

Silence may be golden, and most of the time, it's probably better not to engage with insensitive strangers. But if you can't help yourself, consider these:

♦ *God never gives you more than you can bear.* You don't even know me. How do you know what I can bear?

♦ *Children with developmental disabilities are always so content, aren't they?* Would it make you feel less guilty that you're not me if that were true?

♦ *Your daughter's adorable!* (From a stranger who pretends your special needs son is invisible.) Thank you. This is my son.

Making your own list of nasty comebacks may help vent your frustration.

explanation or excuse, unexpected things can happen to them, too. The emotional reactions of virtual strangers need not be part of your burden. You can choose whether to respond or be silent.

Comments about sainthood and other unsolicited remarks are tiresome. If you choose to respond, consider saying that "I don't have the luxury of whether or not I can cope. I just do the best I can. I'm not special. I'm just like any other parent who loves her child." You may also choose to tell people when their comments are hurtful. No one has the right to judge the circumstances of your life. You do not owe anyone an explanation. Relegate most comments to the "stupid things people say" category and use the energy saved to better advantage.

GENERAL ADVICE FOR SINGLE MOMS OF CHILDREN WITH SPECIAL NEEDS

Keep in mind that you need every ounce of energy you can muster to be up to the task of caring for your child. Here are some other ideas to help you cope.

Seek Support

This is the most important thing you can do. Single moms of children with special needs require the emotional support of friends and extended families. Networking with other parents facing similar challenges provides the opportunity to confide in someone who truly understands your situation. Networking with other parents can also assist the search for physicians with special training, programs, camps, and a host of other resources.

Investigate Alternatives

Some parents spend thousands of dollars investigating therapies that may range from ridding a home of all chemical and environmental toxins to biofeedback, music therapy, and even swimming with dolphins. Proceed with caution with these treatments. Before you take a second mortgage out on your house or run up your credit card balance, do your homework. Investigate these treatments or therapies with the constant question of what evidence or proof supports their benefits to your child. Hearsay or anecdotal report does not offer enough for you to make substantial financial outlay or major lifestyle changes.

Beware of Reading Outdated Books

Check the copyright dates. Look for hurtful and obsolete terms such as referring to children with Down's syndrome as "mongoloids" or children with hearing impairments as "deaf and dumb." These are sure indications that this outdated book is of no value.

Establish Routines

Routines can be lifelines for any single mother of children with special needs. Routines help you get through the days and the weeks—you'll have less time to wonder if you have the energy to do it all if you always know what to do next.

Set the Example

You'll notice that most parents of children with special needs interact with their children in a positive way and rarely seem embarrassed or uncomfortable in public. People will take their cues on how to deal with your child from your attitude and behavior. The discomfort experienced by those unaccustomed to family diversity is not your problem. Teach others to respect and appreciate your child's "specialness." Correct those who offer pity or disappointment.

Embrace Life

If you build your life totally around your child you risk becoming isolated.

It's better to include your child in your activities and other important things in your life.

Allow Yourself to Vent

Your job is a tough one. Despite the rewards, there are times when you just want to scream or collapse from exhaustion. You may sometimes even feel like running away. These feelings are perfectly normal. Find outlets for your frustration that work for you.

PART 4

YOUR CONNECTION TO THE REST OF THE WORLD

20

All about Child Support

Child support is money to be paid pursuant to a court order as part of dissolution of a marriage or around the time that paternity is established for unmarried parents. The purpose of child support is to make sure that children enjoy the same comforts and opportunities they would have enjoyed if their parents were together. Child support is not intended to financially subsidize the mother as an individual or another adult with whom she might choose to live. Single mothers, whether they receive child support or not, must be aware that their long-term survival depends upon becoming financially self-sufficient. Even ample and regular child support will end when the child reaches maturity.

A BLESSING OR A BROKEN PROMISE

Along with an agreement about child support, the court order typically includes stipulations about custody and visitation and other matters related to the care and upbringing of the children. Many fathers fulfill child support and other such obligations freely and responsibly. Some men go beyond "what is ordered" and willingly provide a better life for their children. These men deserve their own peace of mind because their child is secure and stable.

Unfortunately, too many men have walked away from their child support obligations, effectively deserting their children. Many men justify this financial and emotional abandonment with anger toward the child's mother. Some men feel they have no financial responsibility for their children if they are not married to the mother. Some are selfish, refusing to sacrifice their own luxuries or leisure time, in the form of a second job. If the same money that once provided for one household is now providing for two because you are living apart, your children's father may be having trouble compromising his standard of living. Some fathers, certainly, are simply poor. According to the federal Office of Child Support Enforcement, there is upward of $90 billion in unpaid child support payments dating as far back as 1975. The majority of the debt—nearly 70 percent—is owed by noncustodial parents earning less than $10,000 per year. Less than 4 percent is owed by men with annual incomes of more than $40,000.

The bottom line is that physical custody of the children should not mean that you shoulder an undue burden for their financial well-being, but many single mothers do.

THE STATE OF CHILD SUPPORT

Failure to pay child support has gone from a shameful family secret to a topic of public debate and concern. Arising from this public debate and outrage, landmark federal legislation has been passed to assist custodial parents, overwhelmingly mothers, to collect the literally billions of dollars owed in unpaid child support. The number of mothers receiving child support has markedly increased. The good news is that with careful effort and perseverance it is likely that you will be able to collect child support. The bad news is that, given the income level of many fathers who don't pay support, the laws that serve to help you are, at best, insufficient to solve child poverty in the United States.

SHOULD YOU SEEK CHILD SUPPORT?

Some mothers feel that it is easier to raise a child alone than to hassle with the efforts needed to collect child support. Begin by figuring out if attempting to obtain child support is the right decision for you.

Here are some reasons to consider a child support enforcement action against your child's father.

♦ Eighteen years is a long time. Who knows what your financial circumstances may be in the future? Are you being totally realistic about your ability to handle all the expenses involved in raising a child? Remember that your expenses increase as your child gets older. It may take some time for enforcement to succeed—don't wait for a financial crisis.

♦ All children are entitled to support from both parents whether or not their parents were married. This is the law.

♦ Men who pay child support are more likely to involve themselves in other aspects of their child's life and may be more willing to help out with other medical, educational, or recreational expenses.

♦ If the birth father cannot be identified or is in prison, institutionalized, homeless, or dead, seeking child support is probably not worth your trouble. If you knowingly deceived a man who made clear his intent not to have children with you, you may feel it is unethical to pursue child support.

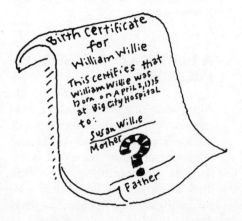

CHILD SUPPORT VERSUS VISITATION

My partner and I split shortly after our two-year old twins were born. He told me he just couldn't deal with the day-to-day responsibilities of children but promised to pay child support. Frankly, I was never interested in letting his chaos become part of our lives, and so I have not encouraged visitation. He has reneged on his promised child support, and I plan to pursue child support collection. Will visitation automatically be required once child support enforcement action begins?

Child support and visitation are separate issues. The children's father is entitled to visitation, and you cannot legally withhold visitation. No court can require that a parent maintain a visitation schedule, however, if that parent is unwilling to spend time with the children. You will be required to get a court order for child support before enforcement action can begin. If you obtain a court order for child support and Dad continues to be in arrears, enforcement action can begin. Child support enforcement action cannot be initiated based on promises or informal agreements.

Bringing and enforcing child support orders can affect visitation in various ways. Occasionally, some men suddenly insist on seeing the children despite your objections, essentially to punish you for seeking financial support. Other dads rightly see child support enforcement as a wake-up call and make the effort to become a more meaningful and integral part of their children's lives. A number of dads make no changes in their current "no visitation" schedule.

Think carefully about what you mean by chaos when you describe Dad. Is he loud, messy, and kind of unreliable? Does he have drug or alcohol addictions, gambling problems, or repeated run-ins with the law? Do you need to protect your children from him, or do you simply need strategies to allow your children contact with him without unnecessarily complicating your life? Your children will very shortly ask questions about their dad. Child support enforcement is essential, but you also need to consider Dad's possible role in your children's life. He will always have the right to request visitation. Unless he is a definite threat to their safety and well-being, talking with Dad about visitation as well as child support might be the right way to go. You will want to be comfortable with what you will tell your children when they ask in a few years why they never see their dad.

WHAT ABOUT SUPPORT OUTSIDE OF THE UNITED STATES?

My son's father has moved to Canada. I was told to give up seeking support if the father is out of the country. Is this true?

By the end of 2004, the United States had gained federal-level agreements with nine countries—plus most Canadian provinces—in the effort to tighten international cooperation among child support enforcement agencies. Contact your local child support enforcement office to get started, visit the National Child Support Enforcement Association *(www.ncsea.org/international/)*, or go to *www.deadbeatparent.com*.

YOU'LL KNOW HIM BY THE HOLE IN THE DOOR

A stiff upper lip, that dry English wit, and some bad history with an ex may account for why some moms filling out applications at a British child support agency responded outrageously when asked where was Dad. One mom wrote:"I don't know his whereabouts. But he does drive a BMW with a hole in the door made by my stiletto; perhaps you can check BMW stations and see if he's had it replaced!"

HOW TO BEGIN

The first step in obtaining child support is getting a legal order for it. This order must spell out the amount of the obligation and how it is to be paid. Many states have arrangements for establishing the support order by an administrative procedure or other expedited legal procedure. The hearing may be conducted by someone other than a judge, such as an administrative hearing officer, master, or referee of the court. An agreement made between the parents and approved by this type of agency generally has the same effect as one established in court. It is legally binding on the parties concerned.

How Is the Amount of Support Determined?

Every state has guidelines for determining the amount of child support to be awarded. When granting support, the judge refers to these guidelines, which take into account the income of each parent and various other factors

like the number of children in a family and costs like medical expenses and child care. Even though support orders are now computed using state guidelines rather than the old-fashioned and faulty method of "gathering receipts" from the custodial parent to justify every expense, you should still compile a list of all the costs involved to raise your child. Consider expenses like shelter, food, education, and clothing, but do not overlook hidden costs or the need to save for large expenses. Future college expenses, special medical or dental needs, summer camp, school field trips, vacations, and memberships in organized programs and clubs are real expenses that will add up!

If a noncustodial parent attempts to get their child support reduced, the judge may grant a reduction for legitimate reasons like serious illness or long-term unemployment. Typically, however, judges are prohibited by law from reducing the support obligation retroactively—that is, future child support may be reduced, but he is still liable for the full amount of past support owed.

IF YOU NEED HELP

You may need to get in touch with the federal government. Title IV-D of the Social Security Act passed in 1975 established a local IV-D child support agency in every state in the union. These local IV-D agencies are federally funded and must help you collect child support if your children are under eighteen or if you apply for help before your child reaches eighteen years of age. Find your local IV-D agency by contacting your local Child Support Enforcement Office. Look in the telephone directory under the state or county social services agencies. These agencies go by different names in different states.

There are some fees charged by the IV-D office depending upon your state, but efforts are underway to eliminate the dubious practice of charging fees to victims of nonsupport. Check with your local agency for a fee schedule.

Your state's child support enforcement program is available to help you find the noncustodial parent, establish legal paternity (fatherhood), establish the legal support order, and collect child support payments. You can also obtain help to establish and enforce medical support. IV-D agencies can enforce alimony if it is in the same order as the child support. IV-D agencies can also enforce court orders though wage withholding, contempt proceedings, judgments, and liens. IV-D agencies can attach unemployment compensation, military wages, retirement benefits, or Veterans Administration benefits as well as federal and state tax refunds. IV-D agencies can also assist if a modification or change is needed in the existing child support order. Other legal issues like custody, visitation, and property settlements are not, by themselves, child support enforcement issues, and child support enforcement programs cannot intervene in such matters.

When the Threat Is Bankruptcy

Child support payments generally cannot be discharged in a bankruptcy. This means that your ex cannot escape his child support obligation by filing for bankruptcy. Bankruptcies do not act as a stay, or hold, on actions to establish paternity or to establish or modify child support. Back child support is never canceled in bankruptcy proceedings. This means that once child support is owed that it will always be owed until it is paid.

When You No Longer Know Where He Lives

To obtain a court order or to enforce a court order for child support, legal documents must be delivered to the absent parent notifying him of the legal action that will take place. This is a constitutional right that protects all of us from having legal obligations imposed without an opportunity to tell our side of the story. If you no longer know where your ex lives, you can obtain help in locating him through your IV-D agency, but you can speed things along by doing a little simple detective work yourself.

♦ *Surf the Web:* The Internet is the best way to locate your child's father. With a few keystrokes and for minimal cost, you will usually be able to find current and previous addresses. Your search will be greatly aided by knowing his Social Security number, birth date, and full legal name. Most colleges and universities and many high schools have sites and try to keep alumni contact information current. Someone doesn't have to be rich and famous for his name to come up if you "Google" him or use any other powerful search engine. If you do not have access to the Internet or are just not computer savvy, try asking a girlfriend for some help. The public library also has computer facilities and the staff to help you. Some sites search many databases, and these sites typically require a credit card.

♦ *Send him a letter at his last known address:* Write Forwarding Address Requested on the envelope. The post office will send you back the letter with either a little yellow sticker on it with your ex's forwarding address or let you know that there is no forwarding address. Your ex will not be notified by the post office of your attempt to locate him. You can also contact the Department of Motor Vehicles, and for a small fee, the DMV will provide you with an address and a list of vehicles registered under his name. You can do this even if you live in a different state. Contact his high school or college alumni office by telephone and see if they have a current address on file. You need not tell the alumni office exactly why you are asking for his address. Just say that you are interested in getting in contact with him. This is certainly not a lie.

When You Must Establish Paternity

There are two ways to establish paternity. The father can voluntarily consent, which means he admits he is the father. Sometimes men may not be so eager to admit paternity. They may be angry at the child's mother, jealous that you may be in another relationship, or simply no longer want to be a father. The father may himself be in a new relationship and now wants to avoid the anticipated child support obligations from a prior relationship.

If he is unwilling to admit paternity, you will need to arrange with either a private attorney or your local IV-D agency to serve him with a summons to appear in court to either acknowledge or deny paternity. If he tells the judge or administrative hearing officer that he is not the father or he is not sure that he is the father, then a paternity test will be ordered. Allegations and denials, once the substance of many paternity disputes, have been replaced with beyond-any-reasonable-doubt laboratory test results. Don't worry that he will get someone else to take the test for him. Laboratories require photo ID with corroborating identification documents.

What about Getting an Attorney?

All the IV-D agencies have attorneys who provide services for child support matters. There are no income eligibility requirements. To use a IV-D attorney, you simply have to fill out a IV-D application. Obviously, this low-cost/no-cost legal representation is a critical benefit, particularly if the lack of child support has led to financial hard times. You need to remember, however, that you are going to be one of probably hundreds of cases the IV-D attorney will be handling. There will be little personal attention, and you will need to be organized and active in keeping your case moving forward.

Representing yourself or appearing pro se may seem like a good idea. You have control on actions taken or not taken and can be sure that paperwork is filed in a timely manner. There are major drawbacks to being your own legal advocate. You will not know all the legal ins and outs and may miss opportunities to place in evidence key information. Child support hearings are emotionally charged events. Think about facing someone in court whom you used to love. Emotions can cloud judgment; this is why even the best attorneys do not represent themselves.

Pro bono attorneys, meaning non–IV-D attorneys, who will take your case for free are few and far between. If you find such an attorney, you will probably find yourself a low priority in her or his schedule. This means even more delay and longer waiting to get the outcome you are working toward. You will still be responsible for filing fees and other court costs.

Private attorneys charge by the hour and are the most costly option. If you are fortunate enough to be able to afford this route, make sure you choose an experienced individual—this is not the time to be paying for someone else's education. Be clear what you expect to gain from court proceedings. Make sure that your expectations are realistic. Understand what the expected fees and costs will be. Look for someone with whom you feel comfortable and who makes the process easy for you to understand. Above all else, remember this person works for you. There is no reason to be apologetic or ashamed of the circumstances that have led you to seek her or his services.

WHEN YOUR FEELINGS THREATEN TO OVERWHELM YOU

When you really need help, you should remember that counseling is not a luxury. In addition to legal assistance, if your single parenthood status is the result of a devastating circumstance (your husband's death, his abrupt departure, his disinterest in his child), counseling for you and your children is essential. Do not allow limited finances to be an obstacle. Investigate what mental health services are available in your community. This is an excellent time to find out what your health insurance benefits cover. You and your children need a safe place to sort out and deal productively with the conflicting and painful emotions that each of you is experiencing. In some cases—for example, if your husband has left you and your teenage child for another relationship—you may need to know how not to get your child mixed up in unhealthy emotional reactions, or your child may need help in understanding how to be involved with both of his parents without hurting one or the other.

The work ahead is difficult. There is nothing more frightening than the prospect of a major life change. Each of you is now confronted with enormous life changes that probably were neither positive nor welcome. You can rebuild your life, and your children can thrive. You must take charge of your life by

---

⭐ SINGLE MOM OF NOTE

Mother of David Lennox

David Lennox, born in 1855, may have inherited his father's mechanical ability, but it was mom who ran a Chicago grocery store to support him after Lennox's father left to join the Civil War. He returned once after three years, but they never saw him after that.

David worked in several machine shops perfecting his mechanical and design skills. In 1881, Lennox designed a staple-making machine, an instant hit. He gained area-wide recognition and later built the first Lennox furnace.

Lennox sold his furnace business in 1904. Today, Lennox International is worth billions.

confronting and working through the powerful feelings that every woman in your circumstances has experienced.

You should let go of the role of victim. Only your own heart can guide you in matters of forgiveness. If you do decide to forgive your ex-husband, you would not necessarily be doing it for his benefit nor would your forgiveness imply that negative actions were morally acceptable.

Constant anger is easy to understand but will only drain your energy and be destructive to your own life. You are not hurting him but are hurting yourself and the children by letting your anger make you bitter and resentful. Your energies are better focused on creating a better life for you and your children. Strive toward having your ex as emotionally absent as he is physically absent from your life.

HELP IN THE TOUGHEST CIRCUMSTANCES

What if your ex lives out of state and the result of your efforts so far is no luck! The dismal record of child support enforcement, particularly when fathers move to a state different from where their children reside or even move to a foreign country, prompted passage of the Child Support Recovery Act (CSRA) in 1992. It was recognized that many of these out-of-state moves by a noncustodial parent were simply to avoid child support obligations. Interstate child enforcement had been notoriously difficult, expensive, and time-consuming. Typically, mothers were frustrated by the time delays and costs and often gave up the fight. The Child Support Recovery Act made it a federal offense to willfully fail to pay a past due support obligation for a child who lives in another state.

The CSRA was amended in 1998 to create the Deadbeat Parents Punishment Act. These amendments create two new first offense felonies that may now be prosecuted under the CSRA. Deadbeat dads (or moms) can be now be sentenced to a two-year maximum prison term and a fine for traveling to another state or foreign country with the intent to evade a child support obligation, if the obligation has remained unpaid for longer than one year or is greater that $5,000. Deadbeats can also be charged with a felony for willfully failing to pay a child support obligation for a child who resides in another state, if the obligation has remained unpaid for longer than two years or is greater than $10,000. Willfully failing to pay means that you must be able to prove that the child's father knew about his child support obligations.

When He Threatens to Cry Poor

The Deadbeat Parents Punishment Act does not require you to prove that your deadbeat ex has the ability to pay. The deadbeat parent must now prove he is unable to pay. This is a subtle but important difference and a great victory for child support enforcement.

This is the practical result of the change in the law. There is no need for you to obtain bank records, pay stubs, back tax returns, or any other type of financial information to collect back child support. The deadbeat must supply the records to prove that he is unable to pay. This important change addresses what many single mothers have learned from painful experience.

It is difficult to prove that the deadbeat dad is earning or acquiring income or assets. Child support offenders are notorious for hiding assets and failing to document earnings. Obviously, if you have any access to such records or can somehow show evidence of the deadbeat's opulent lifestyle, this is helpful information.

The law now makes the assumption that if the deadbeat parent had a legitimate change in circumstance after the court order for child support was put in place, like prolonged sickness or job loss, he would have had his child support order reduced in civil court. If a deadbeat has not tried to have his child support reduced, the law now requires that he puts forth evidence that he cannot pay. Substantial and complete financial records and other documentation are needed by the deadbeat to prove he has an inability to pay. Failure to keep records does not get the deadbeat off the hook. In fact, it may get him in even deeper trouble.

When He Is Not Just a Deadbeat

Priority is given to cases where a pattern of flight from state to state to avoid payment can be demonstrated. Federal officials are also giving priority to cases where frequent job changing, concealing assets, or using false Social Security numbers show a pattern of deception. Failure to make child support payments after being held in contempt and failure to make child support payments in connection with or related to activities like bankruptcy fraud, bank fraud, or tax evasion are of particular interest to federal prosecutors.

When He Would Rather Be Unemployed

Unemployment compensation can be attached for child support under federal law. Working through your local IV-D agency or with a private attorney, you can also ask for a contempt hearing and request that the court order your ex to seek employment and provide proof to the court that he is looking for work.

This is called a "seek-work order." Ask the court to order your ex to report to the court on a different day each week with signatures and telephone numbers of at least ten places where he has sought employment. If he fails to provide this weekly report or the names of the prospective employers on the list cannot be verified, he can be sent to jail after the second contempt hearing is held to show that he did not comply with the seek-work order issued in the first contempt hearing.

When His Wages Are Off the Books

You can arrange through your IV-D agency or private attorney to do a credit check to determine his assets. The court can issue a judgment for back child support. Sometimes you can even collect interest. Once you have an order for the back child support owed, any asset you discover, for example, a house, car, or boat, can have a judgment executed against it.

If he claims to be unemployed while earning money off the books, you can also obtain a seek-work order. Violating this seek-work order will mean that he is in contempt of court and could face jail time. Be aware, too, that if the nonpaying parent is receiving income without declaring it while accepting unemployment benefits that this is viewed as fraud by the unemployment office and is punishable by law.

THE DO'S AND DON'TS OF CHILD SUPPORT

• **Don't** give up because the paperwork seems tedious or because you think you will never find a missing dad.

• **Don't** refuse child support because you feel guilty about the relationship ending. Your child's needs are a separate issue.

• **Do** remember that child support is not a favor; it is the law.

• **Do** remember that you are your own best advocate. Stay informed and take an active role in gathering information and asking questions.

• **Do** know your rights and be persistent when you deal with attorneys and agencies.

• **Do** get organized by keeping copies of every document in a safe place.

• **Do** not use your children as spies or confidants.

• **Do** take the time to take care of the business of seeking or enforcing child support orders. Try to see these efforts as business rather than as a reminder of the pain your ex is continuing to cause.

• **Do** not let attempting to collect child support drain the joy out of everyday living or stop you from pursuing other goals and dreams. Let these efforts be only one facet of your life.

When He Suddenly Owns Nothing

Not only is it unfair, but it is also probably illegal to put assets in someone else's name to avoid paying a valid debt like child support and can be a fraudulent conveyance. If you can prove that he is living in the house or driving the car and is the one making the payments, these assets can be attached to pay back child support. You must also prove that these assets were transferred to another person when the child support payments were due. New federal laws require that states have laws under which fraudulent transfer of assets to avoid child support can be investigated and prosecuted. Speak to an attorney or check with your local IV-D agency.

21

What to Know about Custody and Coparenting

PARENTING TOGETHER SEPARATELY

A minor child must be in the legal custody of someone who serves as his or her primary caregiver, whether that person or persons are the child's parents, guardians, or the state. Generally, sole custody by the mother was the standard in the past for traditional families consisting of a married couple with biological children. Family is now more broadly defined and includes divorced single parents, unmarried mothers, and stepfamilies and blended families. Custody arrangements today can take many forms.

JOINT CUSTODY

Joint custody means the child's mother and father (or legal guardian) share decision-making and responsibility for a minor child's life. Most commonly, one parent, usually the mother, retains physical custody of the children, living with the children most of the week, while the other has visitation rights.

Joint custody is complicated. One common problem is that Mom gets stuck always being the heavy while Dad is the fun and vacation guy. The major burdens and responsibilities of child-rearing are hers; but the ex may have veto power over decisions like whether the children should attend camp, wear braces, or even take certain medications. Different types of decisions are specified in most divorce agreements. One parent is given the "final say" on medical, religious, and educational matters. It can be frustrating to assume the daily responsibilities of parenting, but not be the one in charge. Be sure you understand the limits of your parenting authority, if any, specified in your divorce agreement.

Joint custody is whatever is agreed upon at the time the papers are drawn up. It could mean the child spends the school year at Mom's and summers with Dad, or it could mean that you can live wherever you choose with your child, if your ex agrees. If you and your former partner see eye to eye on most child-rearing decisions, this custody arrangement is workable. In cases where the father and mother plan to coparent, joint custody can be extremely successful and rewarding.

SHARED PHYSICAL CUSTODY

Joint custody is often mistaken for shared physical custody, but the definitions are quite different. Shared physical custody means that each parent has equal physical responsibility and access to the children. Neither parent receives child support because each is paying for the care of the children. This arrangement is gaining in popularity, particularly when the child can live part of the week with one parent and the remainder with the other and still attend the same school. Even though your child may attend the same school, this kind of arrangement can be highly stressful to children. Many mental health professionals believe that because shuffling back and forth from one parent's house to the other

interferes with establishing consistent daily routines that it will interfere with a secure feeling of belonging. There's an element of common sense here: most adults would resist toting a suitcase a few times a week.

SOLE CUSTODY

If your child's father is not reliable or responsible enough to make decisions about your child's future, sole custody with generous visitation is usually the ideal solution. For example, your child may benefit from remaining connected to his father's large extended family. He may be the apple of your child's eye but often is unpredictable, unaccountable, and irresponsible. He may suffer major career lapses, indulge in questionable relationships, or have emotional problems. This doesn't mean he's bad for your child to be around. It just means that you want to be the one making all the major decisions for your child.

TEMPORARY CUSTODY

Temporary custody is sometimes given to one parent or other custodian during an unresolved divorce or when further investigation is warranted to determine custody. Although any custody decision can be contested, temporary custody always means that there will be a court date to settle the custody issue.

WHEN TO DETERMINE CUSTODY

The safest bet is to have all the details of custody specifically outlined in your divorce or separation papers. These negotiations are often expensive and time-consuming but are necessary to insure that privileges and responsibilities relating to custody are clearly spelled out. If your child's father opted out of the picture or you were unmarried when your child was born, file for sole custody immediately.

If you were not married to the child's father, it is still necessary to establish custody because biological fathers have rights in every state, whether or not they were married to the mother. New MOMs (Mothers Outside of Marriage) often make the mistake of assuming that they automatically have sole custody of their child because the father was uninterested or simply disappeared. In some states this may be true, but it's best to check with an attorney to make sure there are no unpleasant surprises if the father should suddenly reappear.

TERMINATING PARENTAL RIGHTS

I have heard stories about men suing for custody for all kinds of crazy reasons and winning but then not wanting to continue raising the children. I want to avoid any problems with my son's father, whom I do not wish to be part of our lives. Besides, I haven't seen him in two years.

In many states if the father does not shoulder parental responsibility for a certain period of time, his rights can be terminated. In most cases, you need to petition the court to terminate the father's rights. Keep in mind that you need to think this out carefully because you can never expect him to pay child support. If you are okay with that, then this is what you should do. Of course, he will have a chance to oppose this, but chances are he won't show up.

Your best bet is to get an agreement signed by the father relinquishing his rights to the child. However, if he is willing to contribute child support but agrees to relinquish custody, you should specify his obligations in this agreement in detail. The two of you can hammer out the details and have an attorney draw up the agreement. Keep in mind, too, that agreements are not always binding. Still, this will provide some protection in the event of a future custody battle.

WHY FATHERS SEEK CUSTODY

A small percentage of men seek custody because they know they are the better parent for the child. Not all women want the responsibility of raising children. Drug or alcohol abuse or other emotional or medical problems may prevent some women from being an adequate and responsible parent. There is no question that many children would thrive with their father as the custodial parent. However, joint custody is more common for fathers who want to be active participants in their child's lives.

LEARN YOUR RIGHTS REGARDING CUSTODY

Your best bet if you are strapped for money is to request a consultation at your local Legal Aid or Legal Services office or at a legal clinic sponsored by your county's bar association For about $40 to $50 (this varies from state to state), you can learn your options for establishing sole custody. Be sure to make a list of all your questions and be very specific. For example, ask if an attorney is necessary or if you can petition the court yourself, how much a custody order would cost, and how much time, if any, must transpire before the father's parental rights are terminated. Keep in mind that many legal clinics that service lower-income clients are unable to handle custody issues unless there is an immediate threat of danger to the children.

CHILD CUSTODY BLACKMAIL

I'm not a single mother but am seriously considering getting divorced. In fact, the only thing preventing me from going to an attorney to file separation papers is the fear that my husband will get the children. We have no relationship. We rarely do anything together, and when my husband is around, all we do is yell and argue, which upsets the kids. But he has said—more than once—that if I try to leave, he will take the kids and not only won't I get a penny, but I'll also have to pay him child support. My job does not pay as well as his, and he couldn't and wouldn't care for the children the way I do. This seems unfair because I feel incredibly trapped, but I don't want to waste my life in this dead-end marriage. Can he really get the kids? He probably doesn't even know that the youngest one has allergies or that the children need lunch money or a snack packed for school!

Custody blackmail is something many attorneys report seeing much of these days. A father will sometimes threaten to take the children in an effort to get the mother to give up certain financial rights. Many attorneys will tell you that fathers sometimes threaten to seek custody as a way to avoid paying child support. Some men actually think it is cheaper to raise the children themselves than to pay child support. Punishing a spouse with threats regarding the children is usually an attempt to try to control that person and, in many cases, a way of prolonging the relationship.

Most lawyers agree that the father usually has no intention of following through on his threat, but many mothers, especially working mothers, often relinquish what is rightfully theirs—for example, part of the house, profits from

investments, a car, or a beach house—for fear that the father will make good on this threat. If you care more about the welfare of your children than you do about money, you are vulnerable to this tactic.

Evaluate where your husband places the emphasis in his threats. For instance, if money and property are repeatedly stressed, as in "I'll see to it that you lose the house and everything unless you let me have the kids," chances are he won't follow through. He doesn't really want custody; he is only using the children as a weapon to try to force you to make financial concessions. Discuss all your concerns with your attorney, who will be familiar with this "kids for money" strategy. Know your legal rights and your chances of winning custody before you sign away any of your marital assets.

WHEN YOU CAN'T AGREE ABOUT CUSTODY

My husband and I are divorcing after years of drifting apart. My ex is Mr. Mom—sort of. He takes care of the children after school and sells insurance. I have worked my way up from secretary to vice president for marketing at a software company. The hours are grueling, and the traveling gets exhausting. But I really love it. No doubt about it, my hard work is what makes our comfortable lifestyle possible. I spend as much time with the children as I can and try to attend all their school functions whenever possible. My husband wants custody of the children and has made it clear that this is not a negotiating tactic. My attorney tells me

that losing custody is a possibility. How could a judge take the children away from me and let them live with my less than ambitious ex? I thought only drug-addicted or prostitute mothers lost custody. How is this going to be resolved? Who is going to decide which of us gets custody?

In all likelihood, the judge assigned to your case will order an Impartial Evaluation of Comparative Custodial Fitness. This means that a mental health professional, often a psychologist and typically called the evaluator, will interview and observe you and your husband as well as the children. Psychological testing is often administered. Questionnaires will also be completed that give the evaluator additional information about you and your husband's background, interests, and perceptions of the children and one another. Share with the evaluator any documents or information you feel are relevant. The evaluator prepares a written report that is sent directly to the judge and reviewed by your attorneys. This report is not a public record. In some jurisdictions, even the parties involved are not permitted to read it. Sometimes the evaluator also testifies in court. The costs for this evaluation are paid according to what the judge orders or the attorneys agree upon. The evaluator also makes recommendations regarding visitation schedules. The judge has the final say, but most often the judge considers the evaluator to be the expert most able to determine what is in the best interests of the children.

In the past, the courts invariably ruled that children belonged with their mothers except when the father could prove that the mother was grossly unfit. Most states now, however, view a husband and a wife in an impending custody dispute as equals. The evaluator will look closely at which parent has the greater psychological bond with the children. A mother with a successful career achieved by hard work, sacrifice, and extended work hours may find herself at a disadvantage in a custody dispute when the children's father has been the "hands-on" parent. Despite the obvious financial contribution, the father may have been more available to parent. Obviously, this is not the only factor upon which an evaluator bases his recommendation, but which parent is available to do the work of parenting and has achieved the closer psychological bonding with the children are two critical issues.

My ex and I cannot come to any agreement about custody or visitation, and the judge has ordered an Impartial Evaluation of Comparative Custodial Fitness. I want to say and do the right things when I meet with the psychologist the judge has assigned. What exactly should I say or do?

Understandably, the custody of your children is of overwhelming importance to you. You are anxious to make a good impression on the person who will be making recommendations to the judge. The best advice is to be you. Of course, like for any important meeting, you want to be on time and prepared. You will want to bring with you any documents the evaluator has requested or any other documents you think are important.

You should keep in mind that children who are given psychological permission to maintain an active relationship with the noncustodial parent are in the long run happier and better adjusted. The evaluator is going to be sensitive to a willingness on your part to cooperate with your former partner to ensure that your children have the opportunity for a meaningful relationship with their father.

During the interview, it is not wise to try to pretend that you have no personal deficiencies or shortcomings as a parent. First, the evaluator is typically a highly trained individual with a lot of experience, and your less than truths are going to be quickly exposed. The evaluator will also be obtaining information about you, your former partner, and the children from other sources to verify and to cross-check what he has been told. These efforts will quickly let the evaluator know if someone has been less than honest. In addition, your former partner or husband is also going to be interviewed and will be asked, as you will be, to discuss the other person's weaknesses and shortcomings. It is better to be up-front about your life experiences and current situation rather than to allow your former partner to give out information about you. A plan to address your shortcomings is usually seen in a favorable light. For example, if you have a lot of trouble disciplining your children, let the evaluator know. It would be helpful if you were attending a parenting class or attempting some other way to improve your disciplinary skills. Do not confuse wishing or planning to do something with actual accomplishment. Pretending or lying is harshly viewed.

Drug and alcohol addictions are certainly investigated because their effects are so devastating to children. Other health and safety issues are also examined. The known effects of secondhand smoke may put a parent who smokes at a disadvantage. Evaluators may take into account which parent actively encourages safety measures like bicycle helmets and wearing of seat belts.

VISITATION

Visitation is almost always allowed for the noncustodial parent except under the most dangerous circumstances. Although most states take into account a child's rights to emotional and/or financial support of both parents, visitation has nothing to do with child support. In other words, the state can enforce child support but can't force a person to visit his child. Likewise, if you are supposed to receive child support but don't, you can't withhold visitation either. Child support and visitation are two separate issues. Experience seems to indicate, however, that fathers who pay support are more likely to be active participants in their child's lives.

Visitation for the "Sometime Dad"

You can establish sole custody and still offer a generous and reasonable visitation schedule to the father. In fact, this is encouraged for a number of reasons. First, men who can see their children usually will pay regular voluntary child support. Second, your child will have all the emotionally sustaining benefits of a meaningful relationship with his father. Third, while your child benefits you also gain some free time.

When child support payments are chronically overdue, less than the amount the court ordered, or nonexistent, the temptation for many mothers is to restrict or deny their former partner's visitation rights. Difficult as it is when you are barely scraping by, it is important to treat visitation and child support as completely separate issues.

Supervised Visitation

If you suspect abuse or worry that the father abuses alcohol or drugs, you can request that the court recommend supervised visitation. You will most likely need legal representation to win this point. If you've already had unsupervised visitation, you will have to show the court reason to mandate supervised visitation. Gather documents, witnesses, and as much information as you can before seeking legal counsel or petitioning the court on your own. This is often a difficult and frustrating process.

SINGLE MOM OF NOTE

Renée Fleming, Soprano Unparalleled
Renée Fleming has been the biggest-selling soprano in the world in recent years, while also being a divorced single mother of two daughters. She performed "Amazing Grace" at Ground Zero during a memorial service for families of victims of the World Trade Center attacks.

Fleming admits she has trouble saying no to work. "Everyone wants a piece of me—managers, the recording people, the press, and, of course, my daughters. Then there is the question of me. I am just beginning to learn what it's like to be a woman on my own. And there is so much that I want to explore for myself."

DROP-OFF CENTERS

If supervised visitation is needed, investigate using a drop-off center. Drop-off centers provide safe havens where children can visit the noncustodial parent. Particularly when there has been a history of violence, exchanging the children in this "neutral zone" is far less likely to escalate or incite violence than if the children are exchanged in a parking lot or fast-food restaurant.

These drop-off centers are also available for parents who have been accused of mental or physical abuse or neglect, as well as parents involved in custody disputes. Noncustodial parents challenged by mental illness, alcoholism, or mental retardation who still want to maintain relationships with their children in safety can also be serviced by drop-off centers. Funded primarily through federal money, these drop-off centers are typically a better alternative than private and often costly supervised visitation facilities.

BREASTFEEDING AND VISITATION

My daughter is still nursing. Her father, with whom I legally agreed to coparent but not marry, is trying to keep her overnight because the drive is so long for him. Should I wean her or talk to him about postponing visitation for awhile?

Talk to him about postponing overnight visitation until she is off the breast and at least onto a bottle, if not a cup. Of course, if he still wants to come for the day, that's fine. The benefits of breastfeeding are so clear-cut that it is likely that he may agree. Your

pediatrician can certainly discuss with both of you the importance of breastfeeding to the health of the baby. You might also try pumping breast milk and supplying your baby's father with bottles. Make sure you have some practice runs using the bottle interchangeably with the breast. Let your baby's father know that babies who breastfeed often reject the bottle despite successful practice runs and that he may be at a loss about what to do should she spend the night at his place. If you don't work this out with him, you may be the one making long-distance, late-night trips in your car!

UNPREDICTABLE VISITATION

The father of my child was very supportive the first two years of my son's life. But now he visits infrequently, popping in and out of our lives whenever he pleases. What can I do about this man? I think it is wrong for someone to just come and go as he pleases. Maybe I should keep my child from him, but my son loves him. How is this unpredictable relationship with his father going to affect my son later in life?

Just because his father sees your son sporadically doesn't mean that your son will automatically suffer problems later in life. But if you prevent him from seeing his father, you are asking for trouble. Your son, as he matures, will have to decide whether or not he wants his father in his life. It's clear that the father is not making the wisest choices regarding visitation, but this is how things are for a great many single mothers. The best thing you can do is to give your son a consistent and predictable home life. If his dad shows up and it's okay with you, let them spend time together. If not, then continue what you were doing before he interrupted you. As your son grows older, be sure to let your son know there is nothing about him that keeps his father away. Tell him that you don't know why his father isn't available to him more, but that is the way it is.

FROM VISITATION TO CUSTODY FOR MOM

Although I felt I was the more suitable parent during our divorce, my husband had the lawyer with the higher price tag and the more convincing mouth, and he got custody of our three children. Actually, he is an excellent parent, and the children have been living with him for five years while visiting me often. Recently, the oldest, my twelve-year-old daughter, has come to live with me, and things have been going very well. Her father agreed with this arrangement, particularly because she's going through "womanly stuff" and he felt my input would be beneficial. However, he hasn't given up sole custody. How can I parent like this?

Since your daughter is living with you full-time right now, you need the authority to make decisions regarding school, health care, and other issues concerning her welfare. You should discuss the need for decision-making authority as well as a possible transference of custody. It sounds as if you can

have a mature discussion with your ex about these critical matters.

EXPLORING COPARENTING

Coparenting simply means cooperating. Coparenting is an activity for grown-ups, with little or no room for immaturity because the well-being of the children is at stake. Keep in mind that each parent will come up with a different set of expectations and a different way to negotiate the rules, but they never abandon the keys to successful coparenting, which are cooperation, respect, and flexibility.

Successful coparenting is what happens when you both realize that divorce may have ended your marriage, but not your roles as parents. Sadly, the majority of couples who have separated have no idea that they can raise their children together successfully, even though they no longer live together. There are basically six steps toward coparenting successfully, and although it may seem that coparenting is impossible, keep in mind that there are degrees of cooperation. In other words, you are not jointly parenting, but rather trying to cooperate with each other to ensure the most consistency and least disruption in your child's life.

If all parents could coparent successfully, divorce and separation wouldn't be so devastating to children. The disruptions that arise when, for example, the family must relocate because income sharply declines complicate children's lives and force them to make difficult and painful adjustments. These disruptions would be greatly minimized by successful coparenting.

THE SIX STEPS OF COPARENTING

1. *Agree on who is the primary parent.* The primary parent is the one who shoulders the majority of the responsibility for all aspects of child-rearing, including health issues, education, financial support, day-to-day challenges, and routine activities. Although being primarily financially responsible is often unfair for the custodial parent, particularly because this parent is less able to advance along the career track than one with fewer home responsibilities, this parent usually does shoulder the majority of expenses. If your ex is not contributing his fair share financially, then coparenting is not happening because you can't honestly cooperate with someone who is deliberately cheating your children!

The best time to think about coparenting is while the separation or divorce agreements are being negotiated. If you decide after the agreement is signed that you want to coparent as the "bottom-line" parent, additional time and energy to rework the agreement will be necessary. Be aware that much of what men may want in agreements when they are the noncustodial parent has to do with control and money and not with concern over the well-being of the children.

If your children's father resists this notion of you as the "bottom-line" parent, point out that it simply must be this way since the children are living primarily under your supervision. Because most of the day-to-day responsibility is yours, you need the authority to make decisions without fear of being contradicted or undermined. Explain that you will certainly listen to his views and respect his opinions, but that this arrangement gives the children the consistency and the immediacy they need in their lives. Be sure to let your ex know that just because you are the "bottom-line" parent doesn't diminish his ability, attributes, and contributions as a person.

Although we are told that relationships must be equal to work best, the truth is that there is no such thing as a purely egalitarian relationship 100 percent of the time. In the healthiest of relationships, there is often a subtle shifting of power, not in an intimidating or controlling way, but rather in an "on call" kind of way. Look at close and comforting relationships you may have with family or friends. Each of you experiences times of need when the other is more "powerful." It is trust in the process of give-and-take that makes apparent the real meaning of relationships. For example, if your ex loses his job and must reduce his child support, perhaps with his extra free time he can help out more by dropping off or picking up the children at their various activities.

The task of coparenting requires different styles of participation. Don't expect the father of your child to behave exactly as you do, but rather enjoy the fact that he is contributing something different yet useful. You can learn something even if you are the primary or "bottom-line" parent.

2. *Vow to keep your feelings about each other out of your children's hearts and heads.* No matter what the extent of the pain, betrayal, or anger you are harboring, if you can't put a lid on it in

front of the children, then you will fail at coparenting. These feelings have to be worked through so that when you are talking with your ex about the children this does not become simply your time to vent. Coparenting requires that you act with maturity and dignity, and often this means putting other feelings on the back burner. Although you shouldn't hide these emotions, you need to find appropriate outlets to express them. Your ex is only interested in the day-to-day matters regarding your children. Intense expressions of anger or rage are not appropriate in a coparenting relationship.

Your ex is also probably not interested in hearing about your feelings. You may still have leftover feelings regarding the breakup and want to tell your ex something like "I still feel so much hurt over your affair." If you try to have such conversations with him, it only signals to him that it is time for the walls to come up. Words like that also mean that you are stuck and not ready to move ahead. It's impossible to work together when one person is stuck and the other person is hiding. Journal writing, joining a support group, either "live" or online, or seeking counseling are better ways of dealing with the emotional pain.

3. *Assure each other that you are doing the best job you can for the children.* Maintain a respect for this person if only because he is the father of your child. If his involvement with coparenting amounts to daily telephone calls and not much more than occasional weekends and holidays with the kids, there is a benefit in his contact with the children. Let him know his efforts are appreciated. He might need to be encouraged, and the carrot always works better than the stick. Being able to praise and show appreciation and respect for the other person often predicts whether or not a coparenting relationship will be successful.

4. *Always keep the lines of communication open.* Communication is the heart of any relationship. That's why it is so important to listen to your kids, your ex, and most of all, yourself. Many marriages and relationships suffered from lack of communication. If yours was one of them, resolve for the sake of the children to find a way to communicate. If you can't come to an agreement about effectively dealing with the children, or find that you chronically disagree, or either of you claims to have been uninformed regarding new rules or changes, then you need to establish clear rules and procedures. Schedule a regular weekly meeting during which planning problems and concerns are discussed. You can keep these meetings informal and on neutral territory where you are likely not to allow the discussion to escalate into a yelling match. Keep in mind, too, that these meetings don't have to take place in person. For example, why not take advantage of e-mail? Voice mail is also an excellent way to keep each other posted.

There has to be both the commitment and the tools by which regular communication takes place. Divorced and separated people, especially if the parting was a particularly bitter one, do not have the desire to talk with one another as friends. Communication will take much effort, but this communication is not unlike the kind that any successful partnership requires. Remember also that your feelings are important and deserve no less consideration and attention than those of your former partner. You will be unable to meet your children's emotional needs during this tricky time if you are emotionally adrift. Stay in touch with how you are feeling and respect the power of your own emotions.

5. *Allow for change and scary feelings.* There is nothing as certain in life as change. Changes will occur in your life as well as in your ex's life. New jobs, new interests, perhaps a return to school, an illness, a promotion, or even a move to a different neighborhood might be some of the possible changes. Your ex may remarry, and your children may have another adult in the picture when their father is in charge. Your ability to coparent successfully depends largely on your willingness to accept that circumstances will change.

True, change of any sort can seem terribly scary. In fact, it is the very fear of change that explains why so many people stay in relationships that are no longer satisfying or are even abusive. Your agreement to coparent represents another change on top of the big change everyone experiences in a major family disruption such as divorce. It's okay to be scared because it means that you recognize the power and potential in creating a whole new lifestyle that includes coparenting. Anyone facing such a formidable challenge would be less than realistic if they did not feel at least a little bit scared. Remember that a healthy bit of stage fright can produce the most astounding performances of a lifetime!

6. *Talk to and listen to your children.* Your children need the opportunity to express their feelings about how their lives have changed and how they feel about the new parenting arrangements. A child might balk at certain decisions. But you are still the parent, and he or she is still the child, which means that you have the final responsibility and final say. However, it is important to respect children's feelings and to listen to their fears and worries. Some of their fears, like who will take care of them when they are sick, can be easily assuaged by giving them the straightforward facts. You can explain to them, for example, that if they get sick that Aunt Linda or your best friend, Jean, will take care of them while you're at work.

Your children will want to know the nuts and bolts of the new arrangements. Younger children will want to know at whose house they will be trick-or-treating or how Santa Claus or the Tooth Fairy will find them. Older children will want to know who will attend parent conferences and sign their report cards and be there to cheer them on at soccer games. Will friends be allowed to sleep over at both Mom and Dad's houses, and can the dog come, too? Be ready with the answers. If you don't know, it's okay to say "Right now I just don't know, but as soon as I discuss this question with your father, I will let you know." Don't expect every single detail to be ironed out in advance. Encourage your children to share their suggestions and concerns with their dad. Better yet, if at all possible, have family meetings occasionally so that everyone gets a chance to be heard.

THE TRANSITION FROM HIS HOUSE TO YOURS

You take care of the kids all week, cooking, cleaning, working, schlepping them to and from activities, and listening to their stories ranging from hating the new teacher to having a crush on the little girl next door. Friday comes around, and you actually find yourself excited to see your ex because the freedom you are going to experience this weekend fills you with visions of pampering yourself, doing a little shopping, or—even more luxurious—sleeping till noon!

The kids are happy, too, because they know that they are getting away from the daily grind of school, chores, and homework. Saturday and Sunday to them mean eating pizza, watching cartoons when they get up in the morning, playing endless video games, and going to bed without taking a bath!

But now it's Sunday evening, and here they are, desperately needing a bath, a decent night's sleep, and a hot, healthy meal. They are exhausted, cranky, and hungry, and guess who has to endure these children-turned-monsters. That's right, it's good old Monday-through-Friday Mom!

You try to get them settled back into

their routine, but pretty soon they are screaming at you "I hate you! I want to live with Dad."

Before you have a total meltdown, think about this. Your ex probably had as much trouble with the kids over the weekend as you do when they are returned to you. He probably lets them do as they want because it is simply easier. You can pretty much count on Monday coming around and things settling back into place.

Try not to lose your temper or express hurt feelings when your children tell you everything that transpired over the weekend. Your children are not trying to hurt you but are trying to find a way to share their weekend lives with you. You don't want your children walking on eggshells around you because you well up with tears if they say that "Dad's girlfriend came by, and he treated us to ice cream sundaes."

Even with the best intentions and a genuine mutual interest in coparenting, transitions from one place to another are inevitably going to be bumpy. Try to make the change go a little more smoothly by:

♦ Establishing some kind of ritual. This ritual can be a signal to get back on track. You might have them take a bath or a shower—wash that dad right out of their hair, so to speak. Younger children may find a touch of aromatherapy soothing. Try adding a little bath product to scent the bath water with a calming fragrance.

♦ Remembering that your kids see the weekend world as one without the Monday through Friday responsibilities. Let your kids know, whether they live with you or Dad, that responsibilities are part of life, even if it means accepting the consequences for being irresponsible at times. For instance, if your daughter won't brush her teeth at Dad's, chances are the next visit to the dentist will cause a consequence that will be her responsibility to shoulder.

- Talking to your ex about trying to set up shared expectations for your kids so that there is some kind of routine despite the transition.

WHEN YOUR EX SETS NO RULES OR LIMITS AT HIS PLACE

My six- and eight-year-old sons visit their father every other weekend. Although I look forward to the break and the opportunity to pursue my own activities, when the boys return, the free time hardly seems worth it. Their father's house is vacation city to them—no set bedtimes, eating lots of take-out food, and constant snacking. The boys will frequently tell me that I am mean and too strict because when they visit Dad they are allowed to do so many things I do not permit. Do not suggest that he and I sit down and negotiate. If we had been able to work complicated and important issues like this out, we would not have gotten divorced. It seems like my children's lives will always be in turmoil because of all the transitions they must make due to our divorce.

Instead of thinking about your sons' need to make transitions as a negative experience, remember that everyone needs to learn to behave differently in different settings. We are not allowed, for example, to speak loudly in church or in libraries, but it is fine and in fact expected and encouraged to shout and make noise at a football game. Helping your boys to make the transition from one household to another—households with different rules, standards, and expectations—is an opportunity for you to teach your children a valuable lesson in life.

Hold a family meeting where you sit down and have a talk with the boys. Acknowledge that there are different rules with Dad than with you. Talk about these differences in terms of context, not personality. For example, tell your children that because Dad sees them only on weekends that bedtime can be flexible because they do not have to get up for school the next day. Since they are not at their dad's all the time, the kind of food they eat there can be an occasional treat. If they lived there all the time, different food standards would probably apply. Avoid discussing differences in terms of personality, such as saying that "your father allows you to eat take-out food because he is too lazy to prepare nutritious food." Although this might be perfectly true, you will only make the situation worse by bad-mouthing your ex and exposing his shortcomings.

Even though children often want to see their parents together, they have a natural instinct to divide and conquer because this manipulation helps them get their way. By making this a personality issue, they will seize the opportunity to pit you against each other in a kind of twisted "who-loves-them-more" or "who-is-the-better-parent" contest. Stick to the simple reality that different rules and expectations will prevail at each house because there are different life circumstances at each house. At your house, bedtime is important because school cannot be missed. Nutritious food is eaten because you are responsible for their good health. Occasional lapses are okay, and those lapses will take place at Dad's. This does not make you the "mean mother"; so refuse to accept this role. This makes you the consistent, caring, dependable parent every child needs. Anybody can be a playmate to a child; it takes a grown-up to be a parent!

CAN I WITHHOLD VISITATION?

I'm tired of being Ms. Nice Guy to my ex and Ms. Bad Mom to the kids. My ex-husband and I had a fairly civil divorce, and he agreed wholeheartedly to me being the custodial parent. But now, after I had been pretty generous about his visitation rights, he's keeping the children later and later in the evenings and even sometimes overnight on Sunday. He thinks he can make up for not being with them all the time by spoiling them. Because he recently got laid off from work, he stopped paying child support but says it is only temporary. It's amazing how he can take them to any restaurant they want, buy them toys and clothes without having a job, and give them money whenever they want for video games. Can I withhold visitation, especially because he is not contributing financially right now?

There is no connection between support and visitation. Legally, you cannot withhold visitation strictly on the grounds of failure to pay child support.

But, if you really believe the amount of time your kids spend with their dad is detrimental to them, you could request that the court order on visitation be strictly enforced. However, it would certainly be better for all involved if you solve this problem together since there will be so many years of coparenting ahead. As calmly as possible and not in front of the children, explain to your ex that his child support obligation has not stopped because he is unemployed. A portion of his unemployment compensation should be going to the support of the children. If he anticipates that he will be out of work for a long time, it is up to him to get his child support obligations reduced in a civil court. Until his child support is reduced by court order, his obligations remain the same, and back support keeps accumulating. He is not helping himself and certainly not helping the children by being Mr. Big Shot with the unlimited supply of money for video games and other toys and treats. If you are not able to work this situation out between you, contact your local child support enforcement agency or discuss this situation with your attorney.

Explain to your ex that the kids being late for school Monday morning or arriving unprepared is only going to cause grief in their future, not necessarily in yours or his. He might be feeling very inadequate right now, after losing his job not long after losing his family, at least in the traditional sense. Generally, spoiling is nothing more than an inconvenience to moms perpetrated by grandmothers, rich aunts, and guilty ex-husbands. If you feel your children are being harmed by the kind of attention your ex is lavishing on them, then certainly a strictly enforced visitation schedule would make sense.

SHARING DISCIPLINE

My ex-husband says that my children behave badly—in ways they never do at home—and that his stepchildren, who now live with him full time, complain about their visits. I just don't buy this. I'm not sure what to do.

First, buy it. Most likely, this situation, common to new stepfamilies, is caused by your ex not enforcing house rules. His new wife may not feel it is her appropriate role to discipline your children.

It's not your house; so it is up to the two of them to establish rules. Your ex needs to figure out if he is indulging his children's every whim and letting them rule the roost because he feels guilty about the divorce. It might help if Dad spent more one-on-one time with the children—it is probably painful to them that he lives with his stepchildren, but not with them. Even though it is also up to the adults of that household to spell out what happens when rules aren't obeyed—for example, loss of TV privileges—you can still talk to your children and explain that this is not how you taught them to behave in other people's homes. Just because this is Dad's house does not mean they have license to behave as if no one else who lives there matters. Make it clear that you don't want to hear any more unpleasant reports about their behavior.

22

The Ex Factor: Handling Him and Your Ex Relations

You probably already know the good and bad about custody and coparenting. Coparenting with a cooperative, considerate, and reliable ex can be heavenly, but if you experience more of the bad, you may be asking yourself "what did I do to deserve this!" Don't lose heart. Dealing with your ex means coping successfully with his friends and family. This is not unlike negotiating your way through any complicated life situation. The key is to set boundaries that prevent others from hurting you and also to prevent you from stepping too far into their camp. You can learn to understand where his friends and family are coming from and then decide where you draw the line.

THE EX FROM HELL

Attempting to cooperate with an ex with whom communication was difficult enough when you were together can be the nightmare from hell. Of course, you're way better off having an ex from hell than a partner from hell. Still, it's best for you, your children, and everyone around you if you learn to manage a difficult ex.

No matter what twists and turns, advances and setbacks appear in most of the stories of divorce and other breakups; your previous relationship will never improve by the mere act of removing yourself. Most likely, the postsplit days will be a continuation of the same problems that ultimately killed the relationship in the first place. Things can get worse. You may no longer be able to depend on his financial contributions. Your ex may become so emotionally unavailable that he slowly disappears forever from your life. Some women, of course, could easily argue that this would really be a plus. If he was financially irresponsible—you shooed the creditors away, kept the lights on, paid the rent or mortgage, and bought food—nothing will have changed. Look at it this way, you might save a buck or two by no longer having a man-child to feed and shelter.

THE NINE MOST CHALLENGING EX-MEN!

Even if you have an impossible ex, there is hope. There are steps you can take to ensure that you can relate to him. Too many women limit their efforts to cope with an ex from hell by fantasizing, but then again, imagination is a powerful coping strategy.

To deal successfully with this guy, instead of imagining impending doom, get clear about why he is such a problem. Ask yourself what you can do differently that might at least enable the two of you to avoid major clashes? How can you change your own behavior? Our own behavior and our reactions to how others behave are the only things anyone can realistically control. Deal with him more successfully by using what you'll learn about ex-men.

Ex-Man #1: The Sperminator

Whatever he said at one time, when it comes to actually parenting, this guy's just gone to places unknown. Don't be surprised if you find out he has children all over the place. He just does not see the realities of fatherhood as his problem or responsibility. He may be one hot guy. You thought you were the one he would cherish forever and want to be the mother of his children. But, he's a lean, mean, baby-making machine and is just too caught up in himself to think about anyone else for too long. This guy is seductive, charming, and alluring, and well, you just couldn't help yourself.

When handling the absence of the Sperminator, take heart in knowing you were a victim of his lies, you weren't the only one who believed in him, and, yes,

he probably did love you best for just that brief moment. Beware: if he does make an appearance, don't be fooled or believe his lies again, or you may get morning sickness again!

Ex-Man #2: The RAT (Really Always There)

The RAT is simply around too much, but always on his own terms. Rather than simply providing adequate child support and spending time with their children, RATs consciously maneuver their former wives or significant others into circumstances, financial and otherwise, that work best for them. The needs, wants, and desires of their former partners are never given any serious consideration. All the behaviors of the RAT can be explained by their need to keep their ex dependent and to maintain control over the family. In all likelihood, they chose to leave their children.

Often there is some kind of dance between former spouses that maintains the connection between them way beyond the point of appropriate cooperation on behalf of the children. The father may see his ex-wife as having a very specific place in his life. Her role in life is to be the mother of his children. Although he would give ready lip service to her entitlement to a life of her own, this man constructs and manipulates the shared parenting responsibilities in such a way that her freedom and decision-making are minimized while his power and control over the children remain unchallenged.

You may feel that accepting this role serves your needs, if you think half (or less) of this relationship is better than none at all. But it will stunt your emotional growth.

It's tempting to keep a RAT around because he appears to do so much for his family. But, little traces of his visits linger long after the RAT is gone, causing contamination of the home. Total extermination isn't the answer, but RAT control is. Firm boundaries must be set: the RAT needs to call first or have set times for communicating with the family. Expectations must be made clear: he's visiting, not living in your home. Finally, the temptation to ask him to help you needs to be resisted: when the faucet is leaking, fix it yourself or call a plumber. RATs don't go away by themselves but will stay away for longer periods when they aren't so welcome.

I've been dating a guy who seems devoted to his kids, but something weird is happening. Even though he's been divorced for ages, I feel like the other woman! He's constantly at his ex's house doing something, while I pull teeth just to get him to go to a movie with me. I care about him, but this is hurting me.

That's because you are dating a RAT. You may at first be impressed with his love and concern for his kids. He may even, in what he sees as a noble gesture, blame himself for the dissolution of his marriage. He may say the divorce was his idea, and because he admits the marriage ended due to his vague reasons of discontent, you may think "Hey, this guy's got his priorities in order because the issues with the ex are largely resolved." Hold on! As you get to know him, you'll see something's out of place. You'll hear more about his ex than you care to know and may be struck by the intricacies of the

arrangements between them. For example, they may still have their insurance policies for their cars tied together, even if they have been divorced for ten years. He's aware of how much money she makes and where she spent her last vacation, and he may even be in a position to veto any home repairs or remodeling in her house.

Some RATs are free to come and go in their ex's home, or his ex may do his laundry or care for him when he's sick. Why? He probably feels guilty about the effects his leaving had on his children. If his identity and confidence are tightly linked to his children but he didn't want to stay married, then he is trying to maintain his role as father and head of the household.

As nice and devoted as the RAT appears, he's really a controlling kind of man who deals with his guilt by keeping his former home's activities close to his standards and expectations, maintaining a distorted kind of tie with his ex.

The ex-wife needs to set clear boundaries for this person—no comings and goings uninvited, no veto power in homemaking decisions. You need to have your expectations met, too, even if it is just getting him to a movie. If you can handle the relationship for what it's worth and enjoy him in the here and now, that's fine. But if what you want is a committed union, it would be better to look elsewhere.

Ex-Man #3: Meet the MAD (Minimal Access Dad)

There are many variations of the MAD (Minimal Access Dad). A MAD typically provides only the bare minimum, whether it is financial support, emotional giving, or both. For him, his children are psychologically and physically in a convenient, safe niche far from the practical realities of his everyday life.

I recently visited a college friend who is the divorced single mother of two teenage boys. She is really struggling—financially, emotionally, and professionally. There is not a nickel to spare, and her family often does without much of what they want and need. Her former husband, a lawyer, has all the trappings of major success—big house, lavish vacations, expensive car, country club memberships, and trophy wife. My friend is the one who put him through law school! How can this man not give a damn and offer only the bare minimum of child support, knowing his children need winter clothes? I'm enraged!

There is more social injustice and unfairness in the world than we are sometimes able to face. This story is a sample of that injustice. However, without rage, social injustice continues, since rage is what powers social change. In spite of recognizing the low priority our society assigns to the welfare of children, it sounds as if you are trying to understand how this becomes an all-too-familiar family situation. Of course, you would like to offer your friend some kind of practical help or advice.

This man can appear not to give a damn about his children because he simply does not think about it at all. MADs are not even aware of, let alone troubled by, the fact that they are taking lavish vacations while their children may not, for example, have sufficient warm clothing. If this inequity is pointed out to them, they may grudgingly take some action, but

typically they don't. MADs lack the essential emotional connection with their children. Their character is simply not linked to the happiness and well-being of their children. They have other priorities.

Your girlfriend shouldn't blame herself. If she looks back at her relationship with a realistic eye, she'll see that what is now obvious—the lack of emotional connection with the children—is part of a long-standing pattern. It probably had a lot to do with why her relationship ended in the first place. Like many MADs, her ex may insidiously communicate that

SINGLE MOMS AROUND THE GLOBE

Support groups for divorced and unmarried moms are cropping up in Israel, China, Thailand, Japan, Iran, Australia, and many North African nations.

European Union (EU) countries already responding to the needs of single-mother families, such as Germany, Norway, Holland, and Sweden, offer affordable housing, benefits to new moms, and even college education. The EU provides free health care, a strong pension fund, and the help mothers need to raise their babies without financial woes. Europeans *practice* the "it takes a village" concept.

Does this mean you should pack up the kid and buy a one-way ticket abroad? Not so fast. Russian single moms, one-fourth of all households, are struggling to survive. There are some real horror stories coming from countries such as Nigeria, where a mom was nearly stoned to death for being a mother outside of marriage. U.S. women and others worldwide petitioned the government, and she was freed.

she got what she deserved because of something she did or didn't do during their relationship. Not true. Even so, it's helpful for all of us to look back on our relationships and come to terms with our part in the difficulties that ended it.

Ex-Man #4:
The Strafe Bomber

Remember those old World War II black-and-white movies? The unsuspecting civilians would be going about their everyday life, and suddenly, without warning, a squadron of bombers would swoop down from the sky. Boom! The countryside was in flames and ruin. The civilians were left to rebuild while at the same time hardly knowing what had hit them or when these same attack bombers might return.

This sad scene pretty much describes life with the strafe-bomber ex. You go along doing the best you can for yourself and your children, trying to hold everything together, and suddenly, without warning, he swoops in with a big noisy show, leaving nothing but emotional destruction in his wake.

A perfect example is the ex who rarely visits with the children but is otherwise a good-time guy. When you try to discuss things like homework, rules, and routines, he turns a deaf ear. He simply seems to take no interest, and when he does, his reactions are always dramatic and, of course, lack any kind of follow-up.

- *Strafe Bombers Are Deaf But Not Mute.* Women with this type of ex learn to handle more on their own because they know that involving the ex only leads to headaches. One such woman reported that when her younger son was diagnosed with attention deficit

hyperactivity disorder (ADHD), her ex was the last person she turned to for help and advice.

Because her son was more distractible than most seven-year-old boys, his attention span, except for video games and TV, was short. He had trouble staying in his seat and listening to directions and suffered a disastrous kindergarten year. Through hard work and lots of reading, this mom became something of an expert on children with this disorder. She worked cooperatively and closely with her son's school to make sure first grade was a better experience for him. The teachers began to see the child in a whole new light, acknowledging his creative side and encouraging his willingness to learn to read. Everyone regarded this particular crisis to be at least under control.

Spending one weekend with his father, the child was accused of being a "space cadet" because he was unable to perform requested tasks. As you might guess, the ex accused this mother of not spending enough time with her son. One thing led to another, and she found herself discussing ADHD and all the reading she had done and all the meetings she had attended.

- *Strafe Bombers Don't Respond, They React.* The strafe bomber only hears what he wants to hear and reacts immediately, inappropriately, and dramatically. In this case, the father decided he was going to the school the very next morning to "have a serious talk with the teachers and straighten this thing out." He arrived at school like a bull in a china shop, intimidating, criticizing, and belittling all involved, and managed to undo at least some of the work the mom and school staff had done to get the child on track.

  The strafe bomber will position himself by declaring "I am the father," as if that gives him the power to attack.

- *The Shelling Can Happen Anytime, Anywhere.* The bombing can happen any day or every day. The strafe-bomber ex may be one of those guys who still feels that the marital residence, now occupied by you and the children, is still his house. The "bomber attacks" may simply be his frequent unannounced visits when he takes the opportunity to make some comment or criticism that leaves everyone present just a little less happy, less content, or less at peace than before he arrived.

  The strafe-bomber ex has a short, selective memory coupled with the need to make grand entrances. Even if he is well-off, when asked for financial help, such as for college expenses, he might reply that he is tapped out. No matter how many jobs you or your children have or how many loans you've taken out, watch what happens when graduation day joyfully arrives. The strafe bomber will show up big as life with a video camera and proceed to document the whole event as if it was his idea and responsibility from start to finish.

- *Damage Control for the Strafe Bomber.* There are ways to control the damage caused by the strafe-bomber ex. Above all else, set boundaries and edit the information and access given to the strafe-bomber ex carefully. Your children will need more careful instruction and guidance regarding what is appropriate behavior and what is not. For example, in the case of the bombing caused by the ex when he showed up at his child's school, Mom should be prepared to explain this to her son. "It was inappropriate for your father to come to school after never having come to any other school event and begin yelling at the teachers. It hurt your teachers' feelings and embarrassed me. A better way would have been for him to come to conferences all along and listen carefully to all the ideas everyone had." Your children will need you to set a good example of the value and importance of day-to-day consistency and the true meaning of commitment.

Ex-Man #5: The "Back-from-the-Dead" Ex

Similar to the strafe bomber, the back-from-the-dead ex suddenly arrives and decides he wants to be part of things. Often their sudden arrival corresponds with your legal demands for child support. These men will sometimes go so far as to try to sue for custody—a real explosion. The difference between a strafe bomber and a back-from-the-dead is that there was always a slight hum in the distance from the strafe bomber, making you aware that he was still alive.

But you won't have heard a single word from this other type of ex for several years. You may begin to grow tired of shouldering all the expenses yourself and take advantage of improved child support enforcement and locate him. This kind of ex might want to be back in his child's life not only because he is now paying support but also because his son or daughter might be at "more of a fun age" than when you all lived together. He might even try to persuade your children to move in with him.

The common thread that binds strafe bombers and back-from-the-deads is the lack of emotional maturity needed to be a productive, contributing, consistent presence in the lives of their children. These men see their "bombing runs" as proof positive that they are good fathers, when actually these runs are their attempt to atone for their lack of consistent involvement with their children. Their typical reaction is to blame you. When pressed about their lack of involvement with their children, typically they will say that their ex-wives kept the children from them. In the companionship of their children, they seek to meet their own emotional needs. They may even describe their children as their best friends. For an older child, the reappearance of Dad and the opportunity to live with Dad with a fresh start in a different part of the country can be very enticing.

Ex-Man #6:
The Cowboy

The cowboy really isn't such a bad guy; he just needs to ride into the sunset every now and then to find himself. Cowboys need room. They need space. They need a change. Like the back-from-the-dead ex, these are men your children barely hear from for years at a stretch. But, when they return, they are all glitter and glamour, electric horsemen with stories to share about adventures on the long and lonely road. The bad news, however, is that every time they show up there is the hope and expectation that somehow things will be different. Children think that maybe this time their father will stay. When children are much older, they will understand the pattern and with support and reassurance will see that it is the limitations of their dad, and not anything they have done, that has caused Dad to pursue the great unknown.

These guys aren't purposely harmful unless their mystique convinces your children to forget their "real life" and run off and join the cowboy dad's nomadic life. Things usually turn out okay, amounting to nothing more than the children, like the ex, watching too many old Westerns. However, to avoid

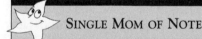

SINGLE MOM OF NOTE

Golda Meier,
Political Leader

Golda Meir was a widow by the time she became the Prime Minister of Israel in 1969, but in fact, the couple had been separated for years before then. Golda said of being a working single mom of two children, "At work, you think of the children you have left at home. At home, you think of the work you've left unfinished. Such a struggle is unleashed within yourself. Your heart is rent."

stepping in his cow patties, stress to your children that his stay is temporary. Saying that "Daddy is just visiting" helps dispel the fantasy that maybe this time it is forever. When their father promises things like a fishing trip or a chance to visit him in his own home on the range, share the children's excitement by affirming that it would be wonderful if they could visit Dad where he lives. But when he gallops off, be ready to give your children an extra measure of love and reassurance.

If your ex has any kind of permanent address, older children should certainly be encouraged to write or e-mail him, if that's possible. You could also create a daddy box where things they would like to show Daddy are stored until the next time he moseys into town. In fact, the daddy box is a terrific idea for any child who has some variation of the Minimal Access Dad.

Ex-Man #7:
The NYPD Blues

This guy is not a policeman. You're blue because he wasn't much of a parent when you were together. Now he's got a new family he seems to dote on, and all you want to do is ask—no, shout— "Now you're playing Daddy?"

I am a thirty-nine-year-old mother. My husband left town after our divorce. Although we hear from him occasionally and sometimes he even sends child support and a rare birthday gift, he basically has a noncommittal relationship with his daughter. Now he's discovered parenting since marrying and becoming the doting stepfather of four-year-old twins. On top of this, his new wife (who was pregnant when they married) recently had a baby, and he tells me they are both thrilled. My daughter took the news of her father's newfound interest in parenting in stride and even thinks it is kind of neat to have a little stepbrother. Where was he for his daughter? I am so angry I can't describe it.

It's justifiable to feel anger for an ex who had so inadequately provided for his child and involved himself so little in her life and now seems so committed to this new set of children.

Most likely, this new development made you think back on why you and your husband divorced in the first place. In many situations, women find that at the time of their marriage their husbands were emotionally impoverished and immature men. They had few emotional resources left after always placing themselves and their needs first.

Maybe, life for your ex had been a progressive lesson in learning how to love. Women unwilling to put up with immature and selfish behavior have dumped men like this more than once. One day, it dawns on them that they have to make some changes or remain alone.

Your ex needed intensive and ongoing tutoring, and his new wife is apparently willing to be his teacher. You and maybe others either have been unwilling to be his teachers or are simply burned out trying to teach the unteachable.

Your daughter is able to accept her father's situation for what it is because you have provided her with the emotional strength to accept his limitations.

- *When His Family Becomes the Only Family.* When a former partner remarries or becomes involved with a new partner as an energetic parent to his new children or stepchildren, it is painful. The pain is greatly magnified when his care and concern for the children you share has been less than adequate or nonexistent. Remember that things are not always as they seem. Some men want you to think that they have become standout dads as a way to hurt or further reject you. They can do little to you directly but can still hurt you through your children. These men may be looking to provoke expressions of outrage from you.

- *What's Ideal for Her Is Not for You.* Women equally willing to parent men as if they were their children have transformed some men into the picture of paternal involvement. This guy may show up if asked and babysit if directed, but the real feelings of attachment and commitment are just as absent for the new set of children as they are for yours. His new wife or partner is simply more willing to put effort into creating the ideal picture than you were.

- *Maybe It's a Miracle.* Some men do change, evolving slowly into the kind of man we hoped they would be when we married them. If this miracle has

actually occurred, it probably took many years and a lot of hard knocks. It is unlikely that if you had stayed with him he would have changed in the same way. You are certainly different than you might have been had you stayed married. The same thing has happened to him.

- *Accept the Changes.* Things are different now. He has changed, his circumstances have changed, and his experiences have made him different. You know that you are different and in many ways better. Accept this change in him. His "improvement" can be a wonderful gift to you and your children. Allow your children to be involved with their father and his new life. Make good use of this unexpected break from daily child care responsibilities to relax and pursue your own interests without worry or guilt. Tell yourself that "his growth is my gain."

Ex-Man #8:
The Under-DOG (Under Darling's Orders to Grovel)

When a former partner commits to a new relationship, you may find the shaky alliance you previously forged as coparents greatly changed. This new wife or girlfriend is clearly calling the shots. The child support checks now bear her signature and arrive late. There is no room to negotiate for one penny more, no matter what unexpected circumstances arise. When your ex calls you from the office or workplace, he is talkative and interested in hearing about the children. Calls made or received from his new home are abrupt. You always get the feeling that you or the children have called at the wrong time.

◆ *This Puppy Was Never Weaned.* Your children's visits to Dad become crises. Your daughter announces that Dad's new wife says that you are fat or a slob or sucking Dad dry. Your son may tell you that Dad is not allowed to do certain things anymore, like have a beer before dinner or see some of his old friends. She yells at your children frequently. You wonder why she does not take the weekend off and visit a girlfriend instead of spending time with children who so obviously annoy her. The change in your former husband's behavior is hard to understand. He seems to have turned into kind of a sissy.

Look beneath the hurt, and this is what you find. Your former husband has been looking for and found what he needed—a mother. He is not able to function in a relationship as an equal partner. He wants to be taken care of, and these needs are so strong that he is willing to sacrifice his relationship with his children to get the care he needs.

◆ *The Controller and Under-DOG Are Sickly Compatible.* The new woman is the type of person who feels adequate only when she is part of a couple. She is controlling and insecure. She does hate having your children visit, but she could never go off and visit a girlfriend. She has to be there so she can continue to be in control. She is insecure in his love and feels jealous and resentful of his attachments to his children and his past relationship with you. She sees you as a constant threat no matter how you really feel about your ex.

This is a tough situation. The more you try to intervene, the more controlling she will be and the more

hostile he will be. By trying to keep things on an even keel for your children, you are interfering with their disturbed little dance. Try to stop the music, and you will know how deeply enmeshed they are. He mistakes her control for the love he never got from Mom. She wants to edit out his children so that she can have him all to herself. There is no maturity or stability here. Attempts to change either one will not meet with success.

◆ *You're Equipped to Play by Her Rules.* Try to play by the new rules while still keeping your children and yourself relatively sane. If you are able to call him at work, do so. Try to keep your children's visits short and with activities planned. Talk to your children about how Dad's new wife may react to what are pretty typical behaviors for their age. Make sure they bring lots of "quiet-time" activities, like games and puzzle books. Do not overreact to the comments made about you, which your children will dutifully report to you. If she could see you laugh off her rude insults, it would make her nuts. That fact alone should give you strength. Show your children how mature adults behave. The lesson will not be lost on them. It will comfort them to know that she does not have all that much power over you.

Do not dignify her name-calling or petty remarks by responding to them. Calling her names and making snide remarks about her in front of the children will not help. If you feel comfortable having your former husband in your home, see if he will visit the children there. She may be more at ease knowing you are not there during his visits; use this free time to pursue your own interests and activities. Resist the urge to share your insights about how screwed up this relationship is. Nothing will be improved for you or your children by telling your former husband that he is a momma's boy or acting like a sissy. Be glad that while the music plays and they dance their little dance, you are singing your own song.

Ex-Man #9:
RUN (Really Ugly News)!

Members of this group include active alcoholics, substance abusers, bigamists, con artists, men serving repeat jail time, and men who disappear for several years at a time without a trace. Your children may see these men only once every several years or may see them often but never for the right reasons. These men may never be sober or capable of recognizing any degree of responsibility toward their children. They can be counted on for nothing.

Contacts with these men almost always bring great emotional pain. There is always the hope that this time things will be different, but somehow things never are. See and accept the truth. Failure to accept the truth will cause your children's hopes to be continually dashed, making it hard for them to trust other people. Help your children to separate what he is from what they are and are capable of becoming. Explain their apparent abandonment in terms of the father's inadequacies or addictions, not theirs. Say that "Your father is not able to care for you because he is always breaking the law and ends up spending a lot of time in jail" or "He has a problem with drugs that makes him very sick. This is why he is not able to help take care

of you." Be vigilant about establishing healthy habits at home, particularly if the problem is drugs or alcohol. Consistent, predictable routines are especially critical for your children. If your children want to maintain contact with their father, phone calls, letters, and e-mails may be possible.

WHEN YOUR EX BEHAVES IRRESPONSIBLY

My ex-husband infuriates me. He takes the children once or twice a month, but he's always late picking them up. (I think he does this just so I can't plan my weekend.) He usually shows up with one of his idiotic chain-smoking friends, knowing that the little one has allergies. He forgets to make the children put on their seat belts, and when I insist that they wear seat belts or he can't leave with them, he mutters and grumbles with a cigarette sticking out of his mouth while adjusting and tightening the children's belts. Then he takes off like a bat out of hell while I'm handing him their medicine or other essentials. To make matters worse, I'm convinced he parties and takes drugs while the kids are at his apartment. He's fairly regular with child support payments so I can't withhold visitation, but I can't believe he's taking good care of them! Any ideas?

It would be surprising if this bad behavior was not the main reason you two are no longer together.

There are some steps you can take to deal appropriately with your ex. The key is to establish communication.

Let him know that you will give him a chance to speak while you listen and that you would like him to listen to you when it is your turn to talk. Many successful negotiators are firm believers in setting time limits. Suggest to him that your discussions about weekend plans be limited to five minutes. Most everyone can hold it together that long.

When your ex comes to pick up the children, make sure they are not waiting outside so he can just pile them in the car and peel out of there without talking to you. Invite him in for a cup of coffee or soft drink (no alcohol) and tell him, very politely, that you need to go over a few things with him regarding his plans for the weekend. Allow him to speak and then say your piece, requesting that no drinking or use of drugs is to take place while the children are in his care. Also explain that the law requires children to wear seat belts. Remember to let him know that it would be best for the children if you could cooperate with each other. Stay calm, and don't let him push your buttons. Finally, know that legally, child support and visitation have nothing to do with each other. If you're convinced that his behavior is a danger to your children, you will need witnesses or proof of his neglect. Are the children injured or sick when they return home?

Do you know for a fact that he abuses drugs and/or alcohol?

For your own peace of mind, if you really believe his behavior endangers the children's safety, speak with your attorney immediately about possible legal options.

Don't let your children ride in a car with an ex who has been drinking or taking drugs. If your ex is impaired and insists on taking your child in his car with him, don't upset him. Call the police or 911 immediately, explain the situation, and give the police all the details, such as the license plate number and the direction he was heading. Protect your children and yourself!

If your ex has been unsafe to be around but is in some kind of treatment program, investigate the safe visitation havens that some cities offer. These are supervised facilities where a parent and his children can meet on neutral territory, thereby sticking to a visitation agreement. Check with your local Department of Social Services or county health department.

WHEN THE KIDS ARE MAD AT YOU

I think it is destructive to bad-mouth or even criticize a child's absent parent, but doesn't there come a time to sit my teenage sons down and tell them that the reason they can't play hockey, join the soccer team, or go away to summer camp is because their father supports them only minimally? It bothers me the way both boys complain about the run-down house and the lack of money to buy clothes, criticizing me while thinking their father has nothing to do with this.

Maybe if I wait it out, they will one day realize the truth.

You're right; relentless bad-mouthing of the noncustodial or absent parent is harmful. However, you understandably have strong feelings of rage, anger, hurt, and disappointment. These feelings need to be expressed but not directed at your children.

Conversely, when we refuse to make any comment regarding the conduct of our former spouse, strong emotions are also at work. The opposite of bad-mouthing the other parent is denying our feelings, which is harmful to you. Many women do this because they fear that if they stated how they really felt that they would become totally out of control, a scary feeling for most of us. When we repress our anger, the result is often depression. Here's the catch-22: depression makes us more vulnerable to the inequities MADs perpetuate. Depression also gives permission to your ex-husband to dish out as truth the idea that you are somehow to blame.

Your children are clearly angry, but they are not exactly sure at what. Because you are their only emotional anchor, guess who hears it? The energy you expend repressing your feelings, coupled with the energy your boys spend complaining, could be put to better use by holding a family meeting and getting to the point regarding your financial situation. Forget the fantasy about some future magical moment of enlightenment when the children recognize and praise you for your many years of silent sacrifice. Even if it did happen, nobody is comfortable around martyrs. Let them know that they are deserving, wonderful kids and that they really have nothing to do with

their father's neglectful behavior. This is just how it is.

WHAT TO DO IF YOUR EX BAD-MOUTHS YOU TO YOUR KIDS

Why is he bad-mouthing you? Is he angry because you are building a new life, perhaps with a new and improved partner? Is this just a continuation of patterns in your previous relationship? Whatever the case, rejoice that you are on your own. Perhaps his new bachelor life is not all that he imagined it would be.

If your children are under the age of eight and report that "Daddy says you are something bad," reply that "I am sorry to hear that Daddy feels that way."

If your children are older, add that "I've noticed that people who bad-mouth other people usually feel bad about themselves. I am sorry your father is feeling this way."

Employ nonemotional responses. Your children will lose interest in reporting these remarks to you. Dad may learn that they did not mention his comments, and the bad-mouthing will lessen because he isn't getting any reinforcement.

Never bad-mouth him back. If you blow your stack, your children will share this information with him when he asks, and the dialog will continue.

If he persists and the children are upset by his words, you can try speaking to him privately and let him know that his words do not hurt you but do hurt the children very much.

RESOLVE TO FORGIVE YOUR EX—FOR THE SAKE OF YOUR CHILD

I have raised my son alone for the past eleven years and have done a fine job. My husband ran off with someone else when I was pregnant and rarely has any contact with me or his child. No birthday presents, no Christmas cards. Other than a couple of phone calls asking to speak to his son (I refused) and one hospital visit when my son had surgery, he has really not shown any interest. Now he wants to see my son more often and actually sent a very expensive Christmas present, which I never gave to my son. What nerve to try to worm his way into our lives now! Where was he when the going got rough? Why on earth should I let this selfish man give anything to my son now?

Why should you let this person give anything to your son? Because your child has a right to know his father—shortcomings and all.

You need to take responsibility for your bruised feelings about your ex before you can even discuss his father with your son. Whatever happened between you and this man has nothing to do with who your child is—rarely do people run off or get divorced specifically for the purpose of harming a youngster. What generally exists is a situation where a father cannot handle the responsibility of raising children or suffers from such a lack of confidence that he has very little to offer a family. Maybe there is a drug and/or alcohol problem, or the irresponsible parent lacks everyday coping skills. Whatever

they can give—whether one phone call a year or an expensive present every ten years—might be the only thing this person is capable of giving and should be recognized as the best they might be able to do.

It sounds incredibly complicated and painful, separating your emotions from the current situation, but any good psychologist will tell you that it is the only way to move on. After all, what's done is done. Why should your child be deprived of any information about the other parent because you still harbor angry feelings toward him? What's painful for you may not be unpleasant for your son. In fact, experts have been saying for years that some knowledge about the absent parent, good and bad, is more beneficial to a child than unanswered questions.

Try forgiving this person for his failings and inadequacies. This doesn't mean giving up the struggle for child support, if that is an issue, or anything else to which your child is entitled. It also doesn't mean letting this person into your child's life without establishing ground rules or dismissing your own emotions toward your ex. It does mean, however, that you are willing to let your child form his own relationship with him without imposing your feelings. This is not the only relationship whose painful and joyous moments your child will have to weather—life is a series of uncertainties. People have a right to experience situations in their own personal way.

DEALING WITH YOUR EX-RELATIONS

Even if your ex is ideal, your ex-relations can be a factor. Your former spouse's or partner's family may previously have been so involved with you and your children that you considered them your family, too. If you've established a relationship with members of his family, maybe his mother or a favorite sister, and you've managed to maintain this connection, you have made great strides for you and your children. The continuing connection to family can be tremendously therapeutic for the children whose parents are ending their relationship.

For the majority of estranged couples, however, the separation also brings the departure of other family members. After the breakup, you may notice a sudden change. Where once you and your ex's sister talked on the phone for hours, shopped together, and complained about the male species with a secret camaraderie, you now find that you are being snubbed, overlooked, or, worse, even made the target of attacks and complaints. Of course, this will affect you because these rejections come at a time when you are especially vulnerable and are in need of support by friends and family.

FIGHTING REJECTION

It certainly would be understandable for you to at least show your disappointment at being rebuffed by people who were once so close to you and your children. Women who have been through this strongly advise against it. The reason? Even though these people may no longer be a part of your life, your child still has a right to remain connected to them. Of course, if they choose to disappear totally, you can't force them to remain family to your child. You can try to arrange time to discuss this issue

and let these individuals know how you feel about their keeping contact with your children. Why not send a letter expressing your hope that a relationship with your children be maintained? A letter makes it impossible for you to be misquoted or misunderstood or for you to say things in the heat of the moment that you might later regret. You may also want to show your children the letter you are sending, or you may wish to keep a copy of the letter to share with younger children at a later time.

HOW TO DEAL WITH FORMER FAMILY MEMBERS

If your desire is to help your children trust other adults and count on them despite changes in the family, you deserve to feel proud and capable.

Here are some tips to help you face your ex's family with pride and self-respect.

- Think about who you are most likely to run into from your ex's family and what it is about them that makes you feel anxious or fearful.

- Try to be well groomed. This doesn't mean being "red carpet ready" or even investing in a new wardrobe. It simply means looking pleasant enough so you won't be embarrassed and feel like you have to offer some excuse or explanation. Freshly shampooed hair and a dash of lipstick can do wonders for your morale.

- Decide what you want from these people. If you feel like a motherless child because you have no family of your own, then you need to develop your own extended family separately. Additionally, if you are emotionally dependent on his family, you will only be more vulnerable to their verbal attacks or faultfinding. If you want these people to remain in your child's life, let them know. Sometimes adults are not quite grown-up enough to continue a relationship with a child despite what has transpired between his parents. In these cases, you need to explain this loss to your child so that he understands that the adult was unable to continue the relationship and this was not because of anything your child has done.

- Rehearse what you would like to say to them. Your ex's father may have taught your son how to bait a hook or use a grass trimmer. Let him know how important you felt his contributions were by saying that "it would really mean a lot to your grandson if you would continue to take him fishing every now and then. Regardless of how you feel about what happened between me and your son, your grandson loves you and would miss you if he couldn't see you." Be aware, too, that even if some of your former family members are willing to continue their relationship with your child that you may have to arrange the visits, make the phone calls, and the plan the outings. However, if your efforts are not reciprocated or even welcomed, it would be better to spend your energy creating your own extended family.

- If a family member wants to continue a relationship with your child, by all means invite her to join a family celebration or outing. Explain again your desire to have the relationship continue and express your willingness to do the driving or whatever legwork is necessary to make it easier for your child and this special adult to remain close.

WHEN GRANDMA WAS YOUR NUMBER ONE SITTER

If your former partner's or husband's mother babysat fairly regularly, let her know that you would love for her to continue. Explain that although she might have offered her services because she wanted to see her son get some free time and you can understand her resentment in doing something extra for you, the benefit would really be for her and her grandchild. She may not realize that by ignoring you that she is probably upsetting her grandchild. The longer she stays away from her grandchild, the greater the loss will be for your child.

Your former mother-in-law may be unable to control her feelings of anger, resentment, or bitterness toward you and cannot keep these feelings separate from her relationship with your child. You may need to rethink this arrangement of letting her see the children without you. If it is likely that she will speak poorly of you to the children, serve as your ex's secret agent, or be unsupportive while you and the children forge a new life, it may be best, for the time being, to include her instead on a family picnic, a trip to the beach, or a day in the park.

FACING AUNTS, UNCLES, COUSINS, AND OTHERS

Other family members on your ex's side may feel the same way. For example, suppose your ex came from a long line of "forever married" or grew up in a large extended family. Maybe they resemble the 1950s type of traditional family, and they think this is the only "normal" kind of family. When divorce does occur, there seems to be a deep sense of disappointment and failure. But who shoulders the responsibility? Blaming the outsider, the person who married into the family, is one way they can remove themselves from any responsibility for the divorce. Additionally, divorce may unnerve some of these family members because it forces them, however briefly, to look at their own lives honestly.

Even if you find it easier to simply stay away and keep them out of your life, chances are there will come a time when you will see each other. This may happen during visitations or at school functions. Health-related emergencies or simply because you all live in close proximity to one another can make unexpected meetings happen. If you feel guilty about ending your relationship to your child's father, you may not be comfortable facing any of these people—at least, not any time soon. Try to remember that regardless of the circumstances surrounding the breakup of this relationship that you are not an evil person or the sole destroyer of men as they may want you to believe. In fact, accepting full blame for this split shows that you are shouldering responsibility far and above what is necessary or realistic.

HOLIDAYS AND CELEBRATIONS

Holidays like Christmas or Chanukah and how and with whom they will be spent are typically part of the divorce agreement. Again, the spirit of the occasions should prevail. It is hardly appropriate to use the spirit of the holiday season as an opportunity to keep your children from people whom they have grown to love. Remember that the generosity and empathy you impart to your children will be returned to you many times over.

Occasions like graduations and weddings mean a gathering of family—from both sides. It's special functions like these that separate the grown-ups from the not-so-grown-up. In other words, even though the graduation ceremony or the wedding preparations should belong to the scholar or the bride and groom, relatives displaying fiendish immaturity commonly challenge their wishes regarding who is invited and who sits where. If your ex's mother threatens not to show up if you do, don't fall prey to this nonsense. True, you don't want to hurt anyone, but if you are invited and you feel like going, go. Have a good time.

As far as who foots the bill for these occasions, there are no hard and fast

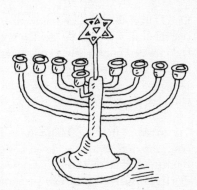

rules. Issues such as who pays for what should be discussed well in advance of the occasion. Write everything down so there is no room for misunderstanding. Many fathers who paid only minimal child support often do like the show of being the father of the bride. Accept this as further proof of his limitations and enjoy the party.

DEALING WITH YOUR EX'S FAMILY

♦ Keep in mind that divorce or the end of a relationship will affect your relationship with members of your ex's extended family.

♦ Don't discuss the personal aspects of your relationship with your ex with his family, unless you have a particularly strong relationship with a family member that would endure whether or not you knew your ex.

♦ Remember that your children's lives will only be made richer by keeping ties with your former partner's family.

♦ Remember that a family is simply people who support and love one another. Feel free to create your own family of choice.

♦ Don't forget that you are the number one adult in your child's life. Do not feel crowded out by new stepmothers or girlfriends. Do not use these relationships as an excuse to give your child less than 100 percent of you.

♦ Try to avoid fighting, blaming, and confrontations with the ex-in-laws. Remember that those in traditional marriages such as your ex's parents'

may still hold the notion that something they did wrong is to blame for your marriage dissolving. Be aware that they just may not know how to behave.

WHEN YOUR CHILD'S FATHER'S FAMILY REMAINS A MYSTERY

Suppose you recently exited a relationship with a husband whose family you barely recognize. If no family members are available to your child, it becomes that much more important to create your own extended family.

If you do have any information on your ex's family, share this with your teenage children at an appropriate time. This is certainly not a casual conversation, and you are going to want to make sure that the timing of your disclosure takes place when there are not other unusual stresses or complications. Let's say your ex has fathered other children, or he is a grandparent. You may choose to show your child a photograph explaining that "Although we may never get to meet Kimberly, she actually is a half sister to you." These "family secrets" should not be hidden from your teenage children. Curiosity and the Internet can easily yield information your children may later feel you unfairly withheld. If you feel other family members may share information about half siblings and other relations without your knowledge, you will want to have these conversations as soon as you feel your child is ready. You may have a trinket or something your ex gave to you that belonged to one of his family members. Tell your child what you do know about her father's extended family. This gives your child the reassurance that you are honest about important things and builds a sense of trust.

RELATING TO YOUR EX'S NEW SIGNIFICANT OTHER

Quite different from the stories you hear about ex-wives and new girlfriends dealing with one another like a pair of mud wrestlers are the tales of the new wife and the discarded wife becoming buddies and even confidantes. When the two women start to console each other and ask why they didn't think they deserved better than this rotten husband, they both dump him for good and start hanging out together.

Is there any middle ground for accepting the new partner of your former partner, even including her in your world and your child's, without becoming best friends? You bet.

Consider what a thankless job— even if only on weekends and other occasions—a stepmother's role must be. She might hear nothing other than "Mom only does it this way," or "Our Mom would never put cinnamon on those," or "Our real Mom would know the answer to that question." It's enough to make her want to pack her bags and head toward the nearest luxury spa. Okay, so you're having a little chuckle to yourself, and deservedly so, knowing that you've wished to get even with this man-stealer for years. Never let these feelings reach your children's ears. Your children need to feel safe when in her care and accept that she is going to be a part of their lives as long as their dad is involved with her. The best thing is to forgive, let go, and move on. Any energy expended on hating her is wasted.

Unless your ex's new mate is physically or mentally abusive to your children, in which case you should take immediate legal action, try to cooperate with her. Communicate important "kid news" with her. If, for example, your child wins an award for a project he worked on while staying with her and your ex, invite her to join Dad to congratulate the child at the award ceremony.

WHEN THE NEW GIRLFRIEND IS A BARRIER BETWEEN YOUR CHILD AND YOUR EX

I am the single mother of a wonderful seven-year-old daughter. Her father lives out of state, and she does not get to see him as much as she did when he lived down the street. When he changed jobs and acquired a new girlfriend, he decided to move. Every few weeks, when my daughter tries to call him, her father tells her rudely not to call him because these calls upset his girlfriend. How do I ease this hurt and explain to her not to call him anymore? My daughter is such a sweet, loving child, and it angers me to have him reject her.

Maybe the best thing for now is to explain to your daughter that at least temporarily she should not try to talk to her father on the telephone. It's obviously not such a good idea. Every time she attempts to call him, she is met with rejection. Why allow this scene to be repeated over and over again? Not because these calls upset his girlfriend, but rather because they hurt your daughter.

The best way to explain to a seven-year-old girl that her father has chosen to be concerned only with his girlfriend's feelings is to stress what her father is unable to do. It probably isn't that your daughter is less loved or less important than the girlfriend, but his actions are emotionally abusive. Dad is probably not able to explain or even understand himself why he is acting in this hurtful way. Maybe he is confused right now with all that is happening in his life—new job, new relationship, and a move. Emphasize to your daughter that even grownups sometimes feel angry, ashamed, mad, and sad all at the same time. Your daughter is not responsible for her father's feelings or his priorities. Tell your daughter she is a wonderful child and that in the best way he can that her father loves her. You can't repeat this last sentence too often.

Your daughter should maintain contact with her father if this is at all possible. You should contact him by telephone at work, since you know he cannot handle calls like this at home, or write him an e-mail. Your daughter is too young to be caught in the middle of all of this, and you need to take action. Let him know that his daughter wants to stay in touch with him and ask how he would like this to happen. Be careful not to place blame, even though you rightly think his behavior is deplorable.

If he continues to place a greater priority on his own selfish needs and his girlfriend's feelings, then, perhaps, the phone calls could be replaced by letters or cards sent to work or even to a post office box he rents for this purpose. If, however, he states that he wants no contact with his daughter, either written or verbal, let your daughter keep writing. Save these notes and other special things in a box labeled "For Daddy Later On." The most important thing is that you allow your daughter to keep a relationship with her father, even if he doesn't respond. Assure her that his behavior is the result of his own limitations and has nothing to do with what a sweet, wonderful child she truly is. Likely, he will return seeking connection and forgiveness from the child he so deeply wounded.

IF YOUR EX IS REMARRYING

Attendance at your ex's wedding should be optional for the children because this may be a rough time for them. Under the best of circumstances, the ceremony will be low key and tasteful. However, if this is a first marriage for the bride, it can be a full-fledged affair just like the one you and he may have had. Good taste and sensitivity dictate that:

- Typically, adult friends—not children—serve as maids of honor or best men.

- Boys are not expected to propose toasts or be ushers.

- You should avoid having your daughter or son be the flower girl or ring bearer if you think this may give them the opportunity to "act out" any negative feelings they might have. (One woman reported that her little girl urinated all over the floor just as the wedding march began.) If your children have gotten through their anger or seem to be handling this well, you may consider letting them have limited roles in the ceremony. If your children are small, picture books on the subject, such as *The Ring Bear*, may be helpful in probing their feelings.

♦ The best roles for your children are as honored guests, with particular attention paid to making the event as comfortable as possible. Some dads make incredible issues out of their children attending and participating because in this way the dads reassure themselves that "we are just one big happy family." You both need to respect your children's feelings.

HOW TO HELP YOUR KIDS' NEW STEPMOTHER

It's important to recognize that when you help your kids' new stepmother, you help your kids. Here are some ways.

♦ When her new partner (your ex) has his daughter every other weekend, they may wind up clashing even if they got along great when she and Dad were dating. Instead of gloating and telling yourself that "I wouldn't want my daughter around that person anyway," tell yourself that as long as your ex has visitation rights and as long as he is involved with her that your child most likely will be a part of her life, too.

♦ Don't tell your ex what a worthless parent and person his new girlfriend or wife is if the kids complain that she doesn't do anything right. Chances are that he still won't appreciate all that you have done.

♦ Be aware that kids tend to harbor a lot of guilt about trying to be nice to a new stepparent because they think it means taking away love from the biological or custodial one. Don't add to their guilt. By promoting a positive relationship between your children and your ex, you are setting an example that the more love you have to share, the more you can produce.

♦ Don't refer to her as the wicked stepmother. This gives permission for her and the children to give you a not-so-flattering title, too. Put an end to the name-calling.

♦ Avoid setting her up for failure. For example, if she is the manager of a seasonal store that gets busiest around the holidays, don't expect her to take the kids on Christmas Eve.

♦ Let her know that she needn't take your kids' behavior to heart too much when they are giving her a rough time. Explain that this is their way of expressing their loss and that they want to be sure they don't lose their dad to her.

♦ Try letting their dad know what is going on and suggest that he ask the kids straightforward questions like "Do you feel disloyal to Mom?" or "Do you feel bad that your Mom and I aren't together or resent having to share me?" Once these feelings are identified, both of you can assuage the kids' fears. You can help by allowing them one-on-one time with their dad and reassuring the new stepmom that eventually she and the children will form some kind of relationship. Tell her to try to set reasonable limits on their behavior and, above all, try to be patient.

YOU'RE STILL THE MOM

Don't worry, you are not being replaced. To children, a new stepmother often is considered an affectionate and supportive person in their lives, but not a substitute mom. At the very best, some stepmoms earn the title "bonus parent."

The danger lies when you worry that this new person will have influence over your children and will probably replace you, and why bother being a parent anyway? Don't withdraw from your child's life! Doing so will actually be setting your children up to turn to the stepparent for the concern and love that you seem to have suddenly withdrawn.

23

A Single Mom's Guide to Sex and Dating

It is a very wise woman indeed who is able to recognize the difference between wanting a relationship and needing physical companionship. For years, leading sociologists and anthropologists have known that physical closeness is a need, not unlike eating, sleeping, and exercise—perhaps not as urgent in the short term, but necessary for physical and emotional well-being. However, through miseducation, religious dogma, and the media, our popular culture has us convinced that sex and love are synonymous, a myth most Americans cling to. One problem with this belief is that it pressures people into entering relationships that may be wrong for them simply because they need to justify the sexual aspects of the relationship. For example, people all too often marry sex partners with whom they have nothing in common to validate the union as something more significant than it is. It is okay to pine for physical closeness occasionally as long as you don't mistake sexual desires for true love. Loneliness that stems

from being in an unfulfilled relationship is far worse.

HOW TO FEEL LESS LONELY

There are subtle yet recognizable signs in a person who is feeling unfulfilled. Because at certain times healthy humans need fulfillment emotionally, spiritually, intellectually, and physically, we mistake a lack in one of these areas for general loneliness and tend to fall into a slump. Many of us were taught that this feeling means we need to find romance.

But this doesn't mean that you should run out and find a lover immediately. On the contrary, you need to find out what you can do for yourself to instill that sense of balance most of us feel when those four needs are being met. In fact, the best time to seek out a relationship with the potential of becoming partnered is when you are feeling fulfilled and have a lot to share and offer another, not when you are feeling empty.

Humans who are creative and empathetic and indulge in a love affair with themselves often state that although they experience times of true solitude that they do not necessarily feel lonely. This doesn't mean avoiding friendships and even romantic encounters with men, especially if you have been living alone for awhile or have been through a series of dead-end relationships. It means engaging yourself physically, spiritually, and intellectually, to be ready for the emotional challenge of entering a relationship.

OBSERVE YOUR SEXUAL NEEDS

Pay close attention to your sexual feelings. When you feel anxious, lonely, or bored, could you be just plain horny? Sometimes when people are under chronic stress, nagging physical needs can seem so overwhelming that many feel the lack of a sexual partner more strongly than usual, leaving them with a sense of utter loneliness. Women ask themselves "How can I have sex? I don't even have a boyfriend!" Yet sexual activity may be just the prescription because, as scientists have pointed out, sex is a great stress-buster. Masturbation may be frequent at times like these, which is perfectly normal. You may have a friend with whom you indulge in sexual play, and this is okay, too, provided that you keep these playful activities separate from your children and use precautions against disease and unwanted pregnancy. After all, you're single, not dead. Ask yourself if it is both physical satisfaction as well as emotional support that you are missing. If you find that you are lonely and need nurturing, see if you have enough loving friends, family, and peers in your life to give you support, empathy, unconditional caring, and acceptance. At certain times, a hug or back rub, a touch of the hand, or a nod of the head is more beneficial than what a sex partner can give.

FIND A CREATIVE OUTLET

Ask yourself "Have I been creative lately?" You may be surprised to learn that many cultures believe that sexual energy and the creative process stem from the same center of the body. In all the latest books that explore the duality of women's nature—the civilized persona and the wild woman within—the wild woman has been revealed to be a passionate artist who needs to express her creativity. Because she demands expression and because time constraints— "I don't have time because of my kids . . . my job . . . my dirty house"—often are used as an excuse to avoid painting, writing, dancing, and making music, the woman within often confuses her passion for creating with romantic passion or, bluntly put, horniness. Because these feelings stem from the same center of our being that produces the urge to create, including the urge to reproduce, women need to recognize the difference between their sexual desires and the need to create something from within themselves.

During part of your life as a single mother, your sexual needs won't be as readily met as they might be if you were in a relationship that includes sex. Use this time as a gift to reveal your creative potential.

During any time that you spend alone and find yourself feeling dry, exiled, depressed, or empty, you must create. Keep a journal on your nightstand, a cassette player at hand, or a sketchbook on your dresser. Don't let lack of money sabotage you. Whether you are working two jobs to make ends meet or your extra cash is going toward your child's piano lessons, it doesn't cost much to sing or dance and bring a little joy into your life. Keep in mind, too, that you are meeting two challenges with a single effort: you're enjoying your creative energy, and you are also encouraging your children to explore their own creativity.

Relax a little and see how much you can accomplish simply by allowing the artist in you to emerge. Try inventing software for children, if your job as a computer programmer becomes routine. Start a newsletter for women artists in your community. Create interesting meals, take up photography, or paint a shelf turquoise. The possibilities are endless.

IF YOUR KIDS WORRY THAT YOU'LL BE AN OLD MAID

My daughter has actually tried to fix me up with her science teacher, but I'm not interested. I'm content with my life, but she acts like something is wrong. I wonder if there is something wrong with me because I don't feel like dating right now.

People do not have to be in tandem with someone else to experience joy and contentment in their lives. This is a major myth, and it has been bought into big-time, especially by girls. Maybe you don't feel like dating because you were involved in an emotionally draining relationship and now you need time to regroup. This could be a good time for you to do something for yourself that you did not have the time or energy to do when you were in a committed relationship. How about taking a cooking class or reading those books you promised yourself you would someday read? Your children may need your full-time attention now, leaving you little energy to pursue or maintain a romantic involvement. Being temporarily uninterested in romance is not a bad thing. It leaves you able to focus your energies elsewhere, and that is good. If your lack of interest is fueled by anger or other unexpressed pain or hurt, then it is time to work toward resolving these feelings in ways that work for you. The romantic respite may simply be your time to heal.

Why is your daughter so interested in your having a boyfriend? Perhaps, particularly if she is a teenager, she feels responsible for your happiness and guilty about leaving you alone to be with her friends or participate in activities or sports. Your children, no matter what their ages, cannot be the sole focus of your universe. You need to give your children permission and encouragement to lead full and happy lives.

THE FEAR OF BEING INEPT AT DATING

I haven't dated in ten years. I feel like an awkward adolescent with sweaty palms, too much cologne, and zero confidence. How do I even begin to talk to another adult? It's been so long. I feel like I only know how to talk to children. Plus, where do I find an eligible man?

The cliché about being yourself probably won't help you at this point. If you are uncertain about what to talk about because you have spent the last few years talking childspeak—"Yes! Mommy sees the ladybug" and "Look who chewed all his food without spitting!"—using few words and mostly facial expressions, don't worry. You just need to be around more adults. Listen to what the other person has to say first. This doesn't mean you have to sit there mutely while he bores you with mundane details of his complicated business life. His focus on business may prompt you to ask him how he plans to use his anticipated profits. If he responds that he'd like to contribute generously to the children's hospital fund, well, you just may listen with renewed interest. If he's strictly into status and male toys, like fancy cars, then maybe you'll decide that this guy is just not for you. The best way to start talking to another person is to hear what is important to that person.

REENTERING THE DATING WORLD

I'm thirty-five years old and have been raising my eight-year-old daughter solo for seven years. During the first four years, I did not have much interest in forming new relationships with men or even in dating for that matter, since my daughter's father was emotionally abusive. I felt I needed time to heal. This period also allowed me to devote more time to my child and more time to learning about myself. The few encounters I've had with dates were disappointing. But now I think I'd like to meet a nice man,

although I'm uncertain whether I'm ready for a relationship or if it's physical companionship I need, since it's been a long time, if you know what I mean. I feel confident at times, but doubtful and confused other times. Any suggestions for sorting out these feelings?

Congratulations. It sounds like you've been examining your feelings and are getting to know yourself pretty well, which is probably the most critical thing one can do to ensure an honest, productive, and meaningful life. You're already doing a great job sorting out your feelings. Maybe it's a combination—occasional release from sexual tension and the pleasures that a committed partnership can bring—that you are now seeking. You seem ready for both.

IT'S OKAY TO WANT A BOY TOY

This cannot be said often enough: you are single, not dead, and deserve a personal life. A personal life means, among other things, sex—doing it, thinking about it, planning for it, dressing or undressing for it.

Having sex does not mean first that you must pledge or feel undying love. As long as you practice safe sex, the kind of sex you choose and with whom is entirely up to you. This may be a time of major experimentation for you. This may be the first time you ever felt "the earth move," even though the guy may possess the IQ of an eggplant. Right now, you may not want or be capable of involvement or commitment. You may just want sex and then to go about your life without entanglements or interference. It is perfectly okay to have a boy toy with whom to play sex games.

WHEN IT'S PLATONIC— BUT YOUR KIDS WISH IT WAS MORE

My best "boyfriend" friend is handsome, intelligent, and good with my kids. However, we have never been attracted to each other in a romantic way. My kids feel disappointed that we aren't going to marry.

There is little here that is a problem. Introducing your children to healthy men who have much to offer in terms of experiences, affection, and support is a positive thing. As the saying goes, "one can't have enough friends." Keep up the good work. There is probably no better way to prepare your children for our changing world than to show by your good example men and women sharing and giving to one another as friends and equals. Explain to your children that one of the most valuable things any human being can have is a friend. Describe the qualities

that make him a good friend. Tell your children that husbands and wives need to be friends above all else but that not all men friends become boyfriends or husbands and not all women friends of men become their girlfriends or wives. When your children become teenagers, explain to them that people who think of members of the opposite sex only as potential bed partners limit themselves significantly. This is a one-dimensional way to think about people.

BEST BETS FOR MEETING MEN

On a first date, arrange to meet in a public place, such as a coffee shop. Never invite someone to your home before you get to know him. If you're looking to meet men, bring a friend who is looking, too. Not only is there safety in numbers, but you can give each other a reality check now and then. Try attending functions or gatherings that would hold an interest for you whether or not you plan to meet someone new. If you're the outdoorsy type, look for opportunities to indulge this passion with others who are equally enthusiastic about the out of doors. You may meet men in places you take your kids, such as sporting events and fairs. Other places to meet men include:

- **Air Shows:** Even if you know nothing about planes, stunt flying is fun to watch and can turn you into an enthusiast. Your kids will love it, too. Often a local Civil Air Patrol (CAP) will sponsor these shows for a small admission cost.

- **Baseball Games:** Not just major league! Almost every community has local clubs sponsoring games, and tickets to minor league games are usually affordable.

- **Beaches:** Even if you don't meet anyone, it's never a waste of time just to look at different kinds of physiques. Who says women can't enjoy just looking?

- **Camping Trips:** Families of all types enjoy the change in routine and the chance to kick back and smell the sunshine. Many campgrounds have family activities. Meeting new people is expected and part of the fun.

- **Chance Encounters:** The fabulous guy next door is often met through a chance meeting in the supermarket when you both reach for the last can of beans. Remember, you'll never meet Mr. Right if you spend your spare time on the sofa watching TV. Get out there and see what happens!

- **Churches, Synagogues, Temples, or Spiritual Associations:** This is one of the best places to meet men with the same spiritual beliefs as yours. Everyone has his or her own path to personal fulfillment, and finding someone traveling on the same road typically means shared values and expectations. Churches have singles groups that often sponsor activities geared to a limited budget.

- **Clubs and Societies:** Follow your own passions and interests. If you are environmentally conscious, you may meet someone terrific by joining one of the many organizations concerned with preserving our environment. If you just like being outside and active, try finding a hiking group or join others who

simply like to explore by foot. If you like wine tasting, tai chi, scuba diving, or any other particular thing, consider joining a club for these enthusiasts.

- **Cooking Classes:** There are more guys than women taking some of these courses, and for good reasons. They are no longer in a relationship where a woman prepares many of the meals. They want to entertain their dates with sophisticated, home-cooked dishes. Not only is it cheaper than going to a restaurant, but a lot of men believe a cooking class is a great way to meet women!

- **Cruises:** If you've got the money and time, go for it. Some cruises for single-parent families offer drastically reduced rates for the kids, plus babysitting services, which can make affordable a vacation full of family fun. Take a singles cruise with a friend and leave the kids home.

- **Dances:** Just look in your local newspaper or entertainment guide, and there will be at least a couple of singles dances held in area hotels or nightclubs on any weekend evening.

- **Dating Services:** There are many types of dating services such as professional matchmakers, newspaper and radio singles personals, speed-dating, and online dating sites.

  A personal matchmaker may charge many thousands of dollars to pair up a potential couple. High-salaried executives and career professionals who use this kind of service feel it is worth the money, similar to the expense employers pay headhunters to search out the perfect person for the job.

Local radio stations and newspapers offer personal classified advertising for singles seeking other singles. They also may sponsor area activities for singles.

◆ **Online Dating:** There are advantages to online or Internet dating. Looking over the different profiles lets you learn a bit about another person before you decide to contact them. It gives you the option to contact someone rather than wait to be asked. Online dating makes it easier and more acceptable for you to make the first move. The idea of getting to know someone first through words rather than actions also seems kind of romantic to many people. Joining an Internet dating service is relatively inexpensive, and some sites are free. Watch out for hidden fees and expensive and time-consuming chat rooms.

There are risks when meeting strangers in any situation. To be safe, don't give out your home or work phone number until you have exchanged e-mails at least a half dozen times. As you exchange e-mails, consider whether this person is looking for a real relationship or is this just a way for him to live out a fantasy life? You probably are not interested in just being someone's latest cyber fling! If he talks about being in a financial pinch, be wary. Don't give any personal information to this person such as bank account or credit card numbers or let them know how much money you earn and only arrange to meet him in a public place after you've had several phone conversations with them. Be sure you get a landline—not just a cell phone—number. Be especially cautious of men who speak too early of commitment and future plans. Look for common experiences and mutual friends. If he becomes angry or hostile if you ask about his schooling or work history, be especially cautious. Report anyone who seems to have a criminal agenda to the dating service, if not the police.

◆ **Education:** Single dads attending PTA meetings is certainly an added incentive to be part of what's going on at your child's school. Why not expand your horizons and take an adult education class, offered in the evening or during your lunch break? Many community colleges also offer on-site child care; don't pass up the opportunity to maybe meet some interesting men as well as advance your education.

◆ **Fishing Trips:** Fishing can be very relaxing for the whole family, and it gives a mom a sense of accomplishment when she can catch dinner with her two hands, a net, and a worm.

◆ **Fast-Food Restaurants:** As some know from personal experience, most weekend custodial dads depend on fast food for at least one weekend meal. The places that have puppet shows, performing mechanical bears, and indoor playgrounds are highly rated spots. Dads are looking for something that will feed and entertain the little ones, and usually there is the opportunity for a little conversation, especially if you can talk above the noise and kid confusion.

◆ **Golf:** The miniature or goofy kind, that is. Of course, if you are a seasoned golfer, by all means get up early on a Saturday morning, send the kids to a sitter or relative, and join a chummy foursome.

◆ **Tennis:** Courts are often available free or at low cost depending upon where you live. Indoor courts are open at hours to encourage play no matter what your schedule. You don't have to be that good at tennis to enjoy the game and the camaraderie. Tennis is also a terrific no stress first date activity.

◆ **Holiday Parties:** As any holiday approaches, make sure every coworker, friend, and relative knows that you are interested in meeting nice men. Gently suggest an addition to the guest list, if you know a man you'd like to meet. Better yet, have a party and encourage your guests to bring along eligible men they know. Make sure you know how many people will be attending so that you can make reasonable arrangements for food and drink. Keep your parties more about food rather than drink to keep the cost and possible complications to a minimum.

◆ **Jogging, Running, or Biking:** Certain parks and sections of towns and cities have jogging paths and biking lanes. Find a place where you could enjoy getting some healthy exercise.

◆ **Kite Flying:** The kids love it, and so will you. It's cheap and guaranteed to get you out of a slump. It's also a great excuse to ask for help when your beagle, daughter, and kite are all wrapped around a tree.

◆ **Skydiving and Other Extreme Sports:** Not only will participation in such activities give you the chance to meet like spirited men, but you can also improve the quality of your life because of the strength and independence you can uncover in yourself. It's a win–win experience because these activities will definitely make you feel powerful and you will probably have developed the guts to talk to anyone without worrying about rejection!

◆ **Lunch:** Make time to have a relaxing lunch with friends at least every other week at a regular gathering place. Befriend the staff, and they might let you know who's who from their regular single male tables. Another lunch tip: when you first start to date a guy, rather than spend money on babysitters, why not meet at a local lunch spot? The added benefit is that, if you don't click with this person, you have the excuse of needing to go back to work.

◆ **Network:** Simply put, network, network, and network some more. Let everyone know that you would like to meet an interesting person with whom you can share fun, ideas, dinner, and companionship. The lady in the apartment down the hall might have an eligible brother, or the sales rep who comes by to service the office equipment may have a friend or neighbor who might be just your cup of tea.

◆ **Personal Ads:** Most singles publications and newspapers have a section for responding to ads or for placing your own. Be sure to follow their instructions or their procedures, particularly if you have never done this before. Because relationship experts liken looking for the ideal relationship to job hunting, placing an ad stating your requirements is a very logical way to seek out someone who shares your interests. Just be sure to use a post office box number or an answering service for initial correspondence. Never, ever, give out your address and telephone number to strangers.

- **Parks:** State parks and recreation facilities are a great, inexpensive getaway for having a picnic or for hiking up the side of a mountain. Bring an extra sandwich in case you run into a hungry park ranger.

- **Auto Races:** Great for moms and kids, but particularly for moms of motor-heads. Interest in everything NASCAR is huge. Plan to come early so you and your family can join all the fun before the races.

- **Sightseeing:** You're the only adult with a camera, and you're wondering how to take pictures of you and the kids together. This gives you a perfectly logical reason to stop the next nice-looking guy you see to ask him if he wouldn't mind taking a snapshot of you and your children in front of the Statue of Liberty, Lincoln Memorial, or while gazing at the Grand Canyon. Single mothers with a passion for photography have a great opening line that leaves little room for rejection because even if a wife emerges from the restroom at least you've got a great picture of you and the kids.

- **Teaching:** This one is in the "kill three birds with one stone" hall of fame! Get all your creative weekend parenting ideas down on paper and then put an ad or flyer in your local paper or on community bulletin boards in your neighborhood announcing your class—Divorced

Dads and Moms—Got the Kids This Weekend? Take a class on how to have cheap, creative fun without losing your wallet or your sanity.

First, maybe you can make a little extra money. Next, you might meet a few interesting people. Last, you will have used your creative abilities and resources to expand your own vision and possibly gotten the inspiration to try something new in your life.

- **Work:** You have an opportunity to get to know male coworkers as friends by talking about company goals, business problems, and personal aspirations. Never gossip or bad-mouth fellow workers or bosses. By becoming personal friends with some of your male coworkers, eligible or not, you are open to the possibility of meeting their available friends. Be familiar with company policy, however, and be aware that sexual harassment allegations can also be made by men.

- **Zoo:** Another great weekend hangout of the single dad set.

Note: Don't lose heart if your attempts at meeting someone special don't bring results right away. Just remember that every meeting holds something to be learned. Rather than seeing the times you strike out as rejection, why not view them as time spent practicing and developing a style?

WHEN YOUR CHILD EMBARRASSES YOU

Here you are, a sophisticated twenty-nine-year-old professional, getting ready for a date with a man you have been seeing steadily for six months. This is his first visit to your home. You have discussed his impending arrival with your four-year-old son, describing him as a special friend of yours. The doorbell rings, you look gorgeous, and the babysitter seems to have everything under control. Except that, despite your careful preparation, your son beats you to the door chattering to your startled date, "Are you going to be our new daddy? Ours never lived here."

Rather than slamming the door in your date's face and hiding under the bed, try not to take this so seriously. Because your four-year-old sees you only as a mommy (even though your résumé is four pages long), it's natural for him to look upon a male as a daddy. Kids pick up on roles that adults play by observing people in your day-to-day life, overhearing your conversations with friends, and from relatives, television, and movies. You might say something lighthearted to your date, if he's still standing, like "this is just a test to see how quick you are on your feet." Anything more than a quick, offhand response might make you sound emotionally needy and or unnecessarily apologetic. You owe him no other explanation other than perhaps agreeing that children can certainly say surprising things. Besides, you two do have some history and have probably enjoyed lots of laughs together. Make this episode just one more laugh together.

WHEN FRIENDS FIX YOU UP

Be grateful for the attention and interest of your friends. One date is not forever, and think of the interesting stories! Turning down the opportunity to spend an evening with someone who clearly sounds strange is one of the perks of being single. Turning down every social opportunity, however, means you are letting many of the interesting parts of life pass you by. Very often, opening yourself up to new opportunities and experiences can be very healing in unexpected and positive ways.

DATING A MARRIED MAN

It is a big shock for many women to reenter the dating scene or return to work after a hiatus at home to discover that many of their single women friends date married men. Some single women find married men a convenience. Scheduling time to see each other is tricky, but this need to make appointments to see each other sometimes fits right in with the hectic life of a single mother. The sex is typically great. After all, these guys know what they are doing. Since they typically have little to offer in the companionship or loyalty department, they go all out trying to please in the bedroom.

Affairs with married men typically begin in the workplace or on business trips far from home. Many single women report that their married lovers are also wonderful mentors, interested and supportive of their ambitions and goals.

Married men are always on their best behavior when they are with you. They always look good, smell good, and sometimes spare no expense to show you a good time. It is all romance and fantasy and is clearly an escape from your responsibility-filled daily life. It is easy to lose sight of the fact that none of this is real. What is real is that you are getting a bad deal. He gets a wife and all the companionship and validation marriage entails, plus whatever extras he is getting from you—and maybe other women as well. You get whatever scraps of time and attention he feels like giving. You will never be in a position to ask for anything. You cannot call him when you are lonely or in a jam unless the crisis takes place during work hours and he is free to take your call. Forget holidays or your birthday. He'll be sorry to hear if you have been sick or hurt, but that is as far as it will go. Most importantly of all, you cannot begin to care for this person without inflicting major hurt on yourself. You can tell yourself that you are a big girl and this is just an adventure, but often it is hard to keep a tight rein on your feelings. Why should you? Don't you deserve better?

Remember that no matter how terrific this guy seems to you—how smart, how successful, how tender, and how supportive—the bottom line is that he is lying to his wife every single day. How terrific can a guy be whose own wife cannot trust him?

DATING A MAN YOU SUSPECT IS GAY

There is a great misconception that men are either exclusively heterosexual or homosexual, both in their fantasies and in their actual behavior. At least one in six men is bisexual, and generally they tell lovers of both sexes what to expect. Few of the approximately 10 percent of men who are exclusively homosexual ever marry. Given that approximately 60 percent of men are exclusively heterosexual, this means that at least 25 percent of men fall somewhere in the middle. Many men live a predominantly heterosexual or homosexual life and then change their social preference because of social pressures or circumstances. Many homosexuals force themselves into a heterosexual lifestyle. Young men face enormous pressures to date and marry, and many young homosexuals want to believe that their feelings are just a passing phase. Many homosexuals want to be fathers and enjoy what they perceive to be a normal family life. Given all these pressures, it is not surprising if you have been dating a gay man. Some women marry gay men and are not even aware of it. Most women, however, do know that a man is gay once the relationship becomes deeply involved or they are actually married.

You need to be clearly aware of what you are getting into if you continue this relationship. If you have a hidden agenda for this person, such as thinking your influence will induce change, you may be disappointed. Be aware of what you can accept and live with, and be true to your own feelings. These relationships can work, but only with an added measure of communication and honesty.

DATING YOUR EX'S BEST FRIEND

Sometimes dating the brother, friend, or cousin of an ex can be a way of holding on and staying part of the family. If these are your feelings, work at resolving your feelings of loss. Do not complicate your life further by trying to bury these feelings in the excitement of a new romance. Everyone involved will be hurt.

If you are simply attracted to a friend or relative of your ex, this is not necessarily bad or wrong. There are rules, however. Respect the privacy of your former spouse. Telling your new boyfriend some less than stellar tale of your ex will charm him for the moment, but later he will wonder what secrets of his you will share for a laugh down the road. Do not frequent places where you will be likely to see your former husband. If you are looking to stick it to your ex by dating his brother or best friend, then you are in the relationship for the wrong reasons. Simply stated, you are just using this man. A little respect for your ex's feelings will be appreciated and will go a long way. Try to keep the conversation with your new love interest future focused. Although you have many past experiences to share, look for new and different things to do together.

DATING YOUR BEST FRIEND'S EX

Dating your best friend's, sister's, childhood buddy's, or college roommate's ex is one of the dating world's more complicated scenarios. So complicated and juicy, in fact, that it is the premise for so many soap operas and made-for-TV movies.

Careful thought is required before you take actions you may later regret. Consider what feelings you may be trying to deal with by thinking about a relationship with this guy. Could there exist just-under-the-surface feelings of jealousy or envy? Do you really believe that despite many nights of listening to your pal complain bitterly about this man that he deserves more credit than she gave him? How will your girlfriend feel about this new relationship in your life? It takes people who have genuinely put the past behind them and are ready

to accept that both they and their partners have a new life. Maybe you or your girlfriend belong in this "grown-up" category, but if you don't both see eye to eye about this situation, it is important to think things over carefully and then proceed cautiously.

Keep in mind that if your best friend or sister ended her relationship with her husband with anything less than grace and humor, more than likely she will not stay your best friend too long after she finds out you two are seeing each other. Remember that boyfriends (and some husbands) come and go, but girlfriends are forever. Do you really want to risk jeopardizing your relationship for the sake of a couple of possibly go-nowhere dates?

True, many relationships flourish and continue to grow in spite of a change in partners, but it takes an extraordinary amount of maturity, acceptance, and consideration on the part of everyone involved.

DATING ANOTHER SINGLE PARENT

The following is some advice on how to comfortably mix a social life with parenting when you both have children:

- Introduce the kids to each other after you have spent a reasonable amount of time with each other's children and everyone feels comfortable. Make sure you don't pressure the kids to like each other.

- Get together for family "dates." For example, movies, ice skating, or a visit to the zoo can involve all family members. Let the kids be part of the decision-making process.

- Let the kids know that they are not going to be included in every activity. Point out that your needing another adult in your life is similar to when they just want to be with their friends and not have you around.

- Don't initially introduce both sets of kids on family dates that last more than a few hours. Save outings such as overnight camping or traveling for when you are fully committed to each other and they know one another a while. If the kids initially feel uncomfortable or threatened, attending a movie or going on a picnic allows everyone the choice of going home to their separate dwellings.

- Don't be despondent if the kids don't click. Children are flexible and resilient, but they need time and patience to get used to an idea. Don't ask too much of them, and don't pressure them into sharing their feelings about your friend's family.

- Don't expect the oldest child to begin babysitting immediately after she or he has met the others. This can lead to resentment and friction. In fact, avoid having one sitter watch the whole bunch until after it has been proven that these kids are really friends. Better yet, wait until you know if this relationship not only will endure but also will remain long term for the kids as well.

SHOULD YOUR NEW LOVER SPEND THE NIGHT?

You are the only one who can and should make the "rules" in your life.

You know your own children better than anyone else. You know what their life experiences have been and their likely reactions to transition and change. Some children are simply by temperament more resilient and hardy. Other children have great difficulty with anything unforeseen or unusual and do not bounce back readily from disappointment, loss, or unexpected disclosures.

Deciding to involve your children in your sex and dating life will naturally have consequences. This is not to say that the consequences will necessarily all be negative, but there is the potential for unexpected fallout. Involving your children in your dating life should be done after you carefully consider your particular family situation and your own tolerance for unexpected emotional reactions.

As you move your personal life ahead, here are some considerations to keep in mind:

Safety. One-night stands may be all the commitment you can handle at the moment. When your partner is a virtual stranger, it is best to be super cautious about bringing him into your home.

Off to the right start. If you plan to bring a man home for dinner or just to watch TV, think about how you will introduce him. Is he a friend, "just a friend," a "special friend," a "friend from work," or your boyfriend? Decide whether you want to create the expectation that your children will see this man again. If you are reasonably certain that you and this man are in a relationship, then you may feel more comfortable in allowing the children to get to know him. Brief introductions are probably best if a guy is just picking you up to go on a date.

Good things take time. A good rule of thumb is to keep your children's involvement with your dating partners a step behind the relationship. In other words, for example, smooching in the kitchen before dinner will probably be okay for the children if they are already comfortable with this man and your commitment to him.

Keep things in perspective. Some long-term relationships are not about "forever after," but definitely work for right now because they meet our adult needs for companionship, shared experiences, and/or sexual fulfillment. Allowing your child to forge an attachment with a "great for right now" guy may not be the best choice. Children have enough trouble making sense and creating order in their world without creating unnecessary confusion and uncertainty. You will know the best way to convey to your children that the man in your life is not forever without spoiling the fun when his presence does add some extra interest and enjoyment to your family life.

Privacy. You may feel that it is acceptable to have the man in your life spend the night. This is strictly a matter of personal choice. Your children may always sleep soundly, letting you feel assured that they will not wake up and demand attention in the middle of the night. You will still want to consider good privacy practices. Locking your bedroom door may not be the best choice. Locked interior doors are a safety hazard and also potentially alert your children that some event of interest in taking place away from their view. Children talk, especially at school and in the homes of friends. Are these tales of locked doors and nameless men really what you want to occupy your children's thoughts and conversations?

The Dad factor. If you are still embroiled in a custody dispute or feel for some other reason that your children's dad could cause difficulties for you, you may wish to rethink bringing your dates home to meet the children. Does Dad still have the habit of dropping in unexpectedly on some pretext? It is not fair or realistic to expect children to be selective or discreet about what they share with Dad during visitation.

Take away messages. Whatever decision you make about what is appropriate, your children will get the message that this behavior is acceptable. You will want to feel confident that your child can handle the same standards of behavior that are being modeled for them. Consider whether you can trust your son or daughter to use contraception, practice safe sex, and not get themselves into situations that are risky or downright dangerous. Consider whether your actions could, perhaps, compromise the respect and authority you hold as a parent.

Timing is everything. Some single moms find themselves inviting men to their homes because they are lonely, but feel guilty about spending time away from the children. Trying to multitask your children's emotional needs and your romantic desires is probably not the best solution. If you feel guilty, perhaps your children have clearly signaled that they are feeling shortchanged; perhaps you haven't resolved the question of whether you even have the right to have your own needs, including sexual ones. Rest assured that you have that right! Being physically present but emotionally unavailable because you are giving your time and attention to a dating partner may not be your best option. If you're having doubts about taking time away from your children for your romantic life, perhaps that's a signal that you aren't ready to have one—for example, because of unresolved feelings about a prior relationship or a seriously out of balance life. Listen to these feelings and work through them. Begin to date when you're really ready.

Men do have feelings. Consider the needs of your partner. Decent men are sensitive to the feelings of others and, delicately put, may feel not up to the experience when children are a thin wall away. Some men will also worry about whether the children's dad is going to show up or if they would be in any kind of trouble if the children do walk in unexpectedly.

Making choices. Finances and child care are realities that must factor into your plans. Artful planning and compromising can solve a lot of potential problems. If your partner is grown-up, he will understand and, perhaps, surprise you with his ingenious and creative solutions to your needs for privacy. Given that male search and conquer gene, there is something about not being so available that tends to pique their interest and add an extra measure of lust and passion to a relationship. Consider your circumstances a plus, not a minus.

DON'T FALL FOR THE MYTH OF ROMANTIC LOVE

In his classic, *The Road Less Traveled*, author M. Scott Peck, M.D., notes that one of the characteristics of "the experience of falling in love" is the illusion that the experience lasts forever. Moreover, he points out how the notion that there is only one man meant for only one woman who can meet each other's every need is a dreadful lie.

Basically, if you subscribe to the myth of romantic love, it means you tend to enter a relationship based on what your hormones tell you, rather than your brain. You might also fall for hype such as the belief that opposites attract, the need for a better half (as if you're incomplete before seeking a partner), and the notion that if sex is no longer new and exciting, then the honeymoon is over or the chemistry is gone.

In actuality, the deepest love is demonstrated through empathy, true concern, and caring enough to want the best for that special person.

OUTGROWING THE BOY TOY

I have been seeing a man on and off for two years. Honestly, the best and probably only thing this relationship had going for it was sex. But now I am bored and plan to break it off. He called the other night, and my son answered the phone. This guy gave my son his name, told him I was a friend of his, and left a message for me to call. I freaked. I have never brought this man anywhere near my house, never mind my son. All this was private and separate from my son. What am I going to say if my son starts asking about this guy?

You have done everything right so far. Why do you doubt yourself now? Obviously, when you and your boyfriend were together, you did not tell your son specifically where you were and what you were doing. There is no reason for any destructive bursts of candor now. Probably your son has forgotten all about this call. If he does ask, just say that he is a friend from work. If your son asks if he knows him or will meet him, tell him probably not because you know for a fact that he is looking to go elsewhere—and you know that is the truth. Tell your soon-to-be-ex to please not call you at home again. Do what is good for you and stop

seeing him when you feel the time is right. Because you have not involved your child in any way, you are free to live your private life as you see fit with no worries about how your actions will affect your child. Congratulations on being such a grownup.

RELATIONSHIPS AND REMARRIAGE

After repeatedly hearing statistics about higher divorce rates for second and third marriages, you may have a gun-shy attitude toward intimacy. But those statistics usually involve people who "jump out of the frying pan and into the fire" or those who enter relationships for all the wrong reasons, such as a crippling fear of being alone or wanting desperately to replace an absent husband and father.

If you have spent your time alone wisely and productively, your chances of maintaining a successful partnership with a new mate are extremely good. In fact, because you are in control of your own life and not overly needy, you have many options when choosing the type of partner and relationship you'd like. Still, all relationships between men and women bring sticky problems that can only be resolved through strong communication, empathy, acceptance of the other person, a willingness to compromise, and the understanding that nothing in life is certain.

ARE YOU READY FOR THE REAL THING?

If you think you are really ready to engage in a long-term, committed partnership, here are some factors to consider:

SINGLE MOMS: MORE SELF-ESTEEM AND "SEX-ESTEEM"

Results from a study of more than 30,000 women nationwide conducted by the online relationship service TRUEBeginnings (now known as True) in 2004 showed that single moms scored significantly higher than single childless women in areas of sexual attitude, confidence, emotional intelligence, communication, and readiness to commit to a relationship.

An article in *True Magazine* stated that: "The challenge is that there is not a lot of recognition that they [single mothers] possess these wonderful character traits. In fact, many single mothers subscribe to society's rather negative views of them instead of accessing the highly developed attributes they possess."

Balancing work, kids, and romance may keep you too busy to realize you have actually developed the skills and traits that make the foundation of a well-balanced relationship.

◆ Are you content and fulfilled by yourself? If you are, you'll have a lot to offer.

◆ Would you want someone with whom you share a lot in common? Men and women are so different by nature. It only makes sense to find someone with whom you can easily share friendship, who approaches life from the same perspective, and has comparable strong values and praiseworthy qualities. If you do have strong disagreements in certain areas, does experience show you that you are able to talk things through without belittling each other?

◆ Are you ready to ask your potential new partner the tough questions? The majority of divorce-causing issues already exist well before the wedding. Having the courage to ask the difficult questions prevents future problems. Maybe you feel that asking, for example, "Is there something you hope I never find out?" is uncomfortable, awkward, and definitely unromantic, but remember that so is divorce.

◆ Do you view a relationship as a separate entity rather than a merging of two people into one being? Two whole beings should create a third entity, an extension of themselves that they can care for without losing the ability to care for themselves. You should be able to keep your own distinct identity so that you can nurture or form other meaningful relationships, such as with your best friend, your child, your family, and your business associates.

Above all, define your own life. If you need to "fix" someone, or need to be taken care of, or are only in the market for a father for your child, then you are not ready. But if your opinion of yourself cannot be changed by someone else's opinion of you, you are ready not only for a relationship or marriage but also for a lot more!

RELATIONSHIP STRATEGIES

When Should Your Children Meet Your Boyfriend

I have been dating a man for about six months and, so far, have kept the relationship separate from my sons, ages six and nine. I am not entirely certain where this relationship is going, but I feel there is the possibility for commitment. What is the right way to gradually introduce this special man into their lives?

You are already on the right track by using the word "gradually," as in slowly and cautiously. A good rule of thumb is to keep your children's involvement with a boyfriend a step or two behind your level of involvement with him. For example, if you are just beginning a relationship, there is no reason for your children even to be introduced to this casual date. If, on the other hand, you are seeing someone exclusively and the potential for commitment is there, it is then time to introduce your children to this new person in your life. Keep their initial meetings simple. Ask your boyfriend to join you for an afternoon in the park or for a picnic. Don't force the children on him and certainly do not expect the boys to instantly bond with your boyfriend. He should be introduced as a guest in your home and a special friend of yours. Your boys should not be your sounding boards on how the relationship is progressing, nor should they be encouraged to think of your boyfriend as a permanent part of your home life. Take things slowly and enjoy the time together.

Showing Affection to Your Boyfriend in Front of Your Kids

When is it appropriate to begin showing affection to each other when the kids are around? My boyfriend and I were holding hands when my daughter tried to pry us apart.

As far as seeing you and your boyfriend hugging or treating each other with affection, start slow and take it one step at a time. Walking arm in arm, hand-holding, or having your partner's arm around you in the movie theater when you are all out as a family is a good start. Some mothers report that when they are holding hands with their significant other that their young child tries to pry them apart. This is probably a signal that your child may not be emotionally ready to see you even casually affectionate with your new boyfriend. Take it easy for awhile and give your child a little added time to adjust. It would be better for the three of you to hold hands, considering that your daughter may be signaling that she feels left out. If your daughter lets go, you can continue holding hands with your boyfriend. If it is an adolescent who is embarrassed by your behavior, keep in mind that at this age almost everything Mom does embarrasses them. Make sure, however, that your adolescent children only witness behavior you are comfortable having

them do publicly. Your own behavior, not your words, is the clearest signal to your children about what is and what is not appropriate.

"My Boyfriend Should Have Warmed Up to My Kids by Now. . . ."

My boyfriend doesn't know when he should start being a little affectionate with my sons, ages three and seven. He's very nice to them but isn't sure how to handle closeness like hugging. We have been dating almost a year.

It's time that your boyfriend showed affection toward your children by reading to them or watching a DVD with his arm around the seven-year-old and maybe the three-year-old on his lap. As things progress, he can help tuck them in at bedtime or even give them a hug or kiss goodnight. If you've all been out late at the zoo or park, he may offer to carry one of the children if they get tired. Be patient, and if the kids aren't receptive when he offers to show some affection, let him give them a little breathing room and try again. Eventually, you may want to introduce them to

a "sandwich hug," where you and your companion hug with the two little ones in the middle. Just keep in mind that although this is sometimes appropriate, your relationship with this man will always retain a component that is completely separate from the kids.

Should Your Kids Ever Get in Bed with You and a Significant Other?

Some single mothers feel that a level of commitment does not depend on legalities and having a boyfriend spend time overnight in their homes feels all right to them. Such single mothers have often experienced a bitter and costly divorce and vow, if only for now, never to marry again despite their love and commitment. Even under such circumstances, unless the boyfriend has become an integral part of the family, it is not appropriate to have even your preschool children join you in bed.

Since you and your partner are not married, you need to be acutely aware that events in your home that may be quite acceptable to you may cause unforeseen consequences to you and your children. For example, allowing even the youngest infant or child to bathe or shower with your boyfriend or to use the toilet together may give your children's father grounds to gain custody of your children. Even if you have no ex in the picture, children relating events like bathing with a boyfriend give school and day care authorities grounds for concern that your child might be the victim of sexual abuse, and they will be legally obligated to report your child's statements to the appropriate state government agency. A report of possible sex abuse will involve intensive home study over a period of time by a social

services agency and, in some states, police investigation complete with blaring sirens and flashing lights. This is a humiliating experience for families.

If you feel that the advantages of having a live-in boyfriend outweigh the possible risks, it might be prudent to discuss this change in your living arrangement with your ex-husband before he finds out from the children. If your divorce proceedings are still ongoing, make sure you discuss your proposed new living arrangement with your attorney. Consider also informing your child's teacher that there will be a new member in the household. Doing so leaves less room for misinterpretation and false allegations.

If Your Kids Hate Your Boyfriend

I'm a single mother with two children, a son five and a half and a daughter who just turned four. Their father and I have been divorced for over two years. I'm now in a serious relationship (we're talking marriage) with a man I've been dating for eight months. Even though this man has tried everything under the sun to please the kids, they are incredibly rude, even obnoxious to him. My daughter once even told him it was time to leave. How should I handle this?

This behavior is fairly typical of the things kids do and say under such circumstances. You and your boyfriend should try not to take their "dislike" too much to heart. It's really nothing personal. It's just that in their eyes, Dad has a continued existence in the family, and your boyfriend's presence reminds them that Dad is no longer at home despite their wish that their parents were still together. Your boyfriend's presence is yet another change, and change is typically among life's greatest challenges.

Consider, too, that your children enjoyed your undivided attention from the time Dad left the scene to the time your boyfriend came into the picture. It's normal for them to have a tough time accepting that the attention that was once theirs alone is now being shared with someone else. Try to understand that your relationship with your boyfriend is a signal that you are ready to move ahead with your life and this may be especially hard for your children to accept.

Maybe You're Ready, But Your Children Aren't. Your children might not be ready to accept a new male presence. By being extra sensitive to their needs, you can help them make the necessary adjustment more smoothly. For example, where once it was just you and your kids cuddling up on Friday evenings to watch a video, now you and your boyfriend join friends for an evening out. This is a loss to your children, and most likely they will resent it. But don't think this means that you are chained to the house forever. It's just a signal that says compromises need to be made.

Schedule Your Boyfriend Around Your Children, Not Vice Versa. Maybe the video can be enjoyed earlier in the evening with a picnic supper around the TV, and you two can go out later. If your boyfriend does not support and accept your children's needs for attention during this time, then maybe he is not too grown-up himself. This big change in your life means that your children will need you more now. Negotiating change is one of the biggest challenges there is in life, and your children really need your help. The time and energy you invest helping them make this adjustment now will pay off handsomely in a smoother transition and happier home life for everyone.

Children Require an Adjustment Period. Children are creative little critters and can find a million and one ways to sabotage a relationship they feel is shutting them out or causing them to lose the attention and care to which they have become accustomed. They need to adjust to the fact that you have a life outside of theirs and that although you may give them a different type of attention, you love them as much as ever.

Sit down alone with the children and allow them to talk about their feelings. Let them know that you understand how they feel, but that it is perhaps not your boyfriend they don't like, but the situation. Emphasize your unconditional love and assure them of your desire and commitment to care for them. Be sure to request that they treat any and all of your guests, including your boyfriend, with respect and politeness, as you have taught them. By allowing your children an environment in which to express themselves and their feelings, you are letting them know that they remain your primary concern and that all your life plans take their needs and feelings into account.

If the problem isn't resolved, you may have to get more assertive by letting them know that you will not tolerate any rudeness. If they choose to behave this way, they will be sent to their rooms or given time out until they decide to apologize.

If He Constantly Puts Down Your Kids. If your boyfriend is constantly criticizing or finding fault with your children, this is emotional abuse. Sometimes because of experiences in our own lives, we are unable to recognize emotional abuse when it is directed at us but are sensitive and aware when this abuse is directed at our children. Take a step back and listen to what he is saying both to your children and to you. You need to discuss what you see going on with your boyfriend in a direct, nonconfrontational manner, out of the children's earshot. Put your statements to him as "I" statements. For example, say to him that "I feel put down when you criticize my . . ." rather than remarking that "you are mean" or "you are abusive." He may simply be replaying old childhood tapes, letting you know exactly how he was treated as a child. This conversation, which should be a one-shot deal, offers your boyfriend the opportunity for growth and change. Remember, however, that you and your children deserve to live

in a peaceable home. His behavior is his responsibility, and it is never your fault or the fault of your children. If he tries to shift the blame to you and the children or seems to always find justification for his actions, this is a clear message that he is an emotionally abusive man. Much as you take responsibility for doing it all as a single mother, you are never responsible for emotional abuse. No one can predict when emotional abusive will turn to violence. Why are you allowing your children and yourself to lose the good things in your life to a controlling, mean, potentially violent man? Take advantage of the resources available to you to end this relationship without delay. If your partner's emotional abuse represents yet another abusive relationship in your life, then if only for the sake of your children, seek counseling and find the specialized resources and support you need to get out of this relationship and move toward the peace and happiness you all deserve.

WHEN CERTAIN THINGS START TO BOTHER YOU

My boyfriend has given me some terrific career coaching, helped me straighten out my credit, and introduced me to activities, like skiing, which I otherwise would never have had the initiative or the available cash to try. Little things are starting to bother me, however. He calls me "Ms. Fat Piggy" in front of my children. He has told me that he does not want me going out with my girlfriends because they are trash and people will get the wrong idea about me. He always says "I have to be the one in control" and demands my undivided attention. I don't like the way these things are making me feel, but I don't say anything. My two teenage children stay as far away from him as they can and tell me he is abusive. Aren't men who are abusive that way all the time? I think I can read him pretty well.

Emotional abuse is a far more potent weapon when it happens unpredictably and you are also enjoying positive experiences with this man. If your boyfriend never did anything to please you or to meet your needs, the relationship would have ended a long time ago. What is confusing and destructive is the subtle mistreatment, which ultimately wears away any feelings of self-worth and sense of control over your own life. You are not confronting him about his behavior because you are scared and rightly so. Believe him when he tells you that he is the one who has to be in control because this need is what motivates everything he does. Single mothers, used to managing unpredictable situations like a suddenly ill child care provider or a constantly changing visitation schedule, are particularly vulnerable to the belief that we can read our partner and figure out what he needs. After all, who solved the child care crisis, and who finally made sense and order out of the crazy visitation schedule? Emotionally abusive men often say to their partners that a situation is "your fault" and "you should fix it," and when the woman does fix it, the abuse only intensifies. Isolating you from your friends and calling you hateful, humiliating names are just two ways for him to gain control. Your efforts will never be enough and will only lead you into possible danger and certain emotional damage. Stop trying to figure out what he needs while bestowing your undivided attention and take care of the most important person—you! The only person who should be in charge of your life is you! Your children surely do not need the further life experience of witnessing their mother being controlled, humiliated, and ridiculed. Think back to the kind of person you were before this relationship. Find that person again by acknowledging the emotional damage this man has inflicted. Find the resources you need to rediscover the capable and confident person you know you can be.

When Your Boyfriend Can't Cope with Your Kids

My boyfriend can't seem to cope with my kids. Any ideas?

How familiar is this man with typical childhood behaviors? Does he know, for example, that all two-year-olds have one favorite word: no! Does he realize that all households have some commotion and resistance around bedtime? Does he know that teenagers are testing you every minute of the day? Does he know that all children have to be reminded about homework, toothbrushing, and picking up their rooms and that whining develops in utero during the first trimester? Perhaps all that is needed is for your boyfriend's world to be widened. Take the opportunity to socialize with others who are raising children and feel free to share your war stories. Think about taking a parent education class together or joining a parent support group.

When Your Boyfriend Doesn't Want Children

My boyfriend has stated that the only obstacle to our future together is the kids. He just doesn't want children, ever.

Your companion is entitled to his own opinion about whether or not to include children in his life plan. Yet, even if he does not see children in his present or in his future, it is still possible for you to continue your relationship with him, as long as you set certain boundaries and limits.

It is disrespectful to your children to invite this man to spend extended periods of time in your home. Does he treat them in a polite but distant manner? That's fine because your children will learn the lesson that you cannot charm all of the people all of the time. But is he hostile or critical? In that case, the only lesson your children would learn is how to tolerate abuse in their own home, which is a lesson better skipped. Can you still enjoy the ballet with him or indulge your passion for silent movies with him? Yes. Might he be the best thing that ever happened between sheets? Perhaps. The point is that his disinterest in your children does not mean no relationship with you. It does mean that you have to remember that it is unlikely that he will change his mind, and that means it is unlikely that this relationship will develop into a permanent one if the total package—husband and father—is what you're after.

When Your Potentially New Boyfriend Needs More Scrutiny

If a man seems overly friendly for the amount of time you have known him, this is a potential red flag. There are people in this world who have no business ever being near children. You want to be open to meeting new people, but always ask yourself why this new male acquaintance is so anxious to befriend you. What does this guy want? Before you even consider inviting a stranger into your home, ask him about his background and see if you share any friends or common experiences. If he balks at questions about his background, ask yourself what he is hiding. It is not unheard of for sexual predators to attempt to date single mothers as a way to gain access to children.

When a New Boyfriend Plays "Daddy"

Be careful if your new boyfriend is already assuming the role of father to your kids. Why is he acting this way? Does he have gigantic control needs and feel that he is in charge no matter what the situation?

Do you encourage this because things may have gotten a little out of hand in your house? Maybe the normal routines became lost in the face of battles between you and your ex. Maybe there is no ex, and you are unwittingly grooming him to be Dad.

Perhaps his playing daddy is simply in response to the chaos that reigns in your home because you have been ill, stressed out, or buried in your work. If so, harness his interest and involvement by accepting his help and suggestions. This is different from letting him

SINGLE MOM OF NOTE

Isadora Duncan,
Modern Dance Pioneer

Born in 1878 in San Francisco, Isadora Duncan loved to dance from the time she could walk. Her free-form method of dance was not appreciated in the United States at the turn of the century, but Isadora found acceptance of her revolutionary dance styles in London during the early 1900s. She is considered the inventor of modern dance. Isadora eschewed marriage in favor of having many lovers, but she was a single mother by choice, first to Deirdre and to Patrick, who drowned in a tragic car accident in the Seine River in 1913, and then to six adopted children.

run things, causing conflict, confusion, and hard feelings with your children—something that is bound to happen no matter what place their biological father has in their lives. Some men like the daddy role but are unable to accept all the commitment and hard work parenting entails, and so they selectively choose the part of parenting they like. For example, your boyfriend may be interested in attending your children's games but totally disinterested in supervising homework.

You must stay in control of your household. You are the parent and already may be in some type of parenting relationship with the children's father. It is up to you to find a place for your boyfriend in this setup, if you so choose, and it is up to the boyfriend to decide if he wants to be included. He can participate and be a valued member of your extended family. Sometime in the future, as your husband, his role

may expand significantly. But for now you need to set the rules.

"My Boyfriend Is Jealous of My Children. . . ."

I am dating this guy who is terrific except for one big thing—he is jealous of my children. He complains that I do so much for them and that there is no time for him and for us as a couple. I think he does not realize that I have to be both mother and father to my ten- and twelve-year-old sons and that it makes me feel good to do everything for them and to make life easy for them. How can I convince my otherwise almost perfect boyfriend that I am right?

Maybe you are both right. It is possible to do too much for children, particularly when we feel that we must compensate for the other parent's lack of responsibility and involvement. Perhaps it is time to step back and see if what your boyfriend is saying better expresses your overprotection and involvement rather than his unjustified feelings of jealousy.

Doing everything for your boys now may make you feel good about yourself, but what kind of message does that send to them about their own capabilities and what will be expected of them in the world? If you are making their beds and picking up their dirty clothes before they even hit the floor, you are sending a clear message that there will always be someone to anticipate their every need. Realistically, unless they plan to wed royalty, this will not happen. Your boys will not develop self-reliance or personal responsibility. There is very little room in this world for people without these skills.

Shortly down the road your sons will resent your efforts, and your boyfriend will tire of always being in second place.

Try to step back and look carefully at your household routines and what you are expecting from your boys. Ask other mothers with children your sons' ages what their expectations are. It may be time to help your boys develop self-reliance by teaching them how to accomplish simple household chores and expecting them to do them. Having the boys pick up their own dirty clothes and do daily chores like the dinner dishes will free you up not only to enjoy more time with your boyfriend but also to pursue your own interests and leisure activities.

IS THIS A MAN OR A FIX-UP PROJECT?

You've heard of him before. This guy is always out of work, has numerous allergies although he continues to smoke, or spends his paycheck on vitamins but has ungodly eating habits. You've witnessed terrible fights with his family, maybe he drinks but just on the weekends, and he can't help flirting with any woman who isn't dead. He is simply afraid of commitment, since his wife left him for a woman, and you chalk it up to bad timing. You say that "he is nice and he loves me, and I know that if I just stick by him he will get better." He just needs someone to help him work on himself, right?

Right. But unless you have doctor in front of your name, charge a minimum of about $150 an hour, and don't get involved with your therapy patients, he needs someone other than you.

Single mothers are particularly vulnerable to hooking up with this kind of "fix-up project." This is because single

mothers routinely handle challenges that would overwhelm less capable individuals and often bring this "I can do the impossible" attitude into their personal lives. No money or poor job prospects—you can help him network. Major drug or alcohol issues—no problem. You hear that you can meet a lot of nice people at those AA meetings and rehab centers. You promise to be there for him even after he steals—excuse me, borrows—the last of your wedding silver and then pawns it to buy drugs. Poor health—you cook for him and get him to like healthy foods. After all, who can make the airplane noises as the spoonful of oatmeal nears the reluctant child's mouth more convincingly than you? Habitually tardy, forgets your birthday, does not keep promises—what can you expect from someone raised in that crazy family of his? Besides, you've cut out that magazine article about how to make your man be on time and taped it to the fridge.

Is this a man or a project? Don't you deserve better? Where are you going to get the energy to build your own nurturing, supportive network or to manage your own career? Why are you so willing to take on all this responsibility? Are you so stuck in the mother role that you cannot see that this is what this guy needs? Sometimes we get so scared of being alone that we grab and hold on tight to the first man who comes along and notices us. Let go of the fear. Work on you, and the kind of relationship you deserve—one of equals and give and take, not just give give give—will come along.

ABUSIVE SITUATIONS

Intimate Partner Violence (IPV) can mean emotional, physical, or sexual abuse. Research studies have shown that IPV is far more prevalent than even many experts believed. Are you allowing your children to be abused? Perhaps you were unaware until you saw the bruises or your child told a trusted adult or teacher. Is your boyfriend physically abusing you in the same way? Does he demean and ridicule you so your confidence is in the toilet? Are you financially dependent on him? Is he just one in a long line of abusive men who have dominated your life? Perhaps your confidence is so shot from the divorce or other difficult life experiences, as well as the perceived stigma of being a single mother, that you seem caught in a vicious cycle that only makes you feel worse about yourself and puts you and your children in danger.

No matter what the circumstance or explanation, you need help to get this person out of your family's life. You are not the first woman to be in this situation, and there is help waiting for you. Your first phone call should be to the National Domestic Violence Abuse Hotline at 800-799-SAFE, which provides twenty-four-hour crisis intervention and referrals to services in your local area. The government section of the phone book will also provide contact information for agencies and hotlines specializing in domestic abuse. If it seems just too hard for you to take this first big step, perhaps a friend or family member can be there to help you make this all-important call. But you must do it. Now.

If Your Boyfriend Mistreats Your Children

My boyfriend is mistreating not only me but also my two young sons. I feel trapped. I don't want to start over from the bottom, but I just don't know what to do.

If you are financially dependent on him, then do what you can to gain your independence now, even if that means getting public assistance. True, there is a certain type of abuse reported by women who have endured the red tape and bureaucratic debasement of waiting on the welfare line, and you may feel that trading in one type for another is just not worth it. But you must remember that you and your children are entitled to any help you can receive and that your lives are worth protecting. Also, it's only temporary.

Be aware that as you get stronger and take more control of your life that he will promise to stop the bad treatment and will profess his undying love and devotion. You will be tempted to take him back because you feel that you need him. You may also confuse love with the exhilarating feelings that often accompany abusive relationships—the highs of the renewed attraction after the lows, the letdown, and the feelings of despair. These emotions are understandable. Every woman who has been in an abusive relationship understands exactly how you feel. Many experts go so far as to say that a chemical change actually occurs, releasing endorphins in the brain, which results in a feeling not unlike a drug high. This accounts for the incredible lovemaking or dramatic romantic behavior that many women say will often follow a brutal attack. If you let him back into your life, he may treat you like a queen for a short time, but almost all abusers will begin the abuse again if they haven't gotten any kind of treatment. Friends and family might even pull away from you because of your inability to stay permanently away from him and because it causes them pain to see you in this predicament.

The sad fact is that sources of financial and emotional support will be less available to you the more often you return to him. The children's father will certainly have every right to protect his children from this abuse and may even call the police. Your child's school or day care staff may intervene and report your situation to the authorities. You could be arrested, or worse, you could lose custody of your children and even lose unsupervised visitation. Your self-respect is worth more than anything this person can give you.

If You Are Abused

I've been in an abusive relationship with a man who has never hurt my children but hurts me. He says he really wants help. Should I believe him? There are so many wonderful things about him if he could get over this.

When you are in an abusive relationship, even if he never hurts your children directly, they are still being severely affected. He may tell you that he was abused himself as a child and just does not know any other way. Sadly, this might be true, but it does not give him the right or excuse to abuse you. He may not be abusive to your children now, but most men who abuse their mates eventually abuse the children, too. Your only priority now should be your safety and that of your children.

Abusive men can change, but they need intensive long-term psychotherapy from professionals with special training and experience. There are also support groups for men who are or have been abusers. These programs are similar to twelve-step programs for other addicts. If your boyfriend is able to make the commitment to such treatment, then you can hold out hope that you two may someday live together without violence. Right now, living together should not be an option. Don't accept promises that he will change his behavior on his own. Experts say this is almost impossible. Remember, you cannot "love these problems away," nor are you to blame.

If you formerly raised your children without help, you are lucky in that you know you can. Make an escape plan as soon as possible. Experts warn that you should never tell an abusing partner that you are planning to leave because this is often when the violence escalates. If you contact a shelter, abuse hotline, or service agency, immediately after you hang up you should dial the local pizza delivery number or some other innocuous number so your boyfriend cannot use *69 or the redial button to trace the call. If you have caller ID, make sure to erase all incoming numbers so he is not tipped off.

IF YOUR PARTNER LEAVES

My boyfriend has been living with my three sons and me for almost a year. The boys and I were really starting to feel like Jake was a member of the family. He would do things with the boys, which was great because their own dad has moved across the country and rarely sees them. Jake and I talked about marriage. I wanted a commitment, but Jake said that things would take care of themselves in time. Last Sunday the boys and I returned from a one-day trip to discover that Jake had moved out. His note said that things had gotten too complicated and he had to move on. The boys are devastated, and I simply do not know what to do.

Unfortunately, you are learning by painful experience that single mothers need to keep a clear head when it comes to allowing a dating partner to move in. It was natural for you to want to be with Jake as much as possible, and your desire to live with him is quite understandable. However, it does not sound as though Jake lied or misrepresented his feelings. No doubt he enjoyed spending time with the boys, and no doubt the boys loved every minute with Jake. The problem is that you held out hope that living together was part of a marriage plan. Things got too intense for Jake. He did not know how to handle the situation that he had helped create. Did he handle things in the most appropriate way possible? No. But rather than blame Jake entirely, perhaps there were things you, too, might have considered.

For instance, a less traumatic way to have approached this situation would have been for you and Jake to have talked out your feelings prior to his moving in and becoming such an important part of the boys' lives. Perhaps Jake would have alerted you that he was ambivalent about his readiness to make a long-term commitment, and you could have given more thought to his moving in. It would have been better, too, to explain to the boys that the future with Jake was precarious and that although you certainly hoped they enjoyed his company that Jake's life might take a different turn. He probably would not be living with them forever the way they live with you. In this way, the boys would have put

certain limits on their feelings, which would have been appropriate given the situation. The difficulty is that the boys, picking up on your cues, trusted Jake in the same manner that they trust you. They believed that he would continue to be a part of their lives. Having lost their father, they have now lost another adult in whom they invested love and trust. But hindsight teaches us a little too late sometimes.

You can still make things better, and here is how: have the talk with the boys now that under better circumstances would have occurred before Jake moved in. Explain to them that men and women sometimes want different things out of relationships and that this sometimes causes hurt and confusion. Tell them straight out that Jake left because you and he did not want the same things. Tell the boys that you are looking for someone to share your life with for a long time, which for adults means marriage. Jake did not want marriage for his own reasons, and this is why he left. Emphasize that Jake's departure had nothing to do with them. They were not in some way not good enough. Tell them that Jake probably misses them a great deal, which is probably very true. This will be difficult, but you will have to put your own hurt aside for now and help your boys get back on an even keel. Take the time to do things together and know that it will take time for all of you to recover from what was an unexpected and disappointing loss.

WHEN A LONG-LOST BOYFRIEND RETURNS

I broke up with my live-in boyfriend literally two days before we were to be married. I found out that he had a serious gambling problem, and I could not bring that kind of chaos into my daughters' lives. He split, and we did not hear from him for two years. Now he is back and wants to take up where we left off. I am confused and do not know what to do.

When you do not know what to do, do nothing. For you this means taking things very slowly. People do change, and it is possible that your boyfriend has completely changed and that his serious addiction no longer is a threat to the stability and peace of your home. If you want to date him again, by all means do so. See him, however, away from your home without involving the girls. Listen to what he shares with you about his life. If he is indeed in control of his addiction, you should expect to hear him say that he has been in treatment and continues to be in some type of support program like Gamblers Anonymous. Statements like "I beat this on my own" or "I still put a few bucks in the football pool every now and again but nothing like I used to" should be red flags signaling that he is still controlled by his addiction. If this is the case, run away and stay away from him. He can only bring you heartache.

Through no real fault of your own, your daughters suffered a serious loss when the wedding was canceled and he left. You cannot change what happened, but you can prevent another loss by proceeding—if you decide to pursue this relationship at all—slowly, cautiously, and with both eyes wide open.

HELPING THE KIDS THROUGH YOUR BREAKUP

I have been dating a man for about four years. He has become an integral part of my children's lives although their father remains attentive, supportive, and involved. My boyfriend lives with me for all intents and purposes, and the children certainly are aware that we sleep together. The problem is that I no longer love him. It is the old sad story. I have grown, and he has not. Breaking up with him will be hard enough for him, but I do not know how to handle the "breakup" of him and my children.

Relationships that are slowly dying often cause the most pain. You are right to be concerned about handling not only your feelings but also those of your children as well. While you and your boyfriend work things out (or do not work things out, as the case may be), the best thing to do is to lessen his involvement and contact with them. Do not stop all contact immediately, but rather begin to include him less in your regular family activities. This means that you may plan your outing to the museum without him, go grocery shopping without him, and generally begin to live your lives more separately. For right now, it is okay to be vague with your children about why your boyfriend is not joining you. The old standby "he has other plans" will work nicely here. When you are absolutely definite about the status of the relationship, then tell your children and help them deal with their feelings about losing someone who has become an important part of their lives.

IF YOUR EX-BOYFRIEND WANTS CONTACT WITH YOUR CHILD

I have broken up with my boyfriend. He is just not relationship material. We want different things out of life. He has gotten so attached to my ten-year-old daughter that he wants to keep coming over to see her. He says he will miss her too much. I am not sure how I feel about this and how I should handle things.

This man may have genuinely grown to love your daughter. He may be able to be a special adult friend to her. On the other hand, he may want contact with your daughter solely to keep some kind of tie to you. Perhaps he cannot satisfy your needs but cannot quite cut the ties with you. If this is the case, asking to keep contact with your daughter reflects a desire to use her to get what he wants. There are men, too, who are unable to make a commitment because they have serious sexual problems. This is not to say that he is a pedophile whose sexual needs are met by contact with children, but all precautions should be taken while investigating why he wants to maintain this relationship. He really may feel that she fills a special place in his life and may have a genuine "fatherly" love for her, but you need to examine his reasons.

You also need to ask yourself how your daughter feels about your boyfriend. If she is unenthusiastic about the idea, then she should not be made to feel obligated or guilty. Have you ever for even a fleeting second had a concern that his actions toward her were even slightly inappropriate? If so, the answer, of course, is that he cannot see her. If, however, you have always felt that these two got along appropriately and you can handle having him be a peripheral part of your life, then you might consider letting him spend some limited time with your daughter. Common sense rules should always be followed. You need to know where they are going and when they will return. Overnight stays are out of the question. If your child returns from this visit telling you that the plans you approved were fully followed and that she enjoyed this visit, then you can know that your instincts were correct in trusting him. If she returns with no details, is sullen and quiet, or tells you that they did not go where you had agreed to let them go after all but just "hung out," then your mother radar should be on full alert. He did not keep his word, and you cannot trust him with your daughter again. You will need to tell him just that and stick to it.

BLENDING FAMILIES

If Your Boyfriend's Mother Treats You Like Excess Baggage

The most important thing to consider in this situation is not what his mother says, but how he reacts to it. If you detect a whiff of agreement or there is no effort on his part to modify his mother's remarks, then it is probably time to reassess this relationship. Nobody wants to feel second-rate. On the other hand, if your boyfriend's mother has fantasies that her son will marry a virgin with no past and begin a fairy-tale family, it is not his fault that Mom lives in romance novel reality. Try saying to Mom that "I think Joe is lucky to be part of all the fun we have as a family." Refuse to be drawn into a discussion with his family about where this relationship might be leading, if anywhere. That is for your boyfriend and you to talk about privately. Prepare your children for remarks they may overhear, and let them know that some people require more than a little extra understanding.

If his family is so nasty or abusive that you or your children have left a family gathering or encounter in tears more than once, then it is time to take a hard look at changes that need to be made and new rules that need to be negotiated. This may mean that he socializes with his family without you and the children. Make room for compromise and accept that not all people are capable of change.

If Your Boyfriend's Family Is Not Receptive to Yours

I'm a single mother of five-year-old twin girls. I've been dating a never-married man I met through work for almost ten months. He recently invited us to his family's house for a holiday celebration. However, when I met his mother briefly a few weeks ago, she made me feel like returned merchandise. Jeff was talking about my girls when she cut him off with a comment about when he has his own children. I know that there will be other kids at her house during Christmas week—nieces, nephews, and grandchildren—but I don't want to feel rejected and especially don't want my daughters to feel left out. What should I do?

Maybe Jeff doesn't respond to his mother's obvious or even subtle pressures regarding his marrying and having children, and so she dumps on you. Try not to take it to heart—Jeff is ultimately the one who has to deal with her, not you.

If Jeff talks about the twins, especially to his family, regardless of the depth of your involvement with him, it sounds as if he has a relationship with the girls, for whatever it's worth. You might want to tell Jeff that you are worried your children will feel isolated at his mother's house and you would appreciate a little extra support from him. Perhaps he could introduce them to the others.

You can also decline the invitation if you feel Jeff won't be supportive and are truly concerned that his mother will make hurtful remarks. But you could also respond to offhand comments that make you feel unwelcome by saying "I thought we were welcome here to share and participate in Christmas week festivities with the rest of the group. I can't help sensing that you are uncomfortable with my children and me being here." Often, people who slip you underhanded remarks suggesting their displeasure need to be asked directly what the problem is.

Most likely, your daughters won't take too much notice of Jeff's mother's feelings about "his own children" and will be happy to have other kids to play with and toys and stories to share. But children do pick up on the body language of adults quite easily. If you worry that they will feel alienated from the others because they might pick up on signals transmitted either by you or by Jeff's mother, you might want to prepare the girls first. For instance, you might tell them that you will be spending time during Christmas week with a lot of new friends. Letting your children know that Jeff's mother sometimes has trouble with new friends will help them understand that it is not because of them that she might appear to be ignoring or rebuffing them. Let the girls know that being around Jeff's mother doesn't make you very happy sometimes, but you are excited about meeting the other "friends." You might initially want to spend a little time with the children organizing a game or activity to serve as an icebreaker. This will help everyone get off on equal footing.

Telling Your Children You Are Getting Married

If you have involved your children appropriately as this wonderful, special relationship has evolved, the fact of your actual marriage and all the planning entailed will probably not come as a big surprise. More than likely, it will seem to your children a natural turn of events. If, however, your circumstances have been such that your husband-to-be has not become an integral part of your children's lives, it is probably best

to let them get better acquainted before springing the big news. Your children will have many questions no matter what. They will ask if they will be living in a different house or if their visitations, if any, with Dad will change. They may want to know if household routines and holiday rituals will be different. You should be ready with answers because you and your fiancé should have settled these kinds of questions as part of your getting to know and love one another.

If your children protest loudly and seem generally devastated and upset by the news of your marriage, ask yourself why. Do they still have hopes that you and their father will get back together again? If so, this is the time to explain gently that your life and that of their father are separate now. Your children may still be grieving and may need a greater measure of love and support to weather this big change in their lives. Your soon-to-be husband may not have formed the most affectionate of bonds with your children, and they may resent what will be his greater presence in your life. This signals the need for clear boundaries about who sets family policy and who is in charge of discipline. The children will do much better if the rules and expectations are clearly set out.

Just as you expect them to adjust, you will have to adjust to the fact that your children may never be more than lukewarm in their feelings for this man you love. The best you may be able to hope for is cordial respect. Remember always that *The Brady Bunch* is fantasy. In real life, the adjustments in remarriage and stepparenting are among the most difficult to negotiate. Many second marriages fail over disagreements concerning the children from prior relationships. Everyone needs a chance to be heard and to have his or her feelings respected. Take things slowly and keep your expectations reasonable. Do not expect instant bonding and immediate togetherness.

Should Your Children Attend Your Wedding?

It depends how they feel about your new marriage. Watching your mother pledge eternal love to a man you can barely tolerate can require more fortitude than some children can muster. Most children of divorce harbor fantasies about their parents getting back together long after there is no realistic flicker of hope left that such a reconciliation might occur. Ask your children directly if they would care to attend and participate. If they seem okay or are enthusiastic about participating, give them a simple role appropriate to their age. Very young children might carry flowers or simply stand by your side. An older child might do a brief reading. Unless your children are adults, the role of maid or matron of honor or best man or simply witness belongs appropriately to an adult friend. You and your husband might choose to include in your vows promises to care for and love the children you bring to the marriage. Including your children in this way can be very comforting and affirming to them. Remember that this is your day of joy. Your children may not be as joyful as you are, but if they choose to attend and participate, they must do it in the proper spirit of the day. Explain that if they feel they cannot be part of this joy, then it is certainly their choice not to attend. This is simply part of proper social training and is not negotiable.

Spending the Night When You're Engaged

When the relationship is a committed one and marriage is planned shortly, it becomes more difficult to know what to do. There are a couple of things, however, to keep in mind. First, the standards you set in your home will be the standards your children will follow. You may, for example, tell your ten-year-old daughter that Robert is spending the night with you because you two love one another and plan to spend the rest of your lives together. Your ten-year-old will accept this, and you will see no immediate repercussions. But, later on, when those hormones hit, she will tell you how much she loves her pimple-faced but ardent suitor and how they plan in just twelve more years to get married and spend the rest of their lives together, too. Your children will not see themselves at this future time so differently than you see yourselves now. If your marriage is postponed because one of you is waiting for those final divorce papers, then the issues become even trickier because, in essence, one of you is still married. You don't want this for yourself, and you certainly do not want to encourage your children to have relationships with married people.

If You Decide to Live Together

For right now, remember that if you decide to live together with your children's full knowledge, your children will feel fine about discussing the circumstances at home with teachers and anyone else. Even though more and more women are sharing their lives with "partners," not spouses, there are huge pockets in our culture where this is slow to catch on. Your little one may have lots to say at "show and tell" that you might have preferred to keep private. Older children, who might still be harboring anger and resentment, may openly refer to your husband-to-be as "the man my mother screws" and give the full report to back up the statement. If this is okay with you, then okay. It's certainly acceptable to live together—as long as you use caution. For example, some noncustodial fathers have been known to take exception to such premarital arrangements and have sometimes sued for custody and/or caused other grief. So it is usually best to avoid living together and to keep your private life separate from your children.

FROM SINGLE PARENT TO STEPPARENT

There are few greater challenges than bringing together two families to create what is now known as a blended family. It is important to remember that the creation of your new family order will require commitment, hard work, perseverance, and a lot of unselfish love. It is equally important to remember that by committing yourself to the creation of this blended family that you are giving your children priceless gifts of resilience, adaptability, and tolerance. These gifts will be their reward for the many compromises all of you will have to make to bring this new family together. There will be change, and change is always difficult and never entirely to our liking. Your children will have mastered the ability to confront the need for change, do what needs to be done, and move ahead. But think about this: what better preparation for life can there be?

Making the Initial Adjustment

Before you can adjust to the challenges of creating a new family structure, you and particularly your children need to mourn the loss of the original family. This could mean grieving for a lost parent, whether dead or divorced, or facing the loss of the cozy little nest you created as a Mother Outside of Marriage. Additionally, kids worry that your attention to your new spouse means that you will have less affection for them. Moreover, they have to face the fact that their biological parents will never unite. Allow everyone some time to get over the past before beginning anew.

Giving Up a Special Place

Remarriage and the creation of a blended family may present special challenges to certain family members. Your child, always the baby of the family, may now lose that distinction and the privileges that role may have carried. Another child may resent no longer being the oldest or the only girl or the only boy. A child may no longer be "the family brain," or the "best athlete" distinction may now belong to another child in your blended family. Comparisons are inevitable; shifting family roles can certainly cause resentment. Ease these expected difficulties by making sure each child is given special recognition as well as the opportunity to spend some "just with Mom" time. Praise each child for what makes him or her unique and what they are striving to achieve. Contributions to harmonious family life, like doing your chores or finishing your homework before the dinner time deadline, should also be warmly praised. Look for opportunities for your children to work together as a team so that all can hear warm words of encouragement and "good job" from both of you.

Financial Considerations

More than just deciding how you are going to divide, share, and handle routine household expenses or who pays for vacations, the cost of rearing children needs to be itemized. Paying for food, housing, college, medical and dental bills, insurance, educational activities, and enrichment are just some of the things that are factored into the cost of raising children. You need to be clear about what your respective contributions will be. Often, a simple written contract clarifies misunderstandings and prevents serious disagreements later.

Feelings about Raising Someone Else's Kids

In an ideal society, it would be the lucky child indeed who not only gets to live with an extended family but also has the support of those who were at one time a part of a previous chapter in his or her life. It seems an incredible fantasy to visualize a room filled with all the people who are connected to one child and who want what is best for that child. Unfortunately, our culture doesn't typically lend itself to this type of lifestyle. Although we feel an extraordinary bond to our biological children, it is important, on a more spiritual level, to recognize that all children belong to the family of the human race. It is our job as adults to mother them all without prejudice, jealousy, resentment, or fear.

SETTING UP HOUSE RULES

To avoid having his kids get away with murder while your kids are constantly complaining that they have no rights, you and your new partner need to first establish rules and boundaries for the basic operations of running a house.

Make a Contract

Putting these rules in plain sight is an important first step. Print the house rules on a piece of poster paper or any large piece of paper and display them in the kitchen for all to see. Some parents find it useful to make the rules into a kind of contract and have all family members sign their names or draw pictures of themselves to demonstrate their agreement to these "Rules at Our House."

Be Specific about Rules

Both you and your partner must agree to these rules. These rules must be capable of being enforced without disagreement about whether or not the rule has been broken. For example, a rule that bedtime must be at a reasonable hour only opens the door for debate and disagreement about what is a reasonable hour. It is better if the rule states, for example, that all children are to be in bed by 9:00 PM on school nights and 10:00 PM on other nights.

Picking up and keeping the house in reasonable order is another common battleground. Try making a rule that all toys should be in the toy box or on the shelves before bedtime rather than a rule that says the house has to be cleaned up before bedtime. "Cleaned up" might not mean the same thing to you that it does to your partner or to the children. In fact, a common bone of contention between men and women is basic disagreement on the definition of "clean"!

The rules need to be clear and enforceable with no room for debate. Start simply and begin with no more than four or five rules.

Choose Your Battles Wisely

It might make you nuts that the toothpaste cap is never replaced, but are you sure this is where you want to make a stand? Wouldn't dirty clothes in the hamper or a less hassled bedtime seem more appealing? Do not hesitate to make a rule forbidding foul language, hitting, or other unacceptable behaviors. Again, remember to be as specific as possible and avoid vague rules like "be kind to everyone."

When possible, try to write the rules in a positive manner. Instead of writing "do not turn on the TV until homework is finished," try writing instead that "the TV may be turned on only after homework is finished." This small difference creates a more positive tone and adds to the general feeling of cooperation for which you and your partner are striving. Remember that if you and your partner disagree that you should work out these disagreements out of earshot of the children.

Present a United Front

When it is time to post and discuss these rules with the children, present a united front. If you and your new partner are not clearly united, the children will sense this, and then divide and conquer games will begin. Remember also that your children will fight. There

will be normal sibling-type disagreements about what DVD to watch or whose turn it is to choose the ice cream flavor at the supermarket or who ate the last chocolate chip cookie. There cannot be rules to govern every possible circumstance.

Let the Children Settle Their Own Disagreements

Do not think that you have to mediate or settle every dispute. The best response is to tell them to work it out themselves. Children love the structure of rules, and you will chuckle at the complex rules they will devise if the decision is left up to them. You really do not care what flavor ice cream the kids ultimately select; let them work it out and save your energy for the important stuff.

Support Each Other

An important part of setting up household rules is to agree on the consequences for breaking the rules. The consequences must be clearly spelled out, and the children must know that their biological parent will support the other in enforcing these consequences. For example, if the rule is no TV until homework is finished and your partner's child has not completed his homework, the child needs to be reminded that he cannot plop himself defiantly in front of the TV. If he responds that "you can't tell me what to do because you're not my real mother," warn him that the rule his father helped to write and will enforce is no TV until homework is complete. Emphasize that this is the rule of the household, not your rule.

It is far less likely that there will be such showdowns if each child knows that the other parent will back up the parent who is in charge for that moment. If the children sense that one parent will soften or not support the other, then there will be defiance and chaos, and nobody, including the children, will have the privilege of living in a happy home. Be ready to back each other up.

Who Disciplines Whose Children?

It is simply not realistic or practical to decide that he will discipline his children and you will discipline your own. What happens when one of you is not at home? Avoid physical punishment. Withholding privileges and using time-outs are the best consequences, but be sure you and your partner agree on them. Better yet, jointly create a system of rewards for positive behavior. The goal is to achieve cooperation, not division.

Altered Lifestyles

Some of your cherished habits like uninterrupted Sunday mornings with the newspaper may need to be revised in the face of new family arrangements. Your partner may suddenly find himself listening to your daughter's endless hours of introductory violin practice,

which sounds more like a chorus of dying cats. Your new living arrangements mean that adjustments and goodwill are necessary. Remember, you are the adults. Your behavior will set the tone and provide the model for your children's behavior. If you and your partner are always complaining, bickering, and keeping score, chances are your kids will do so, too. But if you allow the richness that each of you brings to this relationship to flourish, a stronger family will be the result.

Maintain Connections to the Past

People who were once or still are important need to be accepted in your lives. Your new partner may have a cordial relationship with his former wife or significant other, and you should allow room for this friendship to be woven into the material of your new life. The keys here are accommodation, communication, and respect. For example, spending Christmas Eve with your former in-laws may not be the best arrangement now. Be flexible and creative to schedule opportunities to spend time with all family and friends important to both of you. A positive mental attitude and a willingness to adapt to change must be an integral part of your everyday attitude toward living.

24
Expanding Your World

One of the most remarkable observations made about single mothers is their depth of creativity, inventiveness, and resourcefulness. It's sad that we don't read enough about the achievements of many of these women, but it's not unusual to learn that a particularly successful person had spent many years as a single mom. J. K. Rowling, author of the *Harry Potter* book series, is certainly an outstanding example. Other women, whether they are truck drivers, teachers, police officers, social workers, students, or those undergoing personal or career changes, have found that their experiences as single mothers prompted them to use innovative methods for balancing their personal development with their roles as mothers. Some underwent significant spiritual changes, while others discovered that their relationships with their children helped them grow and learn about the world in ways they had never understood before becoming mothers. This chapter is about defining yourself and finding your place in the world. It's about the ways you can expand your horizons while growing as a parent and as a complete woman.

BALANCING WORK AND FAMILY

Almost all single mothers have to work outside the home. Those who have chosen to return to school see their education as their work. Balancing your work and your family can be difficult, but it doesn't have to be overwhelming if you have a blueprint to follow. Flexibility is a must when combining your career with children.

Life should be more than a hectic blur. Take some time to review your schedules, your child's routines, and the realistic options you have available to you. Some mothers make flowcharts to order their priorities, and others simply keep lists, lists, and more lists. A family activity calendar posted in an accessible place is a must, as are phone numbers of "backups"—people or services that can help out in a crunch.

Keep in mind, too, not to overschedule your child's life, and take every spare moment to reenergize yourself the way you feel is good for you, regardless of what others think. If friends urge you to get away to the beach but you hate the sun, don't do it. If family members insist you take a nap but you're too wired and would rather work on a report, do what your heart dictates. Learning where your center of gravity is or what activities or actions sustain you is the first step toward balancing the demanding life of a single mother.

Returning to Work

Going back to work, whether you have been on maternity leave or you are recently divorced and reentering the workforce after staying at home with the kids, can be emotionally challenging.

For the new mom, even though returning to your job is exciting and is actually a relief from the twenty-four-hours-a-day, seven-days-a-week job of beginning motherhood, it's natural to feel conflicted and sometimes more than a little guilty about leaving your baby. For the mom who stayed home during her marriage and now has to enter the workforce as a newcomer, the excitement and anticipation of this new life also brings with it feelings of insecurity. You may ask yourself "what if I can't cut it?" or "how will I ever make enough money with my limited skills?" These are normal feelings. Rest assured

that your skills will improve while you are on the job.

However, you might also want to consider getting started on a new or modified career path or working out of your home. Make sure you are up-to-date on what is required at your current job. Consider asking your new boss to let you come in a few hours for a couple of days to get settled and organized before your official first day on the job.

Getting Your Career Back on Track

Jump-starting a career can be difficult for mothers who have taken several months of maternity leave or have been staying home to care for the kids for years. Following are tips for getting your career back on track:

- Focus on your goals. Ask yourself what are your assets and weaknesses. Who are your role models? Which three words describe you? Which three words would you like to describe you?

- Network with parents you will meet at your Lamaze class, new moms support group, day care center, child's school, Little League, or other organizations to see what jobs are out there for you.

- Maintain contacts with people with whom you have worked before. Try to get connected to the Listservs that target your particular career or professional area. Visit Web sites for up-to-date information. Don't ignore the importance of staying connected with former coworkers. Schedule coffee or a quick lunch at least twice a month to keep posted on what's new in your field and to keep abreast of potential new opportunities.

- Become involved in volunteer activities in your community. This sounds difficult when you're busy with a child, but one hour per week is really not too difficult to slot out.

- If you're returning to your regular job after maternity leave, consider job sharing if you'd rather work part-time. Like part-time work, job sharing allows you to spend more time with your baby. But there are more advantages for both employees and employers. Job-sharing positions usually include half of all benefits that full-time employees receive. Additionally, the salary is usually more than a similar part-time position. Plus, the employer benefits by getting two skilled people for the price of one. The fields of medicine, education, administration, and human resources are utilizing job sharing, and a number of major U.S. corporations are beginning to catch on, too. However, the best way to arrange job sharing at your place of business is to find another person in your department who is interested in sharing the position and for both of you to make a proposal to your manager. Give serious thought to the career implications of job sharing, if for example, making partner or becoming a department chairperson is a cherished goal.

- Work full-time with modified hours. This is known as flextime, a work policy that is gaining popularity with many large companies. According to "Caring for Infants and Toddlers" by the Peter and Lucille Packard Foundation, while many employers are taking steps to be more family-friendly, higher paid employees are more likely than lower paid employees to receive benefits that help them deal with the dual demands of work and family.

- If you simply can't see eye to eye with your employer and you see no way of balancing your job with your home life, consider starting your own business. More and more women are going the entrepreneurial route as consultants, bookkeepers, copywriters, data processors, or medical transcriptionists; they are earning money through hobbies such as sewing, interior design, catering, or teaching skills like tennis, swimming, painting, or music.

- Work at home. With the advances in telecommunications, working at home is a very viable option. If you have skills such as sewing, writing, illustration, or hairstyling, working at home may be just the solution for you.

- Keep current in your field by reading professional journals or trade publications. They often include an employment section or job-hunting guide.

- Join or rejoin professional organizations. Keep your memberships current—these groups are great for networking and new opportunities.

- Take classes if you need to develop new skills. Your local community college most likely will have courses discussing the latest business trends and computer training, no matter what your level of skill.

- Get in touch with the alumni office

of your college or professional school. Call an old classmate or teacher for ideas.

◆ Look for companies that are hospitable to women. Check out *Working Mother* magazine's yearly "Guide to the Best 100 Companies."

◆ Consider part-time employment or a temporary job in your field or in a field you have wanted to work in that could lead to a full-time position.

Out-of-Town Trips

There will be times when you'll be asked to go out of town, take a business trip, work on a weekend, or put in some overtime. These obligations can present difficult challenges and really tax your support system, especially if you have an infant or toddler or have never been separated from your children. Always remember that the most important thing you can do for yourself and your family is to be who you are. Although it might be the most valued undertaking in your life, being a parent is not the only definition you give yourself. If you have worked hard to score points in your career and want to advance further in your job, then making that overnight sales trip or putting in that overtime as the deadline nears might not only be the right decision but also the only decision in a perilous job market.

What to Do When the Kids Have a Snow Day

When your children have an unexpected day off from school or your babysitter suddenly cancels and you absolutely cannot miss work, are you prepared? First, find out if you work in a kid-friendly place. Inquire about what seems to be the unwritten office rule on bringing children to the office. If you have been with the company only a short time, ask a colleague if children are ever brought to the office when there is a babysitting or weather emergency. Do you see other people bringing their children into the office from time to time? Obviously, some workplaces are dangerous or inappropriate for children—clearly the case if you are an assembly-line worker or a police officer or firefighter. But, in most offices, children are occasionally tolerated and sometimes even welcomed.

If your workplace is able to tolerate your children in such cases, count your blessings and get prepared. Have food set aside to "nuke" for them in the office microwave and have snacks available to bring along. Juice boxes and other such high-priced convenience foods are well worth the price of keeping your children fueled up and content during your workday. You should also think ahead about what your children will bring along to keep them occupied. Even the copying machine loses its fascination after awhile, and you certainly do not want your children becoming pests. The best suggestions are quiet activities like coloring books and board games. You should also plan to discuss ahead of any scheduling emergency the kind of behavior you expect from your children when they accompany you to the office. If your boss wears the most obvious hairpiece in America, discuss this fact with your eight-year-old well ahead of time, rather than have him blurt out, "Your wig is really a funny color. How come it doesn't stick on your head better?"

When You Cannot Bring Your Children to Work

If your workplace is not kid-friendly or even kid-tolerant, you will need a backup plan for bad weather or no-babysitter days. Look for resources close by. Is there an elderly neighbor who might welcome the extra cash and diversion for the day but who is not interested in full-time babysitting? Is there a high school student who might be available to sit on days when there is no school? How about a teacher or other member of the school staff who is off on days when school is closed for weather emergencies? Can you offer her a free Saturday in exchange for the help you need when schools are unexpectedly closed?

Once your plan is in place, make additional preparations at home. Set aside easily prepared, favorite lunch foods for your children to take along, or simply be ready to send along their regular brown-bag lunch. If their destination house has a VCR or DVD player, send along favorite tapes or DVDs, which, incidentally, a senior citizen might actually enjoy watching with them. It is a good idea to send along coloring books, board games, and other quiet activities. Discuss with your children any changes in routine that might take place if your backup plan has to be put in place. For example, if your elderly neighbor is your backup sitter, discuss any special rules she might have like staying away from her not-so-friendly cat. The peace of mind is well worth the efforts this planning involves—not to mention the stress-busting effect of knowing that you are prepared if the unexpected happens.

Should You Call In Sick to Care for Your Child?

Don't just call in sick when your child is sick or family demands overwhelm you. Bosses watch unscheduled absences closely, and your job or career status could suffer. It's amazing how many parents call up the boss claiming that they cannot come to work because their car broke down or a power outage prevented the alarm from going off, rather than admit that they must stay home with a feverish child. Other excuses range from underground gas explosions to attending a relative's funeral for the umpteenth time, rather than saying that a child needs to see a doctor or dentist or is appearing in a school play.

Before you call in sick instead of asking for time off to attend your daughter's school awards ceremony, try to think about the ways you can take time off for your child and function effectively at work.

Take a solution to the boss rather than a problem. Negotiate the time, if possible, and include the specific ways you will make up the time lost from work. For example, can you work out a buddy system with a coworker who can cover for you in your absence? Can you take some work home, make calls outside of the office, or come in earlier one or several days? Once your boss knows that you have made every effort to help the business run smoothly even when you aren't there, he or she may be more willing to negotiate the time you need to meet your commitments to work and family.

If you meet with resistance, perhaps your boss is less than receptive to your needs because you are not completing your tasks or are failing to close certain sales. Does he or she feel that you are not doing your job up to par? How can your performance improve? Does your absence create chaos? Your boss must also be sensitive to the needs of all her employees. Many childless employees resent being asked to pick up the slack during high family demand times, like snow days and summer vacations.

Working During the Summer

Unless you have the budget of a movie star, filling those long summer months with safe, healthy, fun activities can seem like an impossible task. But before you succumb to the "what-am-I-going-to-do-with-the-kids-this-summer" panic, try to realize that most working parents face the same dilemma. Know, too, that there are resources and solutions available if you know where to look.

Keep in mind that because the demand for summer child care is so great

A HOSTEL ENVIRONMENT

Don't bemoan not traveling the world because you're a mom on a budget. Consider visiting places you've never been by staying at youth hostels in this country and across the globe. Hostels aren't just for student backpackers, and they offer more than just a good night's sleep. Many have family rooms with private baths at amazingly low nightly rates. Plus, you'll get to interact with other adults and enjoy family time, too, as hostels invite a wide array of people ranging from new high school grads to retirees. For more information, check out Hostelling International on the Web.

that you need to plan early. Regardless of whether you choose a pricey camp or an inexpensive swim club through your local parks and recreation service, these programs fill up fast. The best strategy is to start planning summer activities between the time you put the last of the Christmas tree decorations away and Valentine's Day!

CONTINUING YOUR EDUCATION

Are you spending too much time wishing you could win the lottery? If you are tired of being strapped for cash or relying on public assistance or undependable or less than adequate child support, you should consider continuing your education. The more education you have, the more money you will make. Nothing will move your life ahead with greater certainty than improving your job skills.

Nobody said that going back to school as a single parent is going to be easy. But nothing worthwhile ever is, and the rewards of getting this valuable education are endless.

For example, you can increase your skills to advance in your job or simply to make yourself employable for the first time. Never forget that knowledge is power. People want to and need to be around people who possess a great deal of knowledge about how things work in our ever-changing world. In addition, you are setting a priceless example for your children as they watch you organize your time efficiently, study for exams, research topics for your homework assignments, and—most important of all—set goals and achieve them. Plus, school-age children who enjoy having a homework buddy actually relish the fact that their moms and they do homework together!

Don't Ignore the Opportunities

There are so many opportunities waiting for you. You might decide to enroll in college classes, sign up for a series of special training seminars at work, take a night course to learn to appraise antiques, get your real estate broker's license, or take correspondence courses. The list of possible educational opportunities is endless.

You're Not Too Old to Start

I have always loved interior design and have helped many friends decorate their homes. I know I have a real flair. The problem is that to get the job I want I must have at least a two-year degree. I can probably only afford to go to the local community college part-time. By the time I get my degree, I'll be forty.

You are going to be forty anyway; so why not go back to college and celebrate forty with a degree? Start planning the future you want and remember that the birthdays come and go, even if we have not begun to move ahead to reach our goals.

"I Don't Want to Be the Oldest Student. . . ."

I would like to earn my bachelor's degree in nursing. I have worked as a nurse's aide for many years. I worry that I will be a lot older than my classmates in the nursing program.

First, it is unlikely that your age will be of great interest to your fellow nursing students. In fact, about one-half of college students today are "older"— thirty-five years and up.

Your fellow students will probably envy your practical knowledge and experience and will be flocking to be your study partners, as so many mature women returning to school soon find out.

Fear of Failing

I have not opened a book in years. I always hated school and got only mediocre grades in high school. My boss wants to send me to a special company training program so that I can upgrade my skills and earn a promotion. What if I can't cut it?

Your experiences as an adult in a career training program will be a far cry from beginning algebra and world history. Probably in high school you saw little point in the subjects you were expected to learn and were distracted by normal teenage concerns like boys, dates, and parties.

Now motivation won't be a problem because education means something else to you—more money, a better life for you and your family. But since you have been out of school so long, you might want to do a little homework before school starts. Bone up on your reading, math, or computer skills. If necessary, find a high school student to tutor you.

If You Never Finished High School

If you never obtained a high school diploma, then look into the General Educational Development (GED) test.

This test is a battery of five comprehensive examinations in social studies, science, writing, reading, and mathematics. This test was developed during World War II to help returning servicemen and servicewomen complete their high school educations. Since then, millions of Americans have received their high school equivalency certification by passing this test.

If this opportunity interests you, your best bet is to call a local community college. Ask to speak with an admissions counselor. It is likely that the college offers classes to help prepare you for taking the GED. If there is no community college in your area, contact your high school guidance office and ask where information about this test might be obtained.

WHAT IS DISTANCE LEARNING?

Distance learning is any learning that takes place with the teacher and the student geographically remote from each other. Distance learning can take place through surface mail, interactive TV, videotape, radio, satellite, or any number of Internet technologies such as message boards, chat rooms, and desktop computer conferencing. Modern distance learning began with correspondence instruction, which began in the United States in the 1870s. Correspondence study pioneered or perfected many instructional methods now taken

for granted, like convenient at-home learning anytime, anyplace, self-paced scheduling, and "action learning" in the workplace, where what is taught matches up with job responsibilities and duties. Distance learning is growing at a phenomenal rate because it has almost limitless potential to bring the finest teachers right to every student's home or office.

College is not just for kids anymore or for those who have the luxury of being able to attend school full-time ,free of demanding family responsibilities! Education is expensive, however, and probably represents one of the biggest investments you will ever make. It is important to check out every option and consider costs carefully.

WHY IS ACCREDITATION IMPORTANT?

First, accreditation is the independent review of an educational program for the purpose of helping to establish that uniform and quality learning standards apply. Accreditation is important if you want to have a public record of your learning that will be widely accepted by employers, professional associations, and other colleges and universities.

Distance Education and Training Council (DETC)

The DETC has been the accreditation standard-setting agency for correspondence study and distance education since it was established in 1926. The DETC member institutions offer more than 500 different academic and vocational courses by mail or by telecommunications. Vocational courses are a good option if your job skills are weak. These programs train you in such specialized fields as locksmithing, interior design, auto mechanics, clerical skills, and landscape design. As a general rule, credits earned from such programs cannot be applied toward a college degree. Many nontraditional learners, such as professional athletes, have earned their high school diploma through DETC accredited agencies. Interested in more information? Get a free copy of the Directory of Accredited Institutions by calling the DETC at 202-234-5100. Be sure to visit their Web site at *www.detc.org* for more information on programs of possible interest to you.

Interested in Academic Correspondence Courses?

Academic correspondence courses designed specifically to earn college credits are ideal for the mom who wants to begin earning college credits while still working and taking care of her children.

Look into programs accredited by the Independent Study Division of the National University Continuing Education Association (NUCEA). NUCEA is a professional organization of approximately seventy colleges and universities offering correspondence courses.

WHAT IS A DEGREE MILL?

You may be warned about degree or diploma mills if you discuss with family and friends your interest in getting a college degree by distance education. Degree or diploma mills prey on a potential student's lack of knowledge and confusion about accreditation. These are bogus universities, which sell college diplomas—the piece of paper itself—rather than the educational

experience. If you pay the "tuition" amount, generally a lump sum of about $3,000 and sometimes more, you will receive a college diploma.

It is important to understand that the term "college" or "university" in many states is not legally restricted to use by accredited agencies. This means that virtually anyone might legally declare himself or herself a "college" and start cranking out phony degrees on the spot.

Diploma mills usually advertise as being "nationally accredited" or "accredited worldwide." The trick here is that these bogus institutions are indeed "accredited" but by phony agencies created by the same people who created the fake college or university.

ARE TOP SEARCH ENGINE LISTINGS RELIABLE?

If your chosen online university appears as a top listing using your favorite search engine, it has to be a "real university," right? Absolutely not. A top search engine listing does not mean academic quality. Top search engine listings often reflect only lots of money spent for online advertising. Anyone can create an impressive Web site with flashy graphics and submit the resulting URL to a search engine. Search engines do not inspect online colleges to determine their accreditation.

DO YOUR HOMEWORK FIRST

◆ Verify the accreditation status of the online college or university you are considering. Visit the Council on Higher Education Accreditation (CHEA) at *www.chea.org.*

Your prospective school must be accredited by an agency recognized by the CHEA. If your online "admissions counselor" tells you that online universities cannot be accredited by the CHEA, you have just been told a lie.

♦ Contact the Better Business Bureau at *www.bbb.org* and see if there are any complaints on file regarding your prospective online university.

Why Distance Learning May Be the Right Choice for You

The majority of online degree seekers are women. The number one cited reason for attending an online program is the need to juggle career with family responsibilities. For single moms, typically with no backup and a shortage of ready cash, online learning offers the chance to avoid babysitting costs while also saving a bundle on gasoline, parking, meals eaten away from home, and all the other costs associated with commuting to a college.

Single moms who chose to dial up their degrees also get a chance to

comparison shop. Women who attend college by commuting realistically may have only one or two choices for their degree and thus have to pay the asking price at their local college. Tuition prices vary widely, and these differences in price do not reflect differences in quality. How much tax revenue a state chooses to distribute to education often greatly affects tuition costs. Online learning favors single moms who aren't afraid to shop around for their best educational buy.

EARNING COLLEGE CREDIT FOR LIFE EXPERIENCE

Are You a Good Tester?

Challenge exams have been developed to evaluate what a student already knows about college-level subjects. Most exams are multiple choice and can be taken for a modest fee.

♦ *College Level Examination Program* (CLEP). The most widely accepted credit-by-exam program is the College Level Examination Program (CLEP). More than 2,900 accredited colleges accept CLEP for undergraduate degree credit. The CLEP program features twenty-nine single subject exams and five general exams. Single subject exams test material that is covered in a single college course. The five general exams cover freshman level knowledge in English composition, humanities, college mathematics, natural sciences, and social sciences. If all five general exams are passed, up to thirty college credits—the equivalent of an entire year of college—can be earned.

Contact The College Board by telephone at 800-257-9558 or at *www .collegeboard.com.*

- *Defense Activity for Non-Traditional Education Support* (DANTES). DANTES exams, originally designed to test military learners, are now available to the public. DANTES covers social science, business, and physical science. Contact the DANTES Program Office by telephone at 877-471-9860 or at *www.getcollegecredit.com.*

- *Academic Portfolio Option.* This may be a better choice for you, if you are not a good test taker and what you know represents applied knowledge rather than textbook theory. You may have artwork, certificates, articles, software, business plans, or videos which attest to your competency in specific subject areas. Credit can be earned toward a degree, provided you document these learning experiences and submit them to the school in the form of a life experience portfolio. Colleges that accept portfolios for review often require students to take a course to learn how to put together an academic portfolio.

  Check out *Earn College Credit for What You Know* by Lois Lamdin and *Preparing the Portfolio for an Assessment of Prior Learning* by Roslyn Snow.

- *College Credit for Corporate Training.* Colleges are not the major providers of adult education. Corporations spend more time, money, and effort teaching adults than all the colleges in the United States combined. This is good news for single moms. Noncollegiate training programs can often be converted to college credit through a portfolio process. Some larger corporations subject their training programs to a special review process sponsored by the American Council on Education's Program on Noncollegiate Sponsored Instruction (ACE/PONSI). If ACE/PONSI finds individual courses are "college level," they recommend that a certain number of college credits be routinely awarded for successful course completion. Some colleges accept these transfer credits; others do not. Check out these opportunities at work.

Don't Overlook Your Local Community College

Your local community college may be your best bet for improving your job prospects by upgrading your skills.

Community colleges typically offer three different kinds of programs:

- *Certificate Programs.* Certificate programs provide you with training for a specific job, such as real estate appraiser, cosmetologist, dental laboratory technician, or legal secretary. For these kinds of jobs you do not need or probably want extra courses in subjects like sociology or political science. Students who enter these types of programs are looking to prepare for new careers, make themselves eligible for promotion, or just stay current with new knowledge in their field.

  The course of study can range anywhere from a couple of weeks to two years, depending upon what coursework is required. The opportunities that such certificate programs provide are very often not available at two- or four-year university-sponsored degree programs.

- *Associate Degree in Applied Science.* An associate in applied sciences (AAS) degree is awarded to students who complete sixty hours of credit—about four semesters—in a specific sequence of courses. These courses are not meant to be the freshman and sophomore years of a traditional four-year degree program. These two-year programs are designed to prepare students for entry into the workforce immediately in fields such as dental hygiene, interior design, and criminal justice.

- *Transfer or Associate in Arts Degree.* Students who think they might wish to obtain a four-year degree eventually often begin by enrolling in a community college to obtain an associate in arts (AA) degree, which generally takes four semesters full-time to complete. Such a degree will transfer to a four-year institution so that a bachelor's degree can be earned. Some students find such a plan a big money-saver—certainly of interest to the strapped-for-cash single mother—and others find they need this first step to gain the confidence and experience to continue their education.

My high school grades were a nightmare. I would really love to begin attending classes at the university part-time, but I know they will not accept me into a degree program with my terrible high school record.

Enrollment in a community college would be a good idea. The good grades you will earn will be considered better evidence of your abilities than your high school grades. In other words, time spent doing well in a community college can prepare you to enroll in a more selective four-year program when your high school record is less than fabulous.

Should I Think about Enrolling in a Private Career School?

I see ads on television all the time for schools that promise high-paying jobs as a professional after you complete their state-of-the-art education program in whatever. What is the story with these schools?

The schools you see advertised on television are called private career schools or proprietary schools. They are private businesses, and their purpose is to make a profit. Some of these schools do grant associate degrees, although the faculty is less permanent than in a community college. On a more positive side, these schools are more sensitive and quicker to change in response to economic forces and changes in the job market than more traditional schools.

These schools will ask you to sign a contract, and their programs will typically be more expensive than community colleges. The courses offered will be very practical and will be oriented toward getting a job upon completion of the program. Some typical courses of study at such schools include auto mechanics, truck driving, and computer technology, but other courses are also available. Hands-on experience is offered, and a new training program usually begins every three or four weeks.

A Word of Caution about Private Career Schools

Before you sign the contract, ask: What will happen if I don't complete the course work? Does the school offer career counseling and placement? What percentages of graduates receive jobs in their field? How long does it take for a graduate to find a job? What are the names of some employers who hire the school's graduates? If the responses are not satisfactory, don't enroll.

Make sure you also take a tour of the school and speak to the current students. They will tell you the real story. Ask for the names of some recent graduates and contact them directly to see how they rate the training they received.

How Will I Pay for This?

Lack of money is the biggest obstacle for a single parent thinking of returning to school, followed by worries over time management. Let's face it; education after high school is not cheap. Not only do you have tuition costs but also there are books and transportation costs and child care to consider. But don't view the money you'll need or the income you'll lose by not working while attending school as a waste. Think of it as an investment.

The biggest sources of financial aid are the state and federal government as well as the colleges, universities, and other types of schools themselves. When you apply for admission to the school of your choice, you must also apply for financial aid.

Plan Ahead

Financial aid is a complicated game. The better you understand the process, the more likely you are to get the money you need. Successful negotiations with the financial aid office are possible, but only if you are well informed and prepared. There are a number of books

---

SINGLE MOM OF NOTE

**Bette Nesmith Graham,
Inventor of Liquid Paper**

In 1951, Bette Nesmith Graham had a young son to support, a love of painting, and typing skills barely adequate to her position as an executive secretary for the chairman of the board of a large Dallas bank. Using her kitchen blender, she mixed up some of her white tempera paint and voilà, Liquid Paper was born. Her son Michael and his friends filled bottles for her customers. Fifteen years later, "Liquid Paper" was selling to the tune of more than 10,000 bottles a day.

Speaking of tunes, that son achieved his own fame as a member of the 1970s pop group, The Monkees.

---

about paying for college on the market that may be of help.

How to Begin

Start by filling out the standardized need analysis form called the Free Application for Federal Student Aid (FAFSA) which can be downloaded from *www .ed.gov*. Many private schools and some state-supported schools may require you to fill out the CSS/Financial Aid Profile Form as well. Promptness is essential. Expect the questions to be personal and prying. The goal of these forms is to figure out what portion of your income and assets you can afford to pay toward your educational expenses in the coming academic year. The difference between what you can pay and what your education will cost is your "need."

Federal Aid

There are six major student financial aid programs through which most students requiring financial aid receive help. These programs are administered by the federal government through the Department of Education. Two are grant programs, which means this is money you will not have to pay back. These grant programs are the Pell Grant and the Supplemental Educational Opportunity Grant (SEOG). Two other programs are loan programs, which means, of course, that you will have to pay this money back with interest, although usually at a rate lower than current rates. These are the Perkins Loan, Stafford Student Loan, and Signature Education Loan. The sixth program is the College Work Study (CWS), which helps colleges provide jobs for students receiving financial aid.

Who Is Eligible to Participate in These Federally Sponsored Programs?

For most programs you must be enrolled at least half-time at an approved college or program of study. You must be a United States citizen or permanent resident. You must use the aid for educational expenses, and you cannot be in default on another student loan or owe a refund on a federal grant. You must qualify on the basis of need.

What to Expect After You Apply for Financial Aid

Your college or university will offer a financial aid package to you. This package will give a breakdown of the campus-based aid you will receive as well as the federally sponsored loans and other grants for which you are eligible. This financial aid package, given to you in the form of a one-page statement, will also tell you at a glance how much money you have been offered to meet the expected costs of books, tuition, and other expenses.

What about Time Management?

Treat going to school as you would going to a job. The same rules that you would apply to showing up at work apply to receiving your education. The pay is different, but the credit you'll earn from school is more rewarding in the long run.

I am scared that I will not be able to handle all the responsibilities of going to school and raising my children. I feel selfish, like I will be shortchanging them, but I really want to go to school.

You're not selfish for wanting to improve conditions for yourself and your children. You may actually become a better role model by showing them how you set goals and deal with conflicting demands. They may wind up more self-reliant, too.

My teenage children are thrilled that I am going to be a student at the local community college. I should be preparing them for the changes my school attendance will bring. What should we discuss?

Talk to them about making compromises. Although they may lose the on-call chauffeur, the always available cook, and the always open ear, they are getting a happier, more successful mother. Prepare your children for what changes in routine and expectations may occur. Reassign chores ahead of time, and go through a rehearsal to see if you can work some of the kinks out of the system before the first day of school arrives.

The key to a successful educational career is time management. You will have to be organized every single day to fit everything in. At the same time, you will have to be adaptive enough to accommodate unexpected changes in routine, like when a child gets sick or the weather is uncooperative.

Ten Tips for Doing Your Best in School

1. **Keep the vision of your goals in front of you.** How will you know when you have achieved your goal? Will it be the moment you are handed your diploma? Will it be the moment you see your name and title on the door? Keep a vision in your mind of that moment and use it to keep you motivated and focused on the task at hand. If your goal is symbolized by a picture, keep that picture handy and look at it often.

2. **Share your vision with others.** Other people cannot help you if they have no idea what your dreams or goals might be. Some people might resent your ability to go after what you want, but most people will support you and help you in ways for which you never would have asked.

3. **Write down your goals.** Make your goals specific. For example, I will have taken all my required courses by the spring of next year.

I will do this by taking two courses each semester and one course during the summer. I will attend every optional career seminar offered, even if it is scheduled on Friday afternoon. Make a contract with yourself and sign your name. Promise yourself to move ahead with a well-thought-out plan.

4. **Plan on paper.** Once something is written down, it is a plan. If you keep it only in your mind, then it is just an idea without form or substance.

5. **Get organized.** Do not think you are going to plop your stuff down on the kitchen table every night. Find a shelf, box, or secondhand file cabinet in which to store all your school materials. The kitchen table can certainly turn into your "school desk" at night, but you need a definite and well-organized place to put everything. Otherwise, you will waste valuable study time looking for things you have misplaced or for things the children have somehow managed to "borrow."

6. **Single mothers do not have the option to procrastinate.** Students without the responsibilities you have may be able to put off studying or writing a paper until the last minute. Guaranteed, the first time you put off an important school paper, your kids will get the flu, and the paper will not be done on time. The best way to manage the inevitable stresses of juggling multiple responsibilities is to do things as they need to be done. Then, when your assignments are

completed, you can enjoy without guilt the time away from the pressures of school.

7. **Rethink your standards.** Does your house have to be spotless? Is watching that TV show really that important? Can you set aside certain hobbies or interests while you are in school? At work, you may volunteer for fewer extra projects or work less overtime. This is a time to concentrate on the task at hand—to finish school so your goals can be realized.

8. **Learn to delegate.** Think about what you absolutely do not have to do yourself and then don't do it. Your children will be infinitely better off as independent creatures capable of packing their own lunches and picking up after themselves.

9. **Learn to say "no."** While you are in school, you must learn to say no to demands that do not help you to move along with your studies or personally benefit you and your children. If this is difficult for you, get a friend to help you role play.

10. **Treat yourself once in a while.** Pat yourself on the back, or buy yourself a candy bar and savor every unhealthy but scrumptious mouthful. Take a walk in the sunshine while reciting in your head recent accomplishments. Enjoy hearing, if only in your head, "Congratulations. Dr. Jones loved your presentation, and you got a B on a quiz that you were sure you failed." If you are not going to say good things about you, who is?

CREATING AN EXTENDED FAMILY

Emotions are contagious. Moods are like social viruses—some people have a natural ability to transmit them, while others are more likely to catch them. Women were reported to be in negative moods almost twice as much as men, although studies indicate that women were generally happier than men.

One way to catch positive feelings is to be around upbeat people. Avoid toxic people—they just pull you into their mood. Another way is to join a support group.

Seeking Self-help Through a Support Group

Support and self-help groups are a great way to balance positive and negative feelings. If you want to try to organize a support group, don't waste your time reinventing the wheel. Visit some support groups to observe how they operate. You can even borrow tips from their material, flyers, and meeting formats. Even if there is no other group in your area for single parents, visiting a new moms' group, sitting in on a regular gathering of divorced parents, or attending, if welcome, a meeting for parents of children with special needs can prove invaluable. Some things to remember:

Don't Overlook the Word "Mutual." You need to find a few others who want to help you start the support group. If you try to manage everything yourself, you will find yourself burning out somewhere down the road. Besides, it is to the other members' benefit to be part of planning activities and tending to the initial tasks required in starting a self-help group.

Select a Steering Committee. A steering committee or core group is necessary to assign chores to other members, particularly if you are planning for fairly large gatherings. For example, one person can handle refreshments, another can be responsible for greeting visitors and handing out name tags, and still others can manage the child care and publicity for the group.

Find a Suitable Place for Your Meetings. Given that this is an opportunity to meet new people, it might not be a good idea for safety reasons to meet at members' homes. Find instead a home for your group, such as a library, community center, church or synagogue, school, hospital, or human service agency. This is probably the best bet, if you plan to regularly invite guest speakers. You can also arrange to have a monthly bring-your-own picnic meeting at a local park or recreation center. Consider the best times for these meetings and try to stick to them. Would daytimes, weekends, or evenings be better for most members? It's easier for people to remember the meeting time if it is always the same day of the week or month. Keep in mind, too, that you can start with very informal gatherings that spend only a few minutes on the business aspects of your support group.

Publicize Your First Meeting. In general, when starting a support group, reaching potential members is not easy, but with all the single mothers out there looking for others with whom to network, it may not be that difficult either. Post flyers or notices where single mothers congregate. Doctors' offices, dental clinics, post offices, schools, day care centers, community centers, hospitals, libraries, pharmacies, and grocery stores are excellent places to publicize your group.

Plan Your Meeting Agenda. Here are the three most important considerations when planning future meetings:

1. *Purpose of the group.* Although you should have this pretty much figured out at your initial meeting, you may learn from members what areas of concern are strongest and what areas do not require much attention. For instance, if most of your members are MOMs and not divorced women, then addressing issues such as finding male role models may be more welcome than discussing methods of coparenting or how to survive a nasty custody battle. Conversely, if your group is primarily composed of divorced women who are having trouble collecting child support, then this would be a stronger area of focus than talking about donor insemination. Defining the purpose of the group will help increase your membership.

2. *Staying in touch.* Give each member approximately three names of people to whom they are responsible for relaying information about group activities or updates. Also, each member should be able to call or e-mail people on their list for mutual support, venting, and even small talk.

3. *Raising money.* Groups charge a small membership fee and at some meetings pass around a basket for funds to help with the cost of hiring babysitters and to pay for paper, printing and/or copying, and other possible incidental costs.

FINDING A SPIRITUAL HOME

Why It's Important to Find a Spiritual Center

Religious scholars have noticed that even though various religious dogmas and beliefs dictate different practices and rituals, most were developed for one basic reason: to give families living under patriarchy (which accounted for most religions founded on Judeo-Christian principles) rules for living morally and with conformity under a set of standards designed to help males and females cohabit. But many are finding that these religious standards don't celebrate the home headed by a single female, whether or not she is a mother. Because of this, there has been a great advancement in what is known as the women's spiritual movement, geared toward more "female affirming" spirituality.

Now, this doesn't mean that you should immediately join a cult of goddess worshippers or study Wicca to cultivate powers against which men have no defense. Nor should you run out and purchase crystals or herbs in search of a New Age religious experience because you feel rebellious against a "Father God." What it does mean is that God does not necessarily take the form of a male entity or father figure. Remember, many of those who need God as a father figure may have had fathers at home but missed the experience of being "fathered." It also means that along with the democratization of society, in which women are gaining more power over their lives, there is a democratizing of religion, too.

For households headed by single mothers, particularly where Mom often feels overwhelmed and lacks a full-time supportive adult with whom to share tasks, the belief that there is something bigger than themselves is very comforting. But you don't need traditional beliefs to be spiritual. God can be anything, look like anything, and be called by any name or not be called by a name at all. Just know that you are not alone. No matter how big some crises you face appear to be, the world will continue. Why not let go of some of the stress and find a little peace by focusing on something bigger than yourself?

Religion is a deeply personal subject, and no one should suggest or urge anyone to move from one place of worship to another or to convert to another religious faith. Whatever way you choose to believe in God is all right for you and your family. It might be helpful, however, for you to be aware that many churches today are actively seeking to meet the needs of their single-parent members. Even if you have not attended church or other place of worship in a long time, explore what is available in your community. Informal, ecumenical services might give you spiritual comfort, or you may find greater solace in traditional worship. Attending one service is not a commitment but may open the door to spiritual renewal for you and your family.

Feeling Out of Place

I am in my late twenties, and my fiancé died while I was in my fourth month of pregnancy. I recently joined a church, but the programs for widows seem to be for elderly women. Also, I feel that because I wasn't married before I became pregnant that I am being unfairly judged. I've tried to establish a support group for single mothers, but no one came. The married women at my church can't seem to relate to this need and make me feel self-conscious and out of place.

You have been through a difficult time with the loss of your fiancé and the challenging adjustments all new mothers face. You may be misinterpreting the reactions of others. Rather than being inconsiderate or judgmental, the women members of your church may not know exactly what to say given the death of your fiancé and then the birth of the baby. Do they console you or congratulate you? Their confused silence can lead you to feel self-conscious and out of place. Maybe trying to start a support group was a bit hasty.

Look for ways as a new member of the church to convey the message that you want to be a part of church activities or at least be accepted in your religious community for who you are. Since your attempts at organizing a support group were not successful, participate in established church activities so that members of the congregation can get to know you as a person, not just as a single mother. Try to connect with one individual at a time instead of trying to win the acceptance of everyone. Be an enthusiastic volunteer, giving freely of your time and talent. If these efforts are ultimately less than successful and you still feel out of place, consider joining another church, one a little more embracing of different lifestyle choices and especially single parents.

GROWING WITH YOUR CHILDREN

Being a parent doesn't mean always being in the position of teacher. We learn about the world around us through the eyes of children if we are just willing to look at what they see. Parent development, like child development, is not a one-way street. It's a growth process that lasts as long as you are willing to let it.

Inasmuch as we are the ones to show children how to hold a paintbrush, how to tie their shoes, and how not to hurt themselves, our children can teach us to create and to heal. They help us establish new routines and ways of thinking and doing things, such as creating new family traditions—sources of joy that can emerge from something that once was painful. As long as you focus on your parental development, your children will continue to grow, too.

Seasonal Celebrations and Holidays

Establishing new traditions is the secret to getting through holidays and celebrations such as birthdays, Fourth of July picnics, and other events. Trying to make things fit a certain scheme or reliving what you did before you became a single mother is only an invitation to disappointment and failure. The flexible person who doesn't try to halt change experiences the most joy in whatever comes her way. For example, if you and your child's father celebrated Mother's Day in bed (after he served breakfast), don't ruin your day by pining for what can't be. Instead, think up new ways to celebrate, such as cooking a spectacular breakfast feast together.

If Memorial Day was a time when

you and your ex had an enormous family cookout at the beach, why not celebrate the family dog's birthday that day instead, and you and your kids can get to indulge in gooey birthday cake, candles and all. If Passover is important to you, learn the Haggadah (available from any synagogue) and conduct a seder with your friends and family with you heading the Passover table!

Thanksgiving was a disaster! My husband moved out about six months ago to live with his girlfriend. The children, a boy and girl ages twelve and fourteen, seemed to adjust okay. Their father and I only speak through our lawyers, but they see him fairly regularly. This helps me keep tabs on him and the girlfriend. The children did not say one word Thanksgiving Day and hardly touched their food. I was embarrassed in front of my family. What do you think is going on with them?

Holidays evoke powerful memories. Your children are remembering past Thanksgivings and feeling sad that their father is no longer a part of the celebration. The lack of meaningful communication between their parents is a strain and, no doubt, a constant source of worry and anxiety. The job of "Dad Monitor" places them smack in the middle of all of the marital issues the two of you could not resolve. There is ample confusion and uncertainty in their lives without demanding reports back on the details of Dad's private life.

Ask your extended family for cooperation. An unwelcome part of many family gatherings is listening to the "family know-it-all." The "I just had

to tell you how I feel about what your father is doing . . ." speech is hurtful and unnecessary. Make it clear to your family that you appreciate their loyalty and concern. Remind them that comments about the children's father and the present home situation are strictly off-limits.

Beating the Holiday Blues

It's just before Christmas, and here it comes—the final assault of television ads flashing their rapid succession of "perfect family" holiday images—where the teary wife finds a diamond in her yogurt perfectly placed by her hunky husband or where eternal happiness is found, if not in a bottle of good scotch, then certainly in a bottle of cologne. Of course, the kids will never again misbehave because they got megacrates of brain-sizzling electronic gizmos and dolls that laugh, cry, and have a more interesting social life than you could ever dream up for yourself.

It's enough to make anyone feel depressed, especially single parents. But a real Thanksgiving, Christmas, Hanukkah, New Year's, or Kwanzaa celebration is what you make it. Here's help for driving away the holiday blues and assuring you and yours a really fabulous time.

◆ Media holidays are a fantasy. It is easy to start to believe that the holiday images we see on television and in magazines are within our grasp, if we would just get organized, spend a little more money, and try harder. The projects you see on television and in glorious magazine spreads are the full-time work of a creative and talented professional staff who has been working on each of these

projects since last spring. Real life is not pyramids made of exotic fruit or desserts that look like houses. Unless you literally have no life and zero other responsibilities, comparing yourself to any media image of a "typical holiday" is setting yourself up for failure.

- Think about fun. What part of the holiday preparations do you really enjoy? If you hate to bake, then why do it? Are you flooded with paperwork at your job? This might explain why you describe holiday cards as "another big job I need to get out of the way."

- What are your children going to tell their children about your family holidays? Toys, fancy decorations, and elaborate food are quickly forgotten. Your children will remember time and attention spent on things important to them. Reading holiday stories together is a free and important family activity. Try watching the TV specials or holiday DVD with your child rather than looking at this time as free babysitting. Think twice and then think again about adding

activities to an already bursting schedule. A stressed-out, exhausted parent quick to scold is a holiday blessing to no one.

- Remember what the holidays really mean. For each of us the holidays have a unique and personal spiritual meaning. Make the sharing of your personal spiritual beliefs a central part of your holiday celebration. Teach your children the values and beliefs that will sustain them now and in the years to come.

- Remember this absolute life truth. Children thrive on routine, clear expectations, calm, and simple pleasures. No holiday preparation or activity is worth causing undue family stress and conflict or dangerously lowering your reserves of energy and good humor.

TRY THESE SPECIAL HOLIDAY EXPERIENCES

- Round up the kids and head down to a shelter or soup kitchen and volunteer to help with a sumptuous holiday meal. You'll be setting a great example for your children by showing them that your family has ample warmth and love to share at the holidays with other families who are currently undergoing some kind of burden. Invite a single mother and her children to dinner. There are also many battered women's shelters with lists of families experiencing challenging difficulties who would love being invited to a holiday get-together in your very gracious household.

- If you're still feeling out of sorts in the face of the media's blaring version of a traditional holiday, have your family enjoy a totally backwards, fabulously silly, nontraditional celebration. Laugh at all the frenetic people rushing around in overdrive, while you maintain a very relaxed, low-key attitude. Be carefree—roll in the leaves or snow with your kids. On Christmas Eve, stay up all night, playing with the stuff you opened the day before. Serve your kids' favorites: hot dogs, popcorn, peanut butter and jelly on crackers, instead of turkey. Eat in front of the TV (hopefully this is something that you rarely do) and make sure you start the meal with dessert. Your kids will always remember such holidays with much fondness.

- Buy gifts that require no batteries. You'll save money down the road and do more for the environment. Give your kids simple things that they'll use often, such as a kite or musical instrument. Furnish gifts that require children to use their imagination, including paper, fabric, and other artists' materials to encourage them to create their own picture books. Make items with your children for relatives and friends. Let your kids color large sheets of newsprint to use for wrapping paper, bearing in mind that "classy" is really the outcome of remarkable creativity. Encourage older children to share a special talent or skill. If your fifteen-year-old son is a whiz in the kitchen, team up and make jars of chilled soups, dips, or salsa to give as gifts. See how innovative you can be.

- Be creative. Make ornaments. String popcorn and cranberries on waxed dental floss. Make photo postcards of your family (pets included, of course) as greeting cards. The postage will also be less. If your children are away during the holidays visiting relatives or the other parent, wait until after the holidays to buy their gifts. They won't even know the difference, and you'll save considerably. Plan next year to celebrate the holidays on a tight budget. Shop the week after Christmas to ensure real savings, usually half price on most items.

- Adopt a grandparent. Celebrate the holidays with a senior citizen at a local center or retirement home.

- Round up all the single and married people you know who are not attending or preparing a holiday dinner this year. Ask everyone to bring a dish and have a wonderful potluck celebration at your place.

- Handprint homemade gift certificates offering such services as dog walking for your neighbor. Wondering about teacher gifts? Most teachers would much prefer a simple homemade gift or a sincere note of appreciation.

- If you can't altogether cut it out, limit television viewing. At this time of the year, most ads are targeted toward consumers who faithfully buy into the commercialization of Christmas. Don't be suckered by toy, cosmetic, and jewelry ads or seductive alcohol spots that suggest you need to be part of a couple to have a satisfying holiday. Remember, the goal of the sellers of these products is one thing—to make lots of money.

The most efficient way for advertisers to rake in the money is to convince viewers that their lives will be complete if only they have an abundance of toys for the kids, a cold beer, a partner who always smells good, or a sexy car. What nonsense. Just say no!

- Invite all the members of your support group to feast. Recruit some teenagers to assist with child care and pay them with the two or three dollars that each parent chipped in. If you don't belong to a support group, then make it your New Year's resolution either to join or start one.

Father's Day

It's Father's Day again, you're a single mother, and your five-year-old comes home from kindergarten asking "What's Father's Day?" Here are some things to remember to ensure that this Father's Day won't have you hiding under the bed avoiding "daddy questions."

It's unlikely that your child is the only one in his class without a father living at home. Half of all children today are raised during some time of their lives in single-parent families.

There is no reason for your child not to participate in creative class projects that recognize Father's Day. Just as it is okay not to have a father heading the household, remember that just because "Dad" lives in the home does not mean a child is being fathered. However, there are a number of fatherly types who can be recognized for overall contributions to children, particularly those serving as healthy role models.

- Send a special man a card. Any male friend or family member who has shown significant fathering qualities, including patience, empathy, and mentoring, can be acknowledged on this day.

- Other men can also be the recipients of homemade cards, drawings, or other objects d'art: the softball coach who first showed your little boy the correct way to bat lefty; the repairman who fixes things with his power tools; the neighborhood crossing guard who helps children cross the street safely every morning on the way to school, or the local pharmacist who paid a little extra attention to your child's needs.

- Some families honor their big, lovable German shepherd—the pet who played daddy by protecting their bodies and their home—with a bag of doggie bones.

  Since all children are connected at least biologically to a "father," even those by adoption and donor insemination, tell your child whatever you know about his or her father and let it be the child's decision whether or not to recognize him on this day. Take it a step further, and rename Father's Day. "Parent's Day" is a creative way to encourage participation by your child and coax out of him another work of art for you!

Traveling with Kids

If you think you can't afford to take a vacation during the summer or any other time you and the kids have off, think again. It takes a lot of preparation and planning, but if you do your homework, you can have a memorable vacation that you and the kids will talk about for many years. Following are seven great ideas:

1. Start out by including your kids in the plans. Your older one can help you request pamphlets and brochures from information services in the areas you'd like to visit, such as chambers of commerce, state tourist bureaus, and automobile clubs. Older children can also use their online skills to hunt up travel bargains. Obviously, mom has the final say, as well as the credit card information.

2. Consider traveling with one or more other adults to share some of the expenses. It's cheaper to rent a whole beach house and split the cost than to pay for daily motel rates. Be sure to investigate travel deals through your church, school, or any organization to which you belong and look for group rates, whenever possible.

3. Think about house swapping. If you're a city dweller, for example, consider spending your vacation in a farm house with plenty of room to spare. If you live in the country, a week in a big city apartment might be quite the adventure. Consider trading "your beach" for time in the mountains.

   Try "house exchange" or "house swapping" in your favorite search engine and see if any possibilities appeal to you. Explore networking with other families to make this money-saving vacation opportunity happen.

4. Investigate hostel accommodations. Hostels offer bargain basement prices on dormlike arrangements

and private rooms all over the United States and abroad. These are not luxury accommodations, and you need to bring along your spirit of adventure. Hosteling is a great way to meet interesting people from all over the world.

5. Remember to check out the features of any hotel or motel. See if the rates include a pool or access to workout facilities, and ask if they offer baby-sitting services of any kind. Try getting a fridge and a microwave in your room to defray the costs of restaurants every time your kids are hungry. Bring along lots of easy-to-carry and nutritious snacks. Remember to keep everyone out of the pricey room minibar.

Above all, lower your expectations and raise your enjoyment threshold. Start preparing now because it's never too early to plan for a good time.

SO YOU WANT ANOTHER CHILD. . . .

I have a five-year-old son by a man I've known most of my life. We're no longer together, but his family is very involved in my son's life. In fact, they are the greatest grandparents, aunts, and uncles ever, even more than my own family. I have always wanted two children and would like another child before I turn forty. I'd like my children to be full siblings, but I'm catching flack from my own family for wanting another child outside of marriage. Is this really so bad?

Even if you became a mom by chance the first time, that's no reason you can't do it by choice the second time. You're not alone. Lots of single women want more children. If the father consents, go for it. Let your family know that this is something to which you've given lots of thought, and you would appreciate their support. Just be sure you're comfortable with this scenario and able to explain to your children why their (paternal) grandma and grandpa are more involved in their lives than their biological father.

AFTERWORD

In the time since the research for the first edition of this book began, I have heard from thousands of single moms. The voices in these letters, e-mails, phone calls, and Internet message board postings echoed uncertainty, strength, and downright fear at times. Yet, most of these women almost always signed off with remarkable relief at just having an ear or a forum in which to be heard. I became even more inspired to ask questions and listen to the joys and concerns of heading a single-parent family and to seek solutions that would make single mothering seem less overwhelming. Sure, it's tough, but anything that challenges us to be alive and as real as possible is tough. The bottom line, however, is that I learned it is simply okay to live any life you are dealt at any given time the best way you know how. Where once I was fueled to challenge the prevailing assumption by "traditionalists" that single mothering is not normal, that need to debate has lessened. The fact is, no matter what the latest political stance is on "family values" (I remember when Newt Gingrich publicly stated that all children born to unmarried mothers should be taken away and put in orphanages), the truth is single mothering can't be summed up by any side of the debate as being right or wrong, healthy or deviant, or even happy or horrible. There is no debate. It is simply okay—meaning that it's as normal as you can get, and what makes your life meaningful is how you think, love, and respond to its challenges.

From your words and from the combined experience of coauthor Leah Klungness—who advises countless single moms in her practice—and myself, I found that single mothering is indeed not only normal but also can provide a healthy environment in which to raise children, particularly compared to the stresses of families suffering from gender inequities. Of course, problems exist in every kind of family (which is why we write parenting books), but these should guide you toward finding solutions that work for you and not present a one-size-fits-all solution. Still, if I could wrap up everything I feel about single mothering in one word to provide you with less anxiety, more hope, and reassurance that your life isn't as impossible as you may have been led to believe, here's the reminder.

It's "okay!"

Really, it is.

So that I may remain current and responsive to the needs of single-mother families and to provide material for new editions of this book, I encourage you to contact me. Send your stories, comments, or questions to:

National Organization of Single Mothers, Inc.
P.O. Box 68
Midland, NC 28107-0068

Or visit Single Mothers Online at *www.singlemothers.org* to post a message in one of the forums.

—A. E.

Former First Lady (and single mother) Jacqueline Kennedy Onassis spoke of the privilege and responsibility of motherhood when she said, "If you bungle raising your children I don't think whatever else you do well matters very much."

I heartily agree.

I feel enormously blessed to have had the confidence and commitment to raise my children successfully as a single mother. I am proud of how well my children turned out. Andrew is a respected attorney living in California with his lovely wife. Sarah graduated from college and is completing a degree in nursing. They are optimistic, responsible, and devoted to family. My children are my pride and joy. Each of them has enriched my life in many special ways. One way, of course, has been the opportunity to write a book about single parenting that originated from our experiences together as a family.

One of the great benefits of writing a book is the opportunity to meet people whose life experiences are truly inspirational. The courage, initiative, and grace of the many single parents I have had the pleasure to meet provided much of the substance of my contribution to this book. Successful single parents are resourceful and resilient. Their ability to focus upon the realistic needs of themselves and their families often set them uniquely apart from the selfishness and preoccupation of those around them.

Counseling these single parents and their families is challenging because much of what is simple and obvious has already been recognized and accomplished. The need for collaborative efforts with attorneys and other professionals has become increasingly apparent. This collaboration, as well as my therapy practice and writing, is now an important part of my professional life.

I welcome the opportunity to hear your personal concerns and challenges. Please contact me at my Web site *www JustAskDrLeah.com*.

RECOMMENDED READING

Adoption

Adopting Natasha: My First Year as a Mother, Carol Lee (Publishing Cooperative).

Adopting on Your Own: The Complete Guide to Adoption for Single Parents, Lee Varon (Farrar Straus Giroux).

The Adoption Resource Book, Lois Gilman (HarperCollins).

Adoption: Your Step-by-Step Guide, Mardie Caldwell (American Carriage House Publishing).

Attaching in Adoption, Deborah D. Gray (Perspectives Press).

The Handbook for Single Adoptive Parents, Hope Marindin (National Council for Single Adoptive Parents).

The Handbook of International Adoption Medicine, Laurie C. Miller, M.D. (Oxford University Press).

How to Adopt Internationally, Jean Nelson Erichsen, Heino R. Erichsen (Mesa House Publishing).

Raising Adopted Children: Practical Reassuring Advice for Every Adoptive Parent, Lois Rusaki Melina (Perennial).

Babies

Baby Bargains, Alan Fields, Denise Fields (Windsor Peak Press).

The Baby Book, William Sears, M.D., Martha Sears, R.N. (Little, Brown).

The Girlfriends' Guide to Surviving the First Year of Motherhood, Vicki Iovine (The Berkley Publishing Group).

The Mother of All Pregnancy Books: The Ultimate Guide to Conception, Birth, and Everything in Between, Ann Douglas (Wiley Press).

The No-Cry Sleep Solution, Elizabeth Pantley (Contemporary Books).

Operating Instructions: A Journal of My Son's First Year, Anne Lamott (Ballantine Books).

365 Ways to Calm Your Crying Baby, Julian Orenstein, M.D. (Adams Media).

What to Expect the First Year, Third Edition, Heidi Murkoff, Sandee Hathaway, Arlene Eisenberg (Workman).

Your Baby's First Year Week by Week, Fifth Edition, Glade Curtis, M.D., Judith Schuler, MS (Da Capo Press).

Breastfeeding

The Breastfeeding Answer Book, Revised Edition, Nancy Mohrbacher (La Leche League International).

The Nursing Mother's Companion, Kathleen Huggins (Harvard Common Press).

So That's What They're for: Breastfeeding Basics, Janet Tamaro (Adams Media).

The Womanly Art of Breastfeeding, Seventh Edition–Revised, La Leche League International Book (Plume Books).

Child Custody and Visitation

Child Custody Made Simple, Second Edition–Revised, Webster Watnik (Single Parent Press).

Custody Chaos, Personal Peace, Jeffrey P. Wittman, Ph.D. (The Berkley Publishing Group).

Divorce Poison: Protecting the Parent-Child Bond from a Vindictive Ex, Dr. Richard A. Warshak (Regan Books).

Joint Custody with a Jerk: Raising a Child with an Uncooperative Ex, Julie A. Ross, M.A., Judy Corcoran (St. Martin's Griffin).

Winning Custody: A Woman's Guide to Retaining Custody of Her Children, Deedra Hunter (St. Martin's Griffin).

Children with Special Needs

The Challenging Child: Understanding, Raising, and Enjoying the Five "Difficult" Types of Children, Stanley I. Greenspan, M.D. (Perseus Books Group).

The Child with Special Needs: Encouraging Intellectual and Emotional Growth, Stanley I. Greenspan, M.D., Serena Wieder, Ph.D. (Perseus Books).

The Everything Parent's Guide to Children with Autism: Know What to Expect, Find Help You Need, and Get Through the Day, Adelle Jameson Tilton (Adams Media).

Expecting Adam: A True Story of Birth, Rebirth, and Everyday Magic, Martha Beck (Berkley Publishing Group).

The Gift of ADHD: How to Transform Your Child's Problems into Strengths, Lara Honos-Webb (Harbinger Publications).

Laughing Allegra: The Inspiring Story of a Mother's Struggle and Triumph Raising a Daughter with Learning Disabilities, Anne Ford (Newmarket Press).

Learning Disabilities: A to Z: A Parent's Complete Guide to Learning Disabilities from Preschool to Adulthood, Corinne Smith, Ph.D., Lisa Strick (Free Press).

The Myth of the A.D.D. Child: 50 Ways to Improve Your Child's Behavior and Attention Span without Drugs, Labels, and Coercion, Thomas Armstrong, Ph.D. (Prume Books).

A Parent's Guide to Special Education: Insider Advice on How to Navigate the System and Help Your Child Succeed by Linda Wilmhurst, Ph.D., and Alan W. Brue, Ph.D. (AMACOM).

Pride Against Prejudice: Transforming Attitudes to Disability, Jenny Morris (New Society Publishers).

Right Brained Children in a Left Brained World: Unlocking the Potential of Your ADD Child, Jeffrey Freed, M.A.T., Laurie Parsons (Simon and Schuster).

Smart Kids with School Problems: Things to Know and Ways to Help, Priscilla L. Vail (Plume Books).

Daughters

Celebrating Girls: Nurturing and Empowering Our Daughters, Virginia Beane Rutter (Conari Press).

Embracing Persephone: How to Be the Mother Your Daughter Will Cherish, Virginia Beane Rutter (Conari Press).

I'm Not Mad, I Just Hate You: A New Understanding of Mother-Daughter Conflict, Roni Cohen-Sandler Ph.D., Michelle Silver (Penguin Books).

Odd Girl Out: The Hidden Culture of Aggression in Girls, Rachel Simmons (Harvest Books).

Raising Strong Daughters, Jeanette Gadeberg (Fairview Press).

Divorce

Divorce and Money: How to Make the Best Financial Decisions During Divorce, Violet Woodhouse (NOLO).

Divorce Casualties: Protecting Your Children from Parental Alienation, Douglas Darnall, Ph.D. (Taylor Trade Publishing).

The Fresh Start Divorce Recovery Workbook, Bob Burns, Tom Whiteman (Nelson Books).

Getting Divorced Without Ruining Your Life: A Reasoned, Practical Guide to the Legal, Emotional, and Financial Ins and Outs of Negotiating a Divorce Settlement, Sam Margulies, Ph.D., J.D. (Fireside).

Helping Children Cope with Divorce, Edward Teyber (Jossey-Bass).

Making Divorce Easier on Your Child: 50 Effective Ways to Help Children Adjust, Nicholas Long, Ph.D., Rex Forehand, Ph.D. (McGraw-Hill).

Second Chances: Men, Women, and Children a Decade after Divorce, Judith S. Wallerstein, Sandra Blakeslee (Mariner Books).

Surviving Separation and Divorce, Loriann Hoff Oberlin (Adams Media).

Surviving the Breakup: How Children and Parents Cope with Divorce, Judith S. Wallerstein, Joan B. Kelly (Basic).

What Every Woman Should Know About Divorce and Custody, Gayle Rosenwald Smith, J.D., Sally Abrahms (Perigee).

Your Divorce Advisor: A Lawyer and Psychologist Guide You Through the Legal and Emotional Landscape of Divorce, Diana Mercer, Marsha Kline Pruett (Fireside).

Donor Insemination

Baby Steps, Amy Agigian (Wesleyan University Press).

Buying Dad: One Woman's Search for the Perfect Sperm Donor, Harlyn Aizley (Alyson Publications).

Experiences of Donor Conception: Parents, Offspring, and Donors Through the Years, Caroline Lorbach (Jessica Kingsley Publishers).

Helping the Stork: The Choices and Challenges of Donor Insemination, Carol Vercollone, M.S.W., Heidi Moss, M.S.W., Robert Moss, Ph.D. (Wiley).

Lethal Secrets, Annette Baran, Reuben Pannor (HarperCollins).

Finance/Saving Money

The Complete Guide to Credit Repair, Bill Kelly Jr. (Adams Media).

Ernst & Young's Financial Planning for Women: A Woman's Guide to Money for All of Life's Major Events, Barbara J. Raasch, Sylvia Pozarnsky, Paula Boyer Kennedy, Andrea S. Markezin, Elda Di Re, Freida Kavouras (Wiley).

Financial Self-Confidence for the Suddenly Single: A Woman's Guide, Alan B. Ungar, CFP (Lowell House).

Free College and Training Money for Women, Matthew Lesko (Information USA).

The Frugal Woman's Guide to a Rich Life, edited by Stacia Ragolia (Rutledge Hill Press).

How to Turn Your Money Life Around: The Money Book for Women, Ruth L. Hayden (Health Communications).

Living Well on One Income in a Two-Income World, Cynthia Yates (Harvest House Publishers).

Miserly Moms: Living on One Income in a Two Income Economy, Jonni McCoy (Bethany House Publishers).

The Money Rules, Susan Jones (McGraw-Hill).

Prince Charming Isn't Coming: How Women Get Smart about Money, Barbara Stanny (Penguin Books).

Saving Money with the Tightwad Twins: More than 1,000 Practical Tips for Women on a Budget, Ann and Susan Fox (HCI).

The Single Person's Guide to Buying a Home: Why to Do It and How to Do It, Elaine J. Anderson, Ph.D. (Betterway Books).

Smart Women Finish Rich: 9 Steps to Achieving Financial Security and Funding Your Dreams, David Bach (Broadway).

Start Late, Finish Rich: A No-Fail Plan for Achieving Financial Freedom at Any Age, David Bach (Broadway).

Suddenly Single: Money Skills for Divorcees and Widows, Kerry Hannon (Wiley).

The Widow's Financial Survival Guide: Handling Money Matters on Your Own, Nancy Dunnan (Perigee Books).

Grief/Widowhood

Being a Widow, Lynn Caine (Penguin Books).

The Courage to Grieve, Judy Tatelbaum (Perennial Currents).

Finding Your Way After Your Spouse Dies, Marta Felber (Ave Maria Press).

On Death and Dying, Elisabeth Kübler-Ross (Scribner).

The Widow's Handbook: A Guide for Living, Charlotte Foehner (Fulcrum Publishing).

Inspiration

If Woman Ruled the World: How to Create the World We Want to Live In, edited by Sheila Ellison (Inner Ocean Publishing Company).

Roar Softly and Carry a Great Lipstick, edited by Autumn Stephens (Inner Ocean Publishing Company).

What Would You Do If You Had No Fear? Diane Conway (Inner Ocean Publishing Company).

Job/Career

Balancing Work and Family, Jacqueline Wallen (Allyn & Bacon).

The Everything Alternative Careers Book: Leave the Office Behind and Embark on a New Adventure, James Mannion (Adams Media).

Flex Time: A Working Mother's Guide to Balancing Career and Family, Jacqueline Foley (Avalon Publishing Group).

Going Back to Work: A Survival Guide
for Comeback Moms, Mary W.
Quigley, Loretta E. Kaufman (St.
Martin's Griffin).

I Don't Know What I Want, But I Know
It's Not This: A Step-by-Step Guide to
Finding Gratifying Work, Julie Jansen
(Penguin Books).

The Mom Economy: The Mother's Guide
to Getting Family-Friendly Work,
Elizabeth Wilcox (Berkley Publishing Group).

The 150 Most Profitable Home Businesses for Women, Katina Z. Jones
(Adams Media).

Seven Secrets of Successful Women: Suc-
cess Strategies of the Women Who
Have Made It and How You Can
Follow Their Lead, Donna Brooks,
Lynn Brooks (McGraw-Hill).

Working from Home: Everything You
Need to Know About Living and
Working Under the Same Roof, Fifth
Edition, Paul and Sarah Edwards
(Jeremy P. Tarcher).

Kids (and for Parents to Read with Kids)

Adoption Is for Always, Linda Wal-
voord Girard (Albert Whitman &
Company).

All Kinds of Families, Norma Simon
(Albert Whitman & Company).

At Daddy's on Saturdays, Linda Wal-
voord Girard (Albert Whitman &
Company).

Beginnings: How Families Come to Be,
Virginia Kroll (Albert Whitman &
Company).

A Chair for My Mother, Vera B. Williams (HarperTrophy).

Did My First Mother Love Me? A Story
for an Adopted Child, Kathryn Ann
Miller (Morning Glory Press).

Difficult Questions Kids Ask and Are
Afraid to Ask about Divorce, Meg F.
Schneider, Joan Zuckerberg, Ph.D.
(Fireside).

Dinosaurs Divorce: A Guide for Changing Families, Laurene Krasny Brown,
Marc Brown (Little Brown).

Do I Have a Daddy? A Story About a
Single-Parent Child, Jeanne Warren
Lindsay (Morning Glory Press).

The Don't-Give-Up Kid and Learning
Differences, Jeanne Gehret, M.A.
(Verbal Images Press).

Families Are Different, Nina Pellegrini
(Holiday House).

Girl Talk, Judith Harlan (Walker and
Company).

Helping Children Cope with Separation
and Loss, Claudia Jewett Jarratt
(Harvard Common Press).

How to Survive Your Parents' Divorce:
Kids' Advice to Kids, Gayle Kimball,
Ph.D. (Equality Press).

Mom's House, Dad's House, Isolina
Ricci, Ph.D. (Fireside).

Our Dad Died: The True Story of Three
Kids Whose Lives Changed, Amy,
Allie, and David Dennison (Free
Spirit Publishing).

The Ring Bear: A Rascally Wedding
Adventure, David Michael Slater
(Flashlight Press).

The Survival Guide for Kids With Learn-
ing Differences, Gary Fisher, Ph.D.,
Rhoda Cummings, Ed.D. (Free
Spirit Publishing).

Two Homes, Claire Masurel (Candlewick Press).

We See the Moon, Carrie A. Kitze (EMK Press).

When My Mommy Died: A Child's View of Death, Janice Hammond (Cranbrook Publishing).

Who's in a Family, Robert Skutch (Tricycle Press).

Why Was I Adopted, Carole Livingston (Lyle Stuart).

Parenting

Controlling the Difficult Adolescent: The REST Program (The Real Economy System for Teens), David B. Stein (University Press of America).

The Everything Parenting a Teenager Book, Linda Sonna, Ph.D. (Adams Media).

Healthy Parenting: How Your Upbringing Influences the Way You Raise Your Children and What You Can Do to Make It Better for Them, Janet G. Woititz (Fireside).

Healthy Sleep Habits, Happy Child, Marc Weissbluth (Ballantine Books).

Hidden Messages: What Our Words and Actions Are Really Telling Our Children, Elizabeth Pantley (McGraw-Hill).

How to Talk So Kids Will Listen & Listen So Kids Will Talk, Adele Faber, Elaine Mazlish (HarperResource).

Parenting an Only Child: The Joys and Challenges of Raising Your One and Only, Susan Newman (Broadway).

Parenting with Love and Logic: Teaching Children Responsibility, Foster W. Cline M.D., Jim Fay (Pinon Press).

The Pocket Parent, Gail Reichlin, Caroline Winkler (Workman).

Positive Discipline for Single Parents, Jane Nelson, Ed.D., Cheryl Erwin, M.A., Carol Delzer, M.A., J.D. (Prima Lifestyles).

Problem Child or Quirky Kid: A Commonsense Guide for Parents, Rita Sommers-Flanagan, Ph.D., John Sommers Flanagan, Ph.D. (Free Spirit Publishing).

Put Yourself in Their Shoes, Barbara Meltz (Dell Publishing).

A Tribe Apart: A Journey into the Heart of the American Adolescence, Patricia Hersch (Ballantine Books).

What About the Kids: Raising Your Children Before, During, and After Divorce, Judith S. Wallerstein, Sandra Blakeslee (Hyperion).

Pregnancy and Childbirth

The Complete Book of Pregnancy and Childbirth, Sheila Kitzinger (Knopf).

Conquering Postpartum Depression, Ronald Rosenberg, M.D., Deborah Greening, Ph.D., James Windell, M.A. (Da Capo Press).

The Doula Book: How a Trained Labor Companion Can Help You Have a Shorter, Easier, and Healthier Birth, Marshall H. Klaus, M.D., John H. Kennell, M.D., Phyllis H. Klaus, C.S.W., M.F.T. (Perseus Books Group).

The Everything Pregnancy Book, Paula Ford Martin (Adams Media).

Exercise after Pregnancy: How to Look and Feel Your Best, Helene Byrne (Celestial Arts).

Knocked Up: Confessions of a Hip Mother-to-Be, Rebecca Eckler (Villard).

Meditations for Pregnancy: 36 Weekly Practices for Bonding with Your Unborn Baby, Michelle Leclaire O'Neill (Andrews McMeel Publishing).

The Mother of All Pregnancy Books: The Ultimate Guide to Conception, Birth, and Everything in Between, Ann Douglas (Wiley).

Motherwell Maternity Fitness Plan, Bonnie Berk, R.N. (Human Kinetics Publishers).

The Natural Pregnancy Book: Herbs, Nutrition, and Other Holistic Choices, Aviva Jill Romm (Ten Speed Press).

The Thinking Woman's Guide to a Better Birth, Henci Goer (Perigee Trade).

What to Expect When You're Expecting, Arlene Eisenberg, Heidi Murkoff, Sandee Hathaway, B.S.N. (Workman).

Raising Boys

The Courage to Raise Good Men, Olga Silverstein, Beth Rashbaum (Penguin Books).

Father Figures: Three Wise Men Who Changed a Life, Kevin J. Sweeney (Regan Books).

Raising Boys: Why Boys Are Different and How to Help Them Become Happy and Well-Balanced Men, Steve Biddulph (Celestial Arts).

Raising Boys Without Men: How Maverick Moms Are Creating the Next Generation of Exceptional Men, Peggy F. Drexler, Ph.D., with Linden Gross (Rodale).

Speaking of Boys: Answers to the Most-Asked Questions about Raising Sons, Michael Thompson, Ph.D. (Ballantine Books).

Strong Mothers, Strong Sons: Raising the Next Generation of Men, Ann F. Caron, Ed.D. (Perennial Currents).

Relationships/Dating

7 Secrets of a Healthy Dating Relationship, Les Parrott (Beacon Hill Press).

Boundaries in Dating, Henry Cloud, John Townsend (Zondervan Publishing Company).

The Courage to Love Again: Creating Happy, Healthy Relationships After Divorce, Sheila Ellison (HarperSanFrancisco).

Encouragements for the Emotionally Abused Woman: Wisdom and Hope for Women at Any Stage of Emotional Abuse Recovery, Beverly Engel, M.F.C.C. (Ballantine Books).

Infidelity: A Survival Guide, Don-David Lusterman, Ph.D. (New Harbinger Publications).

Mars and Venus Starting Over: A Practical Guide for Finding Love Again after a Painful Breakup, Divorce or the Loss of a Loved One, John Gray, Ph.D. (Perennial).

Mom, There's a Man in the Kitchen and He's Wearing Your Robe: The Single Mother's Guide to Dating Well without Parenting Poorly, Ellie Slott Fisher (Da Capo Press).

Sex and the Single Parent, Meg F. Schneider, Martine J. Byer (PerigeeTrade).

Why Men Love Bitches—A Woman's Guide to Holding Her Own in a Relationship, Sherry Argov (Adams Media).

Single Mothers/Single Parenting

50 Wonderful Ways to Be a Single-Parent Family, Barry G. Ginsberg, Ph.D. (New Harbinger Publications).

The Courage to Be a Single Mother: Becoming Whole Again after Divorce, Sheila Ellison (HarperSanFrancisco).

Going It Alone: Meeting the Challenges of Being a Single Mom, Michele Howe (Hendrickson Publishers).

On Our Own: Unmarried Motherhood in America, Melissa Ludtke (University of California Press).

Sing Your Own Song: A Guide for Single Moms, Cynthia Orange (Hazelden Publishing & Educational Services).

The Single Mother Book: A Practical Guide to Managing Your Children, Career, Home, Finances and Everything Else, Joan Anderson (Peachtree Publishers).

Single Mothers by Choice: A Guide for Single Women Who Are Considering or Have Chosen Motherhood, Jane Mattes (Three Rivers Press).

The Single Mother's Survival Guide, Patricia Karst (Crossing Press).

The Single Parent Resource, Brook Noel (Champion Press).

Unbroken Homes: Single Parent Mothers Tell Their Stories, Wendy A. Paterson, Ph.D. (The Haworth Press).

When Baby Makes Two: Single Mothers by Chance or Choice, Jane Stonesifer (Lowell House).

Stepparenting

7 Steps to Bonding with Your Stepchild, Suzen J. Ziegahn, Ph.D. (St. Martin's Griffin).

The Enlightened Stepmother: Revolutionizing the Role, Perdita Kirkness Norwood (Perennial Currents).

How to Win as a Stepfamily, Emily B. Visher, Ph.D., John S. Visher, M.D. (Brunner/Mazel).

My Real Family: A Child's Book About Living in a Stepfamily, Doris Sanford (Multnomah Publishers).

Remarried with Children: Ten Secrets for Successfully Blending and Extending Your Family, Barbara LeBey (Bantam).

Stepfamilies: A Guide for Working with Stepparents and Stepchildren, John and Emily Visher (Brunner/Mazel).

The Stepparenting Challenge: Making It Work, Stephen J. Williams, Sc.D. (Mastermedia Limited).

Travel/Moving

Fodor's Family Adventures: More Than 700 Great Trips for You and Your Kids of All Ages, Fourth Edition, Christine Loomis (Fodor's).

Have Kid, Will Travel: 101 Survival Strategies for Vacationing with Babies and Young Children, Claire Tristram, Lucille Tristram (Andrews McMeel).

How to Take Great Trips with Your Kids, Sanford Portnoy, Joan Portnoy (The Harvard Common Press).

Moving with Children: A Parent's Guide, Thomas T. Olkowski, Ph.D., Lynn Parker, L.C.S.W. (Gylantic Publishing).

The Single Parent Travel Handbook, Brenda Elwell (Global Brenda Publishing).

The Single Woman's Travel Guide, Jacqueline Simenauer, Doris Walfield (Kensington Publishing Corporation).

Magazines, Newsletters, Web sites, and Other Periodicals

About.com Single Parenting
http://singleparents.about.com

Adoptive Families
www.adoptivefamilies.com
1-800-372-3300

American Baby magazine
www.americanbaby.com

Babycenter
www.babycentercom/baby/babysingle/index

Child magazine
www.child.com
515-248-7690

ChildCareAware
www.childcareaware.org/en/

Hip Mama magazine and Web site
www.hipmama.com

iVillage Pregnancy and Parenting
http://parenting.ivillage.com

The National Organization of Single Mothers
www.singlemothers.com

The National Parenting Center
www.tnpc.com

The Pampers Parenting Institute
www.pampers.com

Parenting magazine
www.parenting.com
1-800-234-0847

Parenting with Intention Newsletter
www.parentingwithintention.ca
E-mail: *pwi-subscribe@aweber.com*

Parents magazine
www.parents.com
515-244-1832

The Positive Parenting Newsletter
www.positiveparenting.com
E-mail: *subscribe@positiveparenting.com*
805-648-6846

Single Mother: A Support Group in Your Hands
www.singlemothers.org
704-888-KIDS

SingleRose
www.Singlerose.com

Working Mother magazine
www.workingmother.com
1-800-627-0690

INDEX

ABOUT THE AUTHORS

Andrea Engber is founder and director of the National Organization of Single Mothers and editor-in-chief of its publication, *Single Mother*, hailed by the media as the "best source of available information for single mothers" and honored with many awards including a Parent's Choice Award and a Parent's Guide Award.

She has written for and advised major magazines and newspapers on single-parenting issues, including *Redbook, New Woman, Working Mother, Woman's Own, Parenting, American Baby, American Woman, Parents, The Wall Street Journal, USA Today, Chicago Tribune, Los Angeles Times, Newsweek*, and many others. She has been a frequent guest on national television and radio talk shows and served as America Online's Single Parent Pro.

A former contributing editor to *Working Mother* magazine, Engber wrote a single-parenting column for their two million plus readership. She penned the nationally syndicated weekly column "Single . . . with Children" for eleven years and has authored, coauthored, and written essays for seven books. In 1995, she was honored with a No-nonsense American Woman Award, whose past award winners included Barbara Bush and Oprah Winfrey. Engber also won the Outstanding Single Mother Award from National USA Week in 2002 and received a Heart of America Honor for her work on Single Mothers Online (*www.singlemothers.org*) in 2003.

Currently back to work on her next book after dealing with a long bout of illness, Engber lives in North Carolina with her family along with four cats, five dogs, occasional horses, and several other adopted pets. Her nineteen-year-old son, Spencer, a college student, is also a licensed pilot, a full-time plumber, a gifted jazz pianist, a Navy Reservist, and even speaks three languages. But equally impressive, he "has been doing his own laundry since he was twelve!"

For more information about Andrea, visit *www.singlemothers.org*.

Leah Klungness, Ph.D., is a recognized authority on single parenting and relationship issues. She has been quoted in *Ladies' Home Journal, Redbook, Working Mother*, the *New York Times*, and *Newsday*, and she has appeared on national TV and radio talk shows. She is a regular contributor to *City Parent*, Canada's largest parenting publication, as well as a consultant and frequent contributor to *www.singlerose.com*, one of the most popular single parent Web sites. She is also a single parenting expert for ClubMom (*www.clubmom.com*), a group cofounded by *View* cohost Meredith Vieira. Dr. Leah's expertise comes from her personal experiences as a single parent, as well as her training and experience as a psychologist and elementary school teacher. Dr. Leah earned her doctorate while single parenting her two children. Her son, Andrew, is an attorney, and her daughter, Sarah, is a college graduate completing a degree in nursing. Counseling many single parents and their families, particularly those facing divorce, as well as consulting with attorneys and other professionals, Dr. Leah offers practical advice and solutions. She resides in New York. For more information about Dr. Leah, please visit *www.JustAskDr.Leah.com*.